The Monterrey Elite and the Mexican State, 1880–1940

The Monterrey Elite and the Mexican State, 1880–1940

by Alex M. Saragoza

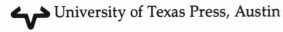 University of Texas Press, Austin

First Edition, 1988

Requests for permission to reproduce material from this work
should be sent to Permissions, University of Texas Press, Box
7819, Austin, Texas 78713-7819.

LIBRARY OF CONGRESS CATALOGING-IN-PUBLICATION DATA
Saragoza, Alex M.
  The Monterrey elite and the Mexican State.

  Bibliography: p.
  Includes index.
  1. Capitalists and financiers—Mexico—Monterrey—
History. 2. Capitalism—Mexico—Monterrey—History.
3. Monterrey (Mexico)—Industries—History. 4. Elite
(Social sciences)—Mexico—Monterrey—History.
5. Garza-Sada family. I. Title.
HG185.M6S27 1988   305.5'234'097213   87-23779
ISBN 0-292-71113-1

The publication of this book was assisted by a grant from the
Andrew W. Mellon Foundation.

Contents

FIGURES

TABLES

Preface

Monterrey, Nuevo León. The city elicits immediate recognition: industries, conservatism, immense economic power, and the base of one of the country's most powerful business groups. As such, the rise and fall of the fortunes of contemporary Mexico seem to be inextricably tied to the city and its leading capitalists, none more so than the clan known collectively as the Garza-Sadas. Indeed, this family and the city have become synonymous, each nurturing the image of the other. "In Monterrey," as one insider has noted, "the myths of business and industry inhibit the seeing of the reality behind its images."[1] Yet the image persists: the city as root of the Garza-Sadas, and they in turn as the center of a web of interests reaching from corporate boardrooms to presidential chambers—the Grupo Monterrey. Used rarely if at all before 1940, this term nonetheless evokes vivid episodes in the national consciousness that seemingly link past and present.

This study intends to illuminate the origins of the Monterrey elite. It is argued here that a decisive stage in the development of the *regiomontano* bourgeoisie takes place between the 1880s and 1940.[2] This formative period in the evolution of the Monterrey Group is marked by three key phases. First, as a result of a series of propitious events and circumstances, close economic and social ties develop among a small group of businessmen, producing a cohesive elite by the conclusion of the Porfirian era. Second, the revolution of 1910 and its aftermath alters the political economy of Monterrey, leading to an increasingly tense relationship between the new state and an elite redefined by the postrevolutionary political context. Third, in the 1930s, under the leadership of the Garza-Sadas, Monterrey's industrialists confront the reformist administration of Lázaro Cárdenas with lasting consequences for both the elite and the state after 1940.

In the wider framework of Mexican and Latin American history, the industrial development of Monterrey and its businessmen possess a number of distinctive characteristics, as discussed in greater detail in the introduction and conclusion of this study. In this respect, the notion of dependency in Latin America finds an exception in the case of Nuevo León. Monterrey's industrialization in its initial stage derived largely from native capital. While the country's economy continued to be essentially dependent, a group of entrepreneurs in Monterrey nonetheless carved out a wide-ranging economic empire, encompassing commerce, industry, and finance before the Mexican revolution. Thus, the roots of their industrial holdings develop prior to the period usually associated with the decisive phase in Latin American industrialization, the so-called import-substitution strategy of the 1930s and 1940s. Second, the social—rather than merely the economic—ties among the *regiomontanos* proved critical to the formation of the elite and its resiliency. In this sense, the Monterrey elite cannot be understood in narrow marxist terms. Third, though this study concentrates on the interplay between the private sector and government, the issue of labor inevitably arises. On this point, Monterrey represents an illustrative, singular case of the rise of company unions. Fourth, the Monterrey example sheds light on the discussion of the authoritarian/corporatist nature of the Mexican state. In this regard, the historical trajectory of the Monterrey elite varies from other economic groups, with implications for the analysis of state-capital relations.

The twists and turns of modern Mexican history and the present crisis have coupled the nation and Monterrey, each one enmeshed in the other's fate, magnifying as a consequence the myths and images of the city and its most visible business family. Certainly there is a measure of validity to this view, as a sketch of recent events amply suggests. The assassination in September 1973 of Eugenio Garza-Sada, captain of the Grupo at the time, dramatized the deepening political strains in Mexico during the tumultuous presidency of Luis Echeverría. After the death of the patriarch, the Garza-Sada empire was divided into four holding companies, two of which became particularly prominent, ALFA and VISA. This partition of the families' companies and interests signified a distinct moment in contemporary Mexico; the short-lived oil boom followed. ALFA and VISA, like the national government as a whole under new president José López Portillo, went on a binge, fueled by the projected abundance of petroleum and the easy credit of avaricious international bankers. The subsequent collapse of oil prices underscored the skyrocketing debt of both the country and the Garza-Sada empire. And, as the crisis took its political and economic toll, ALFA and VISA, as well as the nation, reeled close to bankruptcy. And just as the scion of the Garza-Sadas was compelled to leave the stewardship of ALFA, so the beleaguered head of the Finance Ministry was sacked by current president Miguel de la Madrid.[3]

The historian, however, must sift through the convenient parallels of the present and hold them up to the scrutiny of the past. In the case of the Grupo Monterrey, the "fit" between past and present is a partial one. Monterrey has changed a great deal since the times of the Porfiriato and the revolution that displaced it. Elements of an earlier era appear in the Monterrey Group of today, but it fails to be a duplication or simple reproduction of the city's upper class as constituted in 1940, or before. The present and its perceptions cannot be simply imposed on the past. Still, a legacy remains. This legacy and its origins are the focus of this study.

This manuscript began as a dissertation that covered the years 1880 to 1910. The present work, which takes the story to 1940, required much more additional research and effort. Throughout, the comments and criticisms of others have been crucial to the completion of this book. In this respect, the guidance and counsel of Ramón E. Ruiz, my dissertation advisor and mentor, have been paramount. I am also indebted to Greg Greb, Robert Schaefer, James Wilkie, Ricardo Romo, Manuel Peña, and Andrés Jiménez for their criticisms of earlier drafts of this work. And I benefited greatly from the comments of Ivan Jaksic, Evelyn Stevens, Van Whiting, Jr., Jack Womack, Cesar Gutiérrez, Javier Rojas Sándoval, Ruth Collier, Ramon Chacón, Donald Wyman, Barry Carr, and Abraham Nuncio. I must acknowledge a special note of thanks to Stephen Haber and Mario Cerutti, who shared with me their information, thoughts, and wisdom concerning the businessmen of Monterrey.

The staffs of various institutions were generous with their time and patience in the location of materials. I am grateful for the aid rendered by the staffs of the Archivo General de la Nación, the Archivo Condumex, the Hemeroteca Nacional, the Archivo General del Estado de Nuevo León, and the archive of the newspaper *El Porvenir* of Monterrey, as well as the Latin American Collection at the University of Texas, Austin, the National Archives in Washington, D.C., and the Bancroft Library in Berkeley. I owe particular gratitude to Mr. Richard Gould and Mr. Ronald Swerzck of the National Archives, Irene Moran of the Bancroft Library, and Agapito Renovato of the AGENL for their aid. The research assistance provided by Peter Porritt, Laura Ruiz, Lindie Bosniak, and Kathy Gilbert was very helpful.

This study could not have been possible without the support of the Ford Foundation, UC Berkeley's Faculty Development Grant Program, and a Faculty Travel Grant from the Center for Latin American

Studies. A postdoctoral fellowship from the National Research Council proved especially timely in the completion of the manuscript. I would be remiss without mentioning the clerical aid that I received along the way, including that of Rosa Ramirez, Isabel Mejorado, Rosa Johnson, and Ana Coronado; and Tomás González did yeoman work in putting the manuscript into a word processor. And I am grateful to the University of Texas Press for patience in the completion of the manuscript.

Finally, I must thank Juanita Saragoza, whose companionship, support, and sacrifice make my work possible.

The Monterrey Elite and the Mexican State, 1880–1940

Introduction

I. On the evening of February 11, 1936, Mexican president Lázaro Cárdenas confronted the leadership of the major association of employers in Monterrey, Nuevo León, at a meeting with the directors of the Centro Patronal de Monterrey.[1] This confrontation took place in the wake of several days of massive antilabor demonstrations orchestrated by the leading businessmen of the second most important economic center of the country. At issue was both the presidential authority of Cárdenas and the capacity of the Mexican state to intervene in labor-capital relations. These events marked the political consolidation of Monterrey's largest capitalists as a key power group in modern Mexico and signaled the maturation of this group as an identifiable fraction of the Mexican bourgeoisie. This study focuses on the origins of the Grupo Monterrey and its impact on the relationship between business and government in postrevolutionary Mexico.

The circumstances surrounding the presidential trip to Nuevo León in 1936 pointed to a significant turning point in the pattern of periodic conflict that had underlined the relations between Monterrey's foremost industrialists and the federal government since the revolution of 1910. For over a week, national attention had been drawn increasingly to the mounting labor conflict in Mexico's premier industrial city.[2] Since the inception of the prolabor Cárdenas administration in December 1934, Mexicans had witnessed a rising tide of strikes. But the president's sudden, unannounced journey to Nuevo León signified the unusual importance of the strike at the nation's major glass plant, the Vidriera Monterrey.

The Vidriera belonged to one of Monterrey's most prominent and wealthiest families, the Garza-Sadas. In many ways, the factory epitomized the economic power and prestige of the closely knit, conservative group of businessmen that dominated the city. The Vidriera boasted the latest equipment and technology, monopolized Mexican glass production, thrived without foreign capital or markets, and, in addition, possessed an established company union.[3] Such features characterized the key holdings of the city's reigning entrepreneurs— but none more so than those of Monterrey's "mother" industries, the Cervecería Cuauhtémoc, the brewery also owned by the Garza-Sadas, and the Fundidora de Fierro y Acero, the steelworks controlled by the Prieto family. The stature of these firms in the area and in the national economy magnified the repercussions of the conflict. Insiders realized that the strike represented more than another example of the president's stormy labor policies. A showdown appeared to be in the making between an administration barely a year in office and the powerful, entrenched capitalists of Monterrey.

As well-informed observers recognized, the strike indicated a widening of the rift between Cárdenas and the *regiomontano* businessmen. Indeed, through their local influence, and spearheaded by the Garza-Sada interests, they had waged an audacious campaign to put a candidate into the governorship of Nuevo León six months earlier in July 1935. But federal officials had nullified the election, and a Cardenista governor had been subsequently installed. Shortly thereafter, the governor had reversed the procompany tilt of the local labor board by dumping the old government representatives and appointing new ones. Under these changed conditions, dissident workers moved to challenge the leadership of the company unions.

Organizers soon arrived from the embryonic yet militant CTM (Confederación de Trabajadores Mexicanos). Headed by Vicente Lombardo Toledano, the nascent labor organization had received presidential backing. Not coincidentally, the Garza-Sadas' Vidriera was targeted to break the hold of employers over Monterrey's industrial labor force. By late January 1936, rebellious labor leaders at the glass plant had forced an election over union representation. To the fury of the Vidriera owners and their allies, on February 3, the labor board declared that the company union had lost the election. But Monterrey's businessmen proved equal to the challenge. They had immediately marshaled their vast political and economic resources within and outside Nuevo León to counter the threat to their local ascendancy.

In the days preceding Cárdenas' arrival, a hastily gathered Centro Patronal had staged a series of growing demonstrations to protest "outside agitators," the takeover of Mexico by "communism," and the labor board's "unfair decision."[4] At the urging of the Centro, a "civic association" surfaced to "combat communism." Newspapers and radio stations friendly to Monterrey's industrialists added their voices to the implicitly antigovernment campaign. Furthermore, businessmen, large and small, threatened a "strike" (*paro*) of their own, a lockout of their workers, to demonstrate the "solidarity" of Monterrey against the government-inspired, "communist" attack on Nuevo León. On February 5, a surging, vocal crowd of nearly 60,000 marched to the state government building shouting "death to the Communists" and similar slogans. Violence seemed imminent, and federal troops were called in to assure order. The huge rally also touched off similar antigovernment manifestations in Torreón, León, Mérida, Puebla, and Mexico City: another display of the *regiomontanos'* potent influence.

Then, on the morning of February 6, an ominous quiet prevailed as stores, banks, and factories remained closed. The entrepreneurs' swift mobilization indicated the extent and effectiveness of their influence—and the significance that they attached to the strike. It was clear that, for the Garza-Sadas and their counterparts, the company union composed an essential link in their web of power. The *paro* virtually paralyzed the city; the *regiomontano* capitalists' grip had been reaffirmed. To knowing observers, the president's challenge had been met. Cárdenas was forced to respond: the trip to Monterrey had to be made.

For Cárdenas, the successful *paro* served to reveal the steadfast refusal of the key businessmen of Monterrey to bend to the federal government. Despite his representatives' efforts to deflate the strike's importance, Cárdenas realized the potentially grave consequences for his presidency and for the Mexican state. The *regiomontanos* undermined his drive to break the political hold of ex-president Plutarco Elías Calles. In addition, Cárdenas' tacit approval of the upstart CTM was involved. It was another test of his drive, through the CTM, to destroy the old, corrupt, but recalcitrant CROM (Confederación Regional Obrera Mexicana) labor machine.[5] His efforts to align labor with his administration, however, faced predictable employer opposition, strengthened by the manipulation of workers through company unions.

Yet, more importantly, the *regiomontanos* represented a persistent source of resistance to federal authority. In fact, they had made a bid for national power after the assassination of president-elect Obregón in 1928. But their promotion of the ex-governor of Nuevo León, Aarón Sáenz, for the presidency ultimately failed in 1929.[6] In the same year, Monterrey businessmen opposed the introduction of the federal labor code to congress. And, when the labor bill was nonetheless submitted over their protests, they were instrumental in forming an oppositionist business organization, the Confederación Patronal de la República Mexicana.[7] Moreover, what federal official could forget the caustic condemnation of the passage of the federal labor code by the Centro Patronal in 1931? In addition, they had maintained close ties with the ambitious, opportunistic General Juan Andreu Almazán, head of the federal garrison in Nuevo León, millionaire businessman, and possible presidential aspirant.[8] Finally, there was the flagrant affront to the Cárdenas administration in the elite's attempt to seize the governorship the year before.

The *regiomontanos* were potent adversaries. Their key enterprises involved little if any foreign capital, which robbed Cárdenas of an opportunity to cast them as puppets of foreign companies. Monterrey's businessmen owned reputable firms, visibly successful, and central to the nation's industrial production. Threats of expropriation could not be made lightly and ran counter to the president's push for the "Mexicanization" of the economy. As it was, foreign governments were keenly concerned about the "radicalism" of Cárdenas. A forceful move on Monterrey's industrialists would only raise further doubts among foreign interests about Cárdenas' administration at an early point in his term of office. Nevertheless, such an open display of defiance against the president's authority could not be ignored. Cárdenas' opponents appreciated the damaging implications of his failure to gain the upper hand in the Monterrey strike.[9] With the news of the *paro,* the president decided to travel to Nuevo León and to confront Monterrey's businessmen head-on.

Cárdenas realized that the stakes were high for himself and his adversaries and, above all, for the government he headed. The past had largely shaped the confrontation; the future of his presidency perhaps depended on the outcome.

II.   The forces leading to the Vidriera strike of 1936 and its aftermath contributed importantly to defining the relationship between capital and the state in postrevolutionary Mexico. In this connection, the specific battle between the Garza-Sada family and Cárdenas constituted an escalation in the twenty-year struggle between a maturing economic elite and an emergent state. With the coalescence of the Monterrey elite, effective limits were established on state intervention in the economy and on government control over the private sector. As this study argues, the formative years of the Grupo Monterrey provide a telling story of the development of private sector–government relations during a critical phase in the evolution of the Mexican state.[10]

Furthermore, the changing, often tense relationship between the political bureaucracy and Monterrey's businessmen reflected a process of differentiation within the *regiomontano* elite itself. A close examination of the origins of the Monterrey elite offers a revealing view of the Mexican private sector and its relations with government. The extant literature on this issue has focused primarily on the role of the state. In such studies, the diversity of the Mexican private sector and its significance historically remain unclear.[11] The early history of the Grupo Monterrey suggests the importance of understanding the differences within the Mexican private sector and its implications for Mexico's political economy.

The Monterrey elite possesses several distinctive features within the context of Mexican business history. First, despite the country's historic economic dependency, the *regiomontanos'* basic holdings were built largely through native capital.[12] Second, manufacturing was critical to the economic foundation of the elite, even though the "mother" enterprises—the Cuauhtémoc brewery and the Monterrey steel plant—arose in the late nineteenth century during an era of massive foreign investment in the Mexican economy.[13] Third, the key companies of the *regiomontano* industrialists remained essentially family-run and -owned.[14] Fourth, and most importantly, the major businessmen of Monterrey forged a closely knit complex of economic, social, and political interests cemented through joint ventures, cooperative financial arrangements, interlocking directorates, and extremely propitious marriage and family ties.[15]

Before the revolution, the majority of the Mexican upper class derived its wealth from land, commerce, and mining while foreigners concentrated their investments in extractive activities. Aside from textile mills, manufacturing remained weak until import-substitution dramatically accelerated industrialization in the late 1930s and early 1940s.[16] Contrary to the national pattern, manufacturing has been crucial to the economic development of the Monterrey area since the turn of the century. Founded in 1900, the city's steel plant was the first in Latin America and became an appropriate symbol for the so-called Pittsburgh of Mexico. Thus, the primacy of industry and its Mexican ownership not only distinguished the economy of the city, but the fortunes of its upper class as well.

Moreover, Monterrey's entrepreneurs eschewed the monetary rewards associated with the holding of high political office. Before and after 1910, they preferred indirect influence, behind-the-scene maneuvering, rather than the taking of government positions themselves. Such a stance contrasted with the scores of political and military figures (including "revolutionary" ones) who parlayed their positions into lucrative businesses, profitable investments, and valuable real estate.[17] In this respect, Monterrey's capitalists set themselves apart from the political elite that appeared with the rise of the new state after 1910. Indeed, political corruption after the revolution

provided *regiomontanos* with ample opportunities to condemn un-
scrupulous officeholders and to allege the righteousness of private
businessmen.

Furthermore, the emergent *regiomontano* elite supplied an early,
identifiable, and vociferous defense of "free enterprise" against government intervention in the economy. Monterrey's capitalists apparently desired more than "political stability and proper assurances
that there was a place for a profit-oriented private sector in the new
post-revolutionary Mexico."[18] The *regiomontano*-led foundation of
COPARMEX in 1929 constituted a benchmark in the elite's battle
with the state. Yet, equally important, the Employers' Confederation
served to underscore the aggressive, divergent posture of the men
from Nuevo León within the older, more conciliatory business organizations, notably the Confederations of Chambers of Commerce and
Chambers of Industry established under government auspices in
1917–18.[19]

Finally, the dominance of this elite over the Monterrey region had
few, if any, parallels in modern Mexico. The hold of the elite went
beyond its extensive influence over local commerce, industry, and finance, since the city's powerful businessmen also maintained an ascendant position in the social and cultural life of the area. Its sway
over newspapers, later over radio and entertainment, was matched by
its influence over public education and the church. Company unions,
company cooperatives, company schools, and company recreational
facilities reinforced the elite's ability to affect public life. And social
status in Monterrey stemmed from one's place in the *regiomontano*
pecking order, a social hierarchy regulated by a tight network of clubs
and organizations dominated by the city's elite families.

The social exclusivity of these clubs acted as an essential filter to the
inner circles of the group. Their effectiveness assured an acceptable
stable of grooms and brides for marriageable offspring, an appropriate
pool of in-laws, *compadres*, and *comadres*, and, perhaps most importantly, a like-minded concentration of potentially profitable business
links, associates, partners, and information. As this study shows, the
social dominance of these businessmen complemented their economic
ascent and their efforts to protect their interests. In this sense, the
wealthy families that constituted the *regiomontano* elite represented a
degree of interpenetration that went beyond class interests. Rather, a
particular group of businessmen and their families evolved into an in-
terconnected knot of economic, social, and familial ties that provided a
resilient cohesiveness. The sum of these links anchored the power and
durability of the *regiomontano* elite.[20]

The density of these ties gave an extraordinary coherency to the group's public facade and political views that encouraged a perception of monolithic uniformity among the Monterrey elite. Not unlike a large family, threats from the outside—economic or political—served to promote cohesion and to allow its strongest members to manage its defense. Thus, as the industrialists of Nuevo León increasingly contested the state, the clashes contributed to the tightening of the Monterrey elite's network of resources. Furthermore, the disputes with government developed an ideological character that accentuated their distinctiveness and masked any internally discordant threads or tendencies.

As the federal government grew in institutional strength, free enterprise and local political autonomy became perhaps predictable slogans of the Monterrey entrepreneurs. But they also took special pride in their business accomplishments, in their technical achievements, in their prominence in the nation's industry—the latter a clear refutation of Mexico's blighted past. In their own eyes, despite a studiously modest demeanor, they represented "progress" in a country burdened with the legacies of its historic economic backwardness, including an avaricious political bureaucracy. Indeed, a sense of mission permeated the elite's ideological skirmishes with the state.[21]

With nationalistic zeal, the Monterrey industrialists insistently touted the importance of capitalist values. Authority, discipline, and the work ethic were combined with the glorification of the family, traditionalism, and moral rectitude. In contrast, government meant centralization, despotism, and corruption as well as immorality, laxity, and disorder. Hence, the gleaming, advanced machinery of the Mexican-owned, family-run brewery, for example, took on an added significance. For these men, the distinctive features of Monterrey's industries offered undeniable proof of the acumen of the city's capitalists and confirmation of their vision.[22]

The expressions of the elite's self-image appeared in many ways, at times overtly, on other occasions implicitly: in the suggestive advertising, in the constantly arranged tours for famous visitors to Monterrey's leading industries, in the technical school patterned after the Massachusetts Institute of Technology.[23] Eventually, the ideological conflict between the businessmen of Nuevo León and the state was translated into competing publications, into radio programming, and finally into rival political party platforms. Within the Mexican private sector, the Monterrey elite assumed an unrivaled position of importance. The antigovernment actions of other businessmen in postrevolutionary Mexico paled in comparison to the deep and wide-ranging opposition of Monterrey's industrialists.

As a result, the *regiomontanos* gradually emerged as identifiable spokesmen for similarly disgruntled, but less articulate, native capitalists. Thus, the Monterrey elite acquired a singular notoriety in Mexico's political economy. This visibility tended to further the perception of a near-static homogeneity to the *regiomontano* elite that deflected attention from its inner workings. Indeed, this view has endured, as evidenced in contemporary writings on the Grupo Monterrey.[24] Nonetheless, the apparent uniformity of the Monterrey elite belied the intricacies of its internal dynamics.

III.   Change, as well as continuity, marked the composition of the Grupo in its formative years. Most observers have noted the persistence of certain members of the elite, notably the Garza-Sada family. Yet, over time, a careful analysis reveals that elite membership and standing were subject to change. Some old names lost their glitter, new ones rose in prominence, and still others sustained their luster. Nevertheless, wealth continued to be the primary criterion for admission to elite circles. The composition of this privileged group varied, therefore, over time as the economic fortunes of its members changed, as certain industries thrived while others stagnated, as certain investments prospered while still others failed. The resultant differences, however, were often obscured by the close links among the elite. Nevertheless, if only subtly revealed, diversity occurred within this group in power and status that stemmed from several sources. In this connection, the success of the major industrial holdings of the elite involved several and various dimensions: the characteristics of markets, the significance of imports to the process of production, the importance of the threat of foreign competition, and, most crucially, *the role of the state in the consumption, manufacturing, and protection of Monterrey's industrial products.*

As this study demonstrates, the economic underpinnings of the Monterrey elite possessed an underlying, fundamental rift, best seen perhaps in the differences between the Cervecería Cuauhtémoc and the Fundidora de Fierro y Acero. Government played a critical role from the inception of the Fundidora through government contracts, licensing of necessary, imported equipment, tariff protections, and other forms of support. In short, the Fundidora exhibited a marked dependence on state aid prior to and after the revolution. The Cervecería, in contrast, served markets virtually free of the state and early on took measures to terminate the need for imports. Competition from foreign brewers, particularly from the United States, proved to be minimal in the pre-1910 period. Furthermore, American Prohibition (1918–1933) gave the Mexican brewery a decisive advantage that was compounded by the generally nationalistic, protectionist posture of postrevolutionary governments toward Mexican industry.

The internal differences within the industrialists of Monterrey produced political repercussions as the Porfirian regime ended and a new government emerged. In political terms, the economic relationship of the Fundidora to the new state constrained the ability of the steel plant's owners to challenge government. The Cervecería interests, on the other hand, were economically much less dependent on the state and allowed the Garza-Sadas the capacity to exercise greater political assertiveness than their Fundidora counterparts in relations with government. As noted in this study, through the 1920s the multiplying conflicts between the state and the Monterrey elite found the Fundidora's owners compelled to take a back seat to the Garza-Sadas as the struggles with government unfolded. As a result, the Garza-Sadas exerted increasing influence over the positions of the *regiomontanos* in their intensifying bouts with the federal government.

By the end of the decade, the Garza-Sada family had assumed the political and ideological leadership of Monterrey's capitalists. The Fundidora remained a close, but discreet ally. Still, the Cervecería ownership represented the most stridently conservative voice among the businessmen of Nuevo León. Meanwhile the steel company's leader, Adolfo Prieto, maintained a safer, more conciliatory posture toward the state. Thus, the decade after the revolution witnessed a discernible break in the Porfirian cast of the elite. This change was reflected in the fact that Adolfo Prieto resided in Mexico City and the basis of the Fundidora's welfare largely depended on the state.

The resultant political variation encouraged the ascendancy of the Cervecería clique as the architects of the elite's campaign against the state in the 1930s. The brewery interests assumed a combative stance that was translated into blatant confrontations with Lázaro Cárdenas, including the antilabor demonstrations associated with the 1936 Vidriera strike. The Fundidora, despite its political dissatisfaction with Cárdenas, took a more moderate course—a position underlined by the steel mill's vulnerability to state action. In their contest with Cárdenas, the brewery's owners directed a potent offensive through their support of the right-wing Acción Cívica Nacionalista, their unremitting ideological criticisms of the president's "communism," and, finally, their active involvement in the opposition candidacy of Almazán in the 1940 presidential campaign. Hence, the 1930s cemented the Garza-Sada dominance in the articulation of elite views on state-capital relations. Indeed, as this study suggests, it was this faction of Monterrey's industrialists that figured prominently in the retreat of Lázaro Cárdenas from his reformist policies: a move that redefined the relations between the state and capital in Mexico in the post-1940 era.

IV. The early development of the Grupo Monterrey illuminates the complexities and nuances of the historical interplay between the private sector and the postrevolutionary state. In this regard, the evolution of the Monterrey elite sheds light on the continuing debate on authoritarianism in Mexico and its implications for the private sector.[25] On this point, some scholars have argued that the Mexican state dominates the private sector through the combined use of inducements and constraints.[26] Others have taken the position that Mexican capital possesses much greater autonomy than that implied by the authoritarian framework. Yet such models must be tempered by the historical context in which state-capital relations took place.[27] As the early history of the Monterrey Group demonstrates, the effectiveness of the state's "stick" or "carrot" depended on the specific impacts of state actions. For the Fundidora, for example, the Mexican government played a decisive role in the success of the enterprise throughout the early twentieth century.

On the other hand, the capacity of the state to affect the private sector was not uniform. Given Mexico's weak economy immediately after the revolution, a low tariff on beer, for instance, would have exacerbated the loss of capital to foreign companies. In addition, such an act would have contradicted the fundamental nationalism of the revolution. For practical financial reasons, if not for ideological ones, the use of a tariff to constrain the Cervecería would have been counterproductive. In the case of the Fundidora, because of the centrality of the state to the steel plant's market, a high protectionist tariff could be maintained without sacrificing the influence of government over the steel company. Additional considerations could be taken into account, but the point should be emphasized: state-capital relations after the revolution were fluid and subject to several factors.

These relations were often dictated by the concerns of a state anxious to solidify its control over Mexico's political economy. A volatile political situation compounded a fragile economy beset by the negative consequences of nearly a decade of civil strife from 1910 to 1917, as well as the disruptive repercussions of periodic political upheavals that wracked the country throughout the 1920s.[28] The new government also confronted foreign interests eager to renew their dominant places in the Mexican economy. If this were not enough, the postrevolutionary leadership faced the formidable task of organizing a viable national economic structure—printing currency, regulating banks, servicing debts, setting tax and tariff schedules, balancing rival economic interest groups, implementing labor and land reforms.

The Mexican private sector encountered a similar transition. Native capitalists had to weigh the economic performance of the state, the risks to their businesses of a still-unsettled political scene, and the opportunities (and dangers) of an uncertain market. In this context, few native interests survived the revolution with the resources and internal cohesion of the *regiomontano* elite. In fact, most of Monterrey's industries continued to function throughout the violent phase (1910–1917) of the revolutionary period. After 1917, Nuevo León's industrialists recuperated swiftly as the new state struggled with numerous contending sectors of Mexico's political economy and a myriad of complicated problems.

In short, the postrevolutionary governments did not immediately possess the ability to manage the country and, at the same time, promote economic growth. Eight years after the 1917 constitution, a central bank and a government-supported agrarian credit institution were organized; it took two more years for a formal tariff commission to be established. And it was not until 1934 that a national economic development bank appeared.[29] For governmental leaders, political stability was indispensable to the economy—and to their power. Politics, therefore, of necessity often took precedence over economic reconstruction.[30]

Nonetheless, state intervention in the economy gradually widened and gained in strength. Predictably, clashes with the private sector multiplied as the latter sought to slow land distribution, to limit income taxes, to maintain low wages, to undermine labor reform, and to push for cheap freight rates on government-owned railways. In contrast to bureaucrats, the military, and labor, business interests proved to be difficult for the postrevolutionary regimes to harness under governmental powers. As Roger Hansen has pointed out, the state found that it "could not so easily control the activities of Mexico's growing industrial and commercial elites."[31] In light of their economic assets and interconnections, the members of the emergent elite of Monterrey possessed the resources to take a leading role in the private sector's efforts to limit state intervention in the economy.

Labor policy became the most visible point of contention. The established company unions of the *regiomontanos* allowed them an advantage over the bulk of other businessmen in combating a government-supported workers' organization. Moreover, native capitalists, including *regiomontanos*, successfully thwarted labor's attempt to press for the codification of Article 123 of the constitution of 1917 in 1924, and again in 1926. Although the federal labor code was finally introduced to congress in 1929, the Monterrey-led Mexican private sector stalled its passage until 1931. Thus, the confrontations with the Cárdenas administration were practically inevitable when the reformist president extended the state's reach over labor and, by implication, over government-capital relations. As Arnaldo Córdova has argued, labor, urban and rural, was critical to the institutionalization of state power.[32] Toward this end, the Cárdenas-inspired formation of the Confederación de Trabajadores Mexicanos and the Confederación Nacional Campesina proved essential to the consolidation of government authority.

In the wake of the Vidriera strike, Cárdenas attempted to bring the private sector under the government's wing.[33] In August 1936, a new law compelled all but the smallest enterprises to join the Confederación de Cámaras de Comercio e Industria. The Chambers Law of 1936 extended the state's jurisdiction far beyond previous guidelines that governed such business organizations. The new provisions also gave the state the legal means to blunt the influence of the Monterrey capitalists and similarly antigovernment businessmen within the framework of the Confederación. The *regiomontano* elite joined the reconstructed organization that forcibly combined the Chambers of Commerce and Chambers of Industry into one structure. But COPARMEX remained independent since, technically, it was an employers' syndicate governed, in an ironic twist, by Article 123 and the federal labor code. COPARMEX therefore continued to function as a thinly veiled platform for the *regiomontanos*, while they also maintained a voice within the reconstituted organization. Cárdenas' move failed, however, to intimidate Mexican capitalists determined to resist government encroachments in the economy. Among the opposition, the men from Monterrey stood out as the best organized and, as a consequence, the most prominent.

In sum, the crystallization of state authority in Mexico took place in the face of the potent resistance of capitalists spearheaded by the businessmen of Monterrey, specifically, the Garza-Sada interests. The intensity of this subsequent conflict threatened the state sufficiently to push Cárdenas to look for an accommodation with the private sector. This deal was carried out by Cárdenas' handpicked successor on the eve of the 1940 presidential election. In this process, the Garza-Sadas and their allies played a pivotal role—a role reproduced in the boundaries established between capital and government after 1940.

"An extensive system of bargaining with regard to economic interests," Fernando Henrique Cardoso has stated, "turned the Mexican state into an effective instrument of domination and political control."[34] In this "bargaining," it seems, Mexican business exercised greater weight than peasants and workers. The post-1940 era has revealed disproportionate benefits for Mexican capitalists under a state structure largely shaped by Lázaro Cárdenas. The coalescence of the authoritarian-corporatist Mexican state spanned over two decades from the signing of the constitution of 1917 to the Cárdenas years. The outcome of this process, the evidence suggests, reflected in part the indelible imprint of the struggle between the emergent state and the Mexican private sector. In this light, the history of the Monterrey elite bears significantly on our understanding of the origins and character of authoritarianism in Mexico.

V. Three basic interrelated themes are used here to analyze the formative years of the Monterrey Group within the context of the consolidation of the Mexican state: (1) the economic differentiation within the elite, with particular attention paid to the two "mother" industries, the Cervecería Cuauhtémoc and the Fundidora de Fierro y Acero; (2) the evolution of the elite and its near-hegemonic hold on the city of Monterrey; (3) the development of the *regiomontanos'* ideological positions and the efforts to extend their influence beyond Nuevo León.

These themes are followed through three distinct historical periods that correspond to the major parts of this study. Part one encompasses primarily the Porfirian era (1880–1910) during which the establishment of the brewery and the steel plant occurred under the governorship of the politically prominent Bernardo Reyes. In this section, chapter 1 sketches the background of Monterrey's leading industrialists within the wider context of Mexico's economic history, particularly that of the north. Chapter 2 carefully examines the beginnings of Monterrey's industrialization at the end of the nineteenth century. This second chapter stresses the initial, but decisive economic interrelationships that bound Monterrey's businessmen into an emergent elite. Chapter 3 explores the social ties within the maturing elite through marriages and family bonds as well as the exclusive clubs and activities that served to underscore the social ascendancy of the elite circle of wealthy families. Additionally, this third chapter emphasizes the notions of superiority and paternalism that punctuated the views of *regiomontano* employers toward their workers.

Part two covers the revolutionary years and their aftermath, when Monterrey's businessmen confronted new political and economic realities that precipitated the elite's initial skirmishes with government, especially over labor reforms. This period was climaxed by the formation of the Confederación Patronal de la República Mexicana (COPARMEX) in 1929. Thus, chapter 4 traces the impact of the revolution on Monterrey from 1910 through 1918 and its significance as exemplified by the experiences of the Cervecería and the Fundidora. Chapter 5 covers the economic recovery of Monterrey's leading capitalists and the political relations that ensued with the state in the 1920s. The reestablishment of the elite's social dominance, the continuities and changes in the elite's membership, and the persistent importance of social ties to the concentration of wealth and power in Monterrey are the thrust of chapter 6. The formation of COPARMEX and the emergence of the elite as a national political influence form the basis of chapter 7. In this chapter, particular attention is given to the growing prominence of the Garza-Sadas in the articulation of the interests of the Monterrey elite.

Part three centers on the tense and later blatantly hostile relations between the industrialists of Monterrey and the Mexican government that peaked in the events leading to the presidential election of 1940. Setting the stage for conflict established in the 1920s, chapter 8 traces the major confrontations between the *regiomontanos* and the state during the 1930s. Two key aspects are particularly analyzed to demonstrate the maturation of the Monterrey elite as a principal actor in the definition of state-capital relations in the Cárdenas era: the Vidriera strike of 1936 and its significance for the presidential campaign of 1940. Chapter 9 concludes the study with an analysis of the 1940 elections and the role of the Monterrey elite in the consolidation of an authoritarian state in Mexico by 1940.

In the pages that follow, only the major elements of the origins of the Grupo Monterrey appear. Several crucial events need to be fully explored; various points require further research and clarification that are beyond the scope of this study. In this regard, my intent is not to chronicle the extent of the wealth, income, or assets of *regiomontano* industrialists; rather, the focus is on the basis of their economic prowess and its implications. Similarly, this analysis concentrates on native capital; a detailed examination of foreign investment in Nuevo León, particularly after 1920, awaits the hand of the historian. As the notes will make clear to the careful reader, many questions regarding the Monterrey elite and its relations with the state remain to be completely answered—for instance, the increasingly conservative character of the *maximato* contrasted with the growing tension between the elite and the Calles-dominated regimes after 1928. The question of whether the *regiomontano* case is unique calls for more work on other economic groups in this period. Finally, the contemporary prominence of the Grupo Monterrey in the Mexican political economy tempts one to draw neat lines between the past and present. In fact, as noted in the conclusion, several aspects of the Grupo's more recent political and economic stature suggest characteristics dating from its formative years.

The resilience of the Grupo's power and composition continues to impress most observers and points to an explanation that emphasizes the static, monolithic character of the Monterrey elite. Yet the alleged unchanging nature of the Grupo may say less about the *regiomontano* businessmen and more about a state committed to an economic development strategy wedded to capitalist interests.

1. Commerce and Capital: The Economic Roots of the Monterrey Elite

I. The foundation of the Cervecería Cuauhtémoc in 1890 and of the Fundidora de Fierro y Acero ten years later marked the industrial beginnings of Monterrey, Nuevo León. In an era underscored by the domination of Mexico's economy by foreign interests, native capital nonetheless figured crucially in the establishment of the two firms. In fact, *regiomontanos* often appeared among the investors that made Monterrey into Mexico's leading industrial center by the turn of the century. More importantly, a particular group of local businessmen was inordinately involved in the organization of the city's major industries.

Monterrey's industrialization and its native character reflected the role of the city in the economic history of the region. The evolution of Monterrey as a hub of Mexico's northeastern commerce proved essential to the accumulation of local capital for investment in industry. Three key factors, however, led to the dominance of a few merchants over the area's trade, and the resultant concentration of wealth constituted the economic roots of the Monterrey elite. The first stemmed from the tremendous profits generated by the traffic in cotton during the American Civil War (1860–1865). The Union blockade of the South forced the Confederacy to route its cotton through northern Mexico. Through the influence of the region's ruling *caudillo*, Santiago Vidaurri, Monterrey became the critical link in the trade, and the merchants associated with the powerful *cacique* garnered a disproportionate amount of the cotton trade and its rewards. The second factor derived from the devastating economic depression of the 1870s. In its wake, only a small number of merchants survived, sustained by the profits of the cotton boom, as weaker competitors disappeared. Third, beginning in the 1880s, northern Mexico witnessed a massive influx of foreign investment. The subsequent boom afforded the resilient *regiomontano* merchants an initial but substantial advantage in responding to the internal markets spawned by the region's development. Thus, the nineteenth century, particularly the period after the Mexican-American War (1845–1848), contributed importantly to the economic basis of the Monterrey elite.[1]

II. Adversity stamped much of Monterrey's early history while Mexico was ruled by Spain.[2] On the northern periphery of New Spain, the settlement experienced the trials of a frontier existence after its founding in 1596. Droughts, disease, Indian attacks, and Spanish neglect plagued the little town. The Spaniards were unable to find abundant precious minerals in the area; consequently the Spanish colonial administration relegated Monterrey to serve largely as a defensive post against hostile Indians. Because of its presidio, the village also served as a transit point in the movement of merchandise, and contraband, brought in from the coast to supply the interior mining towns of Zacatecas, Durango, and Saltillo. This commercial traffic, however, faced severe restrictions imposed by the powerful Mexico City merchants, limiting the flow of commerce to the north through Monterrey. Nonetheless, because of the high cost of goods transported overland from Mexico City, smuggling occurred frequently during the colonial period. The settlement grew slowly; subsistence agriculture and pastoral activity reflected the area's underdevelopment. By the middle of the eighteenth century, Monterrey contained just over 3,000 inhabitants.[3]

The colonization of Texas (Nuevo Santander) and Tamaulipas in the 1750s extended the Spanish defensive perimeter. Precipitated by the efforts of the Bourbon kings to reform Spain's colonial administration, the change pushed the line of presidios northward, above Monterrey. The struggling colonists of Nuevo Santander required goods of various types to survive the hardships imposed by distance, weather, and frontier dangers. The increasing commercial traffic to the north allowed *regiomontano* merchants to benefit from the city's function as a chief trading point on the route to the new provinces. In addition to peddling their wares and products to new colonists, Monterrey's merchants and farmers also augmented their trade with the thriving mining centers to the south. The permission to import goods through the nearby port of Soto la Marina furthered the logistical importance of the city. As a result, in the latter part of the eighteenth century, Monterrey practically doubled its population. Over 6,000 residents inhabited the city in 1803.

By the time of independence, the outline of Monterrey's commercial role had been drawn. The turmoil of the decade 1810 to 1821 scarcely touched Monterrey. The end of Spain's colonial rule of Mexico caused little violence or disruption of the town's economy or society.[4] As a source of supplies for both sides, Monterrey benefited from the wars of independence.[5] Confident of their position and eager to discard Spanish controls, the merchants of Monterrey strengthened the city's commercial orientation. Matamoros in particular contributed to Monterrey's position in northern Mexico as a collection center for exports and as a hub of distribution for goods brought in through the same port.[6] Many immigrants from the wartorn central region added to Monterrey's population and further stimulated the town's growth. By 1824, the fledgling city numbered over 12,000 people.[7]

Although Nuevo León escaped the destruction and violence of the wars of independence, the area was not immune to the aftereffects. After the euphoria of independence, Mexico faced a crumbling economy. Agricultural production was severely damaged by the recent strife. Transportation retained its colonial attributes—costly, slow, limited, and uncertain. Mining underwent a long depression due to the lack of capital to restore production to previous levels. Frequent political squabbles underscored the struggle of postindependence Mexico to resolve its crisis, to reestablish a viable political economy. Customs revenues became the main source of income for both federal and state governments. The conditions for contraband and graft flourished in such a situation. Poorly paid public officials, a weak military, and the high prices of legitimate trade produced a smuggler's paradise. With their proximity to ports and their commercial contacts, *regiomontano* merchants capitalized on the weakness of other areas and developed a lucrative business, legal and illegal, primarily the latter, trading with the ravaged interior of Mexico.[8] It was not without risk: confiscation, Indian attack, and bandits constantly endangered the lives and businesses of most traders. Nonetheless, Monterrey sustained a lively, if not impressive, regional economy.[9]

The fortuitous location of Monterrey continued to provide traders with profitable opportunities. The Texas War of 1836 and the subsequent establishment of the Lone Star Republic boosted Monterrey's role as a commercial center. Texas merchants, unencumbered by high Mexican customs duties, transported goods to the Mexican border to sell to their *regiomontano* counterparts. A generally illegal but remunerative trade ensued.[10] In return for gold and silver collected by *regiomontano* traders, Americans sold the Mexicans finished goods, primarily from the United States. As middlemen, the *regiomontanos* earned sizable commissions. The war with the United States in 1845 initially threatened the Texas trade, but the *regiomontanos* turned Mexico's adversity into profit. The disruption of internal trade via

Veracruz and Mexico City produced an incalculable increase in commercial, largely illegitimate, activity.

As a result of the war, Mexico gave up nearly half of the nation's territory. The position of Monterrey, between mining areas to the south and North American products obtainable at the border, favored merchants based in the capital of Nuevo León. Consequently, "the dominant position of Monterrey in the northern region of the country was confirmed after 1848," as one historian has noted, "with its conversion into the center of the regional trade with the neighboring nation."[11]

III.   The political, military, and economic weakness of the central government persisted after 1848 and encouraged the creation of regional *caudillos*. In the midst of this fragmentation, Santiago Vidaurri successfully made northeastern Mexico his personal domain from 1855 to 1865. For Monterrey's merchants, Vidaurri offered political stability, low taxation, and the suppression of contraband and commerce not controlled by *regiomontanos*. In light of Vidaurri's military strength, Monterrey's traders formed a potent alliance with the *caudillo* that monopolized the entire northeast.[12]

Vidaurri shrewdly perceived the potential inherent in Monterrey's commercial role. By incorporating leading merchants as allies, Vidaurri forged a political and economic empire that included Coahuila and Tamaulipas, in addition to Nuevo León. Since Vidaurri based himself in Monterrey as the official governor of the state, the city's advantage redoubled. Prosperity reigned during Vidaurri's rule, and the merchants favored by the *caudillo* garnered the lion's share of the resultant trade.

Several factors contributed to the extraordinary affluence during Vidaurri's tenure as governor. First, the *cacique* permitted the entry of foreign products and facilitated the export of Mexican goods through several new points along the northern border. Second, the creation of a commercial "Free Zone" in Tamaulipas in 1858 added richly to Monterrey's trade. Third, and most significantly, during the U.S. Civil War, the city served as commercial entrepôt for the Confederacy. Fourth, the French Intervention in Mexico (1862–1867) allowed *regiomontanos* to supply both sides, with lucrative results. Nevertheless, the years 1860 to 1865 proved to be especially critical and incredibly prosperous.[13]

A consistent feature of the Vidaurri era was the collusion between merchants and the *cacique*. The substantial rewards from smuggling attracted many would-be contrabandists. Particularly after 1848, smugglers gravitated to the area in the hope of gaining a niche in the thriving illegal trade.[14] *Regiomontano* traders resented the intrusion, that is, the competition. Vidaurri's repression of outside smugglers, and at times legitimate merchants, quickly earned the *cacique* the favor of the city's commercial establishment.[15]

Soon after taking over as governor of Nuevo León, Vidaurri opened several new ports of entry along the Río Bravo for the passage of goods. Despite the economic ills of northern Mexico in the wake of independence, continuing demand for low-cost imports, coupled with high duty rates charged in other parts of Mexico, resulted in astronomical prices. This was especially true of merchandise brought in through the main port of Veracruz, where customs revenues provided much of the central government's funds. By charging low duty rates and establishing new customshouses, Vidaurri successfully increased the volume of trade along the Río Bravo. As a consequence of the *caudillo's* partiality, Monterrey's merchants profited handsomely from the traffic emanating from Reynosa, Camargo, Mier, Guerrero, Nuevo Laredo, and Piedras Negras.[16]

The flourishing border trade offered problems as well as benefits for Nuevo León's traders. Mexican customers quickly realized the advantages of crossing the border, buying on the Texas side, and eliminating the mediating role of Vidaurri's favored merchants and customs officials.[17] The inauguration of the commercial Free Zone in 1858 along the Tamaulipas-Texas border reinforced the position of *regiomontano* interests. The Free Zone allowed the importation of goods from the United States without paying customs duties and deprived Texas smugglers of their key attraction—cheaper goods. Understandably, abuse of the Free Zone occurred immediately, as Vidaurri and *regiomontano* merchants once again had the upper hand on border trade. Products introduced across the Tamaulipas-Texas border were soon appearing throughout northern Mexico. Matias Romero, finance minister of Mexico, lamented the loss in customs revenues due to the extent of smuggling through the mechanism of the Free Zone. Northeastern Mexican merchants found eager allies in congress, however, to dispute and to frustrate Romero's attempts to terminate the Free Zone. Clearly the demarcated area only "facilitated the contraband trade, aside from having other defects," as one observer has stated, but "it undoubtedly benefited the border region."[18]

Given their dominance of the region's commerce, Vidaurri and his merchant friends supported the maintenance of the Free Zone. By 1860, Santiago Vidaurri and a favored group of Monterrey traders largely controlled commerce routed through northeastern Mexico. The *caudillo's* military power enforced the *regiomontanos'* grasp of the region, minimized the appearance of interlopers, and discouraged any interference from the federal government over the virtual domination exercised by Vidaurri and his cohorts. Developments north of the border soon contributed immeasurably to the economic power of Nuevo León's major city.

Because of cotton's importance to the economy of the South and Western Europe, the U.S. Civil War led to an unprecedented period of prosperity for Monterrey's commerce. From the outset of the war, the Union realized the necessity of denying the South the ability to trade cotton for munitions and arms. The Union naval blockade of the Confederacy forced the South to seek an outlet for its cotton. Subsequently, Confederate officials looked to Mexico as a convenient conduit for cotton. President Benito Juárez, however, rejected the proposals since the influence of Union agents effectively counteracted Confederate entreaties. Thus, "when it became obviously useless to expect encouragement from Juárez, Confederate leaders looked elsewhere in Mexico for aid."[19]

The Texas border became the focus of the South's strategy to evade the Union blockade. The period 1848 to 1860 had clearly demonstrated the capacity of the Texas border area to be an avenue for the exchange of cotton for European goods and materials of war.[20] In May 1861, Confederate president Jefferson Davis sent Cuban-born Juan A. Quintero to negotiate with Santiago Vidaurri for an agreement to ship goods through northeastern Mexico. Quintero found Vidaurri eager to cooperate.[21] In response, a delighted Davis instructed Quintero in September 1861 "to establish friendly relations with the Governor of Nuevo León and Coahuila; to express the gratification of President [Davis] upon learning of the amicable disposition of that and adjacent Mexican states; to inquire as to the possibility of securing arms and ammunition; and to seek to induce Vidaurri to interfere in the proposed transportation of munitions and troops of the United States across Mexican territory."[22] Since he was nominally a supporter of Juárez, Vidaurri's cooperation with Davis and the Confederacy incurred the resentment of the central government. Yet, at that time, the governor's troops obviated a direct challenge from the harried Mexican president.

Juárez faced a serious internal political problem as rankled conservatives plotted his ouster by working with agents of Napoleon III of France to return the conservatives to power through the aid of the French army. Napoleon III, of course, had his own designs. In 1862, a large French force arrived and occupied Veracruz, allegedly to collect Mexico's unpaid debt. Despite the Mexican victory outside Puebla on May 5, 1862, Juárez' departure from Mexico City took place a few months later. Thus, an undeterred Vidaurri worked enthusiastically with Quintero and the Confederacy.[23] Because of Vidaurri's support, the *regiomontano* merchants were in a particularly advantageous position. Nuevo León's farmers, ranchers, and textile manufacturers also stood to gain from the opportunities afforded by the Confederate trade.[24]

Within a few months, commercial traffic flourished along the Texas border. To one observer, the volume of the trade took on a near gold-rush intensity.[25] As the shipping point for the Confederacy's cotton, Matamoros became the "one great leak on the Federal blockade,"[26] as fleets of ships disgorged their goods and awaited the loading of the precious white fiber. Money seemed everywhere to be made: haulers of goods, wagon-wheel makers, mule and ox traders, horse sellers, and blacksmiths were among the many attracted to the myriad opportunities spawned by the traffic in cotton. During the Civil War, Matamoros attracted over 20,000 speculators, from Union and Southern agents to English, French, and German representatives.[27] By 1865, Matamoros had become a bustling port of 30,000 people, serviced by countless saloons, several gambling houses, and dozens of brothels.[28]

The commercial activity in Matamoros mirrored the prosperity that was enjoyed by the middlemen of the cotton trade. Monterrey was the essential exchange center of Southern cotton for European and Mexican provisions. In 1862, United States consul M. M. Kimmey noted the constant line of pack trains and wagons between Nuevo León and Texas. In a dispatch, he pointed out that "the trade had grown to such magnitude that enough goods were passing through Monterrey to supply the whole rebel army."[29] Estimates suggested as many as 7,000 bales of cotton passed through the city per month, from which Vidaurri derived 50,000 pesos monthly in customs duties alone.[30] The profits from the trade in taxes, sales profits, and transportation charges were enormous.[31]

An indication of the value of the cotton trade occurred when President Juárez occupied Monterrey in 1864. In just five months, Juárez appropriated over a million dollars in revenues and collected thousands more from local merchants in taxes. Desperate for funds to fight pursuing French-conservative forces, Juárez dropped his opposition to the Confederate trade during his short stay in Nuevo León.[32] In brief, "the commerce of Nuevo León had a splendid epoch," observed the *regiomontano* historian Santiago Roel, "and much capital was amassed as a consequence of the numerous commercial operations that were established at that time."[33]

The French Intervention in Mexico (1862–1867) posed potential hazards to the cotton trade. Vidaurri confronted the choice between the French army and Juárez' ragtag troops, and the northern *caudillo* cast his fortunes with the European invaders. In gratitude, the French named Vidaurri a royal advisor, and, later, minister of the treasury. With the French withdrawal in 1867, however, the era of Vidaurri ended. Later that year, the ex-chieftain of Nuevo León and Coahuila died before a firing squad at the order of a young Mexican officer, Porfirio Díaz.[34] The death of Vidaurri closed a key chapter in the history of Monterrey, but the legacies of that era far outlived the fallen *caudillo.* [35]

Several of Monterrey's merchants, most of them of Spanish descent, emerged from this period greatly enriched. Perhaps the richest beneficiary of the cotton boom era was the Irish immigrant Patrick Mullins (Patricio Milmo). In 1845, the eighteen-year-old arrived in Mexico in the wake of his country's potato famine. He traveled to San Luis Potosí to work for his uncle, a small merchant. After receiving a modest inheritance, Milmo started his own general store in Matamoros in 1848. At the center of the border trade and the Free Zone, Milmo's business prospered, which led to the establishment of another store in Monterrey. The economic turning point for Milmo occurred in 1857 when he married Prudencia Vidaurri, daughter of the powerful *cacique.* Through his ties with the *caudillo,* including managing Vidaurri's financial interests, Milmo became a virtual broker of Monterrey's commercial fortunes. From his business profits, Milmo conducted an important money-lending operation. In return for his loans, Milmo exacted a high rate of interest and a percentage of the owner's profits. By the end of the 1860s, Milmo owned over one million acres spread over the states of Tamaulipas, Nuevo León, and Coahuila, and he remained one of the city's major merchants and its chief source of credit.[36]

Ties to Vidaurri and Milmo also aided other businessmen, among them Santiago Belden, a Milmo crony, as well as Valentín Rivero, Mariano Hernández, and José Armendaiz, a trio of Spanish-born merchants. In addition, Gregorio Zambrano and the Coahuilan merchant Evaristo Madero benefited from the prosperity during Vidaurri's reign. Hernández, for example, began as a small storekeeper in 1855 soon after his arrival from Spain. With Vidaurri's aid and the capital of Rivero, and Gregorio Zambrano, Hernández spearheaded the building of the La Fama textile plant in 1856. The demand for cloth, especially during the Civil War years, earned huge dividends for the plant's owners. At the conclusion of the cotton boom, Hernández maintained two large stores, one in Monterrey and the other in Matamoros. Others who prospered during this era included Bernardino García and Lorenzo González Treviño.[37]

Mexican merchants also gained from the thriving commerce of the period. José A. Calderón, in particular, made a rapid ascent with lasting consequences for the city's industrial beginnings. He was as much an itinerant salesman as he was a merchant in his younger years, bringing products from central Mexico to the north in exchange for goods available in Nuevo León and adjacent states. Trading, selling, and bartering along the way, Calderón crisscrossed roads and trails from San Luis Potosí to Nuevo León, and from Tamaulipas to Coahuila. The American Civil War boom, coupled with his association with Vidaurri and Milmo, transformed his extensive network of contacts into a lucrative source of supplies during the heady 1860s. By the end of the decade, Calderón joined the respected and wealthy members of Monterrey's commercial establishment, with stores in Coahuila and Nuevo León.[38]

IV.   During the cotton boom, the privileged position of Monterrey's merchants allowed them to do business largely unaffected by the troubles afflicting the rest of the country. But the prosperity related to the U.S. Civil War inevitably ended. Nuevo León's commercial golden age was over, and full economic recovery eluded merchants for two decades. In addition to losing the war trade, they also experienced a severe decline of their traditional interior regional markets. The nation's economic problems, due primarily to the destructiveness of the conservative-liberal war, compounded Nuevo León's specific troubles. The Mexican victory over the French and their conservative allies proved to be bittersweet. In its aftermath, President Benito Juárez faced a depressed national economy, a bankrupt government, and a divided society. The north, like the rest of Mexico, confronted the lack of an effective transportation system, rampant banditry, and the consequences of regional political rivalries. Mexico projected a forlorn, chaotic, uninviting image that dampened the spirits of even the most optimistic investors, foreign or domestic.

The merchants of Monterrey encountered several local and regional obstacles to the restoration of their former prosperity. With Vidaurri's death, *regiomontano* traders lost their protective shield and favorable treatment. Without the *caudillo's* troops, wagons and merchandise became much more vulnerable to bandits and Indian attacks.[39] Moreover, Monterrey's traders carried the burden of rising tax rates. The bite of the *alcabala* tax further cut the merchants' profit margins as the need for revenues forced the federal government to charge high duties. Many traders doubled as smugglers in their attempts to avoid payment of customs fees. However, without Vidaurri to discourage outsiders, Monterrey's merchants lost their favored place in the trade emanating from the commercial Free Zone along the Tamaulipas-Texas border. In the hope of expanding their business, *regiomontanos* joined the chorus of northern interests clamoring for an expansion of the Free Zone.[40] In November 1870, congress extended the Free Zone to include Nuevo León, Coahuila, and Chihuahua. Cognizant of the potential for smuggling, the central government countered by greatly increasing its customs border patrols. The extent of previous contraband appeared in the customs duties collected at the major points of entry at the border by determined federal officials. Under the vigilance of its patrols, the customshouses along the Río Bravo more than doubled their revenues between 1869 and 1871. A wail of protests from frustrated northern merchants greeted the tough application of the *contrarresguardo.*[41]

Political contests between rival interests also contributed to Monterrey's commercial woes. A power vacuum resulted when Vidaurri's regime abruptly ended. Consequently, corrupt military commanders, forced loans, and arbitrary confiscations plagued northern traders.[42] To compound the situation, the intense fighting in Nuevo León during the 1872 Noria Revolt particularly hurt the area's economy.

Thus, hostile Indians, bandits, high taxes, hard customs officials, and unsettling political conditions posed serious problems for Monterrey's merchants.[43] Nonetheless, at the heart of the city's economic slump lay the major internal weakness of Mexico: mining composed the core, the motor of the national economy, and the general economic depression in Mexico after 1867 derived essentially from the stagnation in the nation's mining sector. As suppliers of northern mining centers, *regiomontanos* were subject to the negative repercussions of any mining crisis. The precipitous decline in mining production of the nation's leading mining state, Zacatecas, underscored the source of Monterrey's economic ills.[44]

The nation's economic plight paralleled the conditions in Nuevo León. The state's treasury constantly hovered near bankruptcy. In 1879, the director of the Colegio Civil protested to the governor the nonpayment of salaries, in some cases as long as six months, to the teachers and other employees of the Colegio. In the same year the *Periódico Oficial* reported the exodus of hundreds of people from the city. To make matters worse, agricultural production declined as periodic droughts plagued the region's farmers.[45]

Merchants found few customers to buy their wares. Closed shops dotted major streets. Small businesses disappeared, leaving the large merchants to manage the shrinking commerce of the city. The governor's report of 1879 showed 337 commercial establishments in the city. Two years later, the governor's report indicated that Monterrey had only 254 commercial enterprises remaining. Many artisans were forced from their workshops. In 1881, just 57 "industrial establishments" survived of the 185 listed in the 1879 business census, as scores of carpenters, masons, blacksmiths, shoemakers, and the like left the city.[46]

In this depressed economic context, the railroad loomed as the salvation of Mexico. The railroad became, in the eyes of government officials, the "revolutionary element" needed to transform the country's economic life. "Since it was believed without a doubt that Mexico had unlimited riches," as one economic historian has noted, "it was assumed that with the first railroad, once constructed, the national economy would undergo a radical and immediate change."[47] Similar thoughts and expectations reigned in Monterrey. As one newspaper put it, "all that is needed to develop the immense riches of Mexico is to harness it through a railway between Mexico and the United States."[48] The political stability established by Mexican president Porfirio Díaz after 1876 heightened the *regiomontanos'* optimism.[49]

In the face of Mexico's economic disarray, the Díaz administration assumed the necessity of foreign capital in order to develop the Mexican economy. "The substance of the strategy was to take any measures necessary to encourage large amounts of foreign investments to come to Mexico," as Raymond Vernon has pointed out, "on the theory that the capital, skill, and markets which foreigners had at their command were critical for Mexico's growth."[50] Generous railroad subsidies, favorable concessions, liberal mining codes, and government protection successfully induced foreign capitalists to Mexico. Foreign demands, particularly those of an expanding U.S. industrial capitalism, wedded the designs of Díaz with European and American interests.

In 1880, construction of the Mexican National Railroad line began from Laredo, Texas, toward Mexico City, via Monterrey. The city eagerly expected a significant rise in commercial traffic. For the city's merchants, the railway's arrival in August 1882 signaled "a new era of progress and prosperity."[51] But expectations of the benefits of the railroad proved to be more difficult to realize than anticipated by *regiomontano* traders.

By 1884, members of Monterrey's commercial establishment lamented the"disintegration of their rosy hopes."[52] Two years later, the Chamber of Commerce issued a lengthy report on the persistence of the economic crisis and the railway's disappointing results. According to the merchants' organization, the commercial crisis derived from the fact that *regiomontanos* "supplied themselves with all the necessities of life with American articles and products."[53] To put it briefly, the railroad shortened the distance between Laredo and Monterrey's wealthier customers. In the long report on the crisis, the frustrated merchants described a typical situation, where a "passenger takes a large empty bag, without even a change of clothes. The next day he returns newly dressed from head to foot, and in the bag his old clothes and all the new things he can put into it. . . ."[54]

In 1888, the Mexican National Railway reached completion when the northern and southern ends connected in San Luis Potosí. In April of 1890, Monterrey was finally in contact with the International Railway that extended from Piedras Negras to Torreón. Since the International Railway line bisected the Central Railroad (Ciudad Juárez–Mexico City), Monterrey expanded its economic net into Chihuahua and Zacatecas. In the same year, the port of Tampico was about to be incorporated into the iron web emanating from Monterrey. Thus, by 1890, the capital of Nuevo León became a convenient communications hub encompassing the entire northeast of Mexico.[55] During much of this time, however, Monterrey derived few benefits from an incomplete railroad system. Nevertheless, with the railroad's completion, Monterrey was at the center of an extensive railway network that brought to local merchants the long-awaited results. Mexican railways rekindled mining activity with accelerating force during the 1880s. Lower transportation costs, market demand, and new capital prompted northern mining production. As mining towns boomed, the economic tempo of Monterrey quickened.[56]

Yet the imminent prosperity found that only the city's wealthiest merchants had weathered the hard times, among them José Calderón. Unlike some of his counterparts, such as Bernardino García, Calderón had sustained his commercial network and had astutely recruited able, ambitious younger men to run it, including Isaac Garza, Francisco G. Sada, and José Muguerza. In retrospect, Calderón's greatest contribution to Monterrey's industry stemmed perhaps from his bringing together the talent and acumen of these men.

Born in Monterrey, Isaac Garza at twelve years of age was sent to Spain and enrolled in a business school of sorts. He returned in 1870 and went to work for a large merchant in San Luis Potosí, and soon thereafter, on a buying trip, he met José Calderón. Impressed by the young *regiomontano*, Calderón urged him to join his firm in Monterrey. In 1874, Garza took over the accounting duties of the Casa de Calderón. Later, Calderón gave up the management of his business to Garza.

In the midst of the 1870s depression, Calderón married Francisca Muguerza. His sister-in-law, Carmen, was already married to Francisco Sada, a lawyer. Friendship as well as family bonds brought the couples and their children together. Calderón especially admired his sister-in-law's son, Francisco G. Sada, who was well versed in commercial matters early in his life. For five years, in Matamoros, he directed the importing activities of the company headed by José Armendaiz. Sada parlayed his position during the cotton boom into landholdings, saving a sizable amount for other investments. In 1878, he left Matamoros for Chihuahua, bought land in the Laguna area, and became a partner in the commercial house of the González Treviño family. Two years later, Sada moved on to Saltillo to start up his own business. Sada's father managed Calderón's legal matters, and the tie led to close business links as well between the younger Sada and the aging merchant. And, in fact, Sada, in cooperation with Isaac Garza, handled Calderón's commercial affairs in Coahuila.

José A. Muguerza was the brother of Calderón's wife. At twenty-five, after working ten years with Bernardino García, Muguerza joined his brother-in-law's business in Monterrey in 1882. He became a fast friend of Francisco G. Sada and Isaac Garza, especially the latter. Through ties with Calderón, the trio of young yet experienced men represented a deep knowledge of shipping, exports, imports, domestic commerce, agriculture, and the regional economy in general.[57] As a new boom appeared, Calderón and his younger associates possessed the capital and insights necessary to respond to the economic opportunities in the offing. No less importantly, they also enjoyed, along with Valentín Rivero, Mariano Hernández, the Zambrano family, and a few others, the advantages derived by the elimination of numerous potential competitors as a result of the protracted, withering period of economic depression.

V.   The economic problems of Monterrey during the 1870s and early 1880s provided an essential background to an interest in industry. Manufacturing attracted scant attention prior to the 1870s among local businessmen. Nonetheless, as the depression deepened, several *regiomontanos* increasingly considered producing their own goods. The city's Chamber of Commerce constantly counseled members to make new products and reduce imports. As early as 1879, Governor Genaro Garza García called for the establishment of industrial ventures.[58] The new governor two years later, Viviano Villarreal, repeated his predecessor's advice. Villarreal perceptively stressed Monterrey's favorable geographic location: "Because of this, industry will continue to progressively develop, and Nuevo León may perhaps soon follow an essentially industrial line."[59]

Villarreal based much of his industrial hopes on the rudimentary steps taken earlier by local merchants. In 1872, for example, three of the city's major traders pooled their resources to construct the cloth factory El Porvenir. Two of the principals, Valentín Rivero and

Gregorio Zambrano, already maintained an interest in the older La Fama textile plant.[60]

The number of requests for concessions to start new businesses accelerated as the railroad from Laredo neared Monterrey. Expecting the railway's benefits, several enterprises arose throughout 1882 and 1883, from an urban tramway to a paper factory. Exemptions from state taxes ran as long as twenty years.[61] But the disappointing effects of the railroad to Laredo slowed the enthusiasm of Monterrey's incipient industrialists. Nonetheless, the governor's report of 1886 promised to grant tax exemptions and favorable concessions in order to promote more industry.[62] Well-publicized expositions, so popular in the late nineteenth century, added another, though intangible, stimulus to the push toward industrialism. In 1880, and again in 1888, Monterrey hosted industrial fairs, and *regiomontanos* also traveled to American cities to learn about new products.[63]

As railroads extended from Monterrey and as mining activity mounted, the market improved for the city's embryonic industry. The burgeoning mining areas needed lumber, nails, windowpanes, wire, bricks, cement, metalwork of all kinds, wagons, clothing, and foodstuffs. Yet the expensiveness of accessible American goods implied the importance of manufacturing products in addition to importing and exporting. *Regiomontanos* were not blind to the changing situation, as a perceptive local newspaper editor noted: "Before, Monterrey was the commercial center that supplied an extensive surrounding region and enjoyed the consequences of such a position . . . after understanding its new situation, it realized that to maintain its position, it needed new characteristics, that it was not enough to receive merchandise from one point and send it to another . . . that something else is necessary, for example, manufacture and produce articles to export from Monterrey, and not serve simply as an intermediary."[64]

On December 21, 1888, Governor Lázaro Garza Ayala signed into law La Ley Protectora de la Industria. In the effort to promote and attract capital, the proclamation read in part, "all industrial plants with capital of 1,000 pesos or more are exempt from all taxes for seven years."[65] The location of the city put it near highly productive mining areas, particularly in the state of Coahuila. Railroad connections allowed for the easy collection and shipment of mineral products to foreign destinations, and the railway tie with Tampico permitted trade by ship to and from outside countries. Since provisions arrived in Monterrey from within Mexico and from abroad for distribution, the city served as supply center for surrounding towns. Furthermore, local political leaders actively sought foreign investment as well as native capital. The economic attributes of Monterrey were not lost on investors, and, appropriately perhaps, Nuevo León received a fateful push from its neighbor to the north that held significant consequences for the city's industrialization.

The issue of protectionism pervaded the 1890 election campaign in the United States. Western mine owners vociferously blamed Mexican minerals for their diminishing profits. The agitation of the mine operators resulted in higher duty rates for imported ores under the provisions of the McKinley Tariff of 1890. Smelting companies, on the other hand, protested unsuccessfully the increased costs of refining Mexican ores. A storm of criticism greeted the measure in Mexico since it jeopardized mining exports. However, the absence of any significant metal-processing plants in Mexico presented the possibility of establishing smelters in localities with the necessary facilities.[66] In Monterrey, the implications of the tariff were visualized quickly, as the editor of the *Voz de Nuevo León* (May 1890) wrote: "Although the pain [of the tariff] was felt momentarily, the solution was easy to see and it was realized that it would be favorable to Mexico; it was necessary to have within the nation plants similar to those in the neighboring country. . . ."[67] The same article urged American smelter operators to invest in Monterrey, but, as it turned out, little advertisement was needed. The Guggenheims, for instance, moved speedily to lay the foundation for smelting operations in Mexico, and others soon followed their example.[68]

By 1892, the smoke of the city's three smelters signified Monterrey's industrial beginnings. For *regiomontano* merchants, the development of northern Mexico clearly augmented their commercial capital, but the region's economic growth also provided opportunities for the utilization of that capital for industrial ventures. The resources, experience, and connections acquired in the past proved to be critical to the participation of *regiomontanos* in the industrialization of Monterrey.

2. The Making of an Industrial Elite: The Political Economy of Monterrey, 1890–1910

I. The combination of substantial foreign investments and the effective control of the country by Porfirio Díaz produced a period of unprecedented economic growth and stability in Mexico from 1880 to 1910. The prosperity of the Porfiriato, however, exacted high costs: foreign domination of the economy, intensification of the concentration of land ownership, the general oppression of Mexican workers, and the maintenance of a dictatorial political regime.[1] In the midst of this era of economic dependency and political repression, opportunities nonetheless appeared for native capitalists as the Porfirian boom accelerated the integration of the national economy with a corresponding expansion of internal markets. In this context, Monterrey's merchants developed the basis for their transformation into an industrial elite as the city became Mexico's premier manufacturing center.

Capital and access to credit were, of course, indispensable requirements to take advantage of industrial opportunities. And, especially in ventures that called for large capital outlays, government aid and protection through concessions, tax exemptions, and tariffs often proved to be essential to success. Given the grip of Díaz and his cronies over government, political influence was also necessary in many cases for new enterprises to prosper.[2] The costs, supply, and management of labor presented still another consideration for investors. Here again, government played a key role since it provided a check on labor organizing through the control of police and military troops.[3]

The presence of internal markets, therefore, as a consequence of foreign investments, railroad construction, and population growth was not always enough to spur native capital to invest in industry. The participation of Monterrey's native businessmen in the industrialization of the city reflected their ability to organize essential financing, to secure government support, to shape a malleable labor force, and, when necessary, to obtain crucial political favors. Thus, several factors, economic as well as political, contributed to the emergence in Monterrey of an identifiable industrial elite.

The economy of the region afforded Monterrey's entrepreneurs certain advantages. The concentration of foreigners in extractive activities facilitated the entry of *regiomontanos* into industries to meet the swelling domestic demands for goods as a result of the development of northern Mexico. In this regard, the commercial experience of Monterrey's merchants, accumulated over the years, served to identify new markets and the material ingredients necessary to exploit those markets. Moreover, Nuevo León's weak agriculture lessened the attraction of land as a form of investment while mining was, relative to other places, similarly unattractive. Both factors added to the availability of local capital for industrial pursuits. Furthermore, in the context of a thriving area, Monterrey's merchants continued to expand their commercial enterprises and to use the resultant profits for industrial investments. In addition, they astutely manipulated their assets, parlaying them into further sources of capital, such as real estate speculation.[4]

The building of new industries required the acquisition of modern equipment, knowledgeable managers, and able repairmen in addition to capital and markets. Initially, locally financed industries depended on foreigners to provide technical skills, but this early experience was not lost on the city's entrepreneurs. From the beginning, *regiomontanos* worked to lessen their reliance on foreigners for the management and maintenance of plants. And, when possible, they also attempted to manufacture their own equipment, although imported machinery marked virtually all of Monterrey's industries at the time.

Nonetheless, government remained an important factor in the industrialization of Monterrey. Incentives in the form of tax exemptions and the suspension of import duties for equipment were not inconsequential; moreover, at crucial points, the state also provided tariff protection and contracts for Monterrey's manufactured goods. Furthermore, the coercive powers of the state were put at the disposal of Monterrey's employers in their relations with workers. However, as we shall see, for Nuevo León the proximity of the U.S. border had important consequences for labor in Monterrey's major industries. In any case, the state played a role in the city's industrial development that varied, however, in degree and substance from one case to another. In this connection, the political-economic context of Nuevo León contained a distinctive dimension, due to the presence of General Bernardo Reyes.

Bernardo Reyes was governor of Nuevo León from 1889 to 1909. In that capacity, Reyes represented much more than a handpicked agent of Porfirio Díaz' political machine. Reyes rapidly became a nationally recognized candidate to succeed the aging Díaz to the presidency, and his service in the Díaz cabinet as war minister in 1899 enhanced his political standing. As a presidential hopeful, however, Reyes attracted the envy of other aspirants, among them, José I. Limantour, key presidential advisor and Mexico's finance minister. Limantour headed a group of highly placed, wealthy men (the so-called *científicos*) who exercised considerable influence over Díaz, especially on economic affairs. In addition, Reyes' rising political fortunes aroused the mistrust of the suspicious dictator, who jealously guarded his power.[5]

The political triangle of Reyes, Limantour, and Díaz complicated the economic designs of Monterrey's businessmen. As governor and local military chief, Reyes was a powerful, unavoidable political fixture who offered incentives, aid, and protection to the city's nascent industrialists. Indeed, Reyes proved to be ideally suited to the needs of *regiomontano* capitalists. On the other hand, Limantour's economic influence pointed to the necessity of sustaining the finance minister's favor. Finally, Monterrey's entrepreneurs were not blind to the vagaries of power under Porfirio Díaz. Economic interest, therefore, forced *regiomontano* businessmen to navigate carefully through their political surroundings.

In sum, the industrialization of Monterrey and the attendant emergence of a local industrial elite derived from a complex mix of economic and political conditions. Yet, as this chapter stresses, the decisive factor in the industrial roots of the Monterrey elite stemmed from the economic interconnections among the city's major businessmen. Other cities in northern Mexico possessed the basic economic attributes of Monterrey: geographic advantages, access to transportation systems and markets, probusiness political figures with influential connections, large foreign-owned extractive enterprises, and native capitalists of wealth and acumen. Presumably, other types of investments attracted Mexican entrepreneurs in the north away from industrial opportunities, such as the burgeoning agricultural development of the Laguna district, or the rich mining areas of Coahuila, Durango, and San Luis Potosí.[6] But in Monterrey, native entrepreneurs repeatedly pooled their resources in order to initiate costly industrial ventures. And, when capitalization requirements exceeded local resources, Monterrey businessmen demonstrated the capacity to lure outside investors, foreign and domestic, while usually retaining control over new enterprises.

Leading entrepreneurs maintained independent economic interests, but cooperation in various instances led to the distinctive, inordinate participation of native capital in the industrialization of Monterrey. The evolution of the Cervecería Cuauhtémoc and the Fundidora de Fierro y Acero particularly manifested the political and economic nuances of Monterrey's industrial development. This process was not without subtle changes or variation within the dominant business community, as certain men and families assumed ascendant positions in the industrial foundations of the city. For example, some of the old merchants were eclipsed by younger counterparts, while a few new faces appeared among the reigning businessmen of Nuevo León. Nonetheless, as the rise of the two pivotal industries demonstrated, the connections among the city's key businessmen proved to be decisive, with enduring consequences for the relations between Monterrey's capitalists and the state.

II.   The industrialization of Europe and the United States in the nineteenth century fueled an age of economic imperialism as Europeans and Americans pressed their wide-ranging search for raw materials and markets. In Latin America, the resultant profits from exports permitted the greater importation of foreign goods and facilitated the acquisition of the trappings of modernity in transport, architecture, fashion, and related expressions of "progress." Thus, the late nineteenth century, the era of export economies, marked the initial stage of the modernization of Latin America, although the attendant changes were usually confined to major cities and to their upper and middle classes. In the case of Mexico, the aura of peace and order created by the dictatorship of Porfirio Díaz spurred a resurgence of foreign investment as the Díaz government attempted to utilize foreign investments and export revenues to integrate a fractured economy, to stimulate agriculture, and to build a rudimentary industrial base.[7]

The location and distribution of that foreign capital, however, resulted in a lopsided economy. While some regions boomed economically, others remained stagnant since foreign entrepreneurs focused their efforts on those areas that yielded vital raw materials. The types of investments made by foreigners compounded the geographic imbalance of the Mexican economy. By 1910, export-oriented activities represented nearly a third of foreign capital in Mexico, while industry attracted scant attention.[8] (See tables 1 and 2.) In northern Mexico, for example, mining underscored the selective and extractive character of foreign investment.

Geographic proximity encouraged a close relationship between northern Mexico and a U.S. economy that required the acquisition of mineral products such as lead, iron, copper, and zinc (gold and silver maintained their attraction as well, of course). The mining wealth of the region stirred American investors, and, eventually, their investments dominated northern Mexican mining. Moreover, the necessity of transporting Mexican ores accelerated the penetration and extension of

Table 1. *Location of Foreign Investment, 1910*

States	% of Total
Federal District	62.8
Coahuila	9.5
Sonora	7.3
Chihuahua	6.3
Oaxaca	2.3
Nuevo León	2.2
Sinaloa	1.4
Durango	1.4
Total	93.2

Source: *Historia moderna de México, El Porfiriato, la vida económica*, book 2, p. 1134.

largely American-owned railways that furthered the region's development. A mere glance at a map in 1910 testifies to the tremendous expansion of the Mexican railway network and its American linkages, particularly in the north.[9]

As mining activity rose and railway mileage increased, the demand for labor grew proportionately. Population growth added yet another ingredient to the region's economic expansion. The labor force reflected the area's major economic activities; nearly half of the country's workers in extractive-related industries resided in the north. In this connection, higher wages provided an important incentive for the migration of labor to the north from the more populous states to the south.[10] Under such conditions, urbanization in the area understandably proceeded swiftly. In this context, commerce thrived. Customs receipts from the north increased, while they suffered a decline in all

Table 2. *Foreign Investment in Industry, 1911*

	Amount in Pesos	% of Investment in Industry	Investment in Industry as % of Total Foreign Investment
France	71,932,368	55.2	2.1
Germany	26,960,000	20.5	0.8
U.S.A.	21,200,000	16.1	0.6
England	10,855,800	8.2	0.3
Total	130,948,168	100.0	3.8

Source: *Historia moderna de México, El Porfiriato, la vida económica*, book 2, p. 1155.

Table 3. *Percentages of Total Value of Exports and Imports by Location of Customhouses*

| | Exports | | Imports | |
	1888–89	*1910–11*	*1888–89*	*1910–11*
North customs	35.6	57.5	39.5	45.7
Gulf customs	48.2	30.9	48.9	43.7
Pacific north customs	13.3	10.3	9.4	9.2
Pacific south customs	2.9	1.3	2.2	1.4
Total	100.0	100.0	100.0	100.0

Source: Rosenzweig, "Desarrollo económico," p. 417.
Note: Includes maritime and land points of entry.

other parts of Mexico during this period.[11] (See table 3.) Thus, mining and transportation provided the basis for the prosperity of northern Mexico.

Nonetheless, economic patterns in the north were not uniform or invariable. The state of Nuevo León compared poorly with neighboring states in terms of the volume and value of mining activity and agricultural production. Such differences were registered in the composition of the labor force. In 1900, miners numbered 3,500 in Nuevo León, but over 7,000 in Durango and more than 6,000 in Chihuahua. Furthermore, between 1895 and 1910, Chihuahua realized a 43% increase in its agrarian population, and Durango added 40%, while Coahuila underwent a 35% increment; on the other hand, in Nuevo León the rise in population in the countryside amounted to only 16%.[12]

Rather, Nuevo León—and specifically its capital, Monterrey—was distinguished by the industrial character of its development. By 1911, the value of Nuevo León's industrial production exceeded that of Mexico City. (See table 4.) Similar to cities at an initial industrialization stage, Monterrey's early industrial growth derived primarily from the processing of raw materials for export. Yet, in addition, as described below, Monterrey featured the rise of an industrial sector that essentially served internal markets and that developed largely from local capital.[13]

The rhythm and characteristics of Monterrey's industrialization varied over the twenty-year span from 1890 to 1910 as a consequence of larger economic patterns and forces. Export-oriented industrial activity appeared first in response to the repercussions of the McKinley Tariff of 1890. Soon thereafter, however, manufactured and processed goods for internal consumption began to be produced in Monterrey in the midst of a growing population and the area's general

Table 4. *Value of Industrial Production by States*

States	% of the Value of Mexico's Industrial Production	Average Value of Production (in thousands of pesos) Per Worker	Per Factory
Five most important states	54.7	1.5	46.9
Nuevo León	13.5	1.8	42.4
Federal District	11.7	1.3	90.7
México	11.2	2.6	88.1
Veracruz	10.6	1.1	37.0
Puebla	7.7	1.3	26.7
Five least important states	1.2	0.4	3.9
Baja California	0.3	0.6	8.3
Chiapas	0.3	0.3	1.9
Colima	0.3	0.4	10.2
Campeche	0.2	0.3	7.6
Tamaulipas	0.1	0.1	1.4

Source: *Historia moderna de México, El Porfiriato, la vida económica,* book 1, p. 392.

prosperity. Monterrey had to weather several economic fluctuations during this period, but the diversification of the state's economy cushioned the slumps associated with droughts or recessions.[14] Comparatively speaking, Monterrey's economy fared much better than that of other cities that relied more heavily on exports for their prosperity. By the time of the Panic of 1907, for instance, Monterrey's industries had developed to a point where they provided a measure of protection from the consequences of a dependent national economy.[15]

III.   In 1890, Governor Bernardo Reyes granted concessions for the construction of three smelters in Monterrey. The first request came in February from the Nuevo León Smelting, Refining, and Manufacturing Company. Known locally as the Fundición Número Uno, the plant began operations in April 1891 after an investment of 1.5 million pesos. Three Monterrey merchants, led by Francisco Armendaiz, presented their request in May 1890 to establish the Compañía Minera, Fundidora y Afinadora Monterrey, referred to as the Fundición Número Dos. The initial investment of 300,000 pesos merited for the owners a twenty-year exemption from all state and municipal taxes. In October 1890, the Guggenheims made their petition to build the

Compañía de la Gran Fundición Nacional Mexicana, or what became the Fundición Número Tres. Like their competitors, the Guggenheims also received a twenty-year exemption from all local and state taxes. Of the three, the Guggenheim plant anchored Monterrey's smelting production, and it epitomized the initial forces that precipitated the city's industry.[16]

At the urging of Joseph A. Robertson, manager of the Gulf Railroad, Meyer Guggenheim dispatched two of his sons to investigate the possibility of starting smelting operations in Mexico in the aftermath of the McKinley Tariff. The Guggenheim brothers went to Mexico in the hope of receiving a generous concession, and they employed the lawyer Emeterio de la Garza, "who enjoyed the finest connections" with federal officials.[17] After several wine-and-dine meetings with key officials of the Díaz government, the Guggenheims secured the right to import their machinery "free of duty—a notable concession—and the silver tax on the smelter's output was waived—an even greater victory."[18] The location of the smelter was not specified, however, when the agreement was signed with federal representatives on October 9, 1890.

Dan Guggenheim journeyed immediately to Coahuila, but he rejected Saltillo as a possible site; he then turned his attention to nearby Monterrey. The city's railway connections to mining areas, coal deposits, and Tampico convinced the Guggenheims to locate their plant in Monterrey. Daniel Guggenheim's concession request reached Reyes on October 18, 1890, and was accorded virtually the same treatment as those made earlier. The chief distinction of the Guggenheim smelter was the concession received from the federal government. Within a year, Monterrey had become a major center for the processing of Mexican ores.

With the exception of the Fundición Número Uno, smelting operations generally prospered during the two decades following their construction.[19] But the giant of the smelters remained that owned by the American magnates. At the beginning, the Número Tres processed 10,000 tons of ore a month; ten years later, 35,000 tons of ore passed through its furnaces monthly. Only the Guggenheims' mammoth Aguascalientes plant, "the largest in North America by 1908," outstripped the production of the Monterrey smelter. By 1910, the Guggenheim payroll in Monterrey amounted to 1,200 pesos daily to 1,000 workers.[20]

The mineral processing plants of Monterrey soon converted the city into a center of activities tied to mining, smelting, and metallurgy.[21] The demand for metal products, especially finished goods such as nails, wire, sheeting, and pipes, stimulated an interest in the establishment of foundries. More important to local businessmen, the demand for such products indicated the widespread and multiplying signs of the region's expanding internal markets, including those generated in Nuevo León, and Monterrey in particular. The combination of scarce northern labor, the resultant higher wages, the overpopulation of central Mexico, and the availability of railroad transportation led to a consistent pattern of migration to the north. In Nuevo León, by 1895, 16% of its residents were from outside the state, and, attracted by the promise of the city, over 30% of Monterrey's population was composed of immigrants. The census of 1895 indicated that the average wage in Nuevo León was 65 centavos a day, with farm workers receiving as little as 25 centavos daily, as opposed to the 1.00 peso earned by some skilled laborers. By 1902, the average daily wage had risen to 1.00 peso, and by 1906, to 1.25. Wage differentials underlined the attraction of Monterrey.[22] (See table 5 and figure 1.)

Under such conditions, Monterrey's urbanization offered numerous profitable opportunities for its resident businessmen.[23] The primary business district underwent a steady face-lift and expansion that spilled over into the northern part of the city.[24] In 1880, the city contained about 350 commercial establishments; by 1910, 1,100 merchants, large and small, competed for Monterrey's customers.[25] In the years between 1890 and 1910, over 30 million pesos were invested by merchants in Monterrey.[26] By August 1893, the *Mexican Trader* noted that "The *regiomontano* commerce is opulent and prosperous, and the businessmen are in every respect progressive. The great monetary depression, so felt in other localities, appears to really have had little effect on the commercial activity of this city."[27] At about the same time, a local newspaper observed that "about a dozen" large department stores were undergoing extensive refurbishing—clear proof of

Table 5. *Industrial Labor of Mexico, 1895 and 1910*

Zone	% of Labor Employed in Manufacturing		% of Growth between
	1895	1910	1895 and 1910
Mexico (nation)	100.0	100.0	9.5
Central	57.1	58.5	12.6
Gulf	8.8	7.8	−3.0
North	12.0	15.1	37.3
Pacific north	4.4	4.7	15.0
Pacific south	17.7	13.9	−15.2

Source: *Historia moderna de México, El Porfiriato, la vida económica,* book 1, p. 409.

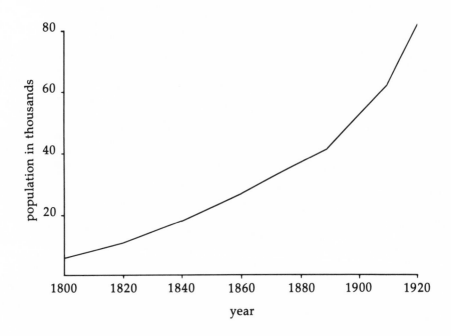

Figure 1. *Population of Monterrey, 1800–1910*

the wealth accruing to Monterrey's merchants.[28] Led by Monterrey, retail sales in Nuevo León nearly tripled during the Porfirian era.[29]

Ideally located on the trade corridor between the United States and central Mexico, Monterrey's merchants continued to gain from the regional dominance of the northeastern city. "Monterrey is the center where all the towns of Nuevo León, and large parts of the neighboring states of Tamaulipas and Coahuila," a report explained in 1910, "send their agricultural, livestock, and industrial products."[30] In fact, businessmen across the border enviously watched the prosperity of the Monterrey market. In full-page newspaper advertisements, store owners in San Antonio, Texas, for example, offered paid, round-trip rail fares for any *regiomontano* who bought more than $1,500 worth of merchandise. Not to be outdone, several Monterrey merchants maintained stores along the Texas border and in surrounding towns.[31]

As a consequence of the city's development, real estate values quadrupled in this period.[32] "The value of landed property in Monterrey has advanced sensationally of late years," an American visitor marveled in 1907; and he further commented that "house property until lately was one of the most stable investments, continually improving in value, while new and handsome buildings, both residential and for business purposes, were being constructed both in town itself and outside it."[33] His observations echoed those made by a local newspaper over a decade earlier. "There is no street where one does not find something being constructed," noted the *Voz de Nuevo León* in 1895, and "it is incredible the value that lots have reached in the city."[34]

Commerce nourished a thriving construction industry.[35] The Monterrey Brick Company began operations in 1890 and was later rivaled by four other competitors. Two cement plants were filling local demands by 1905, and the largest, Cementos Hidalgo, was a major supplier of cement for the entire country. A lumber mill was built in these years, stone masons opened shops, foundries produced a wide assortment of metal products, and carpenters and plumbers were kept busy by the building activity that marked the city's prosperity.[36]

IV.   Within the context of Monterrey's dynamic growth and development, the city's established businessmen extended their dominance of the local economy. Inadvertently, foreigners facilitated the continuation of the *regiomontanos'* economic ascendancy. In general, foreign capital investments went primarily to export-related activities and avoided local investment opportunities that focused on internal demands. For example, the Guggenheims, owners of the largest foreign-owned concern, apparently concentrated their capital on their smelting operations. Thus, with rare exceptions, foreigners like the Guggenheims contributed to the local economic grip of the local merchant families whose wealth derived from the Vidaurri era.[37] The assets of those families and their capital resources, coupled with the prevailing pattern of foreign investment, allowed *regiomontano* businessmen a substantial advantage in exploiting investment opportunities. In this situation, Monterrey's established merchant houses responded by expanding their existing businesses. More importantly, they recognized the industrial possibilities yielded by the region's growing market for manufactured and processed goods.

The major exception among foreign entrepreneurs was Joseph A. Robertson.[38] The Tennessee-born American had foreseen the economic potential of the city while building railroads in the vicinity of Nuevo León in the 1880s. As early as 1890, a local newspaper lauded the efforts and vision of Robertson, "who comprehended what industry could be developed here and worked for it."[39] By 1892, Robertson had translated his business counsel into his own newspaper, the *Monterrey News*. By the turn of the century, Robertson had achieved a wide reputation as a man of enterprise, recognized by Mexicans and foreigners alike.[40] Still, Robertson's foresight, as important as it may have been to the city's development, was matched by the acumen among native capitalists.[41]

Through the years, *regiomontanos* had demonstrated a keen economic sense. In his memoirs of his travels in Mexico, Frederick Obers, for instance, recalled his visit to Nuevo León in 1882, noting that "there has been a great concentration of North Americans in Monterrey and the streets of the city are filled with disillusioned adventurers. They came to this country as if it was new, without taking into account too late . . . that the Mexican . . . has an instinct for commerce and a love for luxury as developed as the most talented Yankee of our country. The Americans . . . have not had much luck in business . . . and do not appear to be making money."[42] Notwithstanding the views of Robertson's zealous admirers, *regiomontanos* clearly possessed their own well-honed entrepreneurial skills and vision. Thus, foreign industrial investments in Monterrey were very quickly superseded by those of Mexicans, primarily from the established business families of the city. By 1900, Mexican capital composed 80% of industrial investments in Monterrey.[43]

In individual terms, entrenched, wealthy native businessmen responded in various ways to the area's economic possibilities. Valentín Rivero and his sons expanded their commercial interests, enlarging their downtown department store and modernizing their textile plant—the largest in Nuevo León. The Rivero clan also increased the productive capacity of their flour mill to take advantage of the growing popularity of bread. And they maintained a thriving credit and deposit operation in their main store as local newspapers constantly implored the city's workers to save money. The Mariano Hernández family paralleled the business activities of their long-standing partners, the Riveros. Lavishly remodeled and enlarged in 1901, the La Reinera store became the showpiece of the family's prosperity. In addition to their Monterrey store, the Hernández family opened branches in Laredo (along the U.S. border) and in Linares in the southern part of the state. As did the Riveros, Mariano Hernández and his sons acquired a flour mill and also offered quasi-banking services in their Reinera store. Francisco Armendaiz, another wealthy survivor of the cotton boom years, maintained a near monopoly on local sugar refining that supplemented his income from his mines, land speculation, smelter, and ranches.[44]

Adolfo Zambrano, spurred perhaps by rising mining activity in the post-1880 era, concentrated many of his resources in expanding the family's mining operations, founded by Gregorio Zambrano. Real estate also figured importantly in the Zambranos' investment. In this respect, they duplicated the activities of Patricio Milmo, who continued to buy mining properties in Nuevo León and Coahuila and to enlarge his vast landholdings. Both Adolfo Zambrano and Patricio Milmo carried with them two constant partners. Zambrano maintained a close business relationship with Vicente Ferrara and his brother, Miguel. Milmo, in a similar fashion, remained an intimate associate of the Belden family. Thus, the Ferraras and the Beldens profited from their association with their older, and wealthier, mentors.[45]

The three businessmen who surrounded José Calderón—Isaac Garza, Francisco G. Sada, José Muguerza—continued to strengthen the interests of the elder Calderón while expanding their individual endeavors. Calderón's son, José, Jr., carried on the family business after the death of his father in 1889. The young Calderón was particularly active in the buying of urban property, especially at the northern edge of the city, near the new industries and recently built railway junction. In these dealings, the young entrepreneur was joined frequently by his uncle, José Muguerza.[46]

These established business families were augmented in the 1880–1910 period by a few others whose wealth earned them inclusion in the select circle of Monterrey's prominent capitalists. Based originally in Coahuila, the economic empire founded by Evaristo Madero during the cotton trade of the 1860s extended with increasing frequency into Nuevo León and Monterrey. Well-acquainted through business ties with the Zambrano and Milmo clans, and related by marriage to the Hernández brothers, Madero and his sons assumed an important position within the city's business establishment by 1900.[47] Manuel Cantú Treviño, as a result of his extraordinary commercial success, also emerged during the era as a member of the city's leading entrepreneurial class. The furniture manufacturers, later department store magnates, Benjamín Salinas and Joel Rocha also edged close to the inner circle of Monterrey's most powerful businessmen.[48]

If the city's major businessmen prospered individually, they also profited from the numerous cooperative ventures in which these men, often in concert with relatives, participated. Native capitalists of Monterrey tended to collaborate on investments as a means to diversify their local interests, and, as a result, to minimize their financial risk. Through a series of relatively modest investments, based upon the profits of their seasoned, lucrative holdings, this group of businessmen moved cooperatively toward industry as a major form of investment, spurred by their perception of internal markets and attendant profits. As noted in table 6, the key families involved used cooperative ventures as a means to span a wide spectrum of business activities.

Table 6. Elite Families and Business Interconnections by Interest Groupings and Selected Firms

Name of Firm	Type	Year	Armendaiz (A) Rivero (R) Hernández (H)			Milmo (M) Belden (B)		Ferrara (F) Madero (Mo) Zambrano (Z)			Sada (S) Garza (G) Muguerza (Mu)		
			A	R	H	M	B	F	Mo	Z	S	G	Mu
1. Cía. Minera de San Francisco	Mining	1890	X					X		X			
2. Cía. Ferrocarril Urbano Monterrey	Urban railway	1891		X	X		X						
3. Banco de N.L.	Bank	1892	X		X				X	X			
4. Cía. Minera de La Fè	Mining	1893	X	X	X		X		X				
(reorganized)		1897		X	X		X	X	X	X			
5. Cía. Minera de San Pablo	Mining	1894		X	X		X	X	X	X			X
6. Fábrica La Fama	Textiles	1895*		X	X			X					X
7. Club Atlético	Club	1895	X			X	X						
8. Cía. Minera La Fortuna	Mining	1895			X		X	X		X			
9. La Esperanza	Mining	1895			X	X	X	X		X			
10. Cía. Minera El Refugio	Mining	1896	X	X	X		X	X		X			X
11. Cía. Minera Azteca	Mining	1897	X	X	X		X	X	X	X			
12. Cía. Minera Carbonato	Mining	1897	X	X	X		X	X	X	X			

Table 6. Elite Families and Business Interconnections by Interest Groupings and Selected Firms (cont'd)

Name of Firm	Type	Year	Armendaiz (A) Rivero (R) Hernández (H)			Milmo (M) Belden (B)		Ferrara (F) Madero (Mo) Zambrano (Z)			Sada (S) Garza (G) Muguerza (Mu)		
			A	R	H	M	B	F	Mo	Z	S	G	Mu
13. Cía. de Baños Monterrey	Club	1897	X	X	X		X	X	X				X
14. Cía. Minera Equitativa	Mining	1897	X				X	X		X			
15. Cía. Minera Maravillas	Mining	1897	X	X			X	X		X			
16. Cía. Minera Dolores	Mining	1897						X	X	X	X	X	X
17. Cía. Industrial de Monterrey	Foundry	1897				X	X	X					X
18. Cía. Minera Norias de Baján	Mining	1897						X	X	X			
(reorganized)		1900						X		X	X	X	X
19. Cía. Minera El Carmen	Mining	1898	X					X	X		X	X	X
20. Cía. El Barco	Foundry	1898	X	X	X		X	X			X	X	X
21. Cía. La Laguna	Soap	1899			X	X	X		X				
22. Cía. del Panteón	Mortuary	1899		X	X		X	X					
23. Cía. Minera Mala Noche	Mining	1899		X			X	X					
24. Cía. Tranvias Oriente	Railway	1899	X	X	X					X			

Continued on next page

Table 6. Elite Families and Business Interconnections by Interest Groupings and Selected Firms (cont'd)

Name of Firm	Type	Year	Armendaiz (A) Rivero (R) Hernández (H)			Milmo (M) Belden (B)		Ferrara (F) Madero (Mo) Zambrano (Z)			Sada (S) Garza (G) Muguerza (Mu)		
			A	R	H	M	B	F	Mo	Z	S	G	Mu
25. Cia. Minera La Luz	Mining	1899		X	X			X					
26. Cia. Minera, Fundidora y Afinadora Monterrey	Metals/ Refinishing	1899	X				X	X	X	X			
27. Banco Mercantil (reorganized)	Bank	1899		X	X	X		X			X	X	X
		1905		X	X	X	X	X			X	X	X
28. Teatro Circo Monterrey	Theater	1900		X			X		X	X			
29. Cia. Minera del Norte	Mining	1900							X	X	X	X	X
30. Cia. Fundidora de Fierro y Acero	Steel	1900	All of the families involved										
31. Fábrica de Cartón Monterrey	Packaging	1900			X				X	X	X	X	X
32. Cia. Ladrillera Unión	Brick	1900	X	X			X		X	X	X	X	X
33. Cia. Ferrocarriles Urbanos Monterrey	Urban railway	1900		X	X		X						X
34. Cia. Tipografía de Monterrey	Printing	1900		X	X		X				X	X	X

Table 6. Elite Families and Business Interconnections by Interest Groupings and Selected Firms (cont'd)

Name of Firm	Type	Year	Armendáiz (A) Rivero (R) Hernández (H)			Milmo (M) Belden (B)		Ferrara (F) Madero (Mo) Zambrano (Z)			Sada (S) Garza (G) Muguerza (Mu)		
			A	R	H	M	B	F	Mo	Z	S	G	Mu
35. Cía. Minera Santo Tomás	Mining	1900	X					X		X			
36. Cía. Industrial Reinera	Mining	1901		X	X			X	X				
37. Empresa Editorial Monterrey	Publishing	1901		X	X		X	X	X	X	X	X	X
38. Cía. Minera El Porvenir	Mining	1901		X	X			X			X	X	X
39. Cía. Minera La Salvadora	Mining	1901					X	X			X	X	X
40. Cía. Minera Providencia	Mining	1901		X	X				X		X	X	X
41. Cía. Carbonifera Monterrey	Coal	1902	All of the families involved										
42. Cía. Minera La Paz	Mining	1902	X	X				X		X			
43. Cía. Minera San Rafael	Mining	1903		X				X			X	X	X
44. Cía. Ferrocarriles de Matehuala	Railway	1903			X	X	X						

Continued on next page

Table 6. **Elite Families and Business Interconnections by Interest Groupings and Selected Firms** *(cont'd)*

Name of Firm	Type	Year	Armendaiz (A) Rivero (R) Hernández (H)			Milmo (M) Belden (B)		Ferrara (F) Madero (Mo) Zambrano (Z)			Sada (S) Garza (G) Muguerza (Mu)		
			A	R	H	M	B	F	Mo	Z	S	G	Mu
45. Cia. Minera Gran Cuadra	Mining	1903		X			X	X			X	X	X
46. Cia. Minera San Francisco de la Soledad	Mining	1903		X				X			X	X	
47. Cia. Minera La Palomilla	Mining	1903	X	X			X	X	X		X		
48. Cia. Minera Tuxtepec	Mining	1903						X	X	X			
49. Fábrica de Vidrios y Cristales Monterrey	Glass	1904*	All of the families involved										
(reorganized)		1909			X		X				X	X	X

Note: The information derives from the records of various notaries who recorded the incorporation of these firms, including the names of the individuals involved. Note should be taken of the close alliances that emerge from these joint ventures (for example, that of Isaac Garza and Francisco G. Sada). I am indebted to Professor Mario Cerutti of the Universidad Autónoma de Nuevo León for help in the location of the relevant materials for this table.

*Reorganized from the earlier plant of 1899.

This collaborative pattern of investment, however, was not untried. Prior to 1890, as noted earlier, these families had participated in joint ventures. Four of the families had pooled their resources in 1856 to construct Nuevo León's first textile plant. The Riveros, with help from the Zambranos, had furthered their textile interests in 1872 with the creation of the El Porvenir cloth factory. The Madero, Zambrano, and Hernández families, moreover, had joint interests that dated from the 1870s. And the Milmo and Belden families worked together on several occasions since their association with Santiago Vidaurri in the 1860s. Finally, José Calderón had been at the center of a hub of interests that encompassed Isaac Garza, Francisco G. Sada, and José Muguerza. Thus, all of the key business figures of Monterrey had experience with jointly owned enterprises, and, in fact, many of them were also linked through family ties. Hence, in light of the sizable capital requirements of new industrial plants, collaboration was a feasible, proven, and sensible approach to industrial and similarly large investments.[49]

In the forefront of such past cooperation, two locally based banking institutions arose to facilitate the financing of industrial ventures. Virtually a complete *regiomontano* effort, the Banco de Nuevo León started operations in 1892 and was administered by Antonio Hernández.[50] The rapid economic development of the city and the continuing need for capital induced the formation of a second major bank, the Banco Mercantil de Monterrey, in 1899. This second banking firm drew the support of Valentín Rivero, Francisco G. Sada, and José Muguerza; and, indicative of the interconnections among the city's upper class, the Hernández and Madero family names also appeared among the Banco Mercantil's investors. Consistent with the growing national economic importance of Nuevo León, the Mercantil Bank's investors included Joaquín Casasús, the well-connected lawyer and wealthy financier, and Enrique C. Creel, governor of Chihuahua and son-in-law to the powerful Terrazas family of the same state. These locally controlled banks easily dominated financial transactions in the state.[51] In a short period of time, the state's booming banks led one newspaper to remark, "Monterrey is, perhaps, the second most important financial center in the nation, given the activity that characterizes it and the incessant exchange [of money] of every size and amount."[52] By 1910, the Banco de Nuevo León's assets had nearly quadrupled, and the Banco Mercantil had posted a similar record of growth.[53] The participation of the wealthiest businessmen of Monterrey in major banks facilitated financial transactions and the acquisition of credit and loans for industrial investments.[54]

The foundation of these key financial institutions pointed to the significance of the collaboration among the city's major businessmen. Furthermore, as a close examination of table 6 demonstrates, the pattern of cooperative investments revealed certain telling nuances in the interrelationships of Monterrey's businessmen. The Milmo interests, for example, well entrenched by 1890, showed relatively less enthusiasm than others in participating in collaborative investments. The Ferraras, in contrast, appeared ubiquitously in cooperative ventures and seemed to have a particular preference for mining-related endeavors. In this regard, the Ferraras' close association with the Zambrano and Madero families complemented the involvement of all three in the processing of minerals and the manufacturing of metal products. Prior to his death in 1901, Francisco Armendaiz, like Milmo, was, comparatively speaking, an infrequent participant in collaborative efforts. Meanwhile, the Garza-Sadas formed a distinct team, rarely acting without the other in cooperatively financed enterprises. In short, certain businessmen tended to merge where familial ties, similar economic interests, or both pulled them together. Consequently, as the evidence clearly shows in table 6, *regiomontanos* diversified their holdings through joint investments far beyond their commercial origins.[55]

The extensive activities of Monterrey's leading businessmen invited new and sometimes greater problems of management. Here again, they turned whenever possible to the established practice of using family members to fill the needs for administrative personnel, accountants, lawyers, and salesmen.[56] Valentín Rivero and Mariano Hernández utilized their sons to help supervise the various firms in which the two patriarchs held interests. Evaristo Madero and Patricio Milmo emulated the same pattern. Vicente Ferrara, on the other hand, enlisted the aid of his brothers, Antonio and Miguel. In this respect, the Italian immigrant family followed the example of their close associates, the Zambranos, who represented a small army of talented help—Adolfo, Eduardo, Eugenio, Ildefonso, and Onofre. If immediate family members were not available, relatives were pressed into service, such as nephews, godchildren, cousins, and sons-in-law. Finally, in order to exercise greater control over their industrial concerns, the *regiomontano* elite realized the importance of lessening dependence on foreigners for technical know-how. Thus, members of elite families were sent to the United States and Europe to learn as much as possible about particular lines of the family business. In this vein, by 1910, several sons of major businessmen were attending universities in the United States with the intent of returning to Monterrey to contribute to the running of family enterprises.[57]

By the turn of the century, the economic interest of these families embraced the entire region, and, in some cases, much of the country as well. This diversity in business activities widened the economic net of Monterrey's leading entrepreneurs and deepened their influence in the local economy.[58] Significantly, primarily through joint ventures, industry marked the expansion of their interests as foreign capital remained largely tied to export-related companies. Most importantly, the interpenetration among these businessmen through collaborative investments tightened the links among a limited circle of men that coalesced into an identifiable economic elite.

V. Not unlike most capitalists, the Monterrey elite desired a predictable and orderly world that was supportive of its welfare. As a result, *regiomontano* businessmen had to contend with the political necessities of their economic interests. The variation of the elite's holdings led to diverse political needs that escape easy generalization. Certain enterprises found political influence secondary to their success beyond the usual incentives. At times, however, the intervention of a government official was essential for the granting of a contract, the lifting of an import duty, or the extension of a tax exemption, and it required the elite to court political favor. Indeed, in the Porfirian era, politics and profits often went hand in hand.

In the years 1880 to 1910, the political economy of Mexico rested on the power and influence of Porfirio Díaz, his supporters, and his agents. Federal, state, and municipal representatives of the Díaz administration frequently mediated the relationship between political and economic interests. In some cases, the arm of government was intimately intertwined with private enterprise where political position also resulted in economic authority and, often, great wealth. In such instances, governors, high-ranking military officers, and public officials doubled as entrepreneurs, realtors, farmers, mine operators, and merchants. Furthermore, control over tax rates, exemptions, concessions, import licenses, and the courts gave government figures decisive influence over private enterprise. As a consequence, bureaucrats and generals used political weight for monetary gain, for the eliciting of bribes, for admission into promising business deals, and for social favors.[59]

Exceptions appeared as some governors, military commanders, and officeholders refused the blandishments offered by the rampant corruption of the Porfirian regime. If a few remained essentially honest, they still demanded political conformity from businessmen. Regardless of their position or integrity, Díaz henchmen held their own requirements of political deference.

Porfirio Díaz desired peace, order, and economic progress for Mexico. The president's design was translated into an alliance between his government and capitalists, foreign and domestic. Such an alliance implied the repression of any threats to the economic welfare of the wealthy and the preservation of their privileges. In turn, Díaz expected the fealty of those who profited from the government's protection and favor. Concerns of the middle class were at best secondary, and those of workers were largely ignored.[60] In this context, and with government sanction, monopolies flourished, peasants lost land to voracious *hacendados*, and Mexican laborers suffered at the hands of their employers. Meanwhile, the rhetoric of economic liberalism endorsed the concentration of wealth and the corresponding impoverishment of the majority of the Mexican population.[61]

Not surprisingly, members of the Monterrey elite recognized the necessity of political attachment to Díaz and of deference to his representatives, particularly those with the capacity to enhance—or endanger—their economic interests. This was not always an easy task. Periodically, the elite confronted situations that demanded caution, tact, and, at times, sizable sums of money. From 1890 to 1910, two fundamental problems plagued elite relations with political authorities. One was essentially local in nature, and the second encompassed national politics; both, however, were frequently entangled and provided Monterrey businessmen with thorny predicaments.

First, for nearly two decades, the chief agent of Porfirio Díaz in Monterrey was General Bernardo Reyes. Over the years, the relationship between Reyes and Díaz blew hot and cold. At times, Reyes seemed to enjoy Díaz' complete support. Indeed, by 1898, political observers touted the governor of Nuevo León as the heir-apparent to the presidency. Two years later, Reyes' career, and his ties with Díaz, appeared bankrupt. But the aging dictator needed Reyes to check the ambitions of other presidential aspirants, and he subsequently engineered Reyes' political recovery. For *regiomontano* capitalists, the governor's up and down political fortunes held certain risks. An excessive demonstration of Reyista fervor invited Díaz' suspicion, yet a manifest break with the powerful Reyes jeopardized the governor's favor, especially if he successfully assumed the presidency.[62]

Second, Reyes' presidential aspirations rankled others with similar ambitions. Two major factions emerged to vie for Díaz' presidential chair. Reyes and José Ives Limantour, Mexico's finance minister, headed the two groups that locked into a bitter contest to succeed Díaz. Limantour represented the so-called *científicos*, a group of intellectuals and professionals, mostly lawyers, educated deeply in positivist ideas. More importantly, in terms of the Monterrey elite, *científicos* came to exert considerable force on the Díaz administration through their seats on important government bodies and their resultant influence over decisions of economic importance.[63] *Regiomontano* businessmen could ill afford to incur the animosity of the *científicos*, and that of Limantour in particular, as the economic net of the Monterrey elite widened and entailed dealings with federal authorities. The struggle between Reyistas and *científicos*, therefore, was not inconsequential to the interests of Nuevo León's leading entrepreneurs.

Nevertheless, Reyes was essential to the elite's local economic hegemony. His troops assured a quiescent labor force; and his fiscal conservatism was appreciated by businessmen well aware of the excesses of officeholders elsewhere in the country. Thus, the elite had to weigh carefully its political posture, especially in light of Reyes' role in the relationship between government and native capitalists.

An energetic and effective administrator, Reyes became an enthusiastic promoter of the city's economic growth. Following the example of Díaz and his predecessors to the governorship, Reyes encouraged business and lured investment to the area. He provided incentives to businessmen, a common practice, and he usually approved requests to establish new enterprises.[64] Most significantly, Reyes avoided intervening in the city's economy for personal gain. In this connection, Reyes differed from government officials who jealously protected the economic prerogatives that stemmed from their positions. Reyes shunned the use of his office to obtain choice properties, to exact huge bribes from businessmen, or to acquire shares in new enterprises.[65] In the case of Reyes, economic self-interest held little importance in his decisions concerning concessions, tax exemptions, or related issues. As a result, Reyes appeared infrequently in the recordings of real estate transactions or among the investors in the ventures that arose in Monterrey during his tenure as governor. In short, Reyes refrained from using his potent powers to rival the local economic ascendancy of the Monterrey elite.

Rather, Reyes hoped to use businessmen as vehicles to display his capacity to fulfill Díaz' grand plans for Mexico's modernization. For Reyes, capitalists (foreign and domestic) represented resources to build a city that would be an illustration of his vision for the country. Reyes' fondness for beautification projects, his support for public libraries, and his renovation of the public schools' curriculum were but a few examples of his intention to make Monterrey a reflection of his leadership, of his faithfulness to Díaz' goals to modernize the nation.[66] Reyes' motivations in promoting economic development allowed the *regiomontano* elite to maneuver easily within the local political economic context. Reyes' political preoccupations, coupled with his personal rectitude, created a situation that furthered the economic grip of the Monterrey elite.

If the elite had any misgivings about the Reyes administration, the objections centered on the lawyers, bureaucrats, and judges who exploited their ties with Reyes to charge high fees or command substantial bribes. The governor's son, Rodolfo Reyes, and the general's brother-in-law, Crispiano Madrigal, were especially involved in such activities. As one victim of a fixed court decision put it, "with the power of Rodolfo Reyes and his clique, they can make a proper representation impossible."[67] Certainly the elder Reyes was not completely ingenuous in such matters, yet Reyes apparently profited little from the corruption of those below him—reason enough evidently for Reyes to shirk any responsibility. Nonetheless, the elite's professed support for Reyes produced significant advantages and few, though perhaps annoying, disadvantages in everyday dealings with Reyes' administration.

Upon Reyes' installation as governor, Monterrey's capitalists affected the expected acts of political deference. Banquets, social honors, and campaign "donations" became routine displays by the elite to assuage the governor's political sensitivities. Through such gestures, Monterrey's large businessmen, with few exceptions, evaded direct and visible participation in Reyes' political organization. Formed and controlled by Reyes, and in consultation with Díaz, the Unión y Progreso party distributed government patronage in Nuevo León. But members of the *regiomontano* elite rarely appeared in the list of party dignitaries, officeholders, or candidates. Within the Reyista machine, the city's leading businessmen maintained a low profile, content to stay in the background in a less identifiable political position.[68]

The elite's economic interests underscored its relations with federal officials. Using Reyes as a buffer whenever possible in politically weighted matters, the elite's contact with bureaucrats in Mexico City occurred in connection with business, such as arranging contracts, making sales, soliciting concessions, and courting customers. Usually, when required, a small delegation of businessmen traveled to Mexico City when concerns required dealings with federal government figures. If possible, *regiomontanos* enlisted the aid of a prominent lawyer to represent their interests in the capital.[69] Visits to Monterrey by federal officials, on the other hand, were apt to provoke lavish dinners, carefully arranged tours of major industries, and a round of meetings with prominent businessmen.[70] In this respect, most of the Monterrey elite showed little interest in business trips, preferring to have others negotiate with government officials outside of Monterrey.

The presence of Reyes precluded extensive, direct interaction with Porfirio Díaz. On occasion, during the 1900 presidential campaign, for instance, the elite staged extravagant displays of homage to the dictator. In October 1899, leading members of the elite held a meeting to raise funds for Díaz' election effort. The gathering included Antonio Hernández, José A. Muguerza, Francisco G. Sada, Isaac Garza, and Manuel Cantú Treviño, among others. The meeting was to orchestrate support for the Díaz reelection, but the elite's effort took place in the midst of a key business deal involving the federal government (as noted below). For the most part, the elite's relations with Díaz were indirect, through intermediaries such as Reyes. Nevertheless, *regiomontanos* were very aware of the center of power in Mexico.[71]

The triangle of Reyes, Díaz, and Limantour, therefore, pushed the Monterrey elite to adopt an expedient political strategy. Making use of Reyes' presidential preoccupations, and mindful of shows of deference to Díaz and the *científicos*, *regiomontano* capitalists charted a political course intent upon circumventing political entanglements while furthering their economic interests. Political opportunism and pliable loyalties marked the political posture of the Monterrey elite. As a consequence, the politics of the elite were calculated to appease political authority rather than to possess it, to influence governmental decision making rather than to control it directly.[72]

The specific interplay of political considerations with economic interests varied according to the particular needs and circumstances surrounding the scores of ventures that appeared in the years from 1890 to 1910. The furniture manufacturers Benjamín Salinas and Joel Rocha, for example, parlayed their original business into a department store that gradually evolved into a chain of outlets beyond Nuevo León. In the early rise of Salinas y Rocha stores, the firm's growth stemmed primarily from the entrepreneurial skills and capital resources of its owners rather than from lucrative government contracts or favorable tariff schedules.[73] On the other hand, political influence and favor figured crucially in the success of other enterprises. In this connection, the Fundidora and the Cervecería Cuauhtémoc represented distinct patterns of development that pointed to the political and economic nuances that surrounded the establishment of Monterrey's major industries.

VI.   The demand for iron and steel products in Mexico multiplied substantially after 1890, and indications pointed to its continuation. Vicente Ferrara had gained valuable experience in metal refining and manufacturing as manager of Fundición Número Dos after its foundation in 1890. Furthermore, the Italian-born immigrant had served as

Italy's consular representative in Monterrey, adding to his knowledge of Mexican trade and the growing importation of iron and steel for rails, trolley lines, bridges, construction beams, and related types of building materials. Moreover, as a partner with his brother Miguel in local commerce, Vicente Ferrara had established a working relationship with most of Monterrey's leading businessmen, often joining them in collaborative ventures. After consulting with the city's key entrepreneurs in late 1898, Ferrara found an interest among them to pursue the possibility of constructing Mexico's first iron and steel plant in Monterrey.[74]

Ferrara visualized a steel mill that called for a 10 million peso investment, a huge sum for that time. Encouraged by the local response, Ferrara set out to acquire the concession for the mill and to organize the required capital from both domestic and foreign sources. Ferrara realized, along with his *regiomontano* counterparts, that the initial thrust of their efforts had to be directed at Bernardo Reyes. In light of the money involved, and the presence of competing foreign interests, government support for the plant was essential to its success.

Effectively exploiting Reyes' ambitions, Ferrara succeeded in securing the governor's dogged backing. In numerous letters to various federal officials, particularly Limantour, in the early months of 1899, Reyes hammered at the importance of the steel mill to Mexico's "national industry."[75] Reyes appreciated the symbolic significance of seeing the first steel plant in Latin America being built in Mexico, in Monterrey. Reyes' letters revealed his determination to have the mill represent his progressive ideas and rule in Nuevo León, although, in his correspondence with federal officials, Reyes emphasized the ways in which the plant signified a crucial step in the modernization of the country. Despite his wooing of foreign capital for Nuevo León, Reyes nevertheless took special pride in Mexico's attainment of *progreso*, of Mexico joining the club of industrialized Western countries. And, of course, Reyes was sensitive to similarly held nationalistic sentiments in Porfirio Díaz. The steel mill, then, came to possess political rewards, not the least of which would be garnered by Bernardo Reyes.[76]

Limantour initially balked at granting his approval to the project. The finance minister was not blind to the benefits that accrued to Reyes if the plant was erected in Monterrey. In a letter in November 1899, Limantour, however, concealed his political opposition by citing his concern over the ability of Ferrara to find sufficient capital for the project.[77] Ferrara, and Reyes, found it easy enough to respond to the expressed reservations of the finance minister.

Headed by León Signoret, a powerful group of French-origin businessmen had shown an interest in Ferrara's proposed steelworks.

Signoret and his partners derived much of their wealth from their holdings in the Mexican textile industry through the CIDOSA conglomerate. In addition, the French capitalists maintained several prominent department stores in Mexico City and had a hand in the highly profitable monopoly on dynamite sales in the country as well. The immense capital resources of Signoret and his group had prompted them to form a finance company in 1898, the Société Financière pour l'Industrie au Mexique. As the name of the firm indicated, the orientation of the company was toward industrial investments, and it had caught the eye of Vicente Ferrara. Of greater importance, Signoret and his clique developed close ties with key banking figures and institutions. Signoret and Julio Limantour, brother of the finance minister and a banker, were good friends, sharing many of the same associates, members of Mexico City's wealthy French colony. Furthermore, Signoret's brother José sat on the board of directors of the Banco Nacional de Londres y México, and, through CIDOSA, León Signoret was also well connected to the president of the Banco de Londres y México, Tomás Braniff. Finally, through Signoret, Ferrara's project attracted the attention of the tobacco magnate Antonio Basagoiti.[78]

Reyes, aware of Limantour's links with the Signoret group interested in the project, assured Limantour that adequate investors had been found. And, playing on the finance minister's anti-American feelings, Reyes also assured him that neither "Americans nor American capital" were part of the Fundidora's backers.[79] (Reyes knew of the participation of Eugene Kelly of New York in the steel-making plant for nearly six months.) Perhaps as a result of pressures from his French associates, Limantour relented a few weeks later. In a letter to Reyes in early December 1899, the chief of the *científicos* gave his approval to the project and agreed to approach Díaz to grant a favorable concession.[80]

In the meantime, Ferrara and his *regiomontano* counterparts were busily at work winning the support of Porfirio Díaz for the proposal. Reyes, as early as May 1899, had attempted to gain the dictator's favor for the project.[81] But Díaz, in a characteristic ploy, apparently waited for the implicit contest between Reyes and Limantour to play itself out on the matter. In the backdrop of the impending 1900 presidential elections, the Monterrey elite formed a local committee to promote Díaz' campaign. In an unprecedented move, with the negotiations on the steel mill concession in progress, the elite decided to travel to Mexico City to fete the president himself. On November 23, 1899, a literal feast was held in honor of Díaz in Mexico City. The owners and managers of virtually every large enterprise of Monterrey attended the festivities.[82]

The effusive demonstration of the Monterrey elite proved to be timely and, apparently, effective. Soon after the display put on by Ferrara's cohort from Nuevo León, as noted earlier, Limantour gave his endorsement to the proposal. At that point, Reyes intensified his effort to acquire presidential approval for the project. In a letter to Díaz in late December 1899, Reyes insistently argued the merits of the project, concluding that the "proposed steel plant is one of the most important industries that the country should possess."[83] Finally, with the elite's November demonstration in mind, Reyes went on to say, "I beg you to give your attention to this matter upon which so many hopes of prosperity have been placed by the businessmen of the capital of the state that I govern."[84] Less than two weeks later, Reyes was thanking Díaz for his approval of the project and for the dictator's suggestions on the wording of the concession request.[85]

The political arrangements made, Ferrara proceeded to finalize the financial organization of the steel-making venture. The mill's capital requirement of 10 million pesos was divided into 100,000 shares at 100 pesos each. As table 7 indicates, Signoret and Basagoiti held about 40% of the shares. With the Kelly shares, nearly 60% of the steel plant's shareholders were from outside Monterrey. Nonetheless, an examination of the underlying links among the investors pointed to the intimate associations between Milmo and Kelly, who were tied by marriage. In effect, the Milmos represented the Kelly portion of the deal. Thus, the effective presence of the Monterrey elite in the new firm approximated that of the Mexico City–based Signoret group. The composition of the plant's administration underscored the extent of *regiomontano* influence. In fact, the steel plant maintained two directorates: a Mexico City group, consisting of Braniff, Signoret, Basagoiti, and León Honnorat, longtime associate of Signoret; and the Monterrey group, including Adolfo Zambrano, Valentín Rivero, Isaac Garza, Ernesto Madero, with Vicente Ferrara as manager of the plant. Thus, despite the prominence of foreign and outside investors, the Fundidora "was, in reality, an internal promotion."[86] (Indicative of the *regiomontano* foundations of the steelworks, a coal-mining venture was organized primarily from local capital in 1902 in order to lessen the costs of fueling the mill's furnaces. See table 8.)

The creation of the mill brought much fanfare in Mexico City and Monterrey. The Fundidora "presents the best manner to employ native capital, it will serve to improve morally and materially our working classes," observed one newspaper at the time, "leaving in its wake, to the commerce of our largest cities, an energy, a spirit that is manifest in all industrial centers and that forms the base of prosperity of all

Table 7. *Major Investors in the Fundidora de Fierro y Acero de Monterrey*

Monterrey Investors by Family Group Name	Shares	Mexico City–Based Investors Name	Shares	Foreign Investors Name	Shares
Milmos		A. Basagoiti	21,500	E. Kelly	13,344
P. Milmo	10,000				
D. Milmo	1,000	L. Signoret	19,000	T. Kelly	4,173
P. V. Milmo	200				
Ferraras				Ed. Kelly	673
V. Ferrara	2,148				
M. Ferrara	1,500				
A. Ferrara	1,000				
Garza-Sadas					
I. Garza	1,200				
F. G. Sada	500	*Summary of Shareholding in Fundidora*			
J. Calderón	400	Monterrey investors		28,098	
E. D. Sada	100	Foreign (Kelly) investors		18,190	
E. Sada Muguerza	100	Monterrey investors and			
A. Sada	100	Kelly shares combined		46,288	
Zambranos		Mexico City investors		40,500	
A. Zambrano	550	Total		86,788*	
I. Zambrano	500				
O. Zambrano	500				
Ed. Zambrano	100				
E. Zambrano	100				
Maderos					
E. Madero	700				
F. Madero	500				
Others					
T. Mendirichaga	3,000				
V. Rivero	1,900				
F. Belden	1,000				
F. Armendaiz	1,000				

Source: Libro de Notarios, 1900, AGENL.
*Remaining shares (of 100,000) sold in amounts less than 100 shares.

nations."[87] On May 5, 1900, chosen no doubt for symbolic effect, ground-breaking ceremonies took place for Mexico's first iron and steel mill in Monterrey, Nuevo León. Iron production commenced in about a year, and the initial batch of steel rolled out of the plant's furnaces two years later. Yet the political concerns of the nascent venture continued to be important to its success.

Table 8. *Companies and Elite Members in the Formation of the Compañia Carbonifera de Monterrey, 1902*

Name of Firm/Individual	Shares*
1. Cía. Mexicana de Carbón y Piedra	2,500
2. Fundidora de Fierro y Acero	1,980
3. Cervecería Cuauhtémoc	1,000
4. Minera Fundidora y Afinadora	890
5. Molinos de Cilindros de Monterrey	600
6. Fábrica de Mantas "La Industrial"	230
7. Fábrica de Vidrios y Cristales	230
8. Fábrica de Mantas "La Fama"	100
9. Ladrillera Unión	100
10. V. Ferrara	650
11. T. Mendirichaga	500
12. V. Rivero y Gajá	300
13. M. Cantú Treviño	300
14. J. Armendaiz	200
15. F. G. Sada	100
16. F. Martínez	100
17. R. Chavarrí	50
18. Constantino de Tárnava	20
19. I. Garza	20
20. F. Izaguirre	20
21. A. Zambrano	20

Source: Libro de Notarios, 1902, AGENL.
*Total shares sold = 10,000.

Mexico's demand for iron and steel at the turn of the century outstripped the productive capacity of Monterrey's Fundidora. Imports of such products persisted as the Fundidora was forced to expand to gain a foothold in the iron and steel trade. (See table 9.) The Fundidora's impressive production statistics concealed, however, the importance of government to the plant's seeming success.

On several occasions, the Secretaría de Fomento sent out circulars regarding requests (usually by foreigners) for permission to initiate businesses that potentially competed with established firms, such as the Monterrey steelworks. Whenever possible, Ferrara attempted to discourage the creation of possible rivals in the iron and steel business. As manager of the plant, Ferrara repeatedly responded to such circulars by pointing out to the Secretaría that the Fundidora was producing (or was about to manufacture) the articles noted in the concession request. Indeed his first effort in this connection occurred the same month that

Table 9. *Production of the Fundidora, 1903-1911 (in tons)*

Year	Iron	Steel
1903	21,583	8,823
1904	35,622	29,552
1905	4,388*	21,613
1906	25,319	33,463
1907	16,328	31,806
1908	16,872	28,900
1909	58,859	59,509
1910	45,095	67,944
1911	71,337	84,697

Source: *Historia moderna de México, El Porfiriato, la vida económica,* book 1, p. 381.
*Furnaces repaired and improved.

construction of the plant began; Ferrara was hardly in a position to cite the mill's line of products, but he nonetheless vigorously protested the granting of a concession by the Secretaría de Fomento to an entrepreneur interested in making metal products.[88] Two years later (1902), Ferrara testily stated that "within a short time" the Fundidora would make the items encompassed by a request for a steel plant concession in Puebla.[89] Manuel Fernández Leal, minister of development, pressed Ferrara on the point in a telegram.[90] In a defensive tone, Ferrara retorted that "the steel-making unit was being finished at the present time, in which all known processes of converting iron to steel would be employed, including the Bessemer type, within a very short time."[91] This last rejoinder apparently satisfied Fernández Leal. About a year later (1903), Ferrara was once again claiming that the Fundidora did not produce sheet metal "at the present time, but it will in a short time."[92] In this case, the minister of development went directly to Governor Bernardo Reyes for an answer—Reyes grudgingly admitted that the Fundidora did not make sheet metal at the moment.[93]

Still, in spite of an occasional setback, the political connections of the Fundidora's founders proved fruitful as they assiduously courted government favor with crucial successful results. Astutely plying the links among Limantour, his French associates, and other influential figures, the Fundidora's owners in 1903 secured federal government approval for a high tariff on iron and steel products.[94] A year later, the Monterrey steelworks obtained the most lucrative government contract in its brief history: to supply the Mexican railway with steel for construction projects and for the replacement of worn rails.[95] Foreign observers clearly understood the significance of government "cooperation" for the sales of the steel plant. Phillip Hanna, for example, U.S. consul in Monterrey, noted in 1904 the importance of governmental protection "against competition of older and richer countries" to the Fundidora's production.[96] Not surprisingly, in light of the steelworks' owners' political connections, the Fundidora "won" the contract to provide steel for the construction of a new port in 1906; a "triumph" for the nation's industry, one press report proclaimed, going on to explain inaccurately how the Monterrey mill in "open competition" beat out its foreign rivals for the contract.[97]

The Fundidora's manager, Vicente Ferrara, was periodically and understandably in Mexico City to drum up business for the plant. In a typical instance, in April 1907, Ferrara attended a banquet in Mexico City while "arranging important deals involving the industrial firms of Monterrey."[98] Among those present at the occasion were Felix Díaz, nephew of the dictator himself, and government officials responsible for the making of contracts for government construction projects. Two weeks later, the director of public works in Mexico City visited the Fundidora "in order to evaluate its ability to meet the demand of Mexico City" for buildings in "actual construction and for those projected for construction in the metropolis [Mexico City]."[99] If this were not enough, the Fundidora employed Rodolfo Reyes, son of the governor, as its lawyer on several deals; and, of course, it continued to plumb the ties among federal officials, such as Limantour, and influential investors in the Fundidora based in Mexico City, such as León Signoret.[100] Thus, the success of the Monterrey steel plant derived in large part from the ability of its owners to obtain political favor, locally and in the highest offices of the Mexican government.

VII.   On December 16, 1890, Isaac Garza and Joseph Schnaider petitioned Bernardo Reyes for permission to build "an industry entirely new to the state" that was the "first in the Republic."[101] Four days later, Reyes approved the request for the establishment of a brewery, and he granted the familiar seven-year exemption from all state and municipal taxes. The new enterprise represented the fruition of an earlier attempt by José Calderón to make beer in Monterrey. The old merchant had imported beer for years and, given the city's lengthy and hot summers, the beverage proved to be popular. But Calderón's initial efforts to produce the beverage had ended in failure. Lack of equipment, of expertise in beer-making, of cheap containers, of easy transportation, and of extensive markets all combined to defeat

Calderón's first foray into beer-making in 1879. The latter two factors, however, changed dramatically with the rapid development of the region's railways and the consequent rise in population, workers, and wages.

Through Joseph Robertson, Calderón came into contact with Schnaider, an experienced brewmaster who had worked at the Anheuser-Busch brewery of St. Louis, Missouri. Determined to try the beer business again, Calderón brought three partners into the venture, his brother-in-law, José Muguerza, his lawyer, Francisco Sada, and Isaac Garza. The group decided to send Enrique Sada Muguerza, a younger relative of the men who spoke English, to St. Louis with Schnaider to look into the buying of necessary equipment, the importation of glass bottles, the supply of malt, and other items related to the production of beer. In the midst of these preparations, José Calderón died in March 1889.

Calderón's widow, Francisca (José Muguerza's sister), agreed to continue the effort. In November 1889, the brewery's founders met to formalize the petition for a concession; they included Garza, Muguerza, Francisca Muguerza del Calderón, Schnaider, Francisco Sada, and Enrique Sada Muguerza. The initial capital amounted to 100,000 pesos. And, in a nationalistic gesture, the brewery was named after the Aztec chief Cuauhtémoc. The following year, the Cervecería Cuauhtémoc began production, turning out 60,000 barrels of beer, 8,000 tons of ice to cool the brew, and 5,000 bottles of beer.[102] (See table 10.)

The popularity of the Cervecería's products mounted quickly and prompted the attempts of the brewery's owners to integrate various aspects of production. Profits were poured back into the enterprise as

Table 10. *Beer Shipments from the Cervecería Cuauhtémoc, 1892–1910 (selected years)*

Year	Quantity (in thousands of liters)
1892	498
1896	2,151
1900	4,866
1904	6,865
1908	11,183
1910	13,275

Source: Stephen H. Haber, "The Industrialization of Mexico, 1880–1940" (manuscript in progress, unpaginated).

its ownership strove to lessen its dependence on imports for glass bottles, for packaging needs, for barrels, and for delivery vehicles. In a short period of time, the Cervecería employed its own glassblowers, made its own wooden boxes and barrels, and maintained a wagon-making shop on its premises. The quality of its product, especially its Carta Blanca brand, spurred sales. In fact, the label won the first of many prizes at the 1893 World's Fair in Chicago.[103] The swift expansion of the company and its activities pushed Isaac Garza, president of the firm, to ask Francisco G. Sada to manage the increasingly complex operations of the plant.

The brewery's growth reflected its ability to establish a predominant position in the Mexican beer market. Proximity to the United States failed to affect the Cervecería adversely since American beer producers were hard pressed to meet domestic consumption, much less export beer to Mexico. More importantly, American brewers commanded higher prices—and profits—in the United States and largely ignored the market potential in Mexico.[104] In addition, entrepreneurs outside of Monterrey were slow to respond to the energetic efforts of the *regiomontano* brewery. By the time other Mexican breweries reacted, the Cervecería Cuauhtémoc had established a firm position in the market, in which the continuing quality of its labels played a definite role. In 1902, and from 1904 to 1907, Carta Blanca won major prizes at expositions outside of Mexico that attracted national attention to the brewery with much attendant newspaper publicity in Mexico City and, of course, in Monterrey.[105] Of greater significance, the Cervecería had created a wide net of distributors, aggressively advertised its products, and pressed its drive to cut down on costs. Competitors lagged behind, leading some to go so far as to engineer special local taxes aimed at the Cervecería while others attempted to imitate the labels of the Cervecería in an effort to confuse customers.[106] Meanwhile, Mexican beer consumption swelled. With an original work force of fifty men in 1891, the Cervecería employed over 500 men a decade later.[107]

In 1899, the Cervecería's ownership made its first major bid to lower substantially the costs of making bottles by organizing a glass-making company, Vidrios y Cristales de Monterrey. But the effort, despite an investment of $600,000 and the importation of scores of European glassblowers, failed to meet the brewery's demand for bottles. The company was reorganized in 1904 with virtually all of the investors from within Monterrey's business establishment. Again the attempt at glass-making ended disappointingly. Finally, through the acquisition of the Owens automatic bottle-making process in 1909, the persistence of the Cervecería's owners, particularly Isaac Garza, paid off with the successful resolution of the glass-making problem. The reconstituted glass plant, the Vidriera Monterrey, immediately became a valuable asset and competitive advantage to the Monterrey-based brewery.[108]

In addition to the glassworks, the Cervecería had developed another company that complemented its beer-making with the formation of Fábricas de Cartón Monterrey in 1900, which made bottle caps, boxes, and packaging materials of various kinds. With its implementation, the Vidriera joined the Fábricas plant in serving the needs of local manufacturing, most prominently the thriving soda works of the city.[109]

In the Porfirian era, the importance of political considerations to the development of the Cervecería paled in comparison to those of the Fundidora. As the evidence suggests, Reyes played a pivotal role in the foundation of the steel plant, and federal officials, such as Limantour, were also enlisted to aid the vulnerable steel-making enterprise. Such governmental favor contrasted with the relative absence of political influence in the success of the brewery. Government support—tax credits, exemptions, concessions—for the Cervecería resembled others in duration and amount, although the tax exemption of the Fundidora exceeded the one granted to the brewery by eight years.[110] The owners of the Cervecería realized, of course, the necessity of meeting the rituals of deference to prominent political figures, and they maintained cordial, if not close, relations with the city's public officials, particularly Reyes. In this regard, the Cervecería's owners held investments in businesses that required much greater political influence, including a sizable interest in the Fundidora. The growth and expansion of the Cervecería, however, occurred essentially without extraordinary government intervention.[111] In short, the nature of the relations between the state and the brewery differed fundamentally from those of the Fundidora.

Several factors contributed to the differences between the two enterprises in terms of their relations with government. First, Reyes took a personal interest in the steel plant since he saw it as a symbol of his own leadership and vision. For Reyes, the Fundidora represented still another, albeit major, opportunity to earn national accolades for his progressive administration. Second, the sheer size of the steel-making venture and the nature of its market implied the necessity of strong governmental backing through tariff protection and substantial government contracts. As a consequence, the courting of officeholders and the application of political pressure marked the development of the Fundidora. And, throughout, political maneuvering invited the complications posed by the subtle battles between Reyistas and *científicos*.

In the case of the Cervecería, Reyes manifested little of the attention and enthusiasm sparked by the steelworks. Moreover, the brewery rarely required more than the usual and practiced forms of respect to Reyes or federal officials. And, unlike the Fundidora, the Cervecería's economic interests found it generally unnecessary to negotiate the fluid conditions within the triangle of Díaz, Limantour, and Reyes. Indeed, for the brewery, Reyes embodied the ideal politician: supportive of business, yet unobtrusive, and available for assistance whenever necessary. And the generally procapitalist policies of the federal government framed the favorable economic climate in which the Cervecería flourished. Yet, in this respect, the brewery was not unique; capitalists throughout the country enjoyed the benefits of Díaz' dictatorship. In brief, the Cervecería's relationship to the Porfirian state reflected the relative insignificance of government to the brewery's market.

The Cervecería and the Fundidora differed in still other ways. Decisions concerning the Fundidora included the consideration of powerful outsiders and foreigners. The importance of French capital to the venture meant a source of influence in Mexico City governmental and financial circles, but such ties also suggested the task at times of balancing diverse interests. As it was, the manager of the Fundidora had to contend with a bifurcated board of directors, with one group in Mexico City and the other in Monterrey. Thus, the clarity of local control in the case of the Fundidora was correspondingly reduced. In addition, as a close examination of the steelworks' shareholders indicates, the plant lacked a clear-cut pattern of ownership and, subsequently, direction. The extensiveness of its financial backing pointed to the fact that the Fundidora's owners were often preoccupied with their additional and more accessible endeavors. Much of the planning and management of the plant fell into the hands of Ferrara, who was forced to consult several people in making major decisions, while he pursued his own wide-ranging interests. The inner workings of the administration of the Fundidora were therefore cumbersome, if not at times inefficient.[112]

The Cervecería, on the other hand, remained largely within the hands of a small, interrelated, and family-connected circle: Isaac Garza, Francisco G. Sada, and José Muguerza. The intimate ties among the three men facilitated the management and development of the brewery. In fact, Joseph Schnaider was bought out of his share in the business in 1896, though he maintained friendly ties with the Cervecería's ownership. Each of the three principal actors of the brewery's ownership continued to have independent economic concerns, but they apparently realized the centrality of the Cervecería to their interests. The cooperation among the three men was manifest in the pattern of investments in which they participated, particularly between Isaac Garza and Francisco Sada.[113] Hence, the management of the Cervecería possessed a degree of control and direction generally unequaled by the Fundidora during its initial stage of development.

In addition, each of the three men took on a distinct function within the expanding web of activities of the brewery and, to a lesser extent, its major subsidiaries. Garza, as president of the Cervecería, took on the larger administrative tasks generated by the brewery, the packaging plant, and the glassworks. Initially, Muguerza's role centered on the financing of the Cervecería and its related activities. Equally important in the management of these enterprises, the triumvirate of the brewery employed a number of relatives, which contributed to the centralization of the administration of business operations. Nevertheless, Isaac Garza and Francisco G. Sada gradually seized the leadership of the Cervecería and its subsidiary holdings. Muguerza, though he remained close to his partners, increasingly devoted himself to other pursuits that reflected the cementing of the Garza-Sada ascendancy within the structure of the Cervecería.[114] Managerial responsibilities fell to Sada, who was well versed in every step of the beer-making process, since he also supervised production and engineered improvements in the brewing equipment and related technical functions. Garza, on the other hand, supplied ideas, vision, planning, and strategy.

The friendship between the two men reinforced a similar outlook and personality that was austere, reserved, prudent, and extremely conservative in thought. The aggressive character of their business initiatives belied the calculated, thoughtful planning that marked their efforts. The Vidriera's first two failures served to demonstrate their tenacity, their conviction that solving the glass-making problem was critical to the enterprise. Their eventual success only confirmed their assumptions about their own entrepreneurship and the soundness of their methods. In this connection, paternalism figured significantly in the management of the Cervecería. The importance of family to the operation of the brewery appeared early on and established a pattern that continued into the contemporary era. Luis G. Sada, for instance, began his career in 1906. Intent on furthering technical expertise over beer-making, Francisco G. Sada sent his son to Chicago to study brewing, and young Luis eventually returned to supervise brewing operations. Later progeny of the Garza-Sadas, as noted in subsequent chapters, followed similar paths.

The tightfisted control of the Cervecería in these formative years contributed to a purposefulness in its operations and a single-mindedness in approach that came from thorough, carefully weighed decisions. If caution characterized the management of the Cervecería, the execution of decisions once made earned the brewery's ownership a bold, enterprising image. The enormous success of the Cervecería, therefore, affirmed in the minds of Garza and Sada the benefits of their paternalistic approach to management and of their business acumen. The experience of the Cervecería's leadership in this era molded its thinking, its approach to problems, and its expectations of the state. In this last respect, the lessons learned in this period differed from those of its sister industry, the Fundidora.

VIII.   The Fundidora and the Cervecería represented two fundamentally different currents in the industrialization of Monterrey that, in the Porfirian era, were obscured by the commonalities shared by the two industrial pillars of Monterrey's elite. Both companies grew out of the response of local capitalists to the internal markets generated by the massive influx of foreign capital in the late nineteenth century into Mexico, and particularly into the northern region of the country. With foreign investors preoccupied with extractive pursuits, Monterrey's businessmen took advantage of their capital resources and established local commercial dominance to extend their economic ascendancy. More importantly, they moved to fill the vacuum created by the concentration of foreign capital on export-related activities and by the rising demand for industrial products induced by the economic growth of the region.

As a result, Monterrey's businessmen collaborated in the formation of industries aimed at fulfilling the region's swelling internal markets. Furthermore, *regiomontanos* incorporated the capital and influence of neighboring, powerful native capitalists into their joint ventures while retaining considerable, if not controlling, interest. The Terrazas of Chihuahua, for example, and the Maderos of Coahuila appeared among the investors in Nuevo León's industries. The Maderos, in fact, moved to Monterrey, and, by the turn of the century, they had assumed an eminent place within the local business establishment. Thus, between 1890 and 1910, the economic web of the maturing Monterrey elite embraced the entire region and members of northern Mexico's wealthiest and most influential families.

Through such ties, especially among themselves, Monterrey's major businessmen to a large extent preempted foreign dominance in the industrial sector of the city's economy. "Monterrey is not, as has generally been believed," *El Imparcial* claimed as early as 1900, "an industrial and commercial center that is given life only by American companies." "Rather," the Mexico City newspaper continued, "native businessmen lead the rapid transformation of the capital of Nuevo

León."[115] By 1903, American investments in Nuevo León were reported to be nearly $11.5 million, yet only $2.5 million of that amount was due to industrial concerns.[116] In 1905, the *Voz de Nuevo León* confirmed the superiority of native businessmen over foreigners in Monterrey's industries. While European investments totaled 400,000 pesos, as the local newspaper reported, those of Americans was 3.36 million pesos. The Guggenheim plant alone represented 2.5 million of the sum. But the value of local industrial capital amounted to nearly 117 million pesos.[117] As a visiting German industrialist noted at the time, "Mexican capital competes equally with American commercial and industrial influence. American preponderance is much greater in Mexico City than in Monterrey. The banks, foundries, factories, and commerce are virtually all in the hands of Mexicans so that assuredly the American element is clearly in the minority."[118] The inability of foreigners extensively to penetrate the manufacturing sector of the local economy reflected the established, wide-ranging interests of a well-entrenched group of Monterrey capitalists. Collaboration, however, among Monterrey's businessmen represented the critical factor in their economic dominance of Monterrey.

The economic success of the Monterrey elite was not without significant political support. In this regard, the Cervecería and the Fundidora shared, in general terms, a political context conducive to the interests of capitalists, foreign or native. Specifically, in Nuevo León, both companies benefited from the probusiness regime of Governor Bernardo Reyes that gave *regiomontanos* virtually free reign in the local economy. The political costs for Monterrey's ascendant businessmen were relatively meager, but the financial rewards were substantial. But here the paths of the Fundidora and the Cervecería parted.

Although initially dependent on foreign technical help, the brewery remained primarily in the hands of the Garza-Sada family. Equally important, in contrast to the Fundidora, political favor was substantively less significant to the Cervecería's success. Reyes and national political figures, such as Limantour, were comparatively inconsequential to the conception and early growth of the Garza-Sada's budding empire, though the brewery's owners observed the requisite forms of political deference. Decision making, however, within the Cervecería occurred free of weighty political considerations and without the inclusion of outside interests. In this sense, the nexus of the Cervecería remained essentially local as opposed to the more diffuse, political nature of the Fundidora's interests. In short, the Cervecería evolved in a distinct pattern from that of the Fundidora, including the relative importance of the state. For the Garza-Sadas, the state played a marginal role. On this point, Reyes loomed crucially in the political perceptions of the *regiomontano* elite, particularly the owners of the brewery.

Reyes failed to force the political hand of *regiomontano* business-men. In contrast to Chihuahua, for example, where the Terrazas family overshadowed the state's political economy, the political visibility of Monterrey's businessmen was blotted out by the overwhelming presence of Bernardo Reyes. The Terrazas developed their economic empire in a political arena in which they personally held obvious, effective authority.[119] This was not the case in Monterrey. Rather, Reyes was used to front the economic aims of the Monterrey elite when his intervention suited the circumstances. In this regard, Reyes avoided thwarting dealings between *regiomontanos* and his political enemies in Mexico City. Reyes even refused to blunt the economic designs of native capitalists by his own personal avariciousness. Hence, Reyes' ambitions and character played into the hands of the Monterrey elite. Reyes was less than a dupe in this respect, but he was hardly an impediment to the calculated intentions of the astute busi-nessmen of Monterrey.

Given its dependence on government support, the Fundidora used Reyes with particular profitable skill. Under the benevolent umbrella of Reyes, the Cervecería also flourished, but without the governor's direct aid as in the case of the Fundidora. Moreover, the lack of sub-stantive outside interests in the primary holdings of the Garza-Sadas reinforced their sense of autonomy. To a much greater extent than the Fundidora, the brewery was able to circumvent two key elements of the Porfirian political economy: the consideration of foreign economic interests and the necessity of national political influence.

For the Garza-Sadas, therefore, their political experiences in the Porfirian era led to an exaggerated sense of the unimportance of the state, to seeing the state merely as an instrument of their interests. Later, after 1910, when political conditions changed drastically, the continued dependence of the Fundidora on government protection dictated, on the surface at least, a conciliatory posture toward the new men in power. The political outlook of the Cervecería clique, nurtured in the Porfiriato, was ill prepared for the changes precipitated by the events after the demise of Díaz. The Fundidora, on the other hand, recognized with well-worn pragmatism the implications of the new order. And, in fact, the assumption of leadership of the steel plant in 1907 by Adolfo Prieto suggested this distinction before 1910. With Prieto, who lived in Mexico City, in control, the Fundidora ceased to be an important extension of the Monterrey elite.

Nonetheless, prior to the revolution the ties among the elite and the fortuitous economic context of Monterrey blurred the underlying differences between the city's foremost industries. Far into the twentieth century, the Porfirian era represented for members of the Monterrey elite a golden age of undisputed local economic power.[120] Their businesses thrived, and the city reflected their image. Monterrey became known as the "Chicago" of Mexico, the "Pittsburgh" of the country. In their own eyes, they personified the future of Mexico—modernity, industry, order. They had succeeded in a way that few Mexicans had before them—Monterrey's belching smokestacks affirmed their superiority and the certainty of their abilities. In the confines of their regional stronghold, unencumbered by a heavy political hand, members of the *regiomontano* elite held sway over the economic fortunes of the city. Indeed, their prominence permeated the life of the city, and the social ties among them served to cement their cohesiveness, their distinctiveness, and their economic power.

3. El patriotismo verdadero: The Social Foundations of the Monterrey Elite

I. A prominent writer of the Porfirian era, Francisco G. Cosmes, claimed in one of his essays that true patriotism in Mexico—*el patriotismo verdadero*—was seen in those who were in step with the "incessant march of progress."[1] For Cosmes, and most of his intellectual counterparts, there existed basically only two types of people: those who were, or were not, "apt" for civilization.[2] The darwinist overtones of Cosmes' view rationalized a society marked by a deepening concentration of wealth in which the pattern of land tenure became the most visible of the inequities of the Porfiriato. Mexican positivism, and its variant ideas, promoted notions of superiority among the rich, leading the Mexican upper class to see less fortunate countrymen with condescension, if not contempt.[3]

In Monterrey, the economic dominance of the city's largest businessmen and their families was furthered by the social and familial ties among them that served to reaffirm their elite status. The resultant insularity of the Monterrey elite underscored its social distinctiveness, but also engendered a sense of control over its world, a world that both shaped and mirrored the outlook of the elite with enduring consequences.

The social primacy of this group of families found expression in the class relations of *regiomontano* society. The peculiar conditions of the labor market in northern Mexico prompted Monterrey's major employers to adopt a paternalistic approach to their workers, where company-supported facilities for employees became an effective means to maintain a dependent, malleable labor force. Reinforced by the generally antilabor posture of the Porfirian regime, the paternalism of the elite formed a key, lasting feature of its view of labor-capital relations. On the other hand, the elite's grip over mobility in the private sector pushed members of the city's middle class to look toward other avenues to reach their material aspirations, such as the acquisition of public office. Rather than challenging the domination of local capitalists, the middle class sought primarily to obtain the trappings of wealth and to enter, if possible, the rich confines of the elite's social life.

An exclusive circle of clubs, organizations, and activities served to enhance the coherence of the elite. There, propitious marriages were promoted, influential *compadres* and *comadres* recruited, and ambitious relatives and acquaintances introduced to appropriate, if not fortuitous, contacts. Nonetheless, the social functions of the wealthy also registered the subtle changes within the elite, revealing the ascent of some and descent of others. Differences due to age and gender also appeared, adding yet another insight into the inner workings of the elite over time. Still, in the Porfirian period, the links, social and economic, among the elite sustained cohesion despite the differentiation that developed among its members.

Unmitigated by an eminent political figure or by the rival presence of foreigners, the ascendancy of the elite resonated throughout the social life of the city. Indeed, not unlike their capitalist counterparts elsewhere, members of the elite perceived their economic power and social power as one, and both as an extension of their acumen. In their own minds, and in the background of the country's history of economic travail, their wealth and status confirmed their importance to the welfare of the nation and its future. They reflected Mexico's promise; they were the true patriots, or so they thought.

II.   The social context that nurtured Monterrey's leading families differed in various ways from that in other areas, such as Jalisco, where economic characteristics and development had produced distinct social structures.[4] The 1860s cotton boom, for example, made for profits that led to the acquisition of vast landholdings by *regiomontano* merchants. Thus, the great *hacendados* of Nuevo León were also often the businessmen of Monterrey; Patricio Milmo, Evaristo Madero, and Francisco G. Sada, to name three, were among those who had invested substantial amounts of their commercial earnings into land. On the other hand, the Zambranos were perhaps the most prominently involved in mining operations. After the depression of the 1870s, Monterrey's major merchants counted among the state's foremost landholders and mining operators. Hence, from the beginning of the Porfirian era, the subtle rivalries often implicit in the divisions between *hacendados* and merchants, such as occurred in San Luis Potosí, failed to materialize in Monterrey.[5]

Early on, the social prominence of local businessmen was enhanced by the fact that major foreign and outside investors resided elsewhere, with the exception of Joseph A. Robertson. The Guggenheims, owners of the largest foreign concern, lived in the United States. Eugene Kelly, though a major participant in the Fundidora, remained in New York, apparently satisfied that the Milmos would manage his investments in the steel plant well. Moreover, León Signoret and Antonio Basagoiti of the Fundidora, and Joaquín Casasús of the Banco Mercantil, continued to make Mexico City their home. The Terrazas, although involved in sundry ventures in Monterrey, stayed in their stronghold in the state of Chihuahua. In Mexico City, on the other hand, at the functions of the Jockey Club, or at the contests sponsored by the French Polo Club, wealthy Mexicans competed with their foreign counterparts for the best seats at the next French opera, or for invitations to the next soirée at the Lyre Gauloise, or for the acquisition of the latest fad in French fashion.[6] This was not the case in Monterrey, where there were few outsiders with whom *regiomontano* elite families had to contend for social recognition.

To the benefit of the established upper class, the chief political force in the state for nearly twenty years, Bernardo Reyes, accommodated himself easily in the social hierarchy of the city. Reyes was a man of modest tastes, more comfortable on horseback and in uniform than sipping cognac in salons furnished in the French style. Reyes shunned ostentation in manner and life, and he seemed to have accepted his social standing more as an obligatory duty of a high officeholder rather than as an enjoyable right and privilege. In this regard, compared to others in similar positions, Reyes appeared as an austere social figure, devoid of the notoriety of a Ramón Corral, governor of the state of Sonora and later vice-president of Mexico.[7] Reyes, in the social life of the city, proved to be an unobtrusive force—his vanity, such as it was, seemed easily placated with honorific posts and gestures from the local elite. Under such conditions, the established, socially prominent families maintained their position, astutely yet selectively admitted new members, and sustained their ascendancy in the face of swelling ranks of workers and an ambitious, growing middle class.

Throughout the Porfirian era, membership in the Casino Monterrey was the imprimatur of elite status and acceptance. The roster of the club indicated both the continuity and change among the wealthy, and its boards of directors suggested the pecking order of Monterrey's leading families.[8] The casino embodied the insularity of the elite, with its own building, its exclusive functions, and its preponderant place in the social life of Monterrey's upper class. Moreover, the casino's composition manifested a two-step process in the evolution of Monterrey's elite. Between 1890 and 1900 or so, the casino incorporated new members while others rose to greater prominence as the city underwent a decade of rapid economic growth. About the turn of the century, a gradual consolidation of the upper class ensued, assimilating recently enriched businessmen, talented, well-connected professionals, and a few high government officials who surrounded Bernardo Reyes. Thus, by 1910, the maturation of the *regiomontano* elite and its changes and continuities were registered in the roster and leadership of the Casino Monterrey. (See table 11.)

The roots of the casino were synonymous with the origins of the city's business establishment. In 1866, in the context of the prosperity and optimism generated by the cotton boom, Valentín Rivero and the

Table 11. *Board of Directors of the Casino Monterrey (selected years)*

1884	*1891*
Francisco Oliver[a]	Juan Weber
Ramón García Chavarrí	Ramón García Chavarrí
Lorenzo Sepúlveda	Tomás Mendirichaga
Ricardo Cellard[a]	Lorenzo Sepúlveda
José M. Videgaray	José A. Muguerza
Fernando Martínez	Nicolas Zerazaluce
Leopoldo Zambrano	Onofre Zambrano
Carlos Holck[b]	José Maiz[c]
Emilio Pautrier[a]	Margarito Garza
Adolfo Zambrano	Entimio Calzado
Tomás Mendirichaga	
1897	*1910*
Bernardo Reyes	Ernesto Madero
Tomás Mendirichaga	Patricio Milmo
Lorenzo Sepúlveda	José L. Garza
Mariano Hernández	Domingo M. Treviño
Juan Weber[b]	Mariano Hernández
José A. Muguerza	Rodolfo G. García
Lorenzo Roel	Manuel Cantú Treviño
Melchor Villarreal	Antonio J. Hernández
Augustín Maiz[c]	Gustavo Madero
Adolfo Zambrano	Benjamin Burchard[b]
Constantino de Tárnava	Joaquin Escamilla[c]
Manuel Cantú Treviño	
José Maiz[c]	

[a]Oliver, Cellard, and Pautrier would be almost entirely eclipsed by others in the 1890s and virtually disappear from elite circles.
[b]From the German colony.
[c]Key figures in the Centro Español.

manager of his textile plant, Antonio Lafón, founded the male-only club, based on local merchants. The 1870s depression led to a hiatus in the club's activities for several years, but the economic regeneration of the city in the 1880s revived the enthusiasm for the casino. In February 1884, the casino was reconstituted with fifty-four members. The number, in fact, was less since several of the members were related: brother and father combinations dotted the rolls of the casino, such as Tomás and Felix Mendirichaga, and Onofre, Leopoldo, and Adolfo Zambrano. The reorganized casino elected a board of directors that suggested the social hierarchy of Monterrey for that period. (See figure 2.)

The arrival of Bernardo Reyes in 1885 as military commander of Nuevo León, and his elevation to governor in 1889, paralleled his social promotion. In October 1887, Reyes received the embrace of the city's social luminaries when he was honored at an extravagant ball attended by the city's leading families. Cognizant of the general's political clout, and appreciative of his probusiness posture, the elite spared little in repeated displays of homage. Banquets, receptions, dinners, and dances also advertised the acceptance of the governor's henchmen, particularly Lorenzo Sepúlveda, Ramón García Chavarrí, and Reyes' brother-in-law, Cipriano Madrigal, into the highest social circles.[9] Not surprisingly, Reyes was elected president of the casino in 1888. Consistent with the elite's "politically tactful and diplomatic" posture toward Reyes, the governor served several terms as president of the club over the next two decades—only in that position and in no other.[10] Regardless of the motivations of its membership, the Casino Monterrey absorbed the social significance of Reyes' power, endowing the club with greater status and legitimacy.

The incorporation of Reyes into the casino was a notable example of the absorption of outsiders whose wealth or prestige merited consideration for admission. Mexicans in general found access to elite circles easier than foreigners. The wealthy Coahuilan family headed by Evaristo Madero complemented its huge investments in Monterrey with a rapid rise socially.[11] Manuel Cantú Treviño represented another notable example of swift social climbing by his debut on the casino board in 1897, seven years after the opening of his prosperous department store.[12]

The lists of guests at casino functions, faithfully reproduced in local newspapers, illustrated the extent to which foreigners participated in the activities of the wealthy. Interestingly, although several Europeans and Americans were extended membership after 1890, the native elite seemingly regulated their inclusion as officers of the casino. In this respect, the leadership of the elite was sensitive to the recognition of

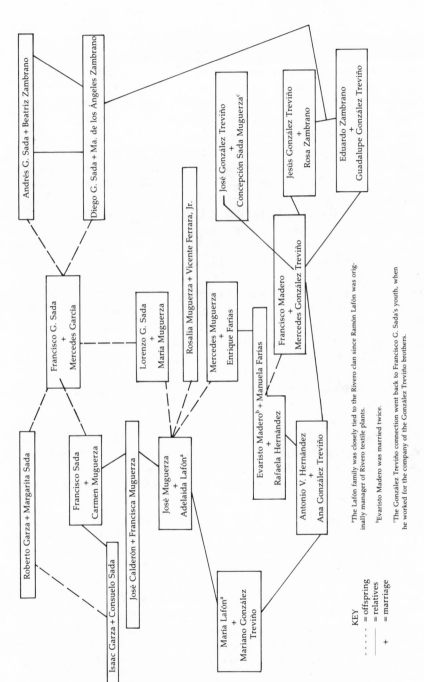

Roberto Garza + Margarita Sada

Isaac Garza + Consuelo Sada

Francisco Sada
+
Carmen Muguerza

José Calderón + Francisca Muguerza

Andrés G. Sada + Beatriz Zambrano

Diego G. Sada + Ma. de los Ángeles Zambrano

Francisco G. Sada
+
Mercedes García

Lorenzo G. Sada
+
María Muguerza

Rosalía Muguerza + Vicente Ferrara, Jr.

José González Treviño
+
Concepción Sada Muguerza[c]

Mercedes Muguerza
+
Enrique Farías

Jesús González Treviño
+
Rosa Zambrano

Eduardo Zambrano
+
Guadalupe González Treviño

José Muguerza
+
Adelaida Lafón[a]

María Lafón[a]
+
Mariano González Treviño

Evaristo Madero[b] + Manuela Farías

Francisco Madero
+
Mercedes González Treviño

Antonio V. Hernández
+
Ana González Treviño

+
Rafaela Hernández

KEY

- - - - = offspring

——— = relatives

+ = marriage

[a]The Lafón family was closely tied to the Rivero clan since Ramón Lafón was originally manager of Rivero textile plants.

[b]Evaristo Madero was married twice.

[c]The González Treviño connection went back to Francisco G. Sada's youth, when
he worked for the company of the González Treviño brothers.

Figure 2. *Garza-Sada Family Ties*

the key "colonies" of the city. Italians, Germans, and Spaniards, immigrants tied to established business families of the same nationality,
made quick appearances in elite functions. Americans, on the other
hand, though the most numerous foreign element of Monterrey, very
rarely entered the inner circle of the elite through election to the casino
board of directors. In contrast, the German colony enjoyed a singular
respect among *regiomontanos* that dated from the 1860s, when certain
German merchants remained in Monterrey after the cotton boom.[13]
The prominent role played by German immigrants in the brewery's
early and spectacular success augmented the number and prestige of
Germans among the resident upper class.[14]

A small number of professionals, lawyers, engineers, and bureaucrats gained admission to elite status. Constantino de Tárnava, for
instance, managed the banking facilities of the Milmo family and
parlayed his position into other investments, leading eventually to
his position as treasurer of the Fundidora. His scaling of the economic structure of the city was confirmed as early as 1892 with his
election to a minor but status-laden office on the casino board.[15] By a
different route, Pedro C. Martínez, municipal president of Monterrey, won acceptance because of his close political ties to Bernardo
Reyes. Similarly, Ramón García Chavarrí, another Reyes crony,
strengthened his high standing when he married into the Muguerza
family.[16] Indeed, marriage provided an expeditious vehicle for admission to elite circles.

For those from middle-class backgrounds, marriage was the surest
way to vault to the heights of *regiomontano* society. Enrique Gorostieta, a lawyer, could serve as a typical example of the use of marriage
as a means to social mobility. As a student at the Law School of Nuevo
León, Gorostieta had the opportunity to establish ties with members
of the Zambrano family and with Francisco Guerra, a relative of
the treasurer of the state under Reyes from 1889 to 1909. Upon
graduation, Gorostieta developed a substantial practice, using his
connections to handle legal matters for the families of wealthier ex-
classmates. In such a capacity, in 1890, he came into contact with
Valentín Rivero y Gajá, scion of the Rivero family fortunes. Social ties
between Gorostieta and Rivero increased soon thereafter, pulling the
ambitious lawyer into the fringe of upper-class society. The links
between the two men were magnified by the gradual relationship
that blossomed between Gorostieta's daughter and Rivero's son.
About the same time, Gorostieta's other daughter was being courted
by Luis G. Sada, son of one of the Cervecería's principal owners.
Through the marriage of his daughters, in 1909 and 1912, respectively, to members of the Rivero and Sada families, Gorostieta

achieved the high social standing that he had diligently cultivated for nearly twenty years.[17]

More often than not, however, marriage among the elite remained within the parameters of upper-class circles, and, through such arrangements, the prevailing patterns of Monterrey's social hierarchy were reinforced. Relative newcomers to Monterrey enhanced their rapid social ascent by marriage to entrenched elite families. The Maderos, for example, augmented their status through their ties with the Belden family, whose wealth and intimate association with the Milmos put them at the pinnacle of *regiomontano* society. Similarly, Manuel Cantú Treviño confirmed his elite status by his marriage to Octavia Rivero, member of the powerful family of the same name. To cite another example, the bonds between the Cervecería's ownership and the Fundidora were tightened by the marriage of the offspring of Vicente Ferrara and José A. Muguerza, respectively, Vicente, Jr., and Rosalia.[18]

As evidenced in figure 2, the Cervecería's triumvirate of Isaac Garza, Francisco G. Sada, and José A. Muguerza composed a hub of propitious marriages that incorporated into the family network the Zambrano, Madero, Hernández, and González Treviño families, as well as the Ferraras. The Garza-Sada-Muguerza clique represented but one link of overlapping, concentric circles of marital ties among the elite.[19] Clearly, the pattern of such connections pointed to the effort made by parents to encourage their offspring to marry appropriately. In this regard, the gatherings and functions of members of the elite, and of their sons and daughters, served the conspiratorial designs of discerning parents.

Parties, church and civic activities, dances, and *tertulias* provided numerous opportunities for romances to bud among the children of the upper crust. By the turn of the century, a clear-cut network of meeting places arose that permitted the establishment of a social routine among members of Monterrey's wealthiest families. For older males, the sumptuously decorated Casino Club, newly built in 1890, remained the favorite watering hole. Operas and plays at the lavish Teatro Juárez, constructed in 1898, offered yet another arena for the rich and powerful to display their finery.[20] The church also allowed for an additional and highly visible avenue for the elite of Monterrey to accentuate social prominence. Visits by important prelates provoked extravagant receptions, usually organized by rich matrons and attended by their husbands. Judging from newspaper accounts, the key families associated with the Cervecería were particularly involved in church-related activities, as were the Zambranos. Church fund-raisers in support of charities such as the St. Vincent de Paul society were apt to spur a newspaper feature with the names of the organizers of the event and the social luminaries who attended.[21]

Over time, as the offspring of the elite families approached adulthood, new clubs and activities appeared in response to the needs of a younger set among the elite. The Sociedad Terpsicore was formed in 1897 with the stated purpose "to have another place for recreation," and it encompassed basically the same distinguished crowd as the casino.[22] Youthful relatives of the elite, often in their employ, as well as a few well-connected, younger members of Reyes' bureaucracy, composed the majority of the society. To a large extent, the formation of the Sociedad Terpsicore stemmed from the establishment of the Monterrey Athletic Club in 1895. The club, along with the male-only bar of the Teatro Progreso, became focal points for the younger members of the casino who found its ambience too stuffy and, in certain respects, old-fashioned. Daughters of the *regiomontano* upper class kept pace through their own organizations and functions. The Club DTUP formally united in 1903 a circle of single, wealthy females who staged picnics, plays, and parties that brought together eligible male and female offspring of Monterrey's leading families. Frequent *tertulias* sponsored by the DTUP and Terpsicore clubs served to sustain the exclusivity of male-female interaction among youthful members of the city's upper class.[23]

The gatherings put on by the Sociedad Terpsicore and its feminine counterpart provided but one vehicle through which the elite maintained its coherence. As the Porfirian era passed into the twentieth century, the powerful business families of Monterrey had established their predominant social presence. In this respect, local newspapers constantly described at length upper-class activities and pointed to the intimate ties between editors and the elite. For example, Joseph Robertson, owner of the bilingual *Monterrey News,* was a close associate of several of the city's businessmen. His newspaper enthusiastically publicized their social life. *La Voz de Nuevo León,* controlled by Bernardo Reyes, and managed and edited by Ramón García Chavarrí, also eagerly reported the activities of the elite, especially so in light of the ties through marriage between the García Chavarrí and Muguerza families. The latter group, headed by José A. Muguerza, were by all accounts the lions of the social scene of Monterrey. Muguerza was very active in the casino, manning a variety of offices during this period, while his nephew, José Calderón, Jr., played a similar role in the Sociedad Terpsicore, serving as president in 1897, 1902, and 1904.[24] And the city's other, though less important, newspaper, the church-dominated publication *La Defensa,* understandably doted on the activities of its patrons, notably dowagers such as Francisca Muguerza de Calderón.[25]

Local sources of information, then, were filled with the social life of wealthy *regiomontanos*, young and old, male and female.[26] Bicycle races sponsored by the Terpsicore, horseraces at the Hippodrome, baseball games between the Fundidora and Cervecería, auto shows featuring the elite's imported cars, musical presentations at the kiosk of the main plaza, operas at the casino, announcements of *tertulias*, and similar stories appeared incessantly in local papers. Where the elite was concerned, winners of contests were listed, boxscores given, auto prize recipients identified, dresses described, and the audience enumerated.[27]

The distinctiveness of the upper crust of *regiomontano* society appeared in still other public ways. On numerous occasions, particularly on major civic and religious holidays (more so the former), parades, marches, and fiestas served to highlight the prominence of the elite. In such events, for instance, the parades celebrating Mexican independence, over 30,000 people attended at times to witness the passing of floats, carriages, and, later, autos carrying youthful members of the elite (usually females) competing for prizes, awarded subsequently with great ceremony. In 1910, for example, the float of the Cervecería Cuauhtémoc, with Luis G. Sada, among others, astride, won first prize in its category; and a marching unit composed of various children of the elite was singled out for praise. Among them were Roberto Sada, Raúl Sada, Jesús Sada Muguerza, Ramón Lafón, and Conchita Calderón, as well as Ricardo Sada Paz and Alicia Videgaray. (The latter two would marry years later.)[28] Such occasions heightened the visibility of Monterrey's wealthy families in the public's eye, if in fact it was necessary.

On a more regular basis, and without as much newspaper fanfare, the elite found ways to express its prominence yet further. On Sundays, for instance, a literal caravan of richly appointed imported carriages made its way to church through the center of the city. Landaus were a favorite, at times driven by chauffeurs clad in the English style: red coats, white gloves, and black boots and plumed, tricornered hats. Alongside carriages with female passengers, male companions often rode on magnificent, well-bred horses, as they made the rounds from the cathedral on the Plaza Zaragoza to the Alameda and then to the broad boulevard Progreso. Later, autos, rather than carriages, continued the practice, as the less fortunate of *regiomontano* society often lined the streets to watch the vehicles of the wealthy roll by, to and from the exclusive neighborhood of the city, El Obispado.[29]

It was a life essentially self-contained, with members of the elite continuously circulating through established, recognized social routines that assured association with the "right" people.[30] Nuances of status occurred, nonetheless, within elite circles, and these took various forms.[31] In this connection, few events in the Porfirian era were as revealing of the pecking order of Monterrey's upper class as the visit of Porfirio Díaz to the city in December 1898.

Politics primarily spurred Díaz' visit of that year, but the president's stay allowed the city's rich families an unparalleled opportunity to display their wealth and, at the same time, their subtle differentiation.[32] The planning commission for the presidential visit, headed by Bernardo Reyes, consisted of Adolfo Zambrano, Tomás Mendirichaga, Antonio Hernández, and Francisco Armendaiz, elder members of the elite. Two younger men, the Cervecería's Francisco G. Sada and the eldest son of the Rivero family, Valentín Rivero y Gajá, and one relative newcomer, Manuel Cantú Treviño, rounded out the commission. The reception committee included Juan Weber, representing the small but highly regarded German colony, H. M. Diffenbach, the German-born manager of the Guggenheim's smelter, and, finally, Vicente Ferrara.

Upon his arrival in Monterrey, Díaz was greeted extravagantly by Reyes and the city's luminaries. That afternoon, wealthy dowagers entertained the president, among them, Guadalupe Zambrano de Treviño, Consuelo Sada de Garza, Carolina Madero de Villarreal, and Adelaida Lafón de Muguerza. Later a delegation of the city's industrial and commercial establishment called on Díaz, but no foreigner appeared among the group, which included the names of Armendaiz, Hernández, Mendirichaga, Sada Zambrano, and Cantú Treviño. Only Melchor Villarreal, selected as much for his family's long association with Nuevo León's politics as for his ties to the Madero fortunes, represented an uncommon face in the elite delegation.

The following night, at an elaborate function planned by Adolfo Zambrano and Francisco G. Sada, the Casino Monterrey honored the dictator. A minuet, danced by several young couples from the cream of Monterrey's upper class, inaugurated the dance. Representatives of the Calderón, Muguerza, Zambrano, and Sada families were among the young dancers, but the names of other adolescents indicated the entry of new families to elite status.[33] Seating arrangements followed the pecking order, with the most important of Monterrey society taking their places near the presidential table. In addition to the members of the visitation committee, these included the Maderos and their compadres, the Villarreals, Sara Milmo, daughter of Patricio Milmo and recently married to the New York financier Edward Kelly, and Doña Francisca Muguerza de Calderón. Resplendent in their finery and jewels, in the midst of a shower of electric lights, decorations, and flowers, Monterrey's high society dined and danced until past three in the morning.

The Díaz visit served to reveal the subtleties of the elite's inner workings. A close reading of the event surrounding the visit pointed to the ascent of the families tied to the Cervecería Cuauhtémoc: Sada, Garza, Muguerza, and Calderón. On the one hand, in a visit imbued with political meanings, the Cervecería clique benefited from the position held by Ramón García Chavarrí as secretary of the state of Nuevo León, particularly given the fact that his father-in-law was José A. Muguerza. On the other hand, the Cervecería's owners possessed one of the most successful businesses of the city. Not surprisingly, Díaz toured extensively only one enterprise in Monterrey—the Cervecería Cuauhtémoc. Thus, compared to the Belden and Milmo clans, the brewery's owners and their families seemed to be on the rise, their prominence magnified by the deaths of the patriarchs of the Rivero and Armendaiz families during this period.

As the economic tempo of the city slowed, the social hierarchy also hardened, with cliques forming and gaps showing, some related to age, others due to nationality, and still others because of close family and economic ties. To take one example, by marriage, the Villarreal and Madero families tightened their links and formed a prominent social tandem of sorts that consistently appeared in elite social functions together.[34] As the *regiomontano* upper class coalesced, its maturing features were reflected in the formation of various clubs, such as the Terpsicore and DTUP clubs mentioned earlier. Significantly, in 1907, to confirm the distinct importance of the German colony of the city, the Club Alemán made its debut. Finally, in 1909, the Centro Español, consisting of "the most distinguished members of the Spanish colony," was formed. It included older descendants of the Hernández and Armendaiz families and, more importantly, recent immigrants such as Juan Escamilla.[35] These German and Spanish clubs, however, remained closely tied to the city's elite, since their memberships were invariably linked to established families whose roots went back to the 1860s. In a sense, the Club Alemán and Centro Español signaled a last hurrah for some of the venerable family names of the city's business establishment, eclipsed somewhat by the accelerating fortunes and stature of others, such as the Cervecería clique. Thus, the casino's leadership during the Porfirian era contained telling changes despite its equally important continuities (see table 11).

In short, more than one rung existed in the social ladder of the *regiomontano* upper class. The top remained a highly select domain, as suggested by the members of the elite who organized the homage to Díaz in his visit of 1898. Another indication of that inner circle came in 1899 in the composition of the committee formed to fete Díaz in Mexico City (discussed in chapter 2). The key men were amply clear: Francisco

G. Sada, Isaac Garza, José Muguerza, Antonio Hernández, Adolfo Zambrano; the participation of Melchor Villarreal pointed to the importance of the Maderos and that of Constantino de Tárnava to the weight of the Milmo clan.[36] In 1910, the Casino Monterrey had approximately two hundred members.[37] The number was somewhat deceiving since some families were represented by more than one member, and still others were joined by marriage—in some cases more than once. Two sons of the Sada family, for instance, were married to two sisters from the Zambrano family. (See figure 2; Andrés G. Sada married Beatriz Zambrano, Diego G. Sada married María de los Angeles Zambrano.) In fact, perhaps only a hundred people in Monterrey counted within the highest circle of *regiomontano* society. In a city of eighty thousand, it was a small circle indeed.

III.   According to a local newspaper, the Casino Monterrey held a masked ball on February 25, 1895.[38] Members arrived in expensive chauffeured carriages, wearing sundry costumes. They entered the gaudily decorated dance hall of the club to the gasps and occasional applause of the crowd that surrounded the entrance hoping to catch a glimpse of the outfits worn by the rich as they made their way into the confines of the casino. In a sense, the people waiting outside symbolized the ambitions of the city's middle class to gain entry into the upper class. Much like their counterparts elsewhere, Monterrey's middling sectors failed to achieve a sense of class; rather, as Ramón E. Ruiz has argued, "the middle-class Mexican was more apt to seek to rub shoulders with the rich, to copy their dress, to live in the most luxurious home his income could provide, and to emulate the life of the country squire."[39]

Such a middle class (if the term can be used accurately) focused much of its aspirations for mobility on the acquisition of government sinecures, hopes compounded by the concentrated control of the elite over the opportunities generated by the private sector. As early as 1903, the city's middle class realized the constraints on its dreams for quick wealth, but it channeled its resentment toward the Reyes administration. The ascendancy of the elite, therefore, largely escaped the criticism of the grasping middle class of Monterrey, and, as a result, the powerful businessmen of the city tightened their grip over *regiomontano* society.

The economic growth of Monterrey fueled a surge in the middle-class elements of the city during the 1880s and into the following decade. The changes in the occupational structure between 1879 and 1895 were dramatic. To take two distinctly different examples, the need for sales clerks was evident in the proliferation of variety stores in this period, from 241 to 484. In the same time span, teachers employed by the city's public schools doubled. Similar increases occurred in the number of lawyers, from 34 to 89, and doctors, from 18 to 62. And certain professions appeared for the first time because of the city's industrialization—over a hundred engineers and a dozen chemists resided in Monterrey by 1895.[40]

Foreigners figured importantly in the rise of technical positions associated with brewing, smelting, mechanical repair, and construction. In this respect, the traditional liberal education of middle-class Mexicans served them badly as Americans and Europeans converged on Monterrey to take many of the well-paid positions produced by the city's burgeoning industries and business. In 1887, 24 German-born residents lived in Monterrey; but in 1895, of Nuevo León's 113 German immigrants, 103 made their home in the capital of the state. The Spanish and British colonies of Nuevo León underwent a similar expansion with Monterrey holding the overwhelming majority. Americans, however, dominated the foreign presence in Nuevo León. The Yankee population more than doubled in just the five years from 1890 to 1895, registering over 1,300, with 900 living in Monterrey alone.[41] As the economy slackened, immigration also slowed, leaving in its wake Monterrey as the primary location of foreigners in the state. The conglomeration of foreigners in the city heightened the concentration of the state's middle class in Monterrey.

Those eager to climb the proverbial social ladder (primarily males) thronged to the city and competed for lucrative jobs, for wealthy clients, and even for fortuitous marriages. But the competition was brisk. Although Monterrey represented less than 20% of the state's population in 1895, a large proportion of Nuevo León's professional groups nonetheless resided in the capital: 80% of the lawyers, 60% of the druggists, 90% of the engineers, 35% of the teachers, 40% of the state's public employees, and nearly 100% of the military officers. Furthermore, of the foreign population in Monterrey in 1895, nearly 70% were male, exacerbating the contest for employment commensurate with the aspirations of the contestants.[42]

The pretensions of higher status among the middle class suggested the hope of making a favorable, propitious impression on potential employers, on possible clients, or on suitably wealthy single women. At times this led many of the middle class to live beyond their means, much to the disdain of wealthier *regiomontanos.* As one newspaper complained at the time, "in general, all those that dress elegantly and excessively are admitted to whatever gathering, although they may be stupid or blockheads."[43] In short, the middle class of Monterrey, much like that of the rest of the country, looked upward toward a more affluent niche in the social structure of the city.

But a key vehicle of mobility, government employment, proved difficult to climb on. A fiscal conservative, Reyes slowly expanded the
state's bureaucracy. Combined with a decelerating economy and the
limited lucrative opportunities yielded by the business establishment,
Reyes' tight grip on patronage provoked a growing resentment against
his administration by 1900. The hotbed of anti-Reyes sentiment centered in Monterrey, particularly at the Law School of Nuevo León, the
main source of bureaucrats for previous gubernatorial incumbents. As
early as 1894, a Mexico City publication noted that Reyes' policy of
filling the "important" and "most profitable" bureaucratic positions
with "strangers from Jalisco" was "naturally hurting the interests of the
regiomontanos."[44] The well-known rivalry between Reyes and the científicos added to the rising political tensions in Nuevo León. Given such
crosscurrents of anti-Reyes sentiment, only an indication of weakness
in Reyes' political standing was needed for an overt opposition to surface; the opportunity came in 1903.

Porfirio Díaz appointed Reyes as minister of war in 1900, leaving
Nuevo León to be governed in absentia from Mexico City for nearly
two years. However, in the wake of a nationally publicized political
imbroglio, Reyes resigned his cabinet post and returned to Monterrey
in December 1902. His critics in Nuevo León, convinced that Reyes
had fallen from political grace in the eyes of Díaz, were quick to
mount a movement to oppose Reyes in the upcoming gubernatorial
elections of June 1903. The subsequent campaign, though essentially a
political episode with overtones of the contest between Reyes and
Limantour, served to reveal two important features of Monterrey's
social context. First, the so-called Revolt of 1903 demonstrated the
deep-seated reluctance of the middle class to attack the concentration
of wealth in the hands of the city's elite. Second, and related to the
previous point, Reyes was cast as the source of the economic and
social disparities of Monterrey.

As might be expected, given Díaz' control over Mexican politics, the
precipitating incident of the 1903 revolt in Nuevo León occurred in
Mexico City. The aging dictator realized that the friction between
Reyes and Limantour stemmed from their ambitions to be president.
"Afraid and jealous of both," Díaz "sought a means to checkmate
both."[45] Limantour's downfall was engineered first. The finance minister's presidential aspirations received a fatal blow when it was made
public that, because of his French parentage, he was constitutionally
ineligible for office. The obvious beneficiary of Limantour's removal
from contention for the presidency was of course Reyes, and the científicos immediately launched a campaign to discredit the minister of
war. Supporters of Reyes responded in kind as the fight raged for

weeks in the Mexico City press. Accusations and criticisms increased
and quickly reached the breaking point. After a meeting with Díaz,
claiming that the country needed "the most perfect tranquillity,"
Reyes submitted his resignation on December 23, 1902.[46] Intent on
erasing Reyes from presidential consideration, the *científicos* looked
toward the elections of 1903 in Nuevo León as a vehicle to bury Reyes
politically.

For Reyes, the signs of opposition presented primarily a political
problem directed from Mexico City by his *científico* enemies. But economic and social conditions in Nuevo León at the time added fuel to the
fires of discontent that met Reyes upon his return. The repercussions of
the 1901/1902 economic recession spelled economic difficulties for
hard-pressed students, fledgling lawyers, poorly paid lower-level bureaucrats, and scores of small businessmen and artisans. By 1903, three
opposition papers made their debut. Emboldened by *científico* aid in
Mexico City, law school students and their supporters distributed mer-
ciless diatribes against Reyes and his political machine, noting his control of local newspapers, his misuse of patronage, his suppression of
labor, the imprisonment of previous critics, and the illegality of his
candidacy for governor, since he was not a native of Nuevo León. The
Reyista press responded with equal fury.[47]

The opposition claimed that the majority of the people of Nuevo
León supported their cause. The governor's following, in contrast, was
composed of "mayors, members of a certain club [Unión y Progreso], of
state and municipal employees, of persons with important posts and a
few others."[48] The anti-Reyistas' posture was ambiguous, however, toward the "others" (i.e., Monterrey's business establishment). This was
in mid-February; by early March, the ambivalence lessened. But the
student-led opposition nonetheless avoided an outright condemnation
of Monterrey's elite. In a March 1, 1903, editorial, the opposition newspaper *Redención* observed:

> Do those banks, smelters, factories result in any usefulness for the work-
> ing class? No . . . the workers, i.e., the Mexican ones, do not escape the
> poverty and misery that they have always had. On the contrary, their
> work is even more difficult. And who is to blame? The government, which
> in an effort to get support from powerful capitalists, forgets that working
> class to whom those capitalists owe their wealth. The government, which
> does not hear the complaints of workers; the government, which gives
> concessions to the powerful and does not demand, however, some bene-
> fits for the workers.[49]

In recurring articles, the opposition attempted to pry businessmen
away from their support of Reyes, emphasizing his unimportance to
Monterrey's economic growth.[50] But Monterrey's major businessmen

apparently remained uncommitted. As a consequence, the attitude of the opposition hardened toward the elite as the patience of the anti-Reyistas waned in the heat of the intense campaign. In a scathing manifesto later in March, the opposition pointed to the collaboration between Reyes and local capitalists. Nevertheless, indicative of the reluctance of the anti-Reyes faction to attack the elite directly, Reyes was still portrayed as the villain, and the city's upper class as victims of his tyranny.[51]

The manifesto signified one last attempt to gain widespread support, from the elite, among others, as a crucial confrontation neared. Appealing to all groups, the opposition called for a massive rally on April 3, 1903, on the pretext of celebrating the anniversary of Porfirio Díaz' victory over the French in Puebla in 1867. But the rally ended in violence as Reyes' police fired on the protesters; opposition papers were subsequently shut down and their staffs jailed. To counter criticisms of the alleged "massacre," Reyes used coercion, bribes, and secret police to produce pro-Reyes letters and petitions that soon flooded the pages of Mexico City and local newspapers. Fear gripped the opposition. With the leadership in prison or exile, the anti-Reyista movement rapidly dissipated.[52]

Liberal groups and the *científico* press attempted to regenerate the anti-Reyistas. Camilo Arriaga and Antonio Díaz Soto y Gama introduced charges against Reyes before the Mexican congress, but the action failed to rekindle local opposition in Monterrey. More importantly, Porfirio Díaz made no gesture to respond or intervene. The president's stance was easily interpreted.[53] On May 29, 1903, to catcalls and hisses, congress found Reyes innocent of any wrongdoing. Three weeks later, Reyes was easily reelected governor of Nuevo León.

Between the April "massacre" and the June elections, the elite for the first time became visibly involved in the campaign for Reyes. One reason for this participation was perhaps Reyes' pressure for more "donations" to cover the costs of bribes in the aftermath of violence in April. Two prominent businessmen, Tomás Mendirichaga and Vicente Ferrara, the latter no doubt appreciative of Reyes' aid on the Fundidora deal, were compelled to form a commission to recruit businessmen to the Reyes campaign, for the purpose of contributing money to Reyes' electoral coffers. Isaac Garza, among others, "donated" over 15,000 pesos, and Mendirichaga "contributed" an even larger amount.[54] Yet a second factor in the elite's unusual political vigor derived from the signs that Díaz had apparently decided to stay with Reyes. With typical calculation, the city's businessmen had lingered in the background of Reyes' campaign prior to the April incident, perhaps concerned about possible *científico* retaliation or Díaz' degree of support for the harried

governor. When the political winds seemed favorable to Reyes, however, Monterrey's elite was quick to join the campaign.[55]

The 1903 revolt was instructive to Monterrey's major businessmen
since Reyes' political prowess was reconfirmed. The larger lesson of the
episode came from the attitude expressed by the opposition toward the
regiomontano elite. The fundamental conservatism of the middle class
was clearly manifest in its aversion to assailing the concentration of
wealth and economic power that marked *regiomontano* society. The
bourgeois mentality of the middle class blinded it to the crucial role
played by the elite in the maintenance of the city's social and economic
inequities. As a consequence, Monterrey's upper class found an inadvertent ally to its social hegemony in a middle class determined to
emulate its wealthy mentors.

IV.   Labor presented a more difficult question to the ascendancy of
the *regiomontano* elite. The general hostility of the Porfirian regime
toward workers, reinforced by the use of police and military troops,
was effective for many years in suppressing the successful organization of Mexican labor. But force proved insufficient and, to some
extent, counterproductive in dealing with a persistent, more basic,
problem for Monterrey's businessmen—the maintenance of a stable,
cheap work force. The effort to solve this problem led Monterrey's
capitalists to develop a paternalistic labor policy, which, eventually,
characterized the elite's attempts to control workers.

A wide variation in working conditions and wages marked labor
in Monterrey. During the 1890s, the city's rapid economic growth
obscured the emergence of a bifurcated work force. At one end, rising
industries, particularly smelting operations, required sizable amounts
of labor, especially skilled and semiskilled workers. With the northern region's swift economic development, demand for such workers
was high, and competition among employers pushed wages upward,
particularly for trained labor. Thus, for much of the 1890s, industrial
workers in the north found continuous opportunities and incentives to
switch jobs. At the opposite end of the spectrum, numerous employers
attempted to pay meager wages and offered even less attractive working conditions. In 1891, for example, textile workers earned as little
as 25 centavos a day despite an average wage nearly twice as high.
Furniture makers, on the other hand, received as much as 4.00 pesos
daily, and mechanics obtained as much as 6.00 pesos a day. Women
were extremely badly paid generally, at times only a peso a week, and
agricultural workers averaged 19 centavos a day. For the minimally
paid, the 3.00 pesos a day earned by some Cervecería workers seemed
very good indeed.[56]

Under such conditions, transiency characterized Monterrey's labor market during the city's initial years of industrialization.[57] Later, as emigration from southern and central Mexico intensified, the competition for labor lessened. Nonetheless, flux continued to mark labor in Nuevo León. In November 1897, a prophetic note appeared in the *Voz de Nuevo León*, briefly describing the abuse of Mexicans by labor contractors, particularly those employed by Americans to take Mexican workers to the United States.[58] The short article pointed to the expanding source of competition for cheap labor in Monterrey: American farmers, railroad owners, mine operators, and industrialists of the Southwest. The availability of higher American wages contributed to the persistent movement of labor to the north. With increasing frequency after 1900, Monterrey newspapers documented the losses of workers to the United States and their adverse effects. A familiar theme in the 1890s, claims of a labor scarcity once again appeared as immigration to the United States mounted. In 1906, one Mexico City newspaper noted the severity of the labor shortage in Monterrey: "the wages that are paid there are not only fair, but more than acceptable, very good, in fact, yet despite it all, the scarcity of labor continues; and the various businesses have suffered greatly."[59]

By 1907, the movement of Mexican workers across the Río Bravo was described as an "exodus" of labor. To stabilize the labor situation, employers were forced to raise wages. As one newspaper summarized it at the time,"the increase is due to the lack of labor in Mexico that forces employers to hold its employees by all kinds of incentives."[60] The differences in the labor market between the 1890s and 1900s failed to change the crucial problem of *regiomontano* capitalists: how to sustain a dependable, cheap labor force.

Over the course of the Porfirian era, Monterrey's larger companies responded by offering free housing, company schools, recreational facilities, and basic medical services to their employees. The Cervecería Cuauhtémoc, for example, appealed to the wives of workers by promoting its day care center and primary school. The Monterrey Brick Company, on the other hand, advertised its enclosed free housing. The Fundidora maintained a hospital and free housing in order to retain its highly skilled employees. A few companies, notably the Cervecería Cuauhtémoc, shortened their workday from the usual twelve to fourteen hours to ten hours.[61] In contrast, smaller firms were unable or unwilling to follow the example of the major employers. As a result, the initial bifurcation of Monterrey's labor force was reestablished.

The inspiration for this labor paternalism stemmed from various sources. Some historians have ascribed it to the papal bull of 1891 (*Rerum novarum*) that, among other things, encouraged harmony be-

tween labor and capital, as opposed to the marxist idea of class struggle. Yet the paternalistic measures of Monterrey's larger industries
were in keeping with previous practices and purposes. First, the
Cervecería and two of the smelting companies early on had supplied
housing for foreign technicians, many of them German immigrants.
The Cervecería expanded this scheme in 1899 when it brought in European glassblowers, again mainly Germans, in conjunction with the
initial glassworks endeavor. Wages for these foreign workers reflected
their special status and the intent of their employer to keep them on
board.[62] The Fundidora followed the Cervecería by erecting special
housing for its skilled foreign workers, the majority from Germany.[63]

The German connection here was not without significance. Ideas
from Germany filtered in via the influx of new German-born merchants into the established, influential German colony of Monterrey.[64]
The labor paternalism of leading *regiomontano* industrialists bore a
striking resemblance to similar practices in Europe, Germany in particular. As one student of European labor-capital relations has noted,

> In the early days, during the industrial revolution, paternalism drew its
> inspiration from the humanitarian and progressive outlook of a minority
> of clear-sighted entrepreneurs; at the same time it did not exclude the
> profit motive. . . . In its second phase, however, paternalism was of a
> defensive nature. . . . It aimed to divert the workers from the political
> temptations held out to them henceforth by the various forms of labour
> movement, trade-unionism or socialism. The attitude of the German in-
> dustrial bourgeoisie after 1870 is extremely characteristic in this respect:
> its gestures to the workers . . . were inspired by a fear of socialism. Ad-
> dressing his employees in 1877, Krupp voiced a feeling prevalent in his
> class: "Enjoy what is given to you to enjoy. Relax, when your work is over,
> in the company of those close to you, your parents, your wife, your chil-
> dren. . . . As for politics . . . spare yourselves that worry. Engaging in
> politics requires more time and experience than it is possible for the
> worker to have."[65]

The sentiments expressed by Krupp cited above were echoed frequently in Monterrey. Exhortations of cooperation between workers
and employers abounded; numerous newspaper articles promoted
family life and condemned drinking, overspending, and immorality
among workers; and in lengthy Sunday special supplements, experts,
often from Europe, recounted the evils of socialism and related ideas.
It was assumed that the need for labor, coupled with its availability,
would result in a fair profit for capitalists and a fair wage for workers.
Complaints of low pay were apt to be met with advice that laborers
increase the quality and quantity of their productivity in order to
merit salary hikes. Not surprisingly, given the darwinist currents of

the time, Mexican workers compared badly with imported foreign laborers, who were often touted for their industriousness and skill.[66]

Regardless of the motives of Monterrey's major employers, their paternalism divided labor into two basic segments: those who enjoyed the benefits provided by the largest companies and those who labored for comparatively lower wages and bereft of any amenities. The interests of the workers with the greatest potential for power—those in the key industries—were generally kept in abeyance by the multitude of workers willing to take the "better" jobs offered by Monterrey's wealthiest employers. When labor activism multiplied in the latter years of the Porfiriato, the paternalistic policies of employers assumed a greater importance and served to protect them from labor protests. Hence, what began primarily as a method to maintain a reliable, malleable labor force became an effective means to undermine independent labor organizing.

This is not to say that Monterrey in this period was without labor activity, strikes, and work stoppages. But the combination of Reyes' antipathy to labor, the paternalism of the elite, and the accessibility of work in the United States made Monterrey an infertile place for advocates of labor.[67] If this were not enough, proponents of workers' organizations faced a host of obstacles inherent in the composition of Monterrey's working class. The range of labor was immense, from highly skilled boilermakers to desperate, recently arrived *peones* from the countryside. Wide discrepancies in wages and working conditions existed that were compounded by the fact that foreign laborers often received higher pay than their Mexican counterparts. In this connection, racism and nationalism only extended the schism among foreign workers and Mexicans. Moreover, certain segments of the labor force tended to identify with their particular regional or national organization. Railroad workers were especially well organized. The importance of Monterrey as a railway center made it a hotbed of labor activity involving rail workers, but their grievances were not necessarily tied specifically to conditions in Monterrey.[68] Textile workers established contacts with labor groups in Puebla, Orizaba, and Veracruz, but local organizations failed to match the success of their counterparts in those areas.[69] In short, despite occasional victories, the diversity in the labor force contributed to its lack of cohesion and potency.[70]

In this context, employees of major companies saw little wisdom in challenging their employers. The impact was decisive on labor's record in Monterrey. Four of the largest companies in the city, all of which utilized paternalistic measures, held over half of the local labor force.[71] (See table 12.) The working class of Monterrey, therefore, was essentially split in two, with crippling consequences for the

Table 12. *Labor Force Concentration, 1902*

Total industrial work force of Monterrey		4,983
Major employers:		
American Smelting (Guggenheim)		1,000[a]
		(1,390)[b]
Minera Fundidora y Afinadora		400
Fundidora de Fierro y Acero		1,000[a]
		(800)[b]
Cervecería Cuauhtémoc		550
	Total	2,950[a]
		3,140[b]

[a]Figure by Guillermo Beato and Domenico Sindico.
[b]Figure by author, based on Correspondencia con el Ministro de Fomento, 1902, Box 1, dated March 27, 1902, AGENL.

solidarity of workers. The paternalism of *regiomontano* capitalists earned them a reputation as enlightened employers. And, although some members of the elite apparently balked at such practices, the owners of the key industries, notably the Cervecería and the Fundidora, remained convinced of the effectiveness and necessity of a paternalistic approach to labor.

V.   In October 1907, businessmen feted Bernardo Reyes at a banquet at the Casino Monterrey. It was an understandable gesture after a tense summer of nationwide and local labor protests and political agitation. In certain instances, Reyes had been forced to exercise his authority to maintain calm in the city.[72] But the prominence accorded Reyes that night belied the social hegemony of Monterrey's elite.

The powerful businessmen of the city sat confidently atop its social and economic structure, their power and prestige unrivaled. As suggested by the events of 1903, the middle class for the most part continued to look upon political change as the key to mobility (i.e., the removal of Reyes and his coterie from the state's government). Labor, though a more complex problem, remained largely in check through a combination of coercion, blandishments, and fear. In this milieu, the social assumptions and thought of wealthy Mexicans found reinforcement and confirmation; and, for Monterrey's industrialists, their special place and mission were raised to near-heroic proportions. This attitude, expressed in various forms, emerged clearly and tellingly in the discussion of labor and capital relations.

Darwinist sentiments rarely failed to surface in describing Mexican workers. Often-cited shortcomings of working-class Mexicans contrasted repeatedly with the exceptional attributes ascribed to Monterrey businessmen. While local capitalists garnered praise for their enterprising spirit, poor Mexicans were constantly chided for their weaknesses.[73] Thus, the elite of the city deservedly held its status and wealth. As one observer put it at the time, in describing the people at the banquet for Reyes in 1907, "the highest classes, the powerful classes of society, the refined and cultured ones . . . are the head of the masses, the head that directs, creates, and gives stability to the social world in which it lives."[74]

Furthermore, local businessmen were frequently cast in a nationalistic light. They became examples of Mexican entrepreneurship, elevated to a plane equal to a Krupp or a Carnegie.[75] In this respect, Monterrey's industrialists were not immune from nationalist stirrings. The overriding presence of foreign capital in the Mexican economy, coupled with the identification of industry with advanced Western countries, spurred patriotic sentiments among Mexicans and invited favorable comparisons between the elite and the future of Mexico. As early as 1900, a local paper noted that foreigners were no longer the only source of enterprise in Mexico. "The Mexicans are as capable as any European," the paper declared, then went on to insist that Mexicans "are not a race that represents backwardness and that is not without intelligence."[76] By 1907, with near arrogance, an observer in Monterrey stated that foreign capital "will find hard competition from Mexicans."[77] Moreover, he continued, "Mexico has reached a point where her own people will invest its capital and gather the fruits as the nation advances on the road of progress."[78]

Hence, in an intellectual climate rife with positivism, the achievements of Monterrey's businessmen took on a special meaning. The invariable tours of local industries given to outsiders pointed to the elite's appreciation of the symbolic importance of the smokestacks that punctuated the skyline of Monterrey. Progress and modernity were embodied, therefore, in the industrialists of Monterrey. The pulsating tempo of the city stemmed from the elite, or so it was thought, and provided clear proof of its rightful claim to occupy the apex of society. For Monterrey's capitalists, their paternalistic outlook was a natural extension of their position and self-evident acumen. Under their aegis, the long-awaited emergence of Mexico as a modern nation was possible, if they were given the opportunity to accomplish such a task.

In 1907, with brimming confidence, a local newspaper headlined the progress of Monterrey and its brilliant future.[79] But events soon destroyed that rosy view. In three years, the country would be plunged into a protracted civil war, marking the end of the thirty-year dictatorship of Porfirio Díaz. Few in 1907, however, could have imagined the impending debacle. From the windows of the Casino Monterrey, overlooking the Plaza Zaragoza, the world must have appeared bright. Protected by the presence of one of the country's most powerful men, the social and economic prominence of the elite seemed complete. It was a safe, comfortable world, insulated by layers of exclusivity and forms of self-congratulation. The times and the context had engendered among members of the elite a sense of superiority vulnerable to myopic pride and self-adulation—a world, as it turned out, they would not easily surrender.

4. The Survival of a Porfirian Elite: Monterrey and the Mexican Revolution, 1910–1918

I. For the businessmen of Monterrey, as for the rest of Mexico, the so-called Mexican revolution went through various phases and embraced several differing aims, leaders, and movements.[1] Consequently, the upheaval of 1910 to 1917 often involved a contest among rival factions, some spurred by ideas for a basic restructuring of Mexican society, others motivated merely by greed and a self-seeking desire for power. The resultant turbulence of those years was not unique to Nuevo León. Yet, from the standpoint of the *regiomontano* elite, the turmoil confirmed its disdain for the rebels and animosity toward the changes precipitated by the end of the Porfiriato. The revolution altered the Porfiriato's political and economic structure, and, as a result, the contours of the relationship between Monterrey businessmen and the state lost their Porfirian cast. For the capitalists of Nuevo León, the changes left bitter memories and a determination to regain their former status.

II. On June 6, 1910, Francisco I. Madero neared Monterrey, Nuevo León, on his nascent political campaign against Porfirio Díaz. The tension heightened as the train approached the city. A large crowd of supporters had greeted Madero two days earlier in San Luis Potosí, and the previous day a thousand people thronged the railway station in Saltillo to voice their approval for the "Apostle of Democracy." Yet the news of the violent repression of Maderista supporters in recent days pressed heavily on the minds of Madero and his aides.

As the train entered the station, only a handful of people appeared to greet Madero. Virtually all of the party consisted of relatives and intimate friends. Madero's car quickly made its way to the family's house on Hidalgo Street, ironically, the former home of Bernardo Reyes. The rest of the day, under the watchful eye of the police—and scores of steadfast supporters—the grandson of Evaristo Madero conferred with members of his family as a stream of visitors went in and out of the mansion. The situation was critical as apprehension, nearly tangible in its intensity, filled the atmosphere. A decision was reached, and Madero prepared to leave for Torreón, Coahuila.

At approximately nine in the evening, Madero, his wife, and his aide, Roque Estrada, boarded a car to take them to the Monterrey railway station. As family and friends clustered around the car to see Madero off, several men appeared suddenly, claiming to be policemen, and demanded that Roque Estrada accompany them. Madero argued with the men and asked them to present their credentials. In the confusion, Roque Estrada bolted into the safety of the Madero home. Flustered, the police retired, and Madero proceeded to the train station.

At the station, the police demanded once again that Roque Estrada turn himself in to the police. Madero refused to give them any information. The train was delayed as the police made an unsuccessful search for Madero's aide. At that point, Francisco Madero was arrested.[2]

Nearly a year later, in May 1911, the leading businessmen of Monterrey sent telegrams to Porfirio Díaz claiming their "unconditional support" for the tottering regime of the dictator. The names were familiar—Garza, Sada, Calderón, Muguerza, Rivero, Cantú-Treviño, Zambrano, Milmo, Elizondo. In six months, however, Francisco I. Madero was elected president of Mexico. On October 19, 1911, the triumphant winner returned to Monterrey, but this time to a raucous welcome as thousands crowded the train station to greet their new president. The members of the Monterrey elite were also noticeably present, their earlier support of Díaz apparently forgotten, if not forgiven. The Sada, Garza, Muguerza, and Ferrara families and others joined the beaming Maderos in staging an extravagant reception. The following night, where thirteen years earlier the elite had celebrated the visit of Porfirio Díaz, President Francisco Madero was honored at a lavish banquet and dance given by the Casino Monterrey, that is, "the families that formed the aristocracy of the city."[3] The reception for Mexico's new president uncannily resembled that held for Díaz in 1898. The focal point of the festivities was a different man, but the stage and cast in Monterrey remained largely the same.

III. The similarities between Madero's triumphant return in 1911 and the Díaz visit of 1898 pointed to the fact that the Maderista movement posed little threat to *regiomontano* businessmen. Madero was not a revolutionary; rather, he was at best an idealistic political reformer. The connections among the Maderos and the local business establishment minimized any substantial change in Monterrey's economic order. The installation of Viviano Villarreal, a familiar face in elite circles, as governor assured receptive figures in state and municipal offices. The beginnings of the Mexican revolution suggested few dangers to Monterrey's leading capitalists.

Unfortunately for Nuevo León's businessmen, the reassuring aura of the Madero administration rapidly dissipated. Within months of the inauguration of the Madero administration in 1911, the loose coalition surrounding the new president fell apart. With the removal of Díaz, the common bond among the contending factions disintegrated. The differences among the leaders of the Mexican revolution led to a violent, destructive civil war that wracked the country for over six years. In this period, disorder reigned as various chieftains in distinct regions of the nation vied for dominance and competed for support within Mexico as well as diplomatic recognition from foreign powers, most importantly, the United States.

The resultant contest produced at times empty pronouncements intended to please a particular constituency, or to create a self-serving facade, or to undermine the popularity of rivals. The political fortunes of key leaders rose and fell, and their rhetoric was at once radical and conciliatory. Stated policies were implemented unpredictably, if at all, or at times with apparent cynicism. Ideological positions, if assumed, derived often from circumstances rather than from well-founded convictions. Inconsistency, contradiction, and confusion marked the political currents embraced by the subsequent phase of the Mexican revolution. Followers of Emiliano Zapata's call for the redistribution of land clashed with Maderista liberals, while Pancho Villa's aims defied clear identification; the ideas of others ranged from anarchosyndicalism to modest liberal reforms.

For the businessmen of Monterrey, the course of the revolution represented two fundamental problems. First was the immediate and practical question of order. The shifting winds of the revolution dashed whatever expectations that *regiomontano* capitalists had for a speedy restoration of the "order and progress" of the Porfiriato. Initially, Monterrey largely escaped the disruptive consequences of the internecine fighting following Madero's election in 1911. But after 1913, and until 1917, Nuevo León experienced the full force of the civil war. Business fell from the burdens of erratic railway service, banditry, confiscations, forced loans, extortion, and corruption, in addition to the vagaries of changing local governments that depended upon which political faction or military chief controlled Monterrey at the time.

Nonetheless, a second question proved more unsettling: what would be the outcome of the revolution for Monterrey's elite? *Regiomontano* businessmen hoped for a political and economic order conducive to their interests, for a restoration of their Porfirian privileges and position, but hope was not enough. Deprived of the protective umbrella of a Reyes, Monterrey's businessmen confronted soon after 1910 a different political order whose interests were not always predictably consistent with those of *regiomontano* capitalists. Particularly after the fall of Madero in 1913, Monterrey businessmen faced a fluid political situation from which they could not escape. Nuevo León's economic elite was compelled to seek direct power in an effort to recreate the old world in a new political and economic setting.

Two key events punctured the expectations of Monterrey's elite of an easy return to a Porfirian world: the takeover of the Cervecería Cuauhtémoc in 1914 by "revolutionary troops" and the strike at the Fundidora in 1918. The takeover of the brewery from 1914 to 1917 stunned Monterrey's businessmen into the realization that the "old days" were over; that deep forces in Mexican society, formerly held in check, would not be easily restrained or suppressed. The Fundidora strike of 1918 indicated clearly that those forces had altered the political economy of the country and of Monterrey. Most importantly, the two events destroyed the confident sense of control of members of the elite. Both events served to push them to regain their previous status, to reclaim their hegemony. Whatever the outcomes of the revolution, Monterrey's elite was determined to renew its grip over the city.

IV. In his masterful examination of this era, *The Great Rebellion: Mexico 1905–1924,* Ramón E. Ruiz describes the underlying causes of the upheaval of 1910. Ruiz notes the yawning inequalities in Mexican society, the landlessness of Mexico's peasantry, the low wages and poor conditions of Mexico's young working class, the increasing rigidity and imperviousness of the political system, the growing resentment of Mexico's avid, swelling middle class, and the lessening capacity of the Porfirian regime to maintain its authority. Nonetheless, the "watershed" of the rebellion derived from the financial disaster of 1907 in the United States.[4] The consequences of the American economic crisis for Mexico "dashed hopes of greater things to come, lowering expectations, and shutting the gates to upward social mobility."[5] The effects of the crisis underscored the dependence of the Mexican economy on external factors, and, as a consequence, the disaster of 1907 affected the ability of the Porfiriato to sustain its legitimacy.[6] The impact of the crisis worsened the inequalities inherent under Díaz' dictatorship and exhausted its sources of support.

Given the export orientation of the economy, industry and commerce absorbed but a fraction of a growing population of educated Mexicans seeking employment. Consequently, the public sector, primarily the government bureaucracy, became the refuge for Mexicans seeking white-collar jobs. According to Roger Hansen, "between 1876 and 1910 the government payroll grew by 900 percent."[7] Indeed, by 1910, of Mexico's educated population, "70 percent were employed in the bureaucracy."[8] As time progressed, however, especially after 1907, the Díaz regime found it increasingly difficult to maintain such mechanisms of control.

To a large extent, government expenditures depended directly or indirectly on revenues derived from Mexico's exports. The pacification of an expanding middle class through public employment similarly relied on the ability of the Díaz regime to open and to fund sufficient numbers of bureaucratic sinecures. The prosperity of Mexico's export economy, therefore, was crucially related to Díaz' policy of cooptation and appeasement. The fortunes of the Mexican economy, of course, nourished others of middling income and status. Thus, recessions or depressions held real and serious consequences for the middle class and its allegiance to Díaz. As the economy worsened after 1907, the negative implications for the Porfirian system became manifest. The ground swell of discontent among the middle class joined the long-standing grievances of Mexican labor against the Porfirian regime. Political opportunities for social and economic mobility diminished: "the coopted grew richer and older; the outsiders grew older and increasingly resentful."[9] Very few posts materialized for those who desired a bureaucratic means to wealth and status, or for Díaz to still the frustrations of the "outsiders."

The growing disaffection with Díaz among the middle class and workers was mirrored within segments of the upper class. The crisis of 1907 "alienated a great number of elite circle families whose economic interests were endangered."[10] In the search for new leadership, the "ruling elite decisively split" during the final years of the Díaz administration.[11] One group allied itself with Limantour and the *científicos;* another group threw its support to Bernardo Reyes, though Díaz relied on Limantour with greater frequency. Thus, the *científico* group, "in conjunction with those foreign interests to which it was often closely attached, controlled literally all the wealth, political power and social position in the country."[12] Consequently, as economic troubles multiplied, "the usefulness of the regime began to be questioned."[13] Public backing of Díaz, his cronies, and the *científicos* eroded throughout Mexico.

The dissatisfaction with the *científicos'* economic leadership intensified among the landholders in the midst of the credit crisis of 1907. In response to a liquidity shortage, banks called in loans and refused credit to drought-plagued and overextended *hacendados.* The Madero family, for example, was especially hurt by the drought's impact on its cotton interests and by the fact that it was over 8 million pesos in debt. The monetary policies dictated by the *científicos* as a consequence of the crisis pushed many elite members, particularly landowners, to seek the removal of Limantour and his cabal.[14]

In an interview in 1908 with an American journalist, James Creelman, Porfirio Díaz stated his intention to retire from office in 1910.[15] A flurry of political activity followed the publication of Creelman's interview. The Reyista forces quickly formed clubs in major cities, while the *científicos* maneuvered to counter Reyes' candidacy. However, it soon became apparent that Díaz "allowed himself" to be nominated for president.[16]

Díaz was seventy-eight years old in 1908, and rumors circulated about his health. Thus, the 1910 election campaign focused on the vice-presidency, on the office whose holder assumed the presidency in the event of Díaz' death. The *científicos* backed Ramón Corral, vice-president since 1904. The Reyes clubs, like their rivals, nominated Díaz for president, but Reyes for vice-president. And in late 1908, the son of one of northern Mexico's wealthiest families, Francisco Madero, launched his campaign for electoral reform. The appearance of his book, *La sucesión presidencial en 1910,* was a prelude to Madero's eventual bid for the presidency.[17] As pressures mounted for Reyes to challenge Díaz directly, the crafty president moved to erase the rising candidacy of the well-known, popular governor of Nuevo León. The continuous harassment of Reyes' supporters was climaxed by the removal of Reyes from his post as regional commander in August 1909. Three months later, Reyes resigned as governor of Nuevo León. The general's subsequent assignment to a military mission in Europe confirmed the political demise of Bernardo Reyes.[18]

V. For the Monterrey elite, the furious political activity following the Creelman interview affirmed the value of an expedient political posture. Appropriately, the elite avoided any overt participation in the electoral campaigns of the Reyistas or the *científicos* as *regiomontano* businessmen remained nominally supportive of Porfirio Díaz. This stance was greatly facilitated by Reyes himself, who refused to challenge Díaz directly. Faithful servant to the last, Reyes avoided an open confrontation with the old dictator.[19] Reyes' vacillation spared Monterrey's businessmen the difficult task of choosing between Díaz and Reyes.

But the Madero campaign was another matter. Initially, the Maderista antireelectionist group seemed inconsequential. Worsening socioeconomic conditions and the political eclipse of Reyes pushed anti-Díaz sentiments in the direction of the Maderista camp.

The antireelectionists gained startling and noticeable momentum by the end of 1909.[20] Monterrey's capitalists realized the possible economic consequences of the impending political storm. Yet the volatile, abrupt political developments of the previous few months underscored the uncertainty of any political forecast.

The uneasiness of Monterrey's businessmen was reflected in the Madero family. Indeed, the "attitude of the family toward the political activity of the eldest son went through several phases."[21] The candidate's parents and grandfather "were convinced only gradually and only as political events unfolded."[22] The Madero family's reaction paralleled the political opportunism of their *regiomontano* counterparts. Evaristo Madero, patriarch of the family, "recognized even more fully than Francisco where his path was leading him and the obstacles and dangers involved."[23] If the Madero family moved hesitantly away from Díaz, Monterrey's elite proceeded with even greater caution and duplicity. Until economic interest indicated a different course, *regiomontano* businessmen maintained their nominal support of Porfirio Díaz.

In late 1909, Bernardo Reyes left Monterrey. The city's leading capitalists failed to express any obvious public remorse for the departing general—a sharp contrast from the glittering welcome accorded a few weeks before to Joaquín Casasús, government lawyer, prominent financier, and an ardent *científico.*[24] The difference was symbolic, the lack of fanfare for Reyes' departure eloquent. The arrival of Casasús and the exit of Reyes signified the pliable loyalties of the elite. The events of 1908 and 1909 reaffirmed the lessons of the past: to participate in direct, conspicuous political activity only when necessary and profitable. As the decisive year, 1910, approached, the influence of Monterrey's businessmen over the city's political economy would face another severe test. As on previous occasions, the elite proved to be flexible, shrewd, and resilient.

VI. The installation of Madero as president failed to pacify the country or to still the insistent demands of various groups and leaders. In November 1911, Emiliano Zapata, stung by Madero's hesitancy on land reform, broke ranks. In rapid succession, a series of revolts headed by sundry men challenged Madero's hold: Reyes in December 1911, Vasquéz Gómez in the same month, Pascual Orozco in March, and Felix Díaz in October 1912. These outbreaks, combined with lesser squabbles among Maderistas, produced an image of an administration seemingly out of control and incapable of providing stability. The radical pronouncements of anti-Madero factions heightened the apprehension over the new president's ability to rule the country. For some, a stern hand was needed to restore order.

While Monterrey's businessmen prudently avoided public discussion of Madero's reformist statements, they were hardly comforted by his performance. As his troubles mounted, *regiomontano* capitalists, with few exceptions, adopted a wait-and-see attitude. No public shows of support for Madero or urgent telegrams offering aid came from Nuevo León's business community.

In February 1913, Madero's skeptics were deprived of their debate. On February 18th, General Victoriano Huerta headed a coup that deposed Madero; subsequently, Huerta assumed the presidency. Three days later, Francisco I. Madero and his vice-president were slain. In the wake of their murder, Venustiano Carranza, in the name of Madero and his movement, announced his opposition to Huerta. Another contest for power was in the offing as, once again, Mexico faced another four years of turmoil. Yet, at the time, Huerta's forces appeared formidable while Carranza's prospects seemed bleak. A former Reyista and ex-legislator in Coahuila during the Díaz regime, Carranza was certainly far from a firebrand radical, and he offered scant hope of success against Huerta's army in February 1913.

Enrique Gorostieta, tied by marriage to both the Sada and Rivero families, joined the Huerta cabinet, an act that pointed to the support of a segment of the Monterrey elite for Huerta.[25] Frustrated by constant political problems and economic disruptions, the owners of the Cervecería, among others of the *regiomontano* business establishment, looked to Huerta to impose a semblance of economic stability and a predictable, if not favorable, political order. Support for Huerta from Monterrey's capitalists hardened when Pancho Villa, the Chihuahuan rebel and Robin Hood–like figure, joined Carranza in March 1913, along with Alvaro Obregón of Sonora, under the banner of the so-called constitutionalist army.

On paper, the Carrancista forces in the north were no match for Huerta's army of 50,000 men. But, within months, the federal army slowly crumbled before the onslaughts of the brilliantly led constitutionalist troops and the debilitating forays by Zapatistas in the south. The declining quality of government conscripts added to Huerta's military woes. Furthermore, and perhaps more importantly, Huerta failed to gain the diplomatic recognition of the United States. President Woodrow Wilson refused to accept the Mexican general, and, as a consequence, fatally weakened Huerta's hand as military reversals multiplied.[26]

Meanwhile, the raging strife through much of the country's central and northern regions crippled the Mexican economy as, for the first time, Monterrey suffered through the effects of Huerta's struggle against Carranza and his allies. Railway service was repeatedly interrupted, slowing the transport of goods and playing havoc with supplies, particularly fuel, for Monterrey's industries. In an effort to sustain production, the Cervecería and Fundidora, for example, bought or rented their own locomotives and railroad cars, used bribery whenever necessary, and maintained their own train crews.[27] Still, the frequent destruction of railway lines and bridges, coupled with a mercurial military situation, proved overwhelming for Monterrey's major businessmen as the year 1913 wore on. Unable to acquire consistent supplies of coke for its furnaces, the Fundidora by the beginning of 1914 was virtually shut down. Other companies were in a similar condition, reflecting the government's inability to stem the rebel tide in the north.

By spring 1914, Huerta's regime tottered toward collapse. Woodrow Wilson's tacit approval and aid to the constitutionalists underscored his unwillingness to grant Huerta recognition. On the basis of a minor incident in Veracruz in April 1914, the American president ordered the occupation of the country's key port—a critical source of revenues and supplies for Huerta's beleaguered government. The American occupation of Veracruz, despite the constitutionalists' disavowal of the act, dealt Huerta a final, climactic blow. Faced with certain defeat, Victoriano Huerta resigned the presidency on July 8, 1914. Huerta's rapid fall surprised his supporters, none more so than the owners of the Cervecería Cuauhtémoc.

Within days of Huerta's resignation, an interim president was selected and a constitutional convention called for October in Aguascalientes. Once again, however, the common thread of the rebel coalition—in this case Huerta—had been eliminated, and the fundamental divisions among Huerta's opponents reemerged at the convention. The meeting at Aguascalientes broke apart as contending factions failed to reach a workable resolution of their differences. Carranza, angered by events at the convention, pulled out his followers, while Villa and Zapata made common cause.

Civil war once more engulfed the country, but the final outcome became clear in April 1915, when Villa's brave troops fell before Obregón at the battle of Celaya. In the fall of 1915, Wilson's recognition of Carranza diminished any hope of victory for Villa and Zapata. With his major rivals in retreat, Carranza called for another constitutional convention in November 1916, in the city of Querétaro.

Reform-minded Carrancistas surfaced at the convention, however, and pushed through two key provisions into the new constitution. Article 27 reaffirmed the need for land reform, and Article 123 responded to labor's long-standing grievances. Out of political expediency, Carranza reluctantly accepted both articles in Mexico's new governmental charter and, subsequently, handily won the presidential election of 1917. A conservative man, an ardent defender of private property, Carranza had no stomach for basic social change. Anxious to assume the presidential reins, he had been forced to make concessions to pacify potent sources of opposition among military chiefs, regional *caciques*, workers, and peasants. Carranza's command over Mexico therefore was tenuous, a patchwork of fragile, volatile alliances, often based on opportunism rather than a common ideology.[28] In such a system and its inherent inconsistencies, no one faction or interest group could be easily or completely satisfied. For the businessmen of Monterrey, financially battered by years of turmoil, the elevation of Carranza to the presidency failed to diminish their distrust of the future or their resentment of the rebellion and its results.

VII.   The dizzying pace of events and changes from 1913 to 1917 forced *regiomontano* capitalists to make difficult decisions as they coped with the consequences of the nation's civil strife. Political predictability proved impossible. Local government became a series of short-lived despotisms, usually headed by military men of the faction that controlled for the moment the area surrounding the city.[29] Federal authority, given the ebb and flow of the fighting, was at best erratic. And economic conditions were subject to constant disruption. While most businessmen transferred large amounts of money to the United States (primarily Texas) and, in some cases, left the country, the majority remained to watch over their properties. As a result, the *regiomontano* elite was repeatedly compelled to pay forced loans, new "taxes," and subjected to fraud, often in the form of sales to rebel leaders, who usually paid with practically worthless scrip. In addition, there were occasional confiscations of horses, cattle, property, and goods, and, as noted earlier, there were the expenses of moving merchandise, materials, and products in and out of Monterrey. In short, the violent years of the revolution embittered Monterrey's capitalists and served to harden their resolve to preserve a semblance of the Porfirian past.

In April 1914, the constitutionalist forces headed by General Pablo González began their March on Monterrey. The owners of the Cervecería fortified the brewery; men, arms, and ammunition were brought in to defend it.[30] Other companies took similar measures, most notably the city's metal refining plants, including the Fundidora. The Garza-Sadas and their counterparts faced the destruction of costly machinery, the confiscation of raw material, and the loss of valuable equipment (e.g., rail cars and locomotives). Moreover, the businessmen of Monterrey were undoubtedly aware of the wild stories of rebel victories—plundering, rape, wanton violence, and wholesale robbery of property, money, and goods. The Garza-Sada clan had additional reason to fear the rebels. Gorostieta's presence in the Huerta cabinet, on the one hand, and his links to the Cervecería's ownership, on the other, added to the apprehension of the Garza-Sadas. Carranza, among others, for example, knew of the intimate links among Gorostieta, Huerta, and the brewery's owners.

Apparently, the city's business establishment hoped to hold on long enough for Huerista troops to arrive and fend off the constitutional-ists. Such hopes evaporated on April 20, when González' men entered the outskirts of Monterrey. After two days of fighting, the federal garrison fell. The defenses thrown up by some of the city's companies also proved to be ineffective and short-lived. The fear of irreparable damage from rebel shells quickly cooled the determination of busi-nessmen to resist González, with one exception—the Garza-Sadas. The Cervecería's money-making potential was not lost on the rebels. (See table 13.) González seemed to avoid damaging the brewery's capacity to make beer, that is, the plant's ability to earn pesos for weapons, munitions, provisions, and the troops' payroll. The thick brick walls of the Cervecería, sand-bagged for greater protection, made the attempts to subdue its defenses more difficult. Nonetheless, on April 25, the plant's defenders surrendered. The Garza-Sadas, however, had escaped and made their way to Texas, where they joined the women and children of the clan in San Antonio.[31]

Others of the *regiomontano* elite were less fortunate. Though several of Monterrey's key businessmen had left prior to the constitutionalist attack, many of them had stayed; as defeat became imminent, they were unable to escape. Immediately after the fall of the city, most

Table 13. *Beer Shipments from the Cervecería Cuauhtémoc, 1910–1920 (selected years)*

Year	Quantity (in thousands of liters)
1910	13,275
1912	16,519
1914–15*	3,359
1918	4,977
1920	14,929

Source: Stephen H. Haber, "The Industrialization of Mex-ico, 1880–1940" (manuscript in progress, unpaginated).
* Combined year.

members of the remaining business establishment found themselves behind bars—the Monterrey penitentiary became known as the "aristocrats' hotel."[32] In exchange for their release, González levied large fines and forced the Banco de Nuevo León to loan the rebels 100,000 pesos. Consequently, business operations were soon returned to the hands of owners. The bulk of the constitutionalist forces subsequently renewed the drive toward Mexico City, leaving Monterrey's businessmen embittered, though relieved, by their short, but costly stay in jail. Although safely ensconced in San Antonio, the Garza-Sadas were hardly spared. Indeed, they would find greater cause for an enduring, deep-seated resentment for the constitutionalist cause.

Within days of his victory, Pablo González ordered the resumption of the Cervecería's operations. Under a government (i.e., constitutionalist) *interventor*, the brewery's production of beer was sold as payment for the uncollected fines from the absent owners. The Garza-Sadas, however, were not resigned to the loss of their most important asset. Living in San Antonio, they were well aware of the heated criticism and overblown claims by U.S. companies as a result of the fighting in Mexico. Moreover, the Garza-Sadas were no doubt cognizant of the generally hostile attitude of the Wilson administration toward the Mexican rebellion.

Three weeks after the takeover, Joseph Schnaider, the former partner of the Garza-Sadas, surfaced in Washington, D.C., hounding American officials at the State Department over the confiscation of *his* brewery. The American-born Schnaider claimed partial ownership of the brewery and argued that its takeover by rebel troops constituted confiscation of his property. Furthermore, he charged that huge loans had been imposed on the Cervecería Cuauhtémoc. Schnaider's visit, a shrewd ploy by the Garza-Sadas, provoked a quick response from the State Department.[33]

On June 2, 1914, Secretary of State William Jennings Bryan sent a telegram to the Monterrey consul, requesting that he seek an "adjustment" with the Carrancistas over the brewery. In a blunt reply, Hanna noted the owners of the Cervecería had contributed to the Huerta cause, and he pointedly asked the amount of money that the Garza-Sadas were willing to pay for the return of the brewery. Bryan immediately responded by instructing Hanna to work with Schnaider in finding an "understanding" with the constitutionalists, as the Garza-Sadas were "perfectly willing to pay a reasonable sum provided that their property is returned to them."[34]

On June 9, 1914, the American consul in Monterrey, Phillip Hanna, dutifully sent a letter to González and requested that the general investigate the matter, with a reminder that American interests should be "respected." With virtually the same text, Hanna also wrote to Carranza about the concerns of the American government, adding that Schnaider would be arriving in Monterrey with a letter for the constitutionalist leader from Secretary of State Bryan. Hanna was an old hand at the Monterrey post, well-informed of the business community of Nuevo León. Hanna knew that the true owners of the Cervecería resided in San Antonio and that Schnaider's claims were at best flimsy and were an ill-concealed attempt by the Garza-Sadas to deny the rebels access to the brewery.

Pablo González apparently anticipated Hanna's letter.[35] In an unusually prompt response, the very next day, González gave a lengthy, cordial, and soundly argued response to Hanna. González pointedly reminded the American consul that the brewery was a Mexican corporation, chartered under Mexican law, and therefore juridically Mexican regardless of the nationality of its ownership. Furthermore, González declared, the Cervecería Cuauhtémoc had not been the subject of a forced loan; rather, the monies collected from beer sales represented a fine for the owners' "very active participation in efforts detrimental to the constitutionalist cause and in favor of the usurpers of the people's power."[36] Spurred by Bryan's instructions, Hanna appealed González' stand to Carranza on June 11, 1914. The American consul asked Carranza, headquartered in Saltillo, to give an audience to Schnaider and the U.S. vice-consul, T. Ayres Robertson. Three days later, Carranza's secretary replied, indicating that he would arrange for a meeting on the Cervecería issue. In the meantime, Hanna made one more effort to persuade González to return the brewery to the Garza-Sadas. In his letter, Hanna argued that any fine for the political activities of the owners should be levied on them as individuals rather than punishing the company. Moreover, Hanna emphasized, the owners of the Cervecería were "men of large personal means."[37] González, stalling for time until Carranza acted on the matter, demanded proof of Schnaider's interests in the brewery. Obviously, the solution was in the hands of the constitutionalist chief.

For three days Carranza kept Schnaider and Robertson waiting. Finally, on June 15, the first chief met with the two Americans. Despite a thick packet of information drawn up for the meeting, Carranza had failed to read it, to the annoyance of Robertson and Schnaider. After a lengthy explanation by the vice-consul, Carranza essentially ignored the entreaties to return the brewery to the Garza-Sadas by referring Robertson to the subsecretary of finance and Schnaider to the military commander in Monterrey. Carranza seemed entirely unimpressed by Bryan's letter or Schnaider's willingness to provide a 150,000 peso loan to the constitutionalist cause. Discouraged by Carranza's apparent indifference, Schnaider wrote to Hanna to thank him for his aid and stated his intention to return to the United States; Carranza's offer to look into the matter when he next visited Monterrey, Schnaider realized, was merely a means of brushing the issue aside.[38] Thus, on June 20, Hanna was forced to communicate the unsuccessful attempt to the State Department. On June 26, with lame bravado, the State Department instructed Hanna to continue to press for a resolution to the brewery question.[39] Schnaider's mission to Washington, D.C., in short, had failed.

For over two years, the Garza-Sada clan was forced to stay in San Antonio; each day a reminder of dispossession, each day a reason to idealize the past.

VIII.   The violence of the revolution subsided markedly in 1917 with the conclusion of the Querétaro convention and the inauguration of Carranza as president. Villa and Zapata had been pushed into their regional bases. Troubles of another sort, however, still brewed for Carranza. Mexico's economy lay nearly prostrate from years of strife. Oil production, a singular bright spot of the economy, remained essentially foreign-controlled. Economic recovery, therefore, loomed prominently on the new president's agenda. Toward this end, and consistent with his bourgeois outlook, Carranza attempted to woo back capital and businessmen to Mexico, offering assurances of cooperation.[40] Sensitive to American pressures and to the image of his administration in the foreign press, Carranza worked to lessen the apprehension created by the potentially explosive economic consequences of a forceful implementation of radical reform (e.g., Articles 27 and 123 of the new constitution). Despite strong nationalist sentiments, Carranza was not adverse to foreign investment, especially from interests of the powerful neighbor to the north. Among several measures designed to minimize his appearance as a radical, Carranza allowed for the return of properties and assets confiscated from businessmen during the constitutionalist campaign.[41]

Monterrey's businessmen moved quickly to take advantage of Carranza's effort to put his administration squarely on the side of capital. Such a policy was not a surprise to several *regiomontano* businessmen. As early as 1914, Carranza had ordered restitution of the properties taken from members of the Monterrey elite, including Patricio Milmo and Francisco Armendaiz. Moreover, Carranza—a former Reyista— helped the Riveros in locating cotton supplies for their textile plant.[42]

In addition, Carranza permitted the Garza-Sadas in late 1916 to return to Monterrey and resume their control of the Cervecería Cuauhtémoc. Encouraged by this act, Luis G. Sada implored Carranza to allow the restoration of the confiscated properties of Enrique Gorostieta, Sada's father-in-law. But, on this point, Carranza balked; he would not forgive entirely Gorostieta's service to Huerta, or the collaboration of the Garza-Sadas with the Huerta regime, regardless of their rationale.[43]

In spite of its probusiness measures, the new administration failed to win the complete confidence of the *regiomontano* elite. The Carrancistas proved incapable of imposing a local political order conducive or acceptable to business interests. The *regiomontanos* were not alone in their complaints. As Ramón E. Ruiz has concluded, "Carranza, a veteran of Porfirista politics, made no serious attempt to transform the political behavior of his countrymen . . . the hated jefe politico disappeared but his successor was not very different. . . . The rigging of elections and the use of terror to achieve political ends went on unabated despite the coming of peace."[44] Monterrey businessmen chafed at the shoddy spectacle of hastily organized, rigged elections. Under Reyes, *regiomontano* capitalists could afford to be smugly complacent over local government, to be assured that municipal and state election results would produce a slate of winners easily amenable to the city's business establishment. Such times, however, had disappeared. The casual confidence of the past was no longer possible. If there were any doubts, they were erased by the unrest among Monterrey's workers and its political implications.

Workers in Monterrey, heartened by the passage of Article 123, in January 1917, moved to realize its potential benefits. Indeed, as the Querétaro meeting debated the labor code in late 1916, the Ferraras and Garza-Sadas witnessed their workers register protests against them. Under the provisions of Article 123, however, states held the authority to delineate the specific measures to implement the basic elements of new labor law. Moreover, disputes over the implementation of the labor code were to be adjudicated by boards of arbitration and conciliation whose membership would be determined by state authorities. In this scheme, the role of the governor assumed special importance for both labor and capital. With restive workers mobilizing with unprecedented vigor, the major employers of Monterrey reached an obvious but grudging conclusion: the new political order required a strategy to renew their grasp of Nuevo León's chief political office and, equally important, of the bureaucratic machinery governing capital-labor relations.

The Fundidora and the city's large smelting plants were initial targets of workers bent on winning recognition of their rights under Article 123. By early 1917, steelmaking and refining operations had started up, spurred by the winding down of civil strife, improving railway service, and, more significantly, the demand for metal products generated by World War I. Nearly three-fourths of the steel plant's production went to highly lucrative external markets in 1917, leading the Fundidora to renege on a contract to supply replacement rails to the Mexican railroads.[45] The resurging activity of the smelters and steel plant led workers to direct their major effort at the most dynamic sector of the city's recovering economy.

Protests at textile plants from January through March 1917 preceded organizing activity at the Fundidora. Citing the recently adopted provisions of Article 123, textile employees pointed out violations of the new measures.[46] Building on the momentum established since January, Fundidora workers in March complained to Governor Pablo de la Garza over violations of the eight-hour workday provision of the labor law. De la Garza immediately requested the Fundidora to comply with the rule. The manager of the plant replied that the main office in Mexico City had not ordered such a change (to conform to the provisions of Article 123); thus, the old schedule of ten to twelve-hour workdays had been maintained. The manager, however, agreed to institute a new work schedule within a week.[47] Workers hailed de la Garza for his aid in their victory, but their triumph was short-lived. The lesson implicit in the Fundidora strike was not lost on the Monterrey elite. The governor's palace had ceased to be a reliable refuge for the interests of local capitalists.

The year 1918 began auspiciously for labor and businessmen with the formation of a Junta Central de Arbitraje y Conciliación (Arbitration and Conciliation Board). Composed of two representatives each from labor and business, and one selected by the governor, the board was organized in March, but its acceptance by businessmen came slowly, reluctantly. The key to the issue was Nicéforo Zambrano, the new governor of Nuevo León.[48] Working through Santiago Zambrano, a relative and prominent member of the elite, the governor apparently convinced the business establishment to participate on the board by arguing its advantage as a mediating agent in labor-capital conflict. Because of his appointive power, Zambrano saw the state government's representative as the tie-breaker in the event of a split on the board between workers and employers. Moreover, Zambrano and his business allies seem to have realized the importance of the board maintaining a "fair" image as opposed to a nakedly obvious instrument of capitalist interests. Such an image, supporters of the board argued, would facilitate the credibility of labor moderates and undermine the appeal of more radical labor elements. In short, the board potentially could be used as an effective bureaucratic mechanism to deflate labor protests.[49] Still, some businessmen balked at the principle of opening their company affairs (i.e., labor disputes) to government intervention. Among those, however, who saw the benefits of participating in the experiment was Luis G. Sada, who joined Santiago Zambrano as business representatives to the first board. Initially, this approach by business to the board worked. Disputes at the American Smelting Company and La Industrial textile mill were resolved by hammering out compromises.[50] But in June 1918, the board faced its first harsh test when a strike arose at the Fundidora.

On paper, the strike stemmed from the firm's refusal to grant days off on holidays to blast-furnace workers. The Fundidora's management argued that the shutdowns of the furnaces for short periods of time were extremely costly. Instead, the company offered to pay double-time to the furnace workers. They refused the offer. The furnace men organized further support from other employees in the plant, and, eventually, their counterparts in the two major smelters in the city. Meanwhile, the furnace men continued to turn down the compromise offers of the board. The businessmen were infuriated by the workers' intransigence, more so because of what they believed to be fair overtures based on sound reasons.[51] The governor was forced to intervene personally to break the impasse, and, as a consequence, his probusiness tilt became manifest.

Zambrano declared that the workers' action "was totally without justification," and he suggested that their efforts were politically motivated.[52] Indeed, it appeared that the leaders of the strike were bent on discrediting the board, on presenting it as a mechanism of control over workers that forced them to use it in order to legitimate their complaints. Zambrano would have none of it. As he indicated in his report on the strike, "only in one great conflict was there the need to use executive power to solve the matter without the cooperation of the board." "Realizing that the rhetoric of the agitation could influence the sentiments [*animo*] of the labor representatives," Zambrano went on to say, "the government assumed an active role . . . and conciliated the interests of workers and employers *without the treacherous influence of the agitators setting a cancerous precedent for the future*" (my emphasis).[53]

For businessmen, the Fundidora strike of 1918 revealed the crucial importance of having a procapital governor in office. Moreover, the conflict underscored the benefits, as well as the limitations, of the board in mediating or minimizing labor disputes. Most significantly, it was clear that former methods of controlling workers were insufficient and that probusiness state officials and agencies were not enough to quell workers' discontent. Luis G. Sada, as a member of the board, perhaps understood from the beginning that such a mechanism, at best, functioned as a buffer between employers and labor. The board failed to assure labor's acquiescence.

In this light, the Cervecería's ownership responded by forming in 1918 a worker cooperative that essentially constituted a company union. The founding of the Cooperativa Cuauhtémoc y Famosa represented an obvious attempt to extend paternalistic practices of the past as a means to forge a more malleable work force, to sustain a measure of control over workers when government authority or agencies proved incapable of squashing dissent among workers.[54]

The approach of the Garza-Sadas was not embraced by all of Monterrey's major employers. Manuel and Florentino Cantú Treviño, for instance, owners of two large textile mills, remained adamantly opposed to any form of appeasement. Florentino Cantú Treviño, for example, seemed to be especially hard-bitten on labor matters. In one dispute in 1917, a local official telegrammed the Department of Labor, explaining his frustration with Cantú Treviño "because he is exceedingly stupid."[55] In fact, the Cantú Treviños would continue to be frequently mentioned culprits in the reports of labor department officials for the next two decades.[56]

IX.   The strikes of 1918 compelled the *regiomontano* elite to face up to a new set of national political and economic realities. Two fundamental problems confronted the reassertion of the hegemony of Monterrey's businessmen. First, local government failed to possess the procapitalist assurances of the past. Despite his generally conservative views, Carranza, beset by a complex host of troubles at the national level, was incapable of exercising a strong hold over local affairs. The weakness of the new regime left the Monterrey elite on its own to cope with state and municipal politics—a stark contrast from the Porfirian era.

Second, the economic dominance of capital was no longer guaranteed. The creation of the Arbitration and Conciliation Board represented a telling indication of a profound change from the Reyista years. Furthermore, the elite found small comfort in Carranza's agreement to go along with the formation of a government-sanctioned labor organization, the Confederación Regional Obrera Mexicana (CROM).[57] *Regiomontano* businessmen seemed unimpressed by the political considerations that dictated Carranza's reluctant concession to labor.

By 1918, the businessmen of Monterrey held few illusions of an easy restoration of their former position under Díaz and Reyes. The assumed certainty of privilege and power under the Porfiriato would have to be recovered; there would be no simple return to the past. Headed by a core group of younger men, members of the Monterrey elite were determined to reclaim their previous place in *regiomontano* society. They continued, therefore, to look back with an increasing and deceiving sense of nostalgia to the time of Reyes as they entered a new and different era.

5. The Redefinition of Power: The Monterrey Elite and the New Mexican State, 1920–1928

I. In the decade following 1918, the political and economic context of Mexico pushed the *regiomontano* elite inexorably toward an attempt to acquire decisive national influence. Without an ally in the Reyes mold, businessmen found no local official to broker an effective and favorable relationship with federal authorities. As their economic activities renewed and spread, members of the elite attempted to negotiate a consistently profitable pact with the leaders of postrevolutionary Mexico. In this respect, an idealized perception of the Porfiriato's clear lines of authority continued to have an effect on the thinking of the elite concerning the new order. In the absence of a sympathetic *caudillo,* the businessmen of Monterrey worked to find a means at the federal level to reestablish their local hegemony and to protect their national economic interests.

Despite their procapitalist orientation, the presidential administrations that followed Carranza were hardly in a position to provide such guarantees to the capitalists of Nuevo León. The leaders of the new state had their own agenda—foremost, to stay in power, to sustain their positions. For much of the 1920s, frustration marked the efforts of the elite to strike a stable *political* bargain with the postrevolutionary leadership. The new state, compelled at times toward populist measures, proved incapable of assuring a local political order conducive to the interests of the resident elite. Nor could federal authority maintain a consistent record of support for business generally, and the concerns of Monterrey employers specifically. Thus, the capitalists from Nuevo León were increasingly pulled into the political vortex of postrevolutionary Mexico. For much of the period spanning the Obregón and Calles presidencies, the elite's search for a power broker proved fruitless, and efforts to negotiate an overarching understanding with the Mexican state were also stymied. Nonetheless, the quest for influence tempered the emergence of a new generation of leaders, among whom the Garza-Sadas figured most prominently. These years provided crucial political lessons for the young captains of the *re-giomontano* elite. What they learned, and what they ignored, during this time laid the groundwork for a fateful moment in the history of the Grupo Monterrey.

II. Mexico, during the presidential terms of Álvaro Obregón (1921–1924) and Plutarco Elías Calles (1924–1928), presented difficult and complex tasks to the ex-generals across a wide front. The clarity of the battlefield, between friend and foe, disappeared among the faces and factions that besieged Mexican presidents for favor, position, opportunities, and influence. Political stability and economic reconstruction preoccupied the Obregón and Calles administrations, but their goals were conditioned by the demands of jealous generals, disgruntled workers, land-hungry peasants, aspiring bureaucrats. And, if this were not enough, Obregón and Calles faced the constant pressures of their foreign creditors, notably those from the United States, and the economic interests that opportunistic foreigners pursued. Throughout, Obregón, then Calles, strove to shore up the strength of the new state while balancing the demands, often contradictory, of various groups and constituencies.[1] In this context, Monterrey's businessmen constituted one element among many that vied for the attention and sanction of presidential approval.

Such efforts on the part of *regiomontano* capitalists invited their accommodation with like-minded groups who sought similar ends. It was a period of political and economic flux, with shifting factions, brittle alliances, and tenuous commitments. Tact and nimble maneuvering were essential for political survival; a miscalculation spelled lost opportunities, disfavor, or worse. If these conditions provided for instability, they also allowed many avenues for businessmen to press their interests and to make the best deal possible.

Obregón and Calles confronted a country devastated by the strife of 1910–1917, an economy riddled with problems. The reorganization of a banking system, the renovation and extension of transportation services, and the regulation of taxes and tariffs were among the major tasks of economic reconstruction and recovery. In addition, both men were committed to further Mexican industrialization and to develop national capital despite an economy decidedly dependent on foreign capital and markets.[2]

On the other hand, workers and peasants made their own demands, as they pressed for the implementation of the promises embedded in the constitution of 1917.[3] Agrarian interests, riding the momentum created by the Zapatista movement, remained weighty contestants in the scramble for influence over policy making. Labor, because of its support for Obregón and Calles at critical moments, earned a recognized voice in government. Not surprisingly, businessmen feared the influence of organized labor and agrarian reformers. Indeed, they often cited the economic nationalism of presidential rhetoric to argue against hiking wages, making costly improvements in the work place, paying taxes, or giving up land. Such measures, businessmen argued, weakened their struggle against foreign competition. In brief, Obregón and Calles frequently faced opposing camps in the formation of economic policy, not to mention the complications of the implementation of government programs.

To compound the problems of policy making and implementation, Mexican presidents had to contend with the overarching and, at times, meddlesome presence of the United States.[4] American recognition was crucial to Obregón and Calles, and the country's economic recovery depended to a large extent on U.S.-Mexican relations generally, and economic relations in particular. These leaders could ill afford an outright conflict with the powerful neighbor to the north. Thus, Mexican economic policies invariably attracted the attention of various, frequently competing, constituencies, not the least of which was the conglomeration of American business representatives in Mexico City that seemingly encircled the American embassy.

Moreover, economic reconstruction was subject to an equal, if not more important, issue—the distribution of the fruits of the revolution.[5] The revolution spawned a bevy of men, primarily from the military, who were eager to enjoy the rewards of their battlefield service and/or their loyalty to victorious chiefs. Officers, especially ex-generals (there seem to have been an inordinate number of "generals" after the revolution), expected compensation for themselves and their men. Failure to receive anticipated privileges invited revolt, political intrigue, or both. Governorships, for instance, became a convenient way to placate ambitious military figures.[6] Most used such positions to grant jobs to retainers, to levy "taxes" for personal use, to dicker with workers and businessmen for favors, and to work out lucrative arrangements with foreign companies located under their jurisdiction. In some cases, governors presided over states as if they were personal fiefdoms. Often essentially free of federal restraints, *jefes de operaciones* participated in politics for economic gain wherever their garrisons existed.[7] Under such circumstances, federal economic policies at times went virtually unacknowledged. Conducting business, therefore, pushed capitalists from Nuevo León among others to enter the political fray to an unprecedented degree in order to achieve their ends.

For Monterrey businessmen (and their counterparts elsewhere), the new state in fact represented two broad but interrelated problems. First, particularly from 1920 to 1927, local politics in Nuevo León played havoc with the attempt of the *regiomontano* elite to establish a clear hold on local governmental affairs and to reach a consistently favorable accord with state and municipal officials. Relations between local political figures and businessmen were apt to swing widely, precipitating momentary conflicts that were compounded by the frequent turnover of officials.

Second, during these years national political affairs also continued to elude the efforts of the Monterrey elite to restore a political order, predictably, on the side of capitalists generally and *regiomontanos* specifically. Through a variety of means, *regiomontanos* constantly badgered the Obregón and Calles administrations for policies and decisions completely to the liking of Nuevo León's capitalists. In concert with other interests, Monterrey's businessmen were quick to score federal policies despite the procapitalist, economic nationalism of Obregón and Calles. Subject to differing pressures, the elasticity of the central government gave the Monterrey elite and its allies numerous opportunities to press for greater concessions, for more favors, for increasing their influence over national economic affairs. Eventually, largely on its own, Monterrey's elite openly confronted the federal government on the crucial question of labor. The timing and circumstances appeared favorable to capital as government-labor relations unraveled in 1928. Buoyed by their economic fortunes and a newly found base of local political support by 1927, members of the Monterrey elite appeared prepared to make a grab at national political power—at the presidency itself.

In these efforts to acquire national political and economic clout, the Cervecería clique assumed a distinctly prominent role. Spurred by their spectacular success and led by able if not brilliant offspring, the Garza-Sadas refused to give quarter to state intervention and disputed the reach of the Mexican state into the private sector. Combative, yet practical, the Garza-Sadas spearheaded the *regiomontano* drive to reestablish a local, then national, economic climate consistent with their aims. Aided by a select group of younger, capable members of the local elite, and undeterred by concerns over state economic reprisals, the Garza-Sadas worked to create a united capital front to pursue their goal of a political economy essentially controlled by businessmen. Implicitly, such an attitude was at odds with the politicians of the state—men too vulnerable in the eyes of the elite to the pendulums of mass appeal and personal aggrandizement. The *regiomontano* capitalists remained convinced that the national welfare was best put in their hands rather than in the sullied, corrupt grasp of greedy men of the new state.

III. Monterrey's businessmen shared the aims of Álvaro Obregón in 1920: political stability and economic reconstruction. Yet, for *regiomontano* capitalists, stability and economic recovery were narrowly construed—namely, whatever was good for their business was good for Mexico. Obregón faced a weightier and more comprehensive task. The one-armed chieftain from Sonora understood the fragile nature of his position. Carranza's removal was a constant reminder that a coup was a real and present danger.[8] Equally important, the United States loomed large for Obregón's administration. American recognition of his government was essential, as well as the settlement of Mexico's huge debt. Nationalist currents, however, pulled at Mexican officials, straining the relations between Mexico and its neighbor to the north.

The relations between Mexican workers and American companies added another complication to U.S.-Mexico relations. Obregón depended on labor support, but he was sensitive to the complaints of American businessmen. Backed by Republican presidents eager to please American business, U.S. companies challenged or neglected Mexican regulations and laws at every turn. Hence, conflicts between American firms and Mexican labor were magnified in importance by the staunch pro-American business posture of the American State Department and Obregón's vulnerability to American pressures.[9] Moreover, the enormous importance of U.S. markets and capital to the Mexican economy made the American presence in Mexico a delicate and volatile problem for Obregón.[10] Mexico's economic reconstruction was inextricably linked directly and indirectly to the United States.

Monterrey's businessmen were not strangers to U.S. interests, and they were keenly aware of the American presence economically and politically. American capital, for Monterrey's businessmen, was essential to the regeneration of the national economy and to the resuscitation of internal markets for Mexican industry.[11] *Regiomontano* industrialists welcomed American investments, in extractive activity particularly, since Monterrey's businessmen enjoyed a dominant position to service the local markets created by American mining, oil drilling, and construction projects. (See tables 14 and 15.) American-paid workers, for example, contributed to the selling of Cuauhtémoc beer and to the purchase of goods from the Salinas and Rocha department stores. Nonetheless, the Nuevo León elite was not blind to the potential threat posed by American competition. When necessary, it was quick to employ the standard of economic nationalism to protect its interests.[12] But

Table 14. *American Investments in Monterrey Consular District, 1920 (selected firms)*

Name of Firm	Value of Investment
Cía. Minerales y Metales (smelting)	$ 5,200,000.00
American Smelting (ASARCO)	3,000,000.00
Derby Lumber Co.	500,000.00
Mexican Lead Co. (Mining)	500,000.00
National Paper & Type Co.	200,000.00
Ladrillera Monterrey (brick factory)	200,000.00
Topo Chico Bottling (Coca-Cola)	75,000.00
Cerralva Mining Co.	60,000.00
J. B. Hibler Ranch	60,000.00
National Candy Co.	25,000.00
B. H. Hill Printing Co.	20,000.00
Azcárraga & Copeland (auto dealership) and several others of smaller value	5,000.00
Total Value of Investments (all interests)	$10,012,500.00

Source: Thomas D. Bowman to Secretary of State, Monterrey, August 30, 1920, NAW.812.503/46.
Note: Those of largest value were selected.

foreign competition proved to be a lesser preoccupation than the elite's concerns over the reordering of the country's political economy.

Working at times independently, in other instances in unison with other native capitalists, the Monterrey elite strove to improve its economic position and interests. These efforts were marked by direct appeals to the presidency. Few attempts were made to use bureaucratic or legislative channels first, if at all. Though the tactic often proved unsuccessful, it allowed Mexican presidents a clear view of the needs of Mexican (i.e., native) capitalists. And such an approach reflected the persistent effort to have an overarching understanding, or agreement, with the state. Rather than dealing with sectors of the state bureaucracy, the elite desired a direct, effective link to the center of power that encompassed the full spectrum of its concerns.[13]

IV.   Mexico's economy received a short-lived respite as a result of the demands for raw materials generated by World War I. But the 1920s commenced under a cloud of economic recession and uncertainty. Oil production offered a singular degree of relief from the nation's economic doldrums. The reintegration of the country's economy suffered from several handicaps, not the least of which was the

Table 15. *Monterrey-Based Industries and Capital Investment, 1922 (selected industries)*

Name of Company	Capital Investment	Comments
1. Cervecería Cuauhtémoc	$840,000	Garza-Sada interests
2. Vidriera Monterrey	150,000	Garza-Sada interests
3. El Porvenir (textiles)	250,000	Rivero interests
4. Black Horse Tobacco Co.	180,000	P. Burchard (German immigrant, merchant)
5. La Fama (textiles)	100,000	Manuel Cantú Treviño interests
6. Cía. Industrial (textiles)	60,000	Ferrara interests
7. Embotelladora Topo Chico (soda works)	60,000	Foreign controlled
8. El Modelo (paper products)	60,000	Foreign controlled
9. La Leona (textiles)	50,000	Florentino Cantú Treviño interests
10. Fábrica de Camas (bedding)	15,000	Salinas y Rocha interests
11. Fábrica de Mosaicos (ceramics)	15,000	Rivero interests

Source: AGN, Departamento de Trabajo, Box 400/Exp. 4.

reorganization of the Mexican railway system.[14] The railway issue provided a telling example of the *regiomontanos'* efforts to pressure government for economic concessions and the state's efforts to balance competing interests.

The American consul in Monterrey in May 1920 noted that the people of Nuevo León, especially its businessmen, "were tired of revolutions."[15] The Obregón rebellion prodded the *regiomontano* Chamber of Commerce to enlist the aid of the consul to maintain order. Assured of his intervention, Monterrey businessmen refused to pay the 100,000-peso forced loan demanded by the outgoing Carrancista governor. A month later, the consul observed, a semblance of order had been restored, to the relief of the local business community. "Once more," the consul's dispatch continued, "business and industry are slowly but perceptively exhibiting a restoration of confidence."[16] It was a fleeting moment, however, in Obregón-Monterrey relations.

The following April, the U.S. consul reported a "serious loss" of confidence in Obregón due to his inability to manage the railway strike and to engineer a favorable outcome for businessmen. The latter, in turn, complained bitterly of the need to pay "outrageous" bribes to ship goods. Businessmen were not sympathetic to the administration's dilemma: a militant, well-organized union and a system of railroads enormously in debt. High rates, intended to pay workers and service the debt, were, however, uneven, lacking uniformity and consistent application.[17] "Only by the purchase and maintenance of their own railroad equipment," the U.S. consul observed, "could the larger industries maintain their operations." "Until some way is found to restore efficiency in the operation of the railways, eliminate sabotage and graft," the consul concluded, "conditions are sure to remain bad."[18]

In July 1921, the Nuevo León Cámara de Comercio, Industria y Minería wired Obregón, beseeching his aid to rectify the railroad situation. But Obregón, wary of the consequences for his labor support, responded the next day that he "would look into the matter."[19] Five months later, conditions had failed to improve substantially.

The railway issue remained a thorn in the side of Monterrey businessmen throughout the 1920s and the source of a series of complaints from capitalists to Obregón and Calles. Finally, perhaps weary of the bickering with the railroads' leaders, and encouraged by Calles' growing support for business, Monterrey's capitalists wined and dined the head of the Mexican railways in July 1927.[20] Undoubtedly, in light of the railway chief's candidacy as secretary of communications, the elite hoped to curry favor by the lavish gesture. The railroad issue provided an early indication of the Monterrey elite's inability to force a visible or easy shift in federal policies.

The badgering of government agencies, and the president's office in particular, was not confined to the railroad question. The circulation of American currency along the border, for example, sparked another test for Obregón and his relations with Monterrey businessmen in June 1921. And, as in the railroad issue, the results disappointed the *regiomontanos'* hopes for a favorable decision. Obregón similarly disappointed Nuevo León capitalists further when he refused to lower mining taxes in September 1921. In that case, the president cited his legal limitations to effect such changes in the tax code. In addition, in a matter especially important to the Cervecería Cuauhtémoc, Obregón refused to reduce the levies on beer despite the entreaties of the brewery's owners in 1922. And later that year, the Cámara de Nuevo León implored Obregón to reduce telegraph rates with little success.[21] In short, in various cases, Monterrey businessmen were unable to change federal economic policies, notwithstanding Obregón's measures to promote Mexican industry.

The Monterrey elite's uneven relationship with the Obregón administration pointed to the president's need to respond to other pressures. The telegraph rate question, for instance, underscored the

122 The Redefinition of Power

federal government's need for revenue for a shaky treasury. Still, *regiomontano* interests maintained an influence in government economic decision making, including the vital area of the development of Mexico's banking structure.[22] The participation of the elite in the Banco de México, for instance, was understandable, given that its organization involved Porfirian acquaintances and men well known to the *regiomontanos*. Nuevo León's industrialists realized the benefits of influencing currency controls, monetary policy, credit, and interest rates. Thus, the involvement of the elite in the Mexican central bank was less a sign of collaboration with the state than it was simply good business with former cronies—an act of self-interest among like-minded friends from a previous era.

The skirmishes between Monterrey businessmen and the Obregón presidency paralleled their running battles with local government officials. And, as it became clear that Obregón would not intervene, the elite was forced to confront local politicos frequently on its own without the aid of the central government. The early encounters in the early 1920s with local officials had enduring effects on the elite's view of politicians and served to reaffirm its general disdain and distrust for them. More importantly, these early, hostile encounters spurred the elite to work actively to bring its power to bear on local affairs. These were frustrating years for the *regiomontano* industrialists, as they despaired at the inability of the state to impose order at the local level.

The successful Obregón coup in 1920 brought in a "collection of chieftains."[23] "Granting the difficulty of demobilizing the many generals who felt that their services should be requited," Ernest Gruening observed in 1928, Obregón "was unnecessarily a 'good fellow'—at the expense of the nation—another survival of personal rule."[24] To the dismay of Monterrey's businessmen, Nuevo León had the "distinction of having had probably the most dishonest governor in all of the twenty-eight states," Gruening concluded, "who, not content to confine his thieving to state taxes collected in advance, defrauded the federal treasury by organizing wholesale smuggling from the United States."[25] From 1920 to 1926, state government in Nuevo León changed hands more than a dozen times like musical chairs. The occupants of the governor's palace were usually the same men, among whom the most prominent was General Porfirio González (see table 16). In the midst of Monterrey's large industries, Governor Porfirio González found abundant opportunities to profit from his corruption.

General Porfirio González early on indicated the nature of his gubernatorial rule. With the Obregonista victory in Nuevo León in May

Table 16. *Changes in the Governorship of Nuevo León, 1920–1931*

Dates of Term	Governor
1. May 1920–February 1921	Porfirio G. González
2. February 1921–April 1922	Juan M. García
3. April 1922–October 1923	Ramiro Tamez*
4. October 1923–December 1923	Anastasio Treviño Martínez
5. December 1923–October 1925	Porfirio G. González*
6. October 1925–October 1927	Jerónimo Siller
7. October 1927–October 1931	Aarón Sáenz

*During this administration, four different men were in charge of the governor's office for various periods of time. Their absences from office were due to health, vacations, or business outside the state.

1920, González attempted to extract a 100,000-peso "loan" from *regiomontano* capitalists. The demand was not granted, due in large part to the intervention of the American consul.[26] Nonetheless, the tenor of the relationship between the elite and state officials, Porfirio González in particular, had been established for the next eight years. And the elite, if any incentive was needed, found the impetus to redouble its drive for local control.

The tensions between government officials and Monterrey businessmen marred the economic life of the city's capitalists. Tax "hikes," graft, bribery marked much of the interaction between the *regiomontano* business establishment and local bureaucrats. The federal government essentially did nothing to stem the corruption that flourished under González and his cohorts (nor in the rest of the country for that matter). Opposition to González' machine was shared by other than *regiomontano* capitalists. In the middle of a sharp recession in July 1925, an opposition bloc formed within the state legislature and met independent of the Gonzalistas. The opposition legislators "elected" General Jerónimo Siller as governor; a shootout between the rival factions finally forced the Secretaría de Gobernación to "recognize" González as the legitimate governor of Nuevo León. As a result, the opposition gave up the fight for the moment. Nevertheless, the conflict drew the ire of Calles. The new president was sensitive to events in the northern state as a result of the marriage of his son, Plutarco, Jr., to the sister of Aarón Sáenz, a native *regiomontano*, an Obregón crony, and Mexico's foreign minister. Two months later, Siller was installed as interim governor and González ousted from office. Significantly, Sáenz had met with local businessmen in June 1925, and he undoubtedly had communicated their complaints to Calles.[27]

In Siller, the Monterrey elite had a man much more to their liking. Though González partisans continued to fight for their positions in the elections of 1926, the crisis passed without the violence anticipated, due in large part to the presence of the new military chief in Nuevo León, Juan Andreu Almazán. Almazán, acting on orders to bring calm to the area, enforced an end to the tensions between Silleristas and Gonzalistas. With Almazán, order was seemingly restored—a point not lost on Monterrey's business establishment. In 1927, Sáenz ran for governor and won.[28] With probusiness men in the governor's palace and in charge of the regional military garrison, the long-awaited days of Bernardo Reyes seemed at hand.

V.   A native of Nuevo León, Aarón Sáenz had coveted the governorship for several years. He had campaigned earlier for the office in 1923, but his bid failed and he was consoled by being appointed to a high federal post. The close ties between Sáenz and the *regiomontano* business establishment were presaged in a meeting in July 1925 that included the leading figures of the city's industries, banks, and commerce. Throughout the period from July 1925 to the elections of 1927, Sáenz frequently visited Monterrey, rarely missing an opportunity on his frequent trips to Washington, D.C., and Mexico City to stop at the northern city. With each visit, Sáenz took the time to meet with local dignitaries and cultivate his political and economic ambitions.

The notoriously probusiness newspaper *El Porvenir* enthusiastically promoted Sáenz, and even suggested him as potential presidential timber. Sáenz, a faithful Obregonista if not a pragmatic politician, maintained his sight on the governorship in light of Obregón's determination to run for president in 1928. In March 1927, Sáenz declared himself a gubernatorial candidate and resigned his diplomatic post the following month.

In one of his first acts as a candidate, Sáenz met with the major businessmen of Monterrey to confirm their support. *Regiomontano* capitalists emerged from the meeting with a glowing, telling enthusiasm for Sáenz' candidacy for the governorship. Three days later, Sáenz lashed out at "professional politicians," a thinly veiled reference to the regime of Porfirio González.[29] With the business community on his side, and, more importantly, with the support of Obregón and Calles, Sáenz was an easy victor in July 1927. Just two weeks later, Sáenz rewarded his business supporters by announcing an ambitious plan for the promotion of local businesses. To be implemented under his stewardship, the plan included a pledge not to introduce new taxes. Upon his inauguration as governor on December 1, Sáenz lifted the taxes on beer. Two months later, Sáenz convened a commission composed primarily of businessmen to review and make recommendations on Nuevo León's tax structure. And, in the midst of directing Obregón's presidential campaign, Sáenz held another meeting with leading businessmen of Monterrey to discuss further ways of promoting commerce, particularly the boosting of tourism to the area. In this regard, Sáenz was responding to an idea long touted by local businessmen. The road construction program in the region had stimulated increasing auto traffic between Monterrey and Texas via Laredo. In June 1928, the probusiness thrust of Sáenz' gubernatorial administration culminated in his submittal of a tax reduction proposal favored by local capitalists and in his pronouncement to contribute toward the construction of a large hotel to boost the city's tourist plans. These acts were roundly endorsed by local luminaries who praised the probusiness policies of the governor. As if this were not enough, Sáenz soon thereafter called on Monterrey's businessmen to formulate an economic plan for Nuevo León.[30]

The apparent, gleeful contentment of the elite with Sáenz was seconded by the presence of the military chief of Nuevo León, Juan Andreu Almazán. Installed as *jefe de operaciones* of the regional garrison in Monterrey in 1926, Almazán avoided political embroglios in the state. Rather, he acted as peacemaker, carefully negotiating to minimize the excesses of the occupants of the governor's chair. Such a stance earned Almazán the admiration of the city's business establishment. For his part, Almazán eagerly sought capital and profitable contacts to promote his own fledgling Anahuac construction company. In return, Almazán endeavored to smother labor organizing, to press the Calles administration for road construction projects via Monterrey, and to garner more funds for military spending in Nuevo León. Local businessmen reciprocated by lending their workers to Almazán's construction projects on occasion and by admitting Almazán into the innermost circles of *regiomontano* society.[31]

Within a year of his arrival, Almazán was a mainstay of elite social life and the object of lavish praise from the city's business establishment. The conjunction of Almazán and Sáenz in Nuevo León from 1927 to 1928 provided the elite, for the first time since 1909, with a political context that approximated its Porfirian ideals. Moreover, given the imminent election of Obregón to the presidency, the presence of Sáenz in Nuevo León augured well for the businessmen in Monterrey. With Sáenz to deflect adverse federal policies and with Almazán to supply the muscle for probusiness designs, the times of Bernardo Reyes appeared to have been reestablished for *regiomontano* capitalists.

VI.   For the elite of Monterrey, the arrival of Sáenz in the governor's palace represented a welcome respite from a decade of intermittent, irritating conflicts, large and small, with local officials. At the national level, the scene had been hardly uplifting; the railway issue was a revealing example of frustration with the federal government. In this regard, as Monterrey businessmen extended their operations into other areas of the country, national labor issues became of increasing concern to *regiomontano* employers. The installation of Luis Morones as minister of commerce and labor in the Calles cabinet failed to elicit much joy from Nuevo León. In short, conducting business for the Monterrey elite in the 1920s was far from a glittering record of state and private sector harmony. Nonetheless, despite the complaints of their owners, the city's foremost industries remained dominant.

As exemplified by the Fundidora and the Cervecería Cuauhtémoc, earlier patterns of business operations and policies among *regiomontano* industrialists continued into the postrevolutionary era. Labor paternalism, for example, persisted as a means of checking independent unionization. In addition, the Cervecería and the Fundidora sustained distinctive approaches to relations between the state and Monterrey's industries. The gravitation of the Fundidora toward an accommodation with the central government reflected the steel plant's greater dependence on state protection and contracts. Not insignificantly, its leader, Adolfo Prieto, resided in Mexico City. For the Cervecería, on the other hand, and its burgeoning sister company, the Vidriera, the 1920s witnessed a surge of growth that was less dependent on government sanction and succor. While the ownership of the two companies remained political and economic allies, the Garza-Sadas invariably took the lead in the bouts with the state over economic policy. Indeed, the 1920s witnessed the crystallization of the leadership of the Garza-Sadas and a small circle of adherents as the spokesmen of Monterrey's business community.

The leading members of the *regiomontano* establishment confronted a number of issues to address in the management of their enterprises that involved government. Two problems particularly loomed large in the minds of the Garza-Sadas and their closest allies: corruption and labor. Graft, fraud, bribery, and "taxes" plagued Monterrey businessmen through the early 1920s and complicated the smooth running of their enterprises. Labor added yet another source of anxiety and potential trouble. In fact, such fears mounted with the rise and influence in national politics of the CROM and its leader, Luis N. Morones. These two broad concerns served to tighten the bonds among the city's capitalists into a concentrated bloc of interests and power.

From May 1920 to February 1921, Porfirio González took full advantage of the governor's office to find several methods of extracting money and favors from local companies. Juan M. García, who followed González into office, so misused his office that he made "previous systems fade into insignificance."[32] Happy to see González out of office, the city's commercial establishment found García's conduct a "keen disappointment." Large businessmen, the American consul in Monterrey noted, "grew so utterly impatient that an attempt was made to develop a strong organization for the purpose of setting up opposition by which to coerce the governor into a more reasonable policy."[33] Indeed, one of the first acts of the García administration was to propose a beer tax that the Cervecería adamantly refused to accept passively. But García was equally determined and had the means to carry out his threat. Finally, in exchange for García's dropping of the beer tax proposal, the owners of the Cervecería agreed to give the governor the brewery's distributorship in Tampico.[34] Understandably, after the beer tax episode, other businessmen avoided a direct confrontation with García for fear of jeopardizing their interests.

García's move on the brewery was not a coincidence. In the grip of the post–World War I recession, the Nuevo León business community contained one real bright spot—the Cervecería Cuauhtémoc. "The only industry that has continued in operation at anything like normal capacity," the U.S. consul observed, "is the brewery and its subsidiary bottle factory."[35] (See table 17 and figure 3.) Fundidora production had slackened, and other businesses, especially commercial-based companies, bordered on bankruptcy. Financial institutions also suffered as three private banks closed by November 1922, leaving the Banco Mercantil and the Banco de Nuevo León as the major survivors

Table 17. *Beer Shipments from the Cervecería Cuauhtémoc, 1920–1930 (selected years)*

Year	Quantity (in thousands of liters)
1920	14,929
1922	13,156
1924	11,564
1926	21,521
1928	22,229
1930	21,760

Source: Stephen H. Haber, "The Industrialization of Mexico, 1880–1940" (manuscript in progress, unpaginated).

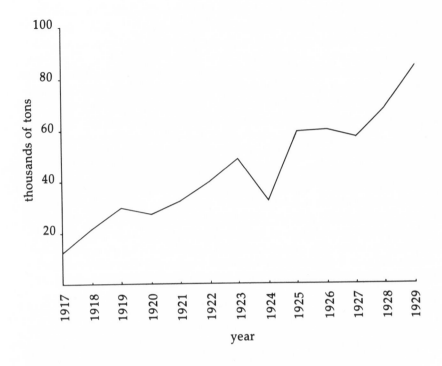

Figure 3. *Total Production of Fundidora, 1917–1919*
(Report, Compañía Fundidora de Fierro y Acero de Monterrey, S.A.,
LAC)

of the Porfirian era.[36] The effects of the de la Huerta rebellion in 1923 compounded the economic woes of the area. Railway service was disrupted, thus hampering business operations throughout the country, with crippling results for the economic recovery of Monterrey.

Nonetheless, the end of the Huertista revolt allowed for a renewal of activity, with the Cervecería leading the way. By early 1924, sales of the brewery's products reached the point that it was unable to satisfy demand at times, forcing full-page advertisements in Mexico City newspapers by the brewery to apologize for the temporary shortfall.[37] (The Obregón administration, mindful of the need for federal revenues, promptly slapped a tax increase on beer.) The recovery of the Fundidora, in contrast, failed to match the rapid pace of the brewery, but 1925 was a banner year for the iron and steel plant. Ironically, the Fundidora's recovery was due in large part to the production of replacement rails for track and bridges damaged by the Huertista rebellion.[38]

Unfortunately, the revival of the *regiomontano* economy pushed González to renew his own schemes of self-aggrandizement. The venality of local officials, however, remained primarily a nuisance that slimmed profits and distracted Monterrey industrialists from other more productive concerns. In this regard, the grasping hands of the governors and their underlings were a constant irritant, but they generally avoided attempts to worm their way into the companies themselves. Nor were these bureaucrats, it seems, interested in establishing their own enterprises. Their ambition was not commensurate with their corruption. In this regard, the conduct of local officials was contemptible to the *regiomontano* businessmen, but their actions were not a threat to the economic dominance of the Monterrey elite.[39]

Labor, on the other hand, presented a greater danger to elite power than graft and bribery. Local government, however, had a part to play in the matter; businessmen were unable to deal with labor unilaterally. Despite their efforts to encapsulate workers, Monterrey's major employers were unable to prevent attempts by workers to break the paternalism and domination of the past. Eventually, the determination of members of the elite to control labor propelled them into the arena of national labor politics.

The strikes of 1918 offered two lessons to the *regiomontano* business establishment. First, Monterrey employers realized the necessity of maintaining an upper hand in the local Junta de Arbitraje y Conciliación, or arbitration and conciliation court.[40] Second, given the authority of the governor to appoint the deciding vote, as it were, the composition of the labor board presented a vexing question; a problem made more so, as it turned out, by the erratic relations between businessmen and state government officials from 1920 to 1927. Hence, the appointment of the government's representative to the labor tribunal often provided a source of tension, if not conflict, between local government and Monterrey's leading capitalists.

In May 1925, for example, a dispute arose involving the governor, the labor board, and the elite of Monterrey. Indeed, *El Porvenir* was moved to lament the wave of labor disturbances that had recently taken place. Against the backdrop of several work actions, the labor board met in July to discuss one of the more intractable disputes, that at the La Leona textile mill owned by the Cantú Treviño family. Smarting from the criticism of businessmen, Governor Porfirio González decided to select a new member for the arbitration board, an appointment considered too prolabor by the Cámara de Comercio. *El Porvenir* immediately seconded the businessmen's position with a nasty editorial against González. To complicate matters, González was in the midst of a fight with an opposition political faction aided by the local commercial establishment.[41] González apparently hoped to use the appointment as a device to discourage business support for his opponent.

A week after the governor's appointment, business representatives, among them Luis G. Sada, withdrew from the labor tribunal, paralyzing further proceedings. The newly selected representative chastised the businessmen and promised that the board would continue to function. González asked the Cámara to reconsider its boycott, but negotiations broke down and both sides stiffened their positions. González threatened to make appointments independent of the Cámara and gave the group a deadline to respond to his offer. Prodded by the Garza-Sadas to hold its position, the Cámara stalled for time, unsure of how to respond to the governor's threat. González, never one to skip an opportunity to parley, consented to "wait a reasonable time" for the Cámara to make a decision.[42]

A week passed, and González, perhaps fearful of losing face, announced that he would soon appoint an entirely new arbitration board. A skittish Cámara relented despite the objections of the Garza-Sadas and chose three men to the labor tribunal. The owners of the Cervecería, incensed over González' bullying of the Cámara (and their inability in this instance to sway the Cámara to their side), refused to recognize the legitimacy of the board.[43] The crisis passed, but its residue undoubtedly remained in the minds of the Garza-Sadas— another item on the long list of grievances held by the Cervecería clique against the state.

Indeed, the events of July 1925 followed on the heels of a confrontation between local officials and the Garza-Sadas a year earlier. Because of an alleged theft of beer, the Cervecería had fired nearly forty workers in June 1924. In fact, the firings represented an effort by the brewery to squelch a drive by workers to establish an independent union. A picket line immediately formed around the Cervecería to protest the firings. The Cámara de Comercio, acting on behalf of the Cervecería, demanded government troops to assure order. Furthermore, the Cámara accused the pickets of threatening workers who were not sympathetic to the strike. An ambivalent González nevertheless sent troops to escort workers through the picket lines. But he also refused to disperse the strikers. Dissident workers appealed to González, but he rejected their request to remove his troops. Unwilling to submit the issue to the arbitration board, on the assumption that it was stacked against them, the strikers took their case to President Obregón. Forced to counter, the Garza-Sadas pressed company union leaders to write to Obregón as well. The *blanco* leadership dutifully wired Obregón, assuring him that "outside elements" were instigating the strike and that the majority of workers were unsympathetic to it.[44] Faced with conflicting evidence,

Obregón asked José Cavazos, the local military chief, to assess the situation. Cavazos subsequently confirmed the view of the *blanco* faction in his report, allowing Obregón to withdraw from the matter. With his retreat, the unionization effort died.[45]

For the Garza-Sadas, the episode reaffirmed their uneasiness over the role of the state in capital-labor relations and over their inability to force the state to take decisive action in their favor. These two events revealed, however, the elite's strategy to use the arbitration board whenever possible to subvert labor activity. Time and again in this period, the labor tribunal moved swiftly to absorb a dispute and render a quick decision. The labor court tended to make speedy compromises rather than risk a mushrooming of work actions. In some cases, strikes were resolved literally in one day. Led by business representatives, the board seemed bent on denying labor activists an issue on which to organize workers. Where such cases involved large companies, businessmen often moved rapidly, at times ruling against the employer. There were exceptions. Generally, nevertheless, the capitalist board members succeeded in suffocating labor problems through the bureaucratic channels of the Junta de Arbitraje y Conciliación.[46] González' tampering with the board's composition in 1925 therefore enraged the elite. His threat endangered a key mechanism for controlling labor.

Elite members of the board, such as Luis G. Sada, took a certain degree of pride in their professed impartiality. The frequent indemnities paid to the workers on approval by the board, for instance, showed an ostensible willingness for the board to come down on the side of labor. But the evidence also suggests that such payoffs to employees were a means to terminate troublesome workers with as little fuss as possible. Arrayed against such powerful enemies and ambivalent about any rewards for their persistence, many frustrated workers apparently took the indemnity rather than pressing their case. Moreover, as letters by disgruntled workers indicate, the dynamics of the board's workings clearly gave the advantage to private sector representatives.[47] Pitted against the training and experience of lawyers such as Virgilio Garza, Jr., labor representatives were hard pressed to match the legalistic powers of their adversaries in a system weighted in favor of businessmen. And, in a city where a Garza or Sada still elicited a measure of awe and fear, the presence of such men in the tribunal was yet another source of the employer's power.

In addition to their shrewd use of the arbitration board, Monterrey's industrialists continued to use forms of paternalism with accustomed ease to undermine labor activity. This approach to controlling workers extended the practices initiated in the Porfirian era, particularly in the larger industries such as the Cervecería, the Vidriera, and the

Fundidora. Thus, in early 1925, the secretary general of the Chamber of Commerce, Manuel Barragán, called attention to the tranquillity of capital-labor relations in Monterrey. Barragán emphasized the fact that the city's "industrialists and other businessmen, with few exceptions, anticipate the needs and demands of their workers contingent upon their work and intelligence."[48] (This was written before the events of July 1925 noted earlier.)

Few could argue with Barragán at the time with his description of the welfare measures provided by Monterrey's major employers. The Fundidora, for example, supplied employees with free medical services, a pharmacy, free schooling for workers' children, a night school adult program, a library, subsidized housing, sports and other types of recreational facilities, a credit union, and even an agricultural tract for those employees who desired to cultivate fruits and vegetables for themselves.

With Isaac Garza on the Fundidora's board of directors, it was not surprising to find virtually the identical services available to the employees of the Cervecería Cuauhtémoc. In fact, the two companies jointly sponsored a housing development for their workers, Colonia Acero, as well as the agricultural tract for workers.[49] Nonetheless, the employers' grip over labor failed to be complete in the minds of Monterrey's largest employers. The ties forged between organized labor and Obregón, and more importantly with Calles, alarmed *regiomontano* capitalists. When Luis N. Morones joined the Calles cabinet as secretary of commerce, industry, and labor, the concerns of the businessmen of Nuevo León deepened.

The relationship between Calles and Morones was a political marriage. Calles needed the solid, disciplined support supplied by Morones' labor organization, the Confederación Regional Obrera Mexicana. With the CROM, Calles acquired a reliable base of support for his own position and for his government. Morones, in exchange, took advantage of the relationship to punish rival labor organizations, to coerce unions to join his organization, to bully Calles' political enemies (i.e., to inflate his own wealth), and to fortify his own political position within government. While labor received some benefits from Morones' political clout, the CROM also became dependent on the state in the process. Its autonomy circumscribed by its links to the state, and Calles specifically, the CROM more often than not became an instrument for Calles to exploit for *his* ends, rather than for the benefit of workers. In this respect, the CROM accommodated the capitalist orientation of the Obregón and Calles administrations. Thus, on December 5, 1924, soon after his entry into the cabinet, Morones announced his intention to make "great efforts toward ending the conflicts between labor and capital in the country."[50] With a figurative sigh of relief, *El Porvenir* of Monterrey lauded the labor leader's call for less turmoil. But the new year witnessed an end to the uneasy optimism of the *regiomontano* businessmen toward the CROM.

The CROM's strength in Monterrey reflected its hold elsewhere in the country—among transport workers, electrical workers, and printers. Perhaps in an effort to augment the organization's presence in the city, a strike was called against the Modelo office equipment and printing company on March 26, 1925. The timing of the strike was no coincidence. Morones apparently had been angered by a stinging editorial in *El Porvenir* condemning his use of his office for personal and political profit.[51] Furthermore, Calles had scheduled a trip to Monterrey for early April 1925. The CROM-backed Modelo strikers pressed for the recognition of their union, hoping that Calles' imminent visit would pressure the company to concede to their demands. The Zambrano family, owners of the printing company, refused to give in to the strikers' demands, and the arbitration board failed to bring either side to the bargaining table. Meanwhile, the printers' union called for a meeting of its membership in Nuevo León and made veiled threats of calling a general strike in support of the Modelo workers. On April 2, 1925, the Unión de Artes Gráficos denounced the workings of the labor board and sent out an appeal for Morones to intervene personally in the case.[52] But the next day, the CROM printers' union reversed its position completely; leaders stated their decision to make one last effort to reach an agreement with the Zambranos through the offices of the arbitration court. For Monterrey's major employers, it was obvious that the Cromistas were trying to use the president's visit to make political capital through the labor dispute. Utilizing *El Porvenir* as a mouthpiece, *regiomontano* businessmen made a caustic assault on the strike on the day of Calles' arrival, April 9, 1925. Condemning the work action as arbitrary and illegal, the city's business establishment charged that the strike was merely intended to exploit the workers for the benefit of labor leaders—an obvious reference to the CROM's flamboyant head.[53]

A lavish reception planned by the city's industrialists greeted Calles upon his arrival. The Fundidora and the Cervecería joined in building a huge metal arch, festooned with light bulbs that spelled out a blinking welcome to the president. In addition, the Calderón family loaned a new car to the president for his personal use while he was in Monterrey. In light of the businessmen's display, Calles apparently signaled his lack of amusement over the controversy at the Modelo plant on the eve of his son's wedding. The day following Calles' arrival, the regional representative of the Secretaría de Comercio,

Industria y Trabajo retreated from his former support for the strike, and he went on to declare that the strike was in fact illegal.[54] Under pressure from an embarrassed Morones, the same representative recanted his earlier statement a few days later to no effect.[55] With Calles' unsympathetic stance clear, the CROM leaders were reduced to sputtering weak threats of a general strike; but the issue sank into sudden oblivion as Calles strolled through the Cervecería and enjoyed another extravagant reception hosted by the Garza-Sadas.[56] Three days later, Calles' son and the sister of Aarón Sáenz married. For two days the society pages of Monterrey and Mexico City newspapers detailed the profuse outpouring of gifts from *regiomontano* elite families, including the Garza-Sadas—there was reason, understandably, for gratitude.[57]

Still, despite the apparent victory over the CROM in mid-1925, Monterrey's business establishment remained preoccupied with the inability of political leaders, including the president, to keep labor, Morones in particular, in check. *Regiomontano* businessmen despaired over Calles' unwillingness to curb Morones' excesses or to block the cabinet minister's encroachment into the nation's economic affairs. Disenchantment with Calles quickly set in within months of the president's visit to Monterrey. "The iron hand that we thought prepared to control the old disorders," *El Porvenir* intoned in November 1925, "turns out to be a fragile gauntlet."[58]

For Monterrey's businessmen, the question of labor and its control extended beyond the confines of their regional redoubt. The postrevolutionary years had witnessed the renewal and spread of their business activities throughout the country. A strong national labor movement menaced their ability to plan and to develop new markets without the harassment of dealing with unions and labor officials outside their control. While *regiomontano* employers had a hold over labor questions in Monterrey, they found such a grasp much more difficult to extend over workers in other sectors and areas of the economy whose labor impinged upon the operation of the industries of Nuevo León. With the ascension of Morones as union kingpin and cabinet member, concern among businessmen swelled over a labor organization capable of influencing the national economy. Morones' preoccupation with rivals and sustaining an ostentatious life-style failed to calm the apprehension of *regiomontano* businessmen. The showy labor leader was no mere buffoon, they realized, and his venality was not a surprise for industrialists accustomed to Nuevo León's history of governors and their underlings. Paying off unions and their leaders was just another inconvenience to be handled and its costs passed on to customers. Rather, Monterrey's capitalists desired a sense of control, of predictability in the operation of their enterprises. In spite of the probusiness measures of the state, Morones cast a pall over the private sector. Moreover, Morones jeopardized progress, endangered the economic revival of the nation, and tarnished the mission of Mexican business, of Monterrey's industrialists in particular.[59]

Borrowing from their experience in the uses of the arbitration board in Monterrey, *regiomontano* capitalists began in 1925 to press for the codification of Article 123 of the constitution.[60] The formulation of a uniform national labor code offered the possibility of a legalistic resolution to labor-capital relations, and, equally important, such a code promised to lessen the authority of local officials to intervene (often for profit) in the economic affairs of businessmen. Moreover, the making of such legislation also provided the private sector with an opportunity to translate its concerns into the federal labor code—an obvious indication of the intent to check the power of Mexico's labor czar.[61]

Such an effort reflected the checkered history of the relations between the *regiomontano* elite and the new Mexican state. The promotion of the passage of a federal labor code was consistent with the elite's determination to bring about a favorable, consistent pact with the state at the highest levels and to end the irritating, time-consuming problems involved in dealing with petty officials, shady bureaucrats, and uncompromising labor activists. Exasperated with the unpredictable whims of local officials, the elite bristled at the thought of Morones' grasping hands in the Mexican economy generally, and in the pockets, as it were, of Monterrey industrialists. The drive for a federal labor code, however, called for political connections, the cultivation of support among congressmen, and a sympathetic lobby within the highest circles of political decision making in Mexico. With increasing urgency, the Monterrey elite intensified the search for the means for national political influence.

The relations between *regiomontano* businessmen and government in the 1920s revealed the inconsistencies of state policies toward Mexican capital. The attempts of Obregón and Calles to balance probusiness measures with political necessities clashed at times with the singular interests of Monterrey's industrialists. The elite of Nuevo León pined for the centralized authority of the Porfiriato and its unambiguous stance toward capital. The incoherence of the postrevolutionary state on matters close to the concerns of *regiomontano* businessmen propelled their entry into politics. The aims of the elite were simple: a stable, procapitalist government that would reassure its local interests and that would provide a profitable context for its enterprises. But the new state found such a task less than simple, compelling the elite to take a hand directly in reaching its ends.

6. Elite and Society in the Postrevolutionary Era

I. On the evening of September 14, 1926, Luis G. Sada crowned the queen of the *fiestas patrias* with a tiara donated by the Cervecería Cuauhtémoc. The event took place before thousands of people at the main plaza of the city. The tiara, and the man who presented it, aptly symbolized the reestablishment and resilience of the social dominance of the elite over Monterrey.[1] Some changes had occurred in the wake of the revolutionary years, but the fundamental contours of *regiomontano* society remained intact as the powerful business families continued their reign. More importantly, the dominion of the Monterrey elite reinforced the persistent sense of mission, of special and unique responsibility for the welfare of the city, and, by extension, the nation. Competent managers, the businessmen of Monterrey wanted the city to reflect their certitude, efficacy, and propriety—an attitude akin to their capitalist counterparts elsewhere, particularly in the United States. In this respect, the nineteenth-century notion of progress endured in the minds of *regiomontano* entrepreneurs, and their desire to extend their view to Mexico endured as well.

The reconstitution of the *regiomontano* society after 1917 revealed the vestiges of the past, so intensely idealized by the elite. The forms of upper-class social life remained essentially the same. Marriages continued to be used as a means to augment financial power and status. Such marital arrangements maintained a pool of candidates from which aging patriarchs selected young captains to guide the family's fortunes. Clubs and activities persisted in their Porfirian mold as practices and routines of a prior era resumed, accompanied by the trappings of change: automobiles, radios, phonographs, and the like replaced carriages, military band concerts at the kiosk, and Sunday promenades. Yet, if the shape of social life had a Porfirian look, the characters involved had changed somewhat. New faces appeared in the most exclusive of elite gatherings, while certain families fell in social prominence. The Porfirian vehicles of social dominance reappeared, though refashioned. The newspaper *El Porvenir* became the conduit of the view of the bourgeoisie and provided a constant source of public visibility for the thoughts and daily life of the city's upper class. Public ceremony and pomp frequently remained in the hands of the elite: holidays, presidential arrivals, passing dignitaries, religious occasions, philanthropic duties, and civic events. Radio stations, movie houses, and fashion added to the means of emphasizing the exclusivity of the elite in the minds and eyes of the city's population.

But the hegemony of *regiomontano* businessmen was, of course, much more tangible and real for thousands of Monterrey workers. The treatment of employees of the city's largest industries underscored the paternalistic perception of employers that resonated throughout *regiomontano* society. Harmony between labor and capital—a favorite theme of the elite—found expression in the emphasis placed on the notion of order. Control permeated the facilities and services offered to workers; dominance pervaded the schemes and promotions of the elite for the improvement of the city for its residents.

The middle class of Monterrey continued voiceless and without confidence, finding solace in the ways of the wealthy and ambition in the search for social status. Mobility, as in the past, often mirrored ties with the businesses of the rich. The seeming disarray and venality of the local government bureaucracy magnified the impressiveness of the elite and discredited its critics, as the beliefs of businessmen found vindication in their wealth, sophistication, and life-style. In short, despite modifications in its composition, the *regiomontano* elite easily reestablished its hegemonic position over the city in the postrevolutionary period.

Nonetheless, Monterrey was not a mere image of the past, for Mexican society changed, however subtle and imperceptible the manifestations. New currents of thought and a visionary rhetoric often at odds with that of the elite punctuated Mexican life in the years following the revolution. At the center of the country especially, disquieting ideas stirred in the pronouncements of labor leaders, in the murals of idealistic artists, and in the cultural forms engendered by the passing of the old regime. The ideological congruence between the elite and the Porfiriato had failed to be renewed under the new state.[2] From Mexico City came troubling allusions to the redistribution of wealth, land, and power, frequently laced with apparent zeal and, at times, tangible effect. The Porfirian sense of concert between polity and businessmen often seemed lost in the residue of governmental rhetoric, inconsistent policies, and the incompetence of the new order.

The conduct of "revolutionary" generals, governors, and federal authorities served to heighten the elite's sense of moral superiority and disdain for the undesirable changes ushered in by the new state. If disorder marked their political and economic preoccupations, *regiomontano* businessmen became increasingly concerned with social order, discipline, and morality. The glorification of the past, tradition, and family represented an ideological translation of their loss of assurance within the new order. Members of the Monterrey elite saw themselves not only as guardians of Mexico's future, but as keepers of a glorious and better past. In charting their course, Nuevo León's entrepreneurs continued to look backward for inspiration, undeterred by the inadequacies of old formulas in coping with the realities of the present. But their attitude, imbued with a deep righteousness and unambiguous confidence, endowed their views and efforts with unassailable certainty. Eventually, the assurance of the elite's vision required an ideological push of national proportions that paralleled, as it turned out, its political mobilization.

II.   The reconstruction of the Casino Monterrey in 1922 signaled the rebuilding of the city's social establishment.[3] A decade of strife showed in the appearance of the crowd that gathered to celebrate the opening of the new building. The young men and women of the Sociedad Terpsícore had grown older, taking their place in the 1920s within adult circles of the casino crowd. In turn, young members of the wealthy formed new clubs, organized new routines, and established their own types of pecking orders. Offspring and relatives of the old elite families increasingly composed the membership of the Casino Monterrey; their wealth and standing derived from the businesses established prior to 1910 by fathers, fathers-in-law, uncles, godfathers, and older brothers. A passing of reins, as it were, was taking place. The presidency of the exclusive club passed from José A. Muguerza to Antonio Muguerza, and to José E. Rivero, who continued the traditional tie between the casino and the family of Valentín Rivero.[4]

This second generation supplanted the venerable men of the Porfirian era and their spouses. The founders of the city's industries were now increasingly surrounded by people of derived wealth rather than makers of companies and profits. The previous exclusivity at the top of *regiomontano* society relaxed to some extent as families extended networks and created new offshoots. In this respect, the familial web of the elite widened, but, in addition, became more dense, with close-knit fractions at times forming from the tight circle of marriages and relationships among a small number of families.[5] (See figure 4.) Hence, the casino witnessed an enlargement of its base of membership that embraced the thickening and proliferation of elite ties.

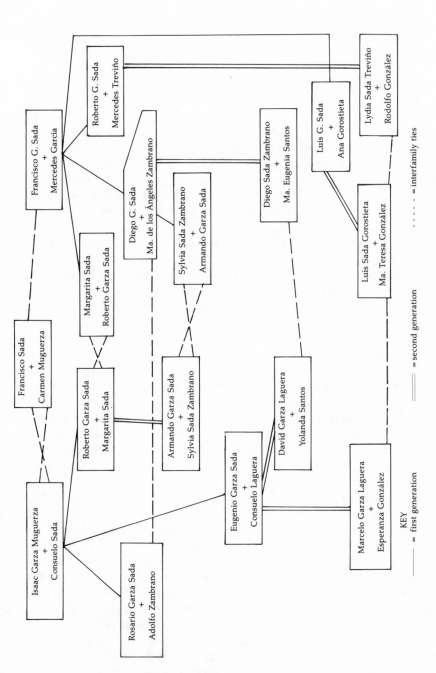

Figure 4. Garza-Sada Interfamily Connections (selected examples)

KEY

—— = first generation

＝ = second generation

- - - - = interfamily ties

As if to demarcate *los hombres de empresa* —the true entrepreneurs— from the others, a new club appeared that brought together the movers of the business community, the cupola of *regiomontano* society: the Rotary Club of Monterrey. It was both business group and social club, and it provided the key men of Monterrey a place to gather to discuss business and to interact socially. Significantly, this new organization had an American connection.[6] In fact, the link stemmed in large part from the schooling of many of its members. Educated in the United States, and influenced by the conservatism of the Rotary Club movement, the business elite of Monterrey found the club an ideal format for creating an inner circle within the larger network of upper-class social and economic relations, such as the Casino Monterrey and the Cámara de Comercio, Industria y Minería (henceforth referred to as the Cámara).

The casino counted over two hundred members by the middle 1920s, swelled severalfold at important social occasions by wives, children, adolescents, and escorts. The Rotary Club, in contrast, was fundamentally male in its orientation, with about fifty members. In its relatively rare social functions, admission was usually confined to members, and their wives on some occasions. The ostentatious openness of Casino affairs was absent at the gatherings of the Rotary Club. The key men of the Rotary Club were the major figures of the elite and successful, effective entrepreneurs in the 1920s—the younger counterparts of the patriarchs who had founded the city's industries a generation earlier. These men included Roberto G. Sada of the Vidriera, Luis G. Sada of the Cervecería, Joel Rocha of the Salinas y Rocha department stores, Manuel Barragán of the Topo Chico soda works, Pablo Salas y López of Cementos Hidalgo, Arturo Padilla of Casa Calderón, and others, as well as relative newcomers such as Emilio Azcárraga, who managed the local Ford dealership in Monterrey.[7]

The prominence of the Rotary Club in the city's life was assured by the economic prowess of its membership. Moreover, the editors of Monterrey's major newspapers, *El Porvenir* and *El Sol,* were among the members of the club, and they conveniently provided an effective source for the club to make known its views. In fact, through the editors, the Rotary Club had a column of sorts virtually every week in the summary of its meetings. Newspapers therefore registered the visitors, meetings, banquets, speeches, and activities of the club, including extensive photos on several occasions. The Sunday supplements of *El Porvenir,* especially, often carried articles on the functions and luminaries associated with the Rotary Club.[8] Through Rotary Clubs elsewhere, the opinions of the Monterrey clique were echoed outside of the city, including Saltillo, Torreón, and Guadalajara. Business ties between Monterrey and the Laguna district, for example, surfaced in the club as well: José Ortíz, for instance, the local representative of the Banco de la Laguna, served as president of the club for a time (as well as for the Casino Monterrey). And, on occasion, *regiomontano rotarios* made junkets to Saltillo on weekend caravans (usually organized by Emilio Azcárraga). In Saltillo, they were met by their *rotario* counterparts from Coahuila. Thus, at a regional level, the Rotary Club functioned as a network of a select group of businessmen who shared a certain outlook of Mexico, and of themselves.[9]

The exclusivity of the Rotary Club also demarcated its members from the larger membership of the Cámara de Comercio, Industria y Minería de Nuevo León. Although the leadership of the Cámara normally fell into the hands of the elite, members of the organization included many men whose holdings paled in comparison to the size, wealth, and economic importance of the enterprises of the premier industrialists of the city. In this sense, the Rotary Club functioned as an inner circle within the Cámara whose interests, social ties, and economic links set it apart from the rest of the organization. The domination of the elite in business matters found expression socially and ideologically through various means.

The legitimacy and weight of the views of members of the elite emanated from their positions as officers of the Cámara, of the Rotary Club, of the casino, or of any number of civic commissions or committees. *El Porvenir*, for example, in 1926 dedicated an entire series to the rise of the city's major industries, with capsule biographies of their owners. The intent of the articles was to showcase the *hombres de empresa* whose entrepreneurial skills had "made" Monterrey the industrial center of the country.[10] The men who were the subjects of the series were invariably members of the Rotary Club.

Moreover, the businessmen of Monterrey supported the publication of a staunchly procapitalist magazine, *Actividad*. The editor of the magazine for several years was Manuel Barragán, a Rotary Club member, manager of the Coca-Cola bottling plant in Monterrey, and future editor in the late 1920s of the Mexico City newspaper *Excelsior*. (He would also serve as president of the Cámara de Comercio, Industria y Minería de Nuevo León.) The monthly publication contained primarily inspirational articles, often by foreigners in translation, that sang the praises of capitalism and the woes of socialism. Not surprisingly, Americans frequently authored the pieces that appeared in the magazine. Distributed primarily in the northern part of the country, *Actividad* articulated the mindset of the Monterrey elite along a wide range of issues. More importantly, the publication reflected the willingness of the elite to take the initiative in the promulgation of probusiness views, and, by implication, in the promotion of antigovernment tracts.[11]

The idealization of the past often surfaced in the views of Monterrey entrepreneurs, a time when they reigned over the city unfettered by the obtrusiveness of the central government. This kind of nostalgia frequently doted on the memory of Bernardo Reyes.[12] The "golden age" image of the Reyes years made explicit the political and economic ideal for Monterrey's businessmen. And, as if to emulate the past—for pragmatic reasons both political and economic—the leaders of the *regiomontano* elite assiduously courted the key *caudillo* of the region, Juan Andreu Almazán.

In this regard, Almazán (then Sáenz after 1927) was a frequent recipient of Rotary Club attention. In addition, the Casino Monterrey often seconded such gestures with its own forms of praise and recognition. Almazán in particular enjoyed the high social life of Monterrey, often mixing with the wealthy at the stream of social activities that emanated from the casino. Indeed, Almazán's treatment contained telling similarities to that accorded to Bernardo Reyes. Like Reyes, Almazán headed civic committees patronized by the city's business establishment, such as the 16th of September celebration of 1926. The Chamber of Commerce, presided over that year by Luis G. Sada, enthusiastically welcomed Almazán's call for industrialists and merchants to lend a hand to the festivities. Sada subsequently joined Almazán on the organizing committee along with Roberto G. Sada, Isaac Garza Sada, and other stellar members of the business community, including Emilio Azcárraga (who was in charge of the car racing committee).[13]

Almazán's popularity with the *regiomontano* elite stemmed in large part from his interest in building his own wealth through various ventures. In this respect, the elite found in Almazán a kindred spirit—that is, a capitalist one.[14] Finally, Almazán's military training and demeanor appealed to the elite's notion of discipline and order. The practical necessity of Almazán as an instrument of the elite's political and economic interests merged with the elite ideal of the type of man to take the reins of government authority.

The search for a new Bernardo Reyes expressed the persistence of the elite's view of its own superiority—that it knew what was best for Monterrey, and, by extension, for the rest of the country. The self-righteousness of Nuevo León's entrepreneurs anchored their paternalistic attitude toward Mexican society. This sense of paternalism was perhaps best understood in their rationalization of labor-capital relations.

III.   In February 1925, *El Porvenir* editorialized that unemployment stemmed in large part from the laziness of Mexican workers. Indeed, the editor went on to say that government, rather than helping workers, should do more for private enterprise since it provided the main source of employment.[15] The comment by the Monterrey newspaper, and similar observations on other occasions, revealed the underlying attitudes of businessmen toward their workers. The constant calls for labor-capital cooperation by *regiomontano* employers belied their near contempt for Mexican labor. *Regiomontano* capitalists exploited their advantages to extend their paternalistic control over their workers and to minimize the introduction of an independent labor movement in Monterrey. Nonetheless, the crude darwinism of the Porfiriato diminished, and, in a sense, the elite struck a different note to blunt the consciousness of workers and to rationalize the use of paternalistic controls.

Solidarity between labor and capital for the national welfare took on added importance in the rhetoric of Nuevo León's entrepreneurs.[16] Strikes, boycotts, slowdowns, picket lines, and other forms of work actions undermined the nation's drive for economic reconstruction in the newfound business philosophy of the *regiomontano* elite. Employer and employee unity, Monterrey industrialists argued frequently, provided the best means to bolster the recovery of the Mexican economy. Cooperation between classes became a manifestation of nationalism, a contribution to the collective welfare of the country. The singular emphasis on the entrepreneur as the motor of progress of the Porfirian years softened to include workers in the altered vision of businessmen in the 1920s. In this regard, Monterrey's employers took a page from the American experience with welfare capitalism to further their practiced forms of paternalism.[17] At the turn of the century in the United States, as the American historian Robert Wiebe has noted, "experiments in welfare capitalism, looking toward a more refined control over the labor force, multiplied each year."[18]

More so than in the past, the Monterrey elite viewed business as a machine in which every part had an important function. With a technician's sensibility, the *regiomontano* industrialist conceived labor problems as an organic dysfunction that needed fixing, or replacement. Workers, as part of the machine, required regular servicing in order to avoid breakdown. Treated in such a way, workers rendered good, loyal service. For the Monterrey elite, such a view was "scientific management," a term derived from the famous book on management by the American Frederick W. Taylor. In this light, it was not surprising that the Fundidora published the book in Spanish and promoted its principles to major political leaders, including Calles and Sáenz.[19]

The Taylor book and the elite's promotion of Taylorism reflected a decidedly American cast to the elite's thinking on business and

government relations generally, and labor-capital relations in particular. The American connection supplanted to a large extent the German influence of the Porfirian era. The speculative fever of the 1920s
in the United States and its prosperity served to confirm the soundness of American enterprise and its principles. The schooling of
many of the elite contributed to the American tone of their views. A
key spokesman of the elite in the postrevolutionary period, Luis G.
Sada, was a graduate of MIT; Roberto G. Sada graduated from the
University of Michigan. These men and their American-trained
counterparts accelerated the American tilt to the elite's political and
economic thought. The offspring of Isaac Garza and Francisco Sada,
among others, were comfortable and familiar with the basic tenets of
American conservatism. Thus, the paternalism fostered in the Porfirian period was endorsed by the movement in American corpora-
tions toward greater efficiency, productivity, and profits through
personnel management, "business administration," and similar notions. "Employers began to study personnel problems, consider
devices for cutting fatigue and improving work conditions," as one
American historian has concluded, "and launched in some cases
upon their own welfare and pension programs and profit-sharing
schemes."[20] The labor practices of the Monterrey elite therefore
found sanction in the success of American companies and in the
ideological underpinnings of American economic thought that produced over 240 books on business management between 1900 and
1910.[21]

In the minds of *regiomontanos*, Monterrey supplied an example for
the rest of the country that pointed the way toward modernity and
economic progress. Hence, the labor practices of the elite acquired a
nationalistic twist that responded by design, or ironically paralleled,
the nationalism of the postrevolutionary period. In the case of Monterrey, labor-capital unity was translated into a program of labor paternalism whose material rewards were magnified severalfold by
the bleakness of the daily life of the Mexican worker. The exodus of
thousands of Mexican workers to the United States in the 1920s gave
oblique testimony to the effectiveness of the elite's offering of picnics,
parties, and paid vacations to employees.[22]

IV. The American influence in the thinking of the elite was not confined to the leading men of the city. By the 1930s, the attraction of
the United States had prompted increasing numbers of Monterrey's
wealthiest families to send their daughters, as well as their sons, to
American colleges and universities (usually religious ones, primarily
Catholic). Going-away parties for the daughters of the elite punctuated

the society pages of newspapers every September and January as they returned to schools in the United States after summer and Christmas vacations. By the late 1920s, elite females easily and with increasing familiarity seconded the American viewpoints of their male counterparts. In more obvious terms, women were also visible conduits of American fashions, fads, and tastes. Sunday supplements in the city's newspapers often carried photographs of the wealthy young women of Monterrey in their American or, less often, European best.[23]

The youth of the elite also added to the American flavor of the elite. American music, especially jazz, was featured frequently in the gatherings of the rich young *regiomontanos*. Fueled by the proximity of Monterrey to American radio stations, and reinforced by recurring visits to the United States by the city's wealthy, American popular culture penetrated the social life of the elite.[24] Moreover, the American presence in Monterrey was given greater visibility and legitimacy through the apparent admiration of members of the elite for their counterparts across the border.

The elite, however, still clung to its own sense of nationalism that contained the remnants of a Porfirian outlook. *Regiomontano* businessmen continued to define achievement, progress, and their own sense of self-worth in foreign terms—and, especially after 1917, American ones. In the early 1920s, the American-style advertising of Monterrey enterprises persisted in its emphasis on technical advancement, cleanliness, and modern equipment in the case of the Cervecería, for instance, production capacity and technological modernity in the case of the Fundidora.[25] The patriotic overtones of *hecho en México* (made in Mexico) would appear only gradually in Monterrey business advertising. In odd, and perhaps defiant, irony, the Cervecería employed a Spanish conquistadorlike character for its promotional announcements and eschewed Indianist symbols despite the company's name. Only later, in the 1930s, would the Cervecería utilize popular, nationalist cultural symbols in its logos and advertisements and push its products under the banner of "buy Mexican."[26] Nonetheless, the elite of Monterrey maintained the use of foreign points of reference to gauge its own success and, by extension, to judge Mexican society. Thus, in a fundamental way, the upper class of Monterrey was at odds with the nationalist currents of postrevolutionary Mexico and found much of the new order's cultural rhetoric and expression contemptible if not pathetic.[27]

In this light, successful businessmen merited nationalistic praise for their ability to carry out the tenets of free enterprise as defined by foreign capitalists, especially in the United States. The identification of national interest with industrial success, therefore, nourished the elite's view of patriotism.[28] Not unlike the Porfirian era, one family particularly exemplified the merger of progress and patriotism: the Garza-Sadas.

Within the reconstitution of the elite in the 1920s, the Garza-Sadas solidified their position at the apex of *regiomontano* society. The social ascendancy of the Cervecería clan stemmed from several causes. First, the comparatively greater financial success of the Cervecería and the Vidriera in the 1920s pushed their owners to the forefront of their business counterparts in the city. Second, the presence of other major enterprises paled in comparison to the powerful industrial plants of the Garza-Sada clan. Their sole rival in this regard, the Fundidora, had its ownership based in Mexico City; its well-known, brilliant leader, Adolfo Prieto, resided there as well. Like the Fundidora, foreign companies had their managers present in Monterrey, but their social prominence was easily eclipsed by the Cervecería group. Third, the Garza-Sada family found within the family highly capable, effective leaders, particularly Luis G. Sada and Roberto G. Sada, who outshone their male peers. Fourth, the Garza-Sada group actively cultivated its social power and influence through participation in a number of endeavors, such as civic celebrations, beautification projects, toy drives, Red Cross fund-raising campaigns, educational projects, roadbuilding, and private philanthropy.[29] Such gestures not only expanded on activities in the past, but also imitated calls of American corporate leaders, such as Andrew Carnegie, for businessmen to use their largesse for the welfare of the masses. In this regard, the women of the Garza-Sada clan, like other elite females, were important adjuncts to the social dominance of their husbands, fathers, and older brothers. With a characteristic sense of social obligation, they actively and conspicuously participated in the civic and religious life of the city. Elite women spearheaded Christmas toy drives for poor children, supported church events of all kinds, and patronized the fine arts, bringing "culture" to Monterrey in various forms, such as operas, music recitals, and dramatic performances.[30]

The prominence of the *regiomontano* elite, in particular the Garza-Sadas, at the local level increasingly extended to the national scene by the conclusion of the 1920s. The success of their companies, their involvement in national political issues, their links with Mexico City economic interests, and their ties with Mexico City publications, especially the newspaper *Excelsior*,[31] pushed the Garza-Sada clan into the national limelight and enhanced its standing in Monterrey social circles. And within the resurgent national bourgeoisie, the connections generated by the Cervecería-Vidriera network elevated the Garza-Sadas to nationally recognized spokesmen for Mexican capital. Thus, in social as well as economic terms, the Garza-Sadas through the 1920s consolidated their position at the top of *regiomontano* society with few if any rivals.

The wealth, success, and cohesiveness of the Garza-Sadas reinforced their social presence in the city; the family name evoked images of vast holdings, extravagant homes, exotic vacations, luxurious possessions, and enormous power.[32] The pinched, sober face of Luis G. Sada—somehow more appropriate to a small shopkeeper—was in contrast to his family's image, and the serious, quiet, yet intense personality of Roberto G. Sada was even more so. Nonetheless, the image remained, permeating the fabric of *regiomontano* society—testimony to the restored dominance of the city by its native elite, among whom the Garza-Sadas were undisputed leaders.

V.   The pattern of marriages among the Garza-Sadas manifested the closed nature of the elite. Still, those outside the circle of the wealthy continued to look toward the residents of the Obispado section of the city with a mixture of envy, admiration, and hope.

The middle sectors of *regiomontano* society remained largely fixed on achieving material status that approximated that of the upper class. The overwhelming economic preponderance of the city's major industries sustained the decidedly Porfirian cast to mobility in Monterrey. Two major avenues existed: association with one of the key companies, banks, or commercial houses, or a lucrative niche in government service. The social polarization that marked Monterrey prior to 1917 endured, with the city's middle class squeezed between a powerful group of entrepreneurs and a large, expanding working class.[33] As a result, members of the city's middling society seemed intent on distancing themselves from workers and/or their own working-class origins. In this respect, Monterrey's middle sectors reflected the situation found in much of the rest of the country. As one historian of Mexico has concluded, the Mexican middle class in the 1920s lived "in a precarious condition but with a certain culture, and whose entire social psychology was oriented to a struggle without quarter for power and material advantages."[34]

The "precarious condition" of the middle sectors mirrored the economic uncertainty and political tensions intrinsic to the 1920s. In the case of Monterrey specifically, the relatively small and vulnerable middle class found few incentives to challenge the power and prestige of the elite. Professionals of various kinds sought attractive salaries by servicing the needs of the city's upper classes. And even here, the offspring and relatives of the elite often circumscribed such possibilities as they became doctors, lawyers, engineers, and architects. Thus, for many of the middle class, serving the city's large working class was the alternative, no doubt heightening the fears of slipping down the social scale and thus providing a constant incentive to find the "break" into quick avenues of status and wealth. Finally, given the fluidity of government in Monterrey and its abject performance, the bureaucracy lost much of its attractiveness as a means to wealth and position, which, once again, redoubled the social significance of the private sector of the city. As for small businessmen, dwarfed by their much larger counterparts, they seemed to find satisfaction in rubbing elbows with the elite in the meetings of the Cámara de Comercio, currying favorable loans, or seeking jobs for relatives.[35]

As in the past, opportunities occurred for a few to acquire easy wealth and prestige. Virgilio Garza, Jr., represented an example of a member of the middle class who gained access to elite circles, in his case, primarily through marriage. Born in 1900 in Monterrey, Garza returned to the city in the early 1920s to practice law after attending law school in Mexico City. His legal skills soon won him a position with businesses that needed an articulate, forceful representative in labor disputes involving the arbitration court. His superlative defense of the Cementos Hidalgo plant before the labor tribunal in December 1924 attracted the attention of businessmen, who were always on the lookout, it seemed, for talented young men. As a result, Garza's career took a spectacular turn when he became the chief counsel of the Cervecería Cuauhtémoc before the labor court in September 1925. In June 1925, Virgilio Garza married Rosario González Sada, and thereby entered the familial network of the Garza-Sadas. The wedding reception took place, appropriately, at the home of Isaac Garza Sada. From that time forward, Garza in effect became the legal counsel for the Monterrey elite, appearing constantly on the side of Monterrey interests at important meetings. As the 1920s wore on, it would be Virgilio Garza, Jr., who was pressed into service to defend *regiomontano* interests in issues involving complex legal questions. In return, Garza commanded enormous fees, and he parlayed his connections into lucrative investments. Eventually, Garza appeared on the board of directors of over fifty companies in Monterrey. By the time he was thirty years old, Garza was a fixture in elite social gatherings. In this regard, Garza provided a rare example of a man of middling society who climbed to the pinnacle of *regiomontano* society and realized the aspirations that many in the middle class had for themselves.[36]

VI.   The social dominance of the elite over Monterrey nourished its long-held sense of superiority. *Regiomontano* businessmen envisioned themselves in their industries—their productivity, efficiency, and technical progress reflecting the acumen of their owners. Monterrey stood in obvious contrast to the apparent disorder, corruption, and ineffectiveness of the state. The workings of the nascent Mexican state vindicated, in the eyes of the elite, the negative perception of government in the postrevolutionary era. Reminiscent of their American counterparts in the late nineteenth century, Monterrey's capitalists sustained the theory that "government maintained order, conducted some public services at minimum cost, and above all did nothing to disrupt the laws of free competition."[37] The meddlesome presence of the Mexican state, in labor relations for example, deviated from the precepts of enterprise and as a consequence invited economic and social catastrophe from the standpoint of *regiomontano* businessmen. From their perspective, economic troubles inevitably led to the doorstep of errant government policies rather than the inadequacies of a capitalist economy. Monterrey's entrepreneurs therefore found it easy to cast themselves as defenders of a fundamental law of nature, of human progress. The darwinist elements of the Porfiriato continued in the minds of the *regiomontano* elite. Monterrey, in this sense, was an example of those principles upheld by its native capitalists. It was their responsibility to make sure that Monterrey would continue to be the example for the rest of the country.[38]

For the elite of Nuevo León, the new Mexican state endangered the progress of Monterrey and, by extension, threatened the model city created by the vision and hard work of its businessmen. Such a self-serving view reflected the narrow-mindedness of the *regiomontano* upper class—an insularity that had survived the Porfiriato and nurtured the inflated self-perceptions of the elite. This attitude produced a persistent defensiveness on the part of entrepreneurs toward the state, which often produced vitriolic criticism of government actions, laced with cataclysmic consequences for the economic welfare of the nation, and for Monterrey in particular.[39] The *regiomontano* business establishment was quick to score government policies deemed inappropriate or misguided and granted the state few accomplishments. The distrust, if not the disdain, for the men of the new state always hovered near the surface of the demeanor of members of the Monterrey elite.[40] But they were practical men, and they realized as the years passed that their hold on Monterrey was best secured through a similar grasp of access to the key sources of political power.

In the Porfiriato, the local hegemony of the elite was based in part on the muted presence of Bernardo Reyes and on the assurance of a government in concert with the fundamental beliefs of the *regiomontano* businessmen. After 1910, government had taken on a different, ambiguous, and at times sinister form that deprived the elite of its sense of order, of control. As a result, the elite turned inward, using its local resources to recoup its economic hold and to retain its grip on *regiomontano* society.[41] Nonetheless, the passive assumption of Porfirian privilege of the past was no longer possible with the rise of the new state. This rival presence, however, compelled the elite to a greater degree of cohesiveness that was reproduced in the increasingly explicit ideological thrust of Monterrey businessmen into Mexican politics.[42] Given their experiences during the revolution, and in the subsequent decade with the new state, the Garza-Sadas not surprisingly took a central role in the reassertion of the elite's dominance of the city. It was a role that prepared them to lead *regiomontano* capitalists in their quest to extend their power beyond the confines of Monterrey.

7. A Fateful Time: The Monterrey Elite and the Mexican State, 1929-1931

I. On July 1, 1928, Álvaro Obregón was elected once again as president of Mexico. He immediately began preparations to assume office six months later; but, within a few days of his victory, he was assassinated. His death convulsed the country's political life. The fragile stability of the political structure threatened to unravel as various factions and interest groups vied to get the upper hand in the selection of a successor. Yet, for Monterrey's businessmen, Obregón's death provided an unexpected, momentary opportunity to acquire direct access to national political power. The hopes of the *regiomontano* elite turned, however, into bitter disappointment; a bitterness deepened by the extent and brevity of its aspirations.

The assassination of Obregón led to two key events for *regiomontano* capitalists. First, the killing of the president-elect elevated Aarón Sáenz to a preeminent position as presidential contender. For the businessmen of Nuevo León, Sáenz' seemingly assured path to the presidency offered them an unparalleled opportunity to wield national influence through the former governor of Nuevo León. Second, Obregón's death precipitated a crisis in the relations between the state and organized labor, that is, Luis N. Morones. The labor leader's presidential hopes, suddenly rekindled by the assassination, were just as quickly extinguished by the immediate political storm generated by Obregón's murder. Eventually Calles was forced to accept a decisive break between Morones' CROM and the federal government. In order to sustain labor support, the state pushed for the codification of Article 123.

In both cases, the promise of favorable changes for Monterrey capitalists became instead a period of jolting political reversals. In March 1929, Aarón Sáenz lost his bid for the presidential nomination of the newly formed, Calles-dominated Partido Nacional Revolucionario (PNR). And, in July 1929, Emilio Portes Gil, provisional president of Mexico, introduced a codification scheme that fell far short of the expectations of *regiomontano* capitalists. The relations between the industrialists of Nuevo León and the government, seemingly on the mend, turned into bitter disappointment. To their chagrin, the man at the center of their frustrations was Plutarco Elías Calles, ex-president and master of a political era that would take his name, *el maximato*.

For his own purposes, Calles undertook actions that damaged his relations with capitalists generally, and the businessmen of Monterrey specifically. The betrayal of Sáenz by Calles at the PNR nominating convention in March 1929 represented, in the minds of the *regiomontano* elite, a biting confirmation of the perception of Mexican politicians as corrupt and self-seeking. The codification proposals of Portes Gil, on the heels of the Sáenz affair, became a culminating blow, forcing a direct response to the Callista regime from the businessmen of Nuevo León. Moreover, from the perspective of the *regiomontano* elite, the political maneuvering by Calles and his cohort imperiled the economic well-being of the country. In this sense, self-interest and patriotism were made one by the industrialists of Monterrey. Regardless of the state's attempts to pacify disappointed businessmen, for the Monterrey elite, the painful disillusionment of the events of 1929 persisted, a disaffection heightened by the eventual passage in 1931 of a federal labor code over the strenuous objections of the Monterrey group.

The formation in 1929 of the *regiomontano*-led Confederación Patronal de la República Mexicana (COPARMEX) signaled the resolve of the Nuevo León elite to play a more forceful role in the political economy of Mexico. Headed by the Garza-Sadas and their close allies, the businessmen of Monterrey pressed for a means to resist the state as the sole arbiter of the nation's political and economic fortunes. The die was cast for the eventual confrontations with the state during the regime of former Callista Lázaro Cárdenas.

II. At the exclusive Café Colón in Mexico City, on the night of November 17, 1928, Aarón Sáenz was the man of honor at a dinner reception given by the elite of Monterrey. Buoyed by the anticipation of a Sáenz presidency, the gathering featured several speeches extolling the virtues and qualities of the ex-governor of Nuevo León. Indeed, Sáenz was accorded the greatest compliment by *regiomontano* businessmen when José Elizondo, speaking for the group, compared Sáenz to Bernardo Reyes. In turn, Sáenz emphasized his desire to extend his policies in Nuevo León to the rest of the country. Nonetheless, one speaker was compelled, tellingly, to deny that Sáenz would be an instrument of the businessmen of Monterrey. But the subheading of one newspaper article describing the reception underscored the importance of the event: "the high political significance of the banquet."[1]

The men from Monterrey had reason to be in a festive mood. Since the assassination of Obregón in July, Sáenz' political ascent had continued unabated. Evidence mounted every day that pointed to his successful bid for the presidency; telegrams, newspaper announcements, and proclamations by sundry groups and organizations trumpeted his candidacy. Playing the gracious candidate, Sáenz through the fall maintained a cautious facade as he maneuvered to receive the presidential nod.[2] In early November, he left the governorship of Nuevo León to be a member of the executive committee of the new political party, the PNR. And, a month later, he left his PNR post, allegedly to avoid accusations of fixing his own nomination at the PNR convention slated for March 1929.[3] Political observers shared the same view that Sáenz would be the next president of Mexico. Confident of his position as front-runner, Sáenz in mid-December stated his intention to abide by the selection of the PNR. The statement by Sáenz was self-serving given the context at the time, but it would be a source of bitter irony for the former governor of Nuevo León.[4]

On December 26, 1928, Pascual Ortíz Rubio arrived in Mexico from his post as Mexican ambassador to Brazil. At the invitation of Portes Gil, and with the apparent assent of Calles, the unknown man from Michoacán was informed of his candidacy for president. Overnight, an opponent for Sáenz had been created. Among those who pledged his support was Lázaro Cárdenas. Within days of his interview with Calles in late December, Ortíz Rubio began his campaign. The fact that he had come from political limbo with a record exceptional only in its obscurity should have been a warning to Sáenz and his supporters that there were deep political stirrings.[5]

Nonetheless, on the eve of the convention, Sáenz remained confident. A preconvention delegate count showed him with a comfortable margin of victory. Sáenz departed from Mexico City to the site of the conclave in Querétaro fully expecting to arrive in triumph. Instead, Sáenz was stunned by the news on March 1 that the delegates from Yucatán, Coahuila, and Chiapas—all of them previously pledged to Sáenz—refused to register their support for him. In addition, the credentials of numerous Saencistas were disallowed and their registration as delegates therefore denied. Shocked, Sáenz issued a statement that blamed certain members of congress for the machinations against him, carefully avoiding condemnation of Calles. Upon his return to Mexico City, Sáenz attempted to present a combative, threatening stance, yet he continued to avoid criticism of Calles.[6] Indeed, the fight was over before it began. The next day, March 3, José Gonzalo Escobar led a group of military men who rebelled against the federal government. Sáenz, forced to make a choice, decided against joining the rebels. Robbed of any momentum by the rebellion, and by Sáenz' decision "to put himself at the orders of the established government," the Saencista presidential movement evaporated.[7]

At the time, the betrayal of Sáenz by the PNR leadership was a surprise, but, in retrospect, the move was not entirely unpredictable. The Sáenz candidacy afforded Calles a cover while he solidified his position in the wake of Obregón's death. The Obregonistas understandably welcomed Sáenz, given his close ties to their assassinated leader; he had been Obregón's campaign manager. Moreover, the suspicions of the Obregonistas were quieted by the business links between Calles and Sáenz as well as their familial ties. Thus, Sáenz seemed to be the ideal bridge between the dashed hopes of the Obregonistas and the Callista regime. The Sáenz campaign and its early success gave Calles time to maneuver, to find a candidate whose political base stemmed directly from Calles.[8] There were risks in the Calles strategy, but the *jefe máximo* had cause for assurance, not the least of which was Sáenz himself.

Calles was apparently convinced that in a political crunch Sáenz would not revolt. The latter's loyalty to Calles was understandable. It was Calles who had made him governor of Nuevo León, who had favored him with profitable business deals, and who had appointed him to prestigious posts. Furthermore, Calles assumed, it seems correctly, that Sáenz' ambitiousness would make him an unlikely source of opposition. Sáenz was an opportunist, most observers agreed, who was willing if not eager to use his position to enhance his own wealth and social standing. In short, Sáenz was a weak man, dependent on men like Calles and Obregón for his socioeconomic rise and political weight, beholden to the political order that nurtured his lucrative career. Sáenz would not revolt, nor join the Escobaristas, Calles gambled, forcing many of his followers to concede defeat. The promotion of Sáenz' candidacy, inflated by Calles' ostensible approval, precluded a search for other alternatives for many in the Obregonista camp. Calles succeeded in making important elements of the Obregonistas invest their political fortunes in the feckless, grasping Sáenz. As for others, less devoted adherents, Calles counted on their greed to still their complaints. The Sáenz candidacy, like the Escobar rebellion, was squashed by the astute political engineering of Calles and his allies.[9]

The weaknesses of Sáenz' character anchored Calles' ploy at the PNR convention. And those same weaknesses, in fact, had facilitated the elite's exploitation of Sáenz as governor. If only inadvertently, Calles had roped the *regiomontanos* along as well, their confidence in Sáenz' victory swelled by the assumption of Calles' support for his *compadre*. And, it appears, the *regiomontanos* pinned a great deal of their hope for a different political and economic order on Sáenz' occupation of the presidential chair. The banquet for Sáenz at the Café Colón had been an expression of the elite's realization, at long last, of a new version of Bernardo Reyes. The abrupt fall of Sáenz' presidential stock was no less stunning to the elite of Monterrey than to Sáenz himself. Crestfallen, bewildered by the sudden turn of events, *regiomontano* businessmen attributed their near-miss defeat to Calles' political cunning.[10]

At the opening of the PNR convention, as Sáenz voiced empty accusations in Mexico City, Pérez Treviño warned the assembly of the right in Mexico, of reactionaries ever alert to subvert the accomplishments and goals of the revolution.[11] Years later, Portes Gil, among others, sustained the view that Sáenz had been unacceptable to the PNR leadership in 1929 because of his ties to *la reacción*, to the conservative businessmen of Monterrey.[12] The charges against Sáenz, then and later, were intended to discredit the governor of Nuevo León and to justify the self-serving actions of the Callistas at Querétaro in March 1929. Calles and his cohorts used Sáenz to extend their own power—indistinguishable from the motives of the men from Monterrey.

III. In May 1929, as the Escobar rebellion ended, Joel Rocha called upon businessmen to participate more forcefully in local and national politics.[13] Rocha's call reflected the disappointment of March 1929 that had spurred the elite to forge an alliance, based on businessmen, to duel with the state. As *Excelsior* echoed the need for an opposition party, *El Porvenir* confirmed the wisdom of Rocha's remarks.[14] If Mexican businessmen were wary of the call by Monterrey's capitalists, an impetus for a businessmen's alliance was provided in July 1929, when Portes Gil announced his plan to push for the codification of Article 123.[15]

The effort to design a federal labor code by the state supplied *regiomontano* industrialists with an opportunity to form a coalition within the private sector to define the state's role in capital-labor relations. In this endeavor, the codification issue propelled the Monterrey elite to the forefront of the organization of Mexican capital. In fact, the vigorous leadership of the elite against the labor legislation served to differentiate certain fractions within the Mexican private sector. In this respect, the codification issue and its outcomes gave shape to the ambiguous political contours of Mexican capital and put into relief the distinct role of the Monterrey group in the relationship between the state and the Mexican bourgeoisie.

The codification of Article 123 had been a recurrent question in Mexican politics throughout the 1920s. Without a uniform federal labor code, officials at the state and municipal level interpreted the provisions of the constitutional article in a variety of ways, if at all. Implementation and enforcement, therefore, were inconsistent and a source of irritation to workers and employers alike.[16] In Nuevo León, the intermittent conflicts between government officials and Monterrey businessmen at times revolved around the unpredictability of labor matters, leading employers to argue for the establishment of a uniform labor code. Indeed, on various occasions, *regiomontano* businessmen had called for the codification of Article 123 in a manner that would lend "stability" to capital-labor relations and that would contribute to the economic development of the country.[17]

Labor leaders, notably Morones, dealt with the question warily since codification offered advantages as well as dangers for the CROM. Given his political strength, especially in certain states, Morones was understandably reluctant to force the issue. With Morones as secretary of industry, commerce, and labor in the Calles administration, codification presented a possible thicket of problems, including the possibility that labor's (i.e., CROM's) power would be diminished. Morones was not unaware of his enemies within the labor movement as well as in the private sector. If implemented honestly, the provisions of a federal labor code on union representation, for instance, held the potential for rival groups to oust the CROM from its dominant position. Finally, in those areas of CROM weakness, codification threatened to preclude any inroads by his labor organization. Thus, Morones' lack of enthusiasm for pushing a federal labor code reflected the uncertain consequences of such legislation for his organization. Without assurances of CROM's ability to control the writing of the code, Morones skirted the problem.[18] Businessmen, including *regiomontanos,* ironically pushed for codification as a means to lessen Morones' grip on labor matters. The meetings held to discuss the issue, however, failed to produce meaningful results in 1925, 1926, and 1928 as each side jockeyed for the upper hand in the writing of a legislative proposal.[19]

In the latter year, with the conclusion of Calles' second term in office drawing near, presidential politics gave the labor code question a greater and new significance. By 1928, Morones fancied himself as the next president of Mexico, but Obregón stood in the way. As the political maneuvering commenced for the nomination of candidates, the tensions between the ostentatious labor chief and the ex-president were well established. Obregón's close ties with agrarian interests endangered Morones' influence in government as well as his grip on vital sources of patronage. For Obregón, his agrarian concerns represented a reversal of his past links with labor, specifically Morones. Obregón, however, realized the need for a political base of support to counter the political weight amassed by Morones and other factions generated by the Calles regime. Former allies, brought together by political necessity, had become implacable enemies for the same reasons. A meeting between the two in April 1928 confirmed the split. Morones bluntly told Obregón that he opposed his candidacy. The endorsement of Obregón by the Morones-led Partido Laborista was an empty gesture that failed to deceive Obregón or his followers.[20]

In this context, the killing of Obregón immediately made Morones a suspect as the instigator of the murder. And, although the evidence indicated otherwise in the days that followed the assassination, Obregonistas nonetheless accused Morones of being the inspiration for the death of Obregón. In the confusion generated by the assassination, Calles strove to maintain a grasp on a volatile situation, while Morones prudently decided to maintain a low profile for the moment. Calles needed to make a gesture to placate Obregonistas eager to vent their anger and frustration on Morones. As a consequence, Calles fired Morones from his post and appointed Emilio Portes Gil, a well-known foe of Morones, as provisional president. Calles, for the time being, had calmed the political waters.[21]

Portes Gil, however, was determined to crush Morones' power. In early November, nearly a month before assuming office, Portes Gil stated his intention to push through congress a federal labor code and called for a preliminary planning session of capital and labor representatives toward that end in late November.[22] Out of position to control the process of codification, Morones was not blind to the motives of the interim president. The incipient conflict between the two men exploded publicly the following month at the CROM convention. On December 4, 1928, Calles addressed the Cromistas, claiming his support for workers and the CROM. The next day, with Calles' speech used as an imprimatur, Morones launched a caustic attack on Portes Gil. The battle was in the open; Calles had to make a choice.[23]

The headlines of Mexico City newspapers on December 8 made clear the choice: Calles turned his back on Morones.[24] Portes Gil moved at once to outflank Morones, to undermine his support among workers, and to make government—not the CROM—the key to labor's protection and welfare. The codification of Article 123 was an element of this strategy, but, to make such a plan viable, Portes Gil had to mount a proposal that would be amenable to labor. In a timely speech to railroad workers on December 7, 1928, Portes Gil declared his intention to treat all labor organizations equally—an obvious repudiation of CROM's favored position in the past.[25] The effects were immediate from Morones' fall from political grace. With Calles' retreat from CROM the following day, CROM affiliate unions began to break away from Morones with each passing day.[26]

A few weeks later, in February 1929, the interim president presented an explicit description of his plan:

> I want to state categorically that the government . . . follows a program that is definitely prolabor, which benefits the workers, and I want also to say . . . that they, within their organizations promote . . . progressive policies, and that these organizations follow these policies rather than a leader who with empty words tries to attract people . . . that they reject the words of those who say that they are leaders who try in fact to weaken organizations in order to dominate them. . . . The working classes should organize themselves. . . . And for that we have progressive laws and we shall be the first to make sure that these laws function. . . .[27]

The speech pointed to the scheme by Portes Gil to isolate Morones and to erase the CROM as a mediating agent between workers and the state. The PNR convention and the Escobarista rebellion delayed the implementation of his plan, but by July 1929 Portes Gil was ready to propose his federal labor code plan, announcing a meeting of representatives of capital and labor to begin July 20, 1929.[28] In the aftermath of the Sáenz affair in Querétaro, and Portes Gil's prolabor rhetoric, the businessmen of Monterrey journeyed with understandable trepidation to Mexico City.

IV.   The fears of the *regiomontano* contingent were heightened by the contrast between the earlier planning session (November 1928) of labor and capital on the same subject. The context had changed radically. Sáenz was no longer the apparent president-elect. Morones was out as secretary of commerce, industry, and labor. Portes Gil was making prolabor statements far too polemical for the comfort of Nuevo León's capitalists. Moreover, the process for the input of businessmen appeared less open than in the earlier meeting. The November conclave had involved long sessions for labor and private sector envoys to present their views on provisions for the labor code. In contrast, for the new round of discussions, Portes Gil seemed bent on rushing through his code scheme, prompting business spokesmen to urge that the codification process be undertaken with careful, deliberate study and with the full participation of the private sector.[29] Labor representatives, especially from the sagging CROM, approached the parley with caution if not hostility given the fact that Portes Gil was directing the effort. Independent unions, often victims of Morones' reign while he was in office, were particularly suspicious of the newfound commitment to workers by the provisional president. More importantly, they were determined to remain outside government control.[30]

The battle lines involving the labor code proposals were immediately drawn at the onset of the meeting. On July 26, newspapers in Mexico City published the protest of the private sector organizations (known as the Grupo Patronal) to Portes Gil over his codification scheme. From the beginning of the document, the antagonism of the Grupo Patronal was manifest. "We wish to bring to your attention," the initial statement read, "points of undeniable importance that we have defended, apparently without success. . . ."[31] What followed was a seventeen-point argument that detailed the objections of the patronal group to Portes Gil's proposed labor code. A few days later, enacting its role as mouthpiece of the private sector, *Excelsior* published an editorial supporting the businessmen's position, calling the labor code proposals overwhelmingly tilted in favor of workers.[32]

Control over business operations represented the fundamental issue for the Mexican private sector in the labor code debate. The ability to employ, to fire, and to make decisions was at stake, or so the business organizations argued, since certain provisions of Portes Gil's proposals impinged upon the issue of control over collective bargaining, employment of foreigners, and the degree of government authority over the decision of owners to close their plants. For good measure, industrialists also requested greater concessions and a relaxation of regulations in the importation and export of goods. The impact of the worldwide depression further deepened the concerns of businessmen over several aspects of the codification proposals. Factory owners, for example, worried over the enactment of those provisions that would restrict their ability to shut down unprofitable plants, forcing them to pay workers while the enterprise sank toward bankruptcy.

In a more general criticism, the private sector organizations emphasized that the passage of the proposed labor code would multiply the adverse effects of the nation's economic downturn. The repercussions of the depression, they warned, for employers and workers would be enormously intensified by a labor code that punished the pillar of the Mexican economy—the Mexican capitalist. Nonetheless, the most important concerns hinged upon the issue of control that underlined the legalistic strategy pursued by businessmen in confronting the labor code proposals. For their defense, businessmen argued that they should be guaranteed "control over their respective companies and the development of their initiatives that promote the progress of the country."[33] In short, by emphasizing the issue of property rights, the private sector organizations intended to draw the parameters of state intervention, limiting the sphere of its influence in a vital area of contention in the past.[34]

On his part, Portes Gil attempted to play on the dislike of the businessmen for Morones. In the Senate Committee's report on the code, the machinations of Portes Gil became manifest. "Mexico had gone from the tyranny of capital to the tyranny of labor," the Senate report stated, "and the labor measure was calculated to create an equilibrium between the two."[35] Such statements failed to earn the support of most businessmen for Portes Gil's proposals. Worse for the interim president's effort, such remarks only fueled the wrath of labor representatives, especially that of the Cromistas, but other labor groups also worried over the threat of government domination of workers' organizations and their demands. Still, Portes Gil doggedly pressed the labor code issue, and, as a consequence, the private sector redoubled its drive to thwart the legislation's passage.[36] In the campaign to scuttle the proposed code, the men from Monterrey, Nuevo León, took the lead.

The *regiomontano* delegation to the hearings on the labor bill consisted of Luis G. Sada, Joel Rocha, Prisciliano Elizondo, and Alberto Santos, but the key men were Rocha and Sada. As the debate on the codification wore on from July into August, Sada and Rocha became fixtures in Mexico City newspapers as spokesmen for capital. The business organizations that composed the Grupo Patronal included the Confederations of Chambers of Commerce and Chambers of Industry and the foreign-dominated Asociación de Empresas Industriales y Comerciales, yet the resources and determination of the Nuevo León representatives led to their constant presence at the debates over the labor code. Moreover, the Monterrey delegation made frequent and effective use of the *Excelsior*'s front pages to mount criticism of the legislation.[37] Thus, by a combination of aggressiveness, tenaciousness, and connections, the Monterrey representatives assumed a preponderant position as spokesmen of Mexican capital on the codification question.

Unlike the labor organizations, with clear hierarchies of leadership, the Confederations of Chambers were at best a loose conglomeration of diverse interests. The nominal officers were primarily responsible for coordinating annual meetings and orchestrating campaigns (usually through telegrams) when necessary to pressure government on business-related issues. But, in fact, little leadership was exercised by the officers of these organizations prior to 1929. As a result, a consistent, intense drive against the labor code by the private sector was no easy matter.[38] The effort was further complicated by the distinct concern by certain companies of possible retribution for too vociferous a criticism of the provisional president's policies. Those companies where state expenditures figured largely in their profits found it prudent to stay in the background in the legislative bouts over the codification question. (Business organizations provided a cover for disgruntled companies, but the committee hearings on the code proposals forced certain individuals to present the side of capital.) The men from Monterrey, steeled by the recent Sáenz affair, showed scant fear publicly and sustained a steady barrage of criticism at the congressional committee hearings discussing the labor code proposals. By default, if nothing else, the leadership of the private sector over the labor code issue gravitated to the *regiomontano* contingent. Newspaper stories on the private sector's reaction to the labor code clearly reflected the high visibility of the Monterrey elite in spearheading capital's drive against the codification scheme presented by Portes Gil.[39] Indeed, it seemed that the *regiomontanos* welcomed their place at the forefront of Mexico's businessmen on the labor code question.

On September 10, 1929, *Excelsior* featured a front-page interview with the Monterrey representatives that laid out their objections to the labor code proposals.[40] The article also revealed that a meeting of industrialists was to take place to formulate a position paper on the codification plan that would be presented to congress on September 20. (This occurred after the review of the congressional subcommittee that had heard testimony on the proposals.) Significantly, the invitation to the meeting originated from Monterrey's leading capitalists. The call for a conclave of industrialists on the labor code by the Monterrey elite attracted nineteen delegations, representing primarily key manufacturing areas and cities of Mexico.[41] The timing of the meeting was intended to coincide with the conference of the Confederations of Chambers of Commerce and Chambers of Industry. The latter organization, however, composed the main source of representatives that responded to the invitation of the *regiomontanos*. It reflected the weighty influence of the *regiomontanos* in the Confederation of Industry as opposed to the larger and more diverse Confederation of Commerce. Luis G. Sada attempted to soften the apparent differences within the business organizations over the handling of the labor code issue, that is, the impatience of the Monterrey elite with the hesitancy of its counterparts in the confederations. Sada inaugurated the initial session and briefly noted that his delegation "had felt it was necessary to make the invitation so that businessmen could present their ideas and complement the thoughtful observations made by the Confederation of Industrial Chambers. . . ."[42]

To mollify criticism from the established private sector groups, Sada stated that the *regiomontano* group "did not intend to direct" the antilabor code campaign. Nonetheless, Sada went on to say that this new initiative by businessmen reflected the enormous importance of the codification of Article 123 for the nation, and he intimated that the confederations lacked the resources to deal with the issue adequately.[43]

Sada's comments notwithstanding, the program committee of the meeting called by the *regiomontanos* clearly revealed the crucial role of Nuevo León's industrialists in planning and leading the gathering of businessmen. Of the five members of the executive committee, two were from Monterrey. And the representatives to the meeting selected Sada to preside over the proceedings. For the moment, the meeting was dubbed the "convention of industrial delegates." In fact, the meeting marked the beginnings of COPARMEX, the Confederación Patronal de la República Mexicana (also referred to as the Employers' Confederation). The meeting represented a splintering of the previous front presented by the private sector under the banner of the Patronal Group. Nonetheless, the *regiomontanos* continued to participate in the deliberations of the larger organization. But the initial step of the organization was not auspicious. Several key areas (i.e., chapters of the Chambers of Industry) failed to attend the first meeting of the organization. Nevertheless, the nineteen delegations present at the initial proceedings were joined by others over the course of the four days of meetings from September 13 through September 17.[44]

The group worked feverishly to produce a document that would satisfy the assembly. The rabidly probusiness *Excelsior*, however, implicitly acknowledged the disagreements that apparently occurred at the sessions.[45] A statement nonetheless was produced and turned over on September 19, 1929, to the congressional commission studying the codification issue.[46]

The statement focused on five cardinal points surrounding business labor-capital relations: (1) collective bargaining, (2) the right to strike, (3) the composition and procedures of the arbitration boards, (4) indemnities, and (5) the obligations and responsibilities of employers to their workers. A few days later, the industrialists pressed their case directly before the commission, reiterating their points and emphasizing the negative consequences of the code if passed as proposed by Portes Gil.[47] In addition, timed to coincide with the oral presentation to the legislative commission, congressmen were subjected to a well-orchestrated assault of telegrams from business organizations throughout the country concurring with the position statement of the industrialists' convention.[48]

If there was any doubt as to the force behind the industrialists' convention, it was clarified on September 21, 1929, with the announcement of an executive committee to stay in Mexico City to push the positions contained in the statement concerning the labor code. (In an effort, perhaps, to placate the *regiomontanos*, Portes Gil traveled to Monterrey in late September to plead the necessity of the law in order "to end the series of conflicts between labor and capital.") This committee consisted of six members, four of whom were from Monterrey: Luis G. Sada, Joel Rocha, Virgilio Garza, Jr., and Francisco Doria Paz.[49] Then, on September 26, 1929, the executive committee of the "convention of industrial delegates" formally proclaimed the formation of a new organization, the Confederación Patronal de la República Mexicana.[50] In order to distance themselves from the chambers confederations, COPARMEX based its bylaws on provisions of Article 123 as an employers' syndicate (in contrast to the quasi-official status of the chambers accorded to them by government in a series of meetings in 1917 through the fall of 1918). Four major points framed the purpose of the organization: (1) to gather information for efficient business-labor relations; (2) to disseminate such information to businessmen; (3) to work toward the improvement of capital-labor relations; and (4) to protect the interests of business.[51]

The key, however, to the organization was the attempt of the *regiomontanos* to form an aggressive alliance of capitalists to dispute state intervention in the economy. Though many businessmen were undoubtedly sympathetic to the COPARMEX stance, they hesitated to join an organization so visibly willing to duel with the state. Hence, "the new organization found it difficult to enlist members."[52] Thus, even though over twenty different delegations were present at the founding of COPARMEX, less than half actually formed chapters upon their return to their respective cities. Significantly, the powerful industrial interests based in Mexico City failed to form a chapter of COPARMEX in 1929. The absence of a Centro Patronal in the country's economic center perhaps reflected a fear of government retaliation at a time when state-dependent firms were especially vulnerable. The Fundidora interests, for instance, remained at the margin of the proceedings of the industrialists' convention. Federico T. Lachica, manager of the steel plant, attended the initial sessions of the meeting. But the Prieto family, major stockholders in the company, and eminent members of the Mexico City business establishment, assiduously avoided a direct association with the *regiomontanos'* drive to kill the proposed labor code. In a meeting two weeks after the founding of COPARMEX, the Chamber of Industry of the Distrito Federal met to discuss its stand on the codification question. The resultant tepid statement made clear the vacillation of the Mexico City group, which contrasted starkly with the vitriolic pronouncements of the organization headed by the

Monterrey elite.[53] On the other hand, the industrialists from Nuevo León sustained their membership in the Patronal Group. Consequently, the Monterrey elite remained in a position to use the Patronal Group whenever possible to ratify the more belligerent stands of COPARMEX.[54]

The scathing attacks on the codification proposals from the *regiomontanos* matched the intensity of those made by labor groups.[55] Portes Gil continued to push the issue, but time was running short since his term as provisional president ended at the conclusion of November. The heated sparring over the labor code persisted into October, punctuated by the relentless, withering criticisms from both labor and the private sector, led by the newly formed COPARMEX. (The other business organizations also protested, though generally in a more tepid manner.) Although the congressional commission voted in October to support the proposed legislation in principle, the labor code remained in legislative limbo as Calles' ominous silence on the issue dimmed its prospects for passage.[56] To compound matters, foreign criticism of the code flared in the wake of the congressional commission's vote in favor of the code's objectives. Henry Ford, for example, talked threateningly of removing his auto plant from Mexico if the proposed code became law. First made in August, the threat was repeated a month later as Calles received pressure from U.S. Ambassador Dwight Morrow to brake the law's passage.[57]

In the absence of a clear-cut stand by Calles in support of codification, and pressured on all sides by labor and business, the Mexican congress moved indecisively on the Portes Gil measure; the vote to support the legislation in principle by the commission was an apparent sop that allowed the interim president to save face. Stalled by congressional inaction, the labor bill ground to a halt without passage as Portes Gil's term ended. It was a victory for the opponents of the codification proposals and a blow for Callistas expecting to reap the political rewards of Morones' fall.[58] Portes Gil had failed to woo labor support for the state in the aftermath of the expulsion of the CROM from the "revolutionary family." On the other hand, the effort to defeat the codification scheme by workers demonstrated the disarray within Mexican labor, its lack of unity in the face of the unraveling of the CROM.[59]

Significantly, however, the labor code proposals had facilitated the political consolidation of a segment of the private sector led by the Monterrey elite. In this sense, the government's preoccupation with the political fallout from Obregón's assassination, and Morones' place in government in particular, had inadvertently led to the crystallization of a tightly organized, combative business organization. In the case of the Monterrey elite specifically, the labor code battle deepened the bitterness over the Sáenz presidential debacle. The labor code proposal channeled the frustrations of the *regiomontanos* over the Sáenz affair into an organization that embraced important fractions of Mexico's private sector. Accepting the lead, they became a rallying pole for disgruntled businessmen who were unwilling, or unable, in the past to risk open confrontation with federal authority. As Morones and his influence precipitously waned, such businessmen, with Monterrey's industrialists at the helm, were emboldened openly to dispute government policy. In short, the maneuvering among political factions in the aftermath of the Obregón murder presented the *regiomontanos* with an opportunity to extend their influence, to enlist the aid of other disaffected businessmen, and, most importantly, to become the principal capitalist critics of the Mexican state.

V.   The reintroduction of the labor code bill under the presidency of Pascual Ortíz Rubio in 1931 served to draw the Grupo Patronal closer to the *regiomontano*-led COPARMEX. Economic conditions and political concerns motivated the Callistas to raise the codification scheme once again. As the adverse consequences of the depression mounted, Callistas seized the opportunity to increase their influence over capital, and, more importantly, to exert government authority over workers given the weakened state of organized labor. Mindful of the CROM's past political clout, particularly in key areas such as Veracruz and Mexico City, the Callista leadership aimed to use the federal labor code as a means of furthering the centralization of state power. Thus, on the one hand, government offered certain incentives to business, while, on the other, it sought to extend its reach over labor organizations and their political force. The Callista labor strategy, however, was of secondary interest to businessmen at the time.

The economic situation had worsened considerably for Mexican business by 1931, including that of Monterrey. The Rocha and Salinas furniture factory, for example, considered closing down because of a surplus inventory.[60] In fact, the *regiomontanos* had launched a "buy Mexican" campaign in an attempt to animate sagging sales.[61] Furthermore, the government's enactment of a 1% tax on gross receipts in 1930 contributed to the grievances of businessmen as the new round of talks on the codification of Article 123 approached.[62] The fragile economic conditions of most businesses, therefore, made the antigovernment posture of COPARMEX much more palatable to capitalists in 1931. In this regard, the Callistas added to capital's ire by their apparent determination to pass some form of a federal labor code regardless of the political costs. Angered by this attitude, the private sector groups that composed the Grupo Patronal moved closer to the position of the Monterrey elite. As a result, the labor code debate of 1931 witnessed a degree of unity within the private sector missing in 1929. Not surprisingly, COPARMEX registered the change by more than doubling its membership (from seven to eighteen chapters) during 1931.[63]

The Callista-dominated Ortíz Rubio administration apparently hoped to win over capitalists with a watered-down version of the legislation put forward by Portes Gil two years earlier. In a series of meetings in January 1931, a strategy was worked out by Callista congressional leaders and the Calles-controlled cabinet of Ortíz Rubio; Aarón Sáenz, secretary of industry, commerce, and labor, assumed primary responsibility for shepherding the bill through the congress.[64] The plan called for a quick process of approval of the code, minimizing the ability of labor or capital to mount an adequate defense. In March, the code scheme was turned over to a committee of the lower house for discussion of its provisions. The Patronal Group reacted immediately to the bill, with the Nuevo León contingent leading the way.[65]

Labor, however, was the chief target of the Callistas' ploy, and the intense, caustic response of workers' organizations forced Sáenz to make certain concessions that were translated into changes in the bill. The prolabor revisions incensed businessmen, and they intensified their pressure on the committee to retreat from the alleged bias of the bill toward employees.[66] But the Callistas refused to bend; the day following a special plea by the Patronal Group, the committee instead closed off discussion and began preparing the code proposals for submittal to the lower house of congress. The criticisms by labor met with similar results.[67] In the wake of Sáenz' defense of the bill on June 10, the Nuevo León businessmen came out publicly, and alone, to endorse the position of the Patronal Group and to offer their own condemnation of the bill.[68] Two weeks later, the *regiomontanos* succeeded in mobilizing several other local and regional business groups to do the same.[69]

Nonetheless, with Calles himself involved in the movement for passage, congress began its consideration of the code in mid-June.[70] Within ten days, congress voted to approve the legislation in principle as Callistas rammed through the bill; in one session, over eighty articles met approval. In less than three weeks, congress concluded its deliberations with the entire code—over 600 articles of provisions—approved. On August 5, 1931, Sáenz celebrated its passage in the lower house with a reception for Callista congressional leaders and predicted that the Senate would move for speedy approval.[71] In one last-ditch effort, the Grupo Patronal sent urgent pleas to the Senate and to Ortíz Rubio to block passage of the labor code; their entreaties were echoed by those from various labor organizations.[72] The pleas of both groups were to no avail. On August 17, the Grupo Patronal lamented the passage of the code by the Senate that, the private sector assured, would lead to disastrous economic consequences for which the state would be solely responsible.[73] Five days later, the Secretaría de Gobernación received the code from congress. A week later, the federal labor code legislation became law.[74]

VI.   The labor code debate of 1929–1931 represented a turning point in the political alignment of the Mexican bourgeoisie in which the Monterrey group assumed an eminent position in the relations between the private sector and the federal government. In this process, the labor code debate also confirmed the dominance of a small circle of men within the *regiomontano* elite. Invisible to most observers, the events of 1929 had forged the maturation of a new generation of leadership within the Monterrey elite, completing a transition marked by the rise of the Garza-Sadas and their close allies to the forefront of the *regiomontano* business establishment. Spanning the years since 1910, this shift witnessed the passing of an aging group of men who clung to a Porfirian vision of the future—a vision passed on to younger men.[75]

The roles of Luis G. Sada and Joel Rocha in the labor code battle signified the continuity as well as the change in the cupola of the *regiomontano* structure of political and economic power. Sada sustained the prominence of the Garza-Sada clan. Rocha, on the other hand, epitomized the elevation of new elements into the core of the Monterrey elite. Bespectacled, short, with thinning hair, and rather slight in stature, Sada fit the image as the shrewd tactician of the *regiomontano* elite. Well-tutored by the founders of the Garza-Sada interests, Luis G. Sada astutely maneuvered his connections with various business organizations to mount the foundation of COPARMEX, including the use of Barragán's *Excelsior* as a veritable propaganda sheet for the *regiomontanos*. Nonetheless, the efforts of Luis G. Sada were based on the ability of others to run and to augment the family businesses while his energies were channeled into other matters such as the labor code issue. In this respect, Roberto G. Sada, who assumed full control of the Vidriera in 1929, held the business operations of the clan together, providing direction and purpose to the Garza-Sada empire as his brother was distracted by the elite's political preoccupations.

Both men were capable, conscientious, hardworking in their respective endeavors—a remarkable resemblance to the working relationship of Francisco G. Sada and Isaac Garza Sada, patriarchs of the clan. As in that previous, fortuitous relationship, Luis and Roberto Sada represented a successful meshing of capabilities and personality to maintain the economic strength and vitality of the Garza-Sada empire. The presence of these two evidently competent men at the head of the Garza-Sada interests was a critical factor in the maintenance of the family's dominance in the political economy of Monterrey. At a critical juncture, members of the *regiomontano* elite possessed the talent necessary to command the respect of their counterparts elsewhere in Mexico for their abilities as businessmen as well as for their wealth.[76] Yet more than intelligence, foresight, and business acumen were required in the world of politics. Flair, rhetorical ability, and charisma also counted for much in the political arena.

Joel Rocha supplied the *regiomontano* elite with an attractive, articulate spokesman. A learned man, often referred to as "el profesor Rocha," and an effective if not gifted speaker, Rocha earned his role through his lucrative partnership with Benjamín Salinas in the building of the Salinas y Rocha department store chain. While Salinas presided over business operations, Rocha seemingly enjoyed the part as voice of the *regiomontano* elite, as was evident in the protracted debates over the labor code issue.[77] The 1929 legislative sessions on the codification of Article 123 permitted Rocha to occupy the public limelight in the name of Mexican capitalists.

Particularly in the decisive month of October 1929, as Portes Gil's term neared its end, Rocha displayed an unerring touch for dramatic, memorable catch-phrases in arguing the case for COPARMEX. On one occasion, at the hearings of October 3, 1929, Rocha declared that he would rather turn over his factories to the state than submit himself to the provisions of the proposed labor code.[78] Newspapers, especially *Excelsior*, ballooned the significance of Rocha's remark into a symbol of the desperation of Mexican businessmen to save Mexico from socialism.[79] (Cárdenas would echo, not coincidentally, Rocha's remarks in the visit to Monterrey in February 1936.) The comment by Rocha touched off an outpouring—its spontaneity debatable—of messages to congress by businessmen around the country in agreement with the *regiomontano's* stand.[80] Whether in fact any of these men were willing to give up their factories was questionable, but the brash declaration succeeded in making the codification question for several days one of near-national urgency. The attention given to Rocha's comments earned him a tumultuous welcome in Monterrey three days after his notorious assertion. Hailed by workers and businessmen alike, according to newspaper reports, he was paraded for several minutes on the shoulders of his supporters through the Monterrey railway station.[81] For the next two weeks, Rocha became a central figure in the debate between labor representatives and business over the provisions of the labor bill, featured on the editorial pages of *Excelsior,* and his comments even made their way into American newspaper reports.[82]

Rocha's emergence as the voice of Monterrey businessmen paralleled his full incorporation into the inner circle of the *regiomontano* elite. In this respect, Rocha indicated change within the upper echelon of the Monterrey business community, and he personified the capacity of the Nuevo León industrialists to renew themselves with leadership that was at once old and new. As with Rocha, others had broached by 1929 the exclusive confines of the elite whose names would be associated in the coming years with the most powerful of *regiomontanos:* Elizondo, Santos, Laguera, among others.[83] These new men augmented the economic clout of the Monterrey elite and contributed to the reservoir of resources, acumen, and energy available to the more established members such as Luis G. Sada, Virgilio Garza, Jr., or Joel Rocha.

VII. The events of 1929–1931 provided an opportunity to test the mettle of the new generation of *regiomontano* business leaders. The Sáenz affair tempered their determination to seek a political response to the state's economic intervention, and the labor code battle tested their resources and organizational ability. In both respects, those years witnessed a fateful turning point in the political and economic development of the *regiomontano* elite. The disappointment at Querétaro destroyed any shred of confidence or trust in the leadership of the new state, and in Calles specifically, a conclusion reinforced by the introduction of labor legislation that failed to meet the demands of Nuevo León's entrepreneurs. The latter effort prodded the elite to mobilize elements of the Mexican private sector into an organized opposition to counter government policy that went beyond previous forms of criticism of the state. The suspicion and disdain toward politicians generated by these events among the *regiomontano* elite culminated over a decade of frustration for the businessmen of Nuevo León in their dealings with local and national government.

The *regiomontano* elite therefore entered the 1930s equipped with capable, battle-tested leadership, as it were, and, perhaps more importantly, with a clear vision of its goals. The businessmen of Monterrey possessed an unflinching resolve to limit the authority of the state. Ironically, as the state's reach stifled democracy in Mexico, it would be capitalists that would defend dissent.[84] Members of the *regiomontano* elite failed to appreciate the irony; their aim was a state structure subordinated to capital and its interests. Still, with a labor movement in disarray and on the defensive, with a peasantry poorly organized and dependent on the state for relief, the men of Monterrey sustained an explicit, coherent, and singular resistance to the encroachments of state power.

8. Confrontation: The Monterrey Elite and Cardenismo, 1934-1940

I. On February 14, 1936, Lázaro Cárdenas left Monterrey, Nuevo León, after a week in the political storm generated by the strike at the glass plant owned by the Garza-Sadas. Despite presidential claims of a resolution to the dispute, the situation remained tense, volatile. The visit of the president had in fact intensified the antigovernment views of the businessmen of Monterrey, specifically toward Lázaro Cárdenas. A local battle between *regiomontano* capitalists and workers had taken a larger, more threatening turn for both sides. For the Garza-Sadas and their allies, the intervention by Cárdenas rekindled a drive for national political power that reached its climax six years later. The Vidriera strike of 1936 was a critical event in the history of the Monterrey elite, and its outcomes laid the groundwork of a new era in capital-state relations.[1]

The dramatic appearance of the popular president renewed the elite's search for a political figure with the capabilities to contend for the presidency, to take up the standard for capital, and that of the men of Monterrey in particular. In the wake of the events of February 1936, the *regiomontanos* played a key if not primary role in the formation of a forceful opposition to the Cárdenas administration. At every turn, the implacable elite of Monterrey attempted to define the limits of state power in the private sector and to thwart the consolidation of a regime where capital was subordinated to the interests of the state. Single-minded in its pursuit, the elite sustained its quest despite the substantial economic gains afforded by the Cardenista administration. Eventually, the businessmen of Nuevo León lost their bid for the presidency. Nonetheless, while the contours of state power fashioned by Cárdenas remained intact, the character of government policies after 1940 carried the indelible imprint of the industrialists of Monterrey. In losing the presidential election, the *regiomontano* elite won a profitable bargain with the post-Cárdenas state.

II. Two key problems came together in Monterrey in February 1936, the results of which produced a larger, more significant conflict. For the elite of Monterrey, the origins of the clash extended back to the break with Calles in 1929, a break reaffirmed by the passage of the labor law of 1931 and subsequent events. The estrangement of the *regiomontanos* from the postrevolutionary leadership found fresh inspiration with the gubernatorial elections in Nuevo León of 1935 that took place in the midst of increasing tensions between Calles and the new president, Lázaro Cárdenas. This second issue contributed decisively to the special political importance of the events in Monterrey of February 1936, for it precipitated a pivotal confrontation between the men of Monterrey and the Mexican state under Lázaro Cárdenas.

For Cárdenas, his visit to Monterrey in February 1936 reflected his determination to deal with several interlocking problems at once. First, Cárdenas desired a demonstration of his independence from Plutarco Elías Calles and to make clear the populist, reformist orientation of his administration. Second, Cárdenas needed an extraordinary demonstration of his prolabor stance in order to cement worker support in his political struggle with Calles. Third, for such a show, Cárdenas required an opponent easy to cast as villain. Fourth, Cárdenas wanted to channel labor into the fledgling organization headed by Vicente Lombardo Toledano as a means to exercise greater control of labor as a political instrument of his presidential regime.[2]

On the surface, Monterrey was not a propitious site for the president's ploy.[3] The company unions were well entrenched. The power and influence of the elite were pervasive, its sources of control and public sway enormous and well honed. Local newspapers and radio stations were firmly in their grasp. Moreover, the Monterrey businessmen were closely interrelated through organizations such as the Knights of Columbus, Rotary Club, Chamber of Commerce, and Centro Patronal, and they possessed strong links with surrounding areas through their business ties. Finally, the *regiomontano* capitalists represented a capable, tested adversary that constituted perhaps the most cohesive fraction of the Mexican bourgeoisie.

On the other hand, from Cárdenas' point of view the showdown in Monterrey made much political sense. First, an attack on the political stronghold of capital promised important dividends from workers made skeptical by government lip service in previous administrations. Second, given the attempt of Calles' son to bid for the governorship of Nuevo León, Monterrey provided a means to confront the Callistas head on. Third, Lombardo Toledano's labor organization lacked support among industrial workers and needed to expand its base to include labor in manufacturing; a key place for such a membership drive outside of Mexico City was Monterrey. Fourth, the businessmen from Monterrey possessed national visibility tinged with negative characteristics—their support of Sáenz, their conspicuous opposition to the labor law, and their vocal criticism of state policies. Finally, and it appears most importantly, Cárdenas saw an opportunity to exploit the division between the Callista regime and the *regiomontano* elite. By exploiting this split, Cárdenas hoped to reap crucial political gains.

In his struggle with Calles, Cárdenas apparently decided to risk the opposition of a portion of Mexican capital in exchange for the staunch support of workers. His agrarian base seemingly in place and growing, Cárdenas moved to garner labor's allegiance and to use Lombardo Toledano as his vehicle toward that end. Monterrey therefore offered a perfect stage to mount his strategy; the city assured him of massive attention and enormous political play. And, not insignificantly, the move on Monterrey allowed Cárdenas the opportunity to settle old scores.[4]

As head of the PNR before his nomination for president, Cárdenas realized the weakening of the foundations of his party and its hold. As spokesman of the party, Cárdenas was forced to defend or gloss over the venality of the bureaucracy, and that of several voracious governors in particular. Calles seemed oblivious to the unraveling of popular support.[5] The impact of the depression heightened the resentment of workers, farmers, and peasants. Cárdenas' subsequent tenure as governor of Michoacán served to deepen his awareness of the estrangement between a disconnected party leadership and large segments of its former constituency. His organization of workers, small farmers, and peasants in Michoacán laid the groundwork for his efforts once in office as president.[6] The six-year plan passed at the PNR convention of 1933 provided a platform for Cárdenas, and it reflected the thinking of certain elements of the PNR that the state needed to shore up its bases of support.[7]

As a result, Cárdenas immediately gave workers and peasants an encouraging signal to press their demands. The apparent sanction by Cárdenas touched off a wave of strikes and worker actions that were seconded by the prolabor acts of the new administration. An old hand at party politics, Cárdenas was keenly aware of the political benefits of possessing a well-organized core of support among agrarian interests—as Obregón held in 1928—as well as the rewards of possessing leverage over a disciplined labor organization—as Calles had held with the CROM. In order to sustain his program, Cárdenas set out to establish a solid base of support within labor and agrarian sectors of the population.[8] Such an effort put him at odds with Calles since it created a source of political power for Cárdenas independent of the *jefe máximo*.

The series of strikes in 1933–34, following the election of Cárdenas, signified in political terms much more than labor discontent. Rather, it revealed that the direction of the state was slipping out of the hands of Calles and into those of the new president. Cárdenas was not blind to the consequences of his actions; he quickly set into motion several moves aimed at protecting his position from an easy military coup.[9] Nonetheless, Cárdenas tried to salvage his relationship with Calles. A good soldier of the party, he strove to prevent an open division within party ranks. The split became unavoidable, however, when, on June 12, 1935, Calles publicly deplored the surging tide of labor disturbances in the country. It was, despite any direct reference to Cárdenas, a repudiation of the president's reformist policies.[10] Cárdenas' political survival was at stake. But the political lessons of the past decade were not lost on the *michoacano*. Calles, perhaps overconfident of his power, was ill prepared for the challenge.

Cárdenas initiated his preparations by maneuvering his sympathizers in the military into strategic posts.[11] More importantly, Calles' anti-Cárdenas statements provided the president with an inadvertent boost from labor. Self-interest, if nothing else, dictated that labor organizations set aside their squabbling to support Cárdenas. Only the old, Moronista CROM, seeing an opportunity to exploit an alliance with Calles in a showdown, failed to join the Comité Nacional de Defensa Proletaria (CNDP).[12] This act of solidarity by organized labor with the Cárdenas administration contradicted his relations with labor at the onset of his administration. "In fact, in the first months of his administration, Cárdenas did not have labor support nor did it appear to have the possibility of establishing a labor policy," Alicia Hernández Chavez has noted, "a serious situation due to the fragmentation that the labor organizations had suffered and the divisions and differences that existed among them."[13] The disarray in the labor movement underlined the first meeting of the CNDP that immediately followed Calles' rebuke of Cárdenas.[14]

Cárdenas, for his part, understood that opportunism conditioned much of his support among the military and bureaucracy rather than loyalty or principle. In the impending confrontation with Calles, the new president bolstered his defense by shuffling his cabinet, reconstituting legislative blocs, and removing governors.[15] Still, labor represented a key weapon against a Callista comeback in the tense aftermath that followed the crisis of June 1935. Cognizant of the differing currents in the labor movement, Cárdenas needed a broker to organize his control of labor—Cárdenas was a Callista long enough to appreciate the value of a labor leader who functioned as an instrument of the state. As Calles had used Morones, Cárdenas needed

Lombardo Toledano. And as it turned out, the ex-Cromista needed the president for his own ends.[16]

Lombardo Toledano emerged as the key figure of the CNDP meeting as the ex-Cromista lieutenant brought into the fold the splintered remnants of the CROM and the newly formed CGOCM (Confederación General de Obreros y Campesinos de México). Yet it was clear that the strength of the CNDP rested on the independent, powerful unions of miners, electricians, and railway workers.[17] The old divisions and differences of tactics and goals died slowly. Nonetheless, the CNDP planned for a convention in February 1936 formally to integrate into a larger labor organization. The maneuvering for the leadership of the proposed labor confederation began soon after the Comité's first meeting in June 1935. Given the importance and clout of the independent unions, Lombardo Toledano realized the necessity of enlarging his base, especially among skilled industrial workers, an element missing in the CGOCM. Such a constituency provided a possible counterweight to that of the independent unions. In this respect, Lombardo Toledano stood to benefit from any event that elevated his prominence on the eve of the convention. Tutored by Morones, Lombardo Toledano knew the power to be derived from being the man to mediate labor's unified power with the state.[18]

In the context of the repercussions of the public break between Calles and Cárdenas of June 1935, the gubernatorial elections in Nuevo León took on a larger significance. With the Calles interests openly involved in the race, they presented Cárdenas with the problem of preventing a Callista victory. The participation of the Monterrey elite, through Zuazua, on the other hand, offered yet another challenge to Cárdenas' political hold; but the situation in Monterrey also offered both Cárdenas and Lombardo a crucial, though risky political gamble. For Lombardo Toledano, the Nuevo León situation afforded him an opportunity to show his value to Cárdenas and to enhance his bid to head the emergent labor confederation. For Cárdenas, Monterrey presented a means to consolidate his political base by dramatizing his support for labor and by erasing the Callista faction from the gubernatorial race. The president and ex-Cromista made a political marriage that for the moment served the aims of both men.

III.   For the Monterrey elite, the move into the gubernatorial fray of July 1935 had little to do with the Calles-Cárdenas conflict. When Cárdenas won the presidency in 1934, the elite perceived Cárdenas as merely another lackey of Calles. Indeed, its initial opposition to Cárdenas stemmed from the estrangement between Calles and the *regiomontano* elite. The period following the Sáenz affair added further strains to relations between Callistas and the elite. Anger over the labor code law of 1931 deepened with a proposed federal tax increase on imported lumber—an obvious slap at Joel Rocha's furniture business. Pleading financial problems, the state fueled the flames by proposing in August 1931 a 1% tax of gross corporate income. The levy was another transparent swipe at the private sector for its harsh criticism of the government during the passage of the labor code. A sharp meeting with federal officials in September 1931 in Monterrey failed to mollify the *regiomontanos* completely. Both Sáenz and Calles subsequently salvaged a fragile rapprochement with the men of Nuevo León, but the relationship had lost all of its former strength. As the economy hit bottom in 1932, relations between the *regiomontanos* and the Callistas' regime reached a similar low.[19]

In that same year, Francisco Cárdenas (no relation to Lázaro Cárdenas) became governor of Nuevo León and at first met only the disdain of the city's leading industrialists. But Francisco Cárdenas was an ambitious man who attempted to ingratiate himself with the businessmen of Monterrey, perhaps in emulation of Almazán.[20] As the new governor put down labor protests and blocked the efforts of the Communist party to extend its activities, the relations between the governor and the business community quickly warmed. Francisco Cárdenas found the post to his liking, and he was unhappy with the prospect of losing the office to Calles, Jr., in the fall of 1933. Seizing an opportunity to get back at Calles, the elite unsuccessfully but forcefully backed Francisco Cárdenas against the younger Calles. The attempt by Sáenz to resolve the split failed miserably; he had lost much of his credibility among the elite. The move to oust the governor by the Callistas provoked mass demonstrations by workers orchestrated by employers in support of Francisco Cárdenas. Furthermore, the rising tensions between Calles and Almazán emboldened the elite's anti-Callista activities.[21]

The opposition of the *regiomontanos* to Calles found further fuel in the selection of Lázaro Cárdenas—as opposed to Almazán—as the presidential nominee of the PNR for the elections of 1934. The fervent promotion of a platform clearly at odds with the views of the *regiomontano* capitalists added to their grievances against Calles. The campaign stop of the presidential candidate from Michoacán produced a sullen response in Monterrey—employers put their workers under wraps and assailed the PNR candidate for his "socialistic" views on education.[22] Intent on seeing his son as governor of Nuevo León in 1935, Calles reached the breaking point in his feuding with the elite following the Lázaro Cárdenas visit to Monterrey. The *jefe máximo*

publicly took the *regiomontanos* to task for their "inhumane exploitation" of workers and went on with his criticism by citing their lack of
appreciation for what the Calles government had done for them. For
good measure, Calles included some nasty anti-Semitic remarks as
well in his furious attack on Monterrey's industrialists. Calles' repri-
mand of the elite was intended to respond to its treatment of the
presidential nominee. In fact, the main cause of Calles' consternation
was the elite's determined drive against his son's quest for the governorship of Nuevo León. The feud heated up further when government
authorities ousted the conservative faculty of an upper-class girls'
school in Monterrey and then nationalized the school's property. The
fury of the elite over the affair was matched by that of Almazán.[23]

With the PNR primary election for the nominee of the party for the
gubernatorial post slated for May 1935, the elite threw its support
to Fortunato Zuazua, an old, but popular veteran of the revolution, to
oppose the Callistas. Zuazua, neglected by the postrevolutionary
leadership, relegated to trivial duties, was flattered and emboldened
by the elite's offer of support. The spring of 1935 witnessed a tense,
dirty campaign as Zuazua and Calles, Jr., engaged in a wide-ranging
effort to capture the PNR nomination. Although Zuazua garnered the
most votes, the younger Calles "won" the primary election and dubi-
ously earned the nomination of the PNR for the general elections to be
held in July 1935. The obviously fraudulent vote count embittered the
elite, as Zuazua protests to Cárdenas were made to no avail.[24]

The month before the elections the celebrated break of June 1935
between Calles and Cárdenas took place, and it undoubtedly surprised
most businessmen—especially in light of the apparent resolution of the
conflict on June 7 when the two men met, allegedly to iron out their
differences. Hence, Calles' criticisms of the Cárdenas administration
five days later were puzzling to Monterrey's entrepreneurs.[25] But the
memories of past betrayals were too fresh for the elite to reembrace
Callistas easily. With elite backing, Zuazua maintained his candidacy
for governor under the banner of the Liberal party of Nuevo León that
had the "tacit support" of Almazán.[26] As the Cárdenas-Calles feud
widened, the possibility arose for the Monterrey businessmen to "sneak
in" their own man as governor. By promoting Zuazua, the elite hoped
perhaps that Cardenistas would be forced to support Zuazua and thus
deny Calles, Jr., the governorship. From the beginning of the campaign,
it was clear that the aging general's popularity was genuine, further
inflated by the money and aid of Monterrey's industrialists. In an honest election, Zuazua would beat anyone. Thus, the contest for control of
the governor's palace became a three-way affair among Zuazua supporters, Cardenistas, and Callistas.[27] For Cárdenas, the situation in

Nuevo León was a delicate one and became more so as his relations with Calles reached a critical stage. For the capitalists of Monterrey, the clash between the president and his former mentor added a new, absorbing factor in their dispute with the state.

IV. Cárdenas faced a quandary as the events in Nuevo León had become enmeshed in the larger struggle between himself and the *jefe máximo*. In the wake of the ex-president's blast at the administration, a Callista victory in Nuevo León would be interpreted as a capitulation to Calles, but Zuazua was equally unacceptable. With Portes Gil, the old enemy of the elite newly installed as head of the Secretaría de Gobernación, Cárdenas made a decision. On August 19, 1935, Portes Gil announced the nullification of the election due to "irregularities" and called for a new election for April 1936.[28] The solution pleased no one faction in Monterrey, except of course Cárdenas and his supporters. Yet the solution was at best a temporary one to buy time for the Cardenistas to mount a response to Callistas and Zuazuaistas. Cárdenas was determined to hold onto the governorship of Nuevo León.

Cárdenas appointed Gregorio Morales Sánchez interim governor on October 4, 1935, as the PNR made Anacleto Guerrero their candidate to oppose Zuazua in the gubernatorial elections of the following spring. Calles left Mexico for health reasons subsequent to the crisis of June 1935. (He would return in December, as noted later in this chapter.) The Callistas, with Calles out of the country, retreated to the background, waiting for their opportunity to make a comeback. The battle lines thus drawn, the campaigning immediately escalated in its virulence and violence.[29]

In this context, Lombardo Toledano (among other labor leaders) appreciated the opportunities presented by the situation in Nuevo León. Organizers from the CGOCM scurried to Monterrey, and work actions multiplied as scheduled contract talks between companies and workers in the area came due.[30] Both sides attempted to use workers to buttress their aims, but in this endeavor the elite held the decided advantage; paternalistic controls became political instruments. To acquire any legitimacy for Guerrero's candidacy, Cardenistas needed to make a dent in the elite's manipulation of its work force. Thus, the obvious drive by the PNR to make inroads into the elite's control over workers raised the stakes to a new and more volatile level. The *regiomontanos* responded in kind. On November 18, 1935, gunfire erupted between the two sides as the fight for votes intensified.[31] The PNR harassed Zuazuaistas at every turn while industrialists redoubled their pressure on workers to support Zuazua.

The businessmen of Monterrey, particularly the Garza-Sadas, formed the heart of the Zuazua movement. Not surprisingly, Lombardo decided to focus his attack on one of the enterprises of the Garza-Sadas, the Vidriera.[32] It had a recent record of labor troubles, its sophisticated technology was vulnerable to work actions, and its recovery from the depression was conspicuously evident. The Vidriera had made a rapid return to health from a critical moment in 1931. Swallowing their pride, the Garza-Sadas had gone to Sáenz, then secretary of commerce, to ask for aid. But Sáenz, still smarting from the elite's criticism for passage of the labor law, refused to even give the group an audience.[33] By 1932, however, the recovery had begun, and by the turn of the new year the American consul in Monterrey was reporting the exceptional activity of the glass plant and its sister industry, the brewery (fueled in part by the repeal of Prohibition in the United States, which immediately opened markets along the Texas border). And as the economy as a whole picked up by mid-1933, the Vidriera took the lead in the city's industrial recovery.[34] (See table 18.)

The dramatic recuperation of the glass plant prompted a response from employees denied pay increases over a long period of time, forced to work much overtime, and pushed continually to raise their productivity. Work actions flared periodically in 1933 and broke out openly in November 1934. But the disturbance was squashed for the moment. Reports, however, revealed that troubles existed under the tranquil facade of the Vidriera.[35] In April 1935, Lombardo visited Monterrey and spurred the local Centro Patronal to press for a membership drive to stave off any eruption of labor activity. Two weeks later, in the background of a rising tide of strike activity in the country, the Centro Patronal called a meeting to organize a

Table 18. *Beer Shipments from the Cervecería Cuauhtémoc, 1930–1940 (selected years)*

Year	Quantity (in thousands of liters)
1930	21,760
1932	14,367
1934	24,305
1936	36,355
1938	43,483
1940	54,709

Source: Stephen H. Haber, "The Industrialization of Mexico, 1880–1940" (manuscript in progress, unpaginated).

"committee of civic action" in order "to take measures to forestall any local difficulties."[36]

Thus, as tensions mounted on the national political stage in 1935, with its ramifications for Nuevo León, a parallel issue concerning labor dogged the *regiomontanos* as well. As a capstone to the elite's local political worries, a new government representative to the labor board was to be selected in December (1935), and every indication from the Cárdenas administration pointed to a prolabor appointment.[37] Then, on December 15, 1935, yet another ingredient entered the boiling political kettle when Calles, along with Morones, returned to Mexico from the United States. When Cardenista supporters organized a mass rally against the return of Calles in mid-December 1935, the concerns of the elite deepened.[38] A successful Calles comeback augured badly for the elite, and Cárdenas offered equally dismal prospects; restive workers seemed to be everywhere, the labor board promised to be another problem, and the gubernatorial elections were just around the corner. Christmas afforded the elite, besieged on all fronts, a lull in the impending storm that exploded in mid-January 1936.

In a series of decisions in which the government representative's vote was critical, the arbitration board came down decisively on the side of labor. Businessmen on the labor tribunal conceded the decisions in the apparent attempt to avoid giving labor an issue around which to rally workers.[39] But three events soon followed that confirmed the worst fears of the *regiomontano* capitalists. On January 30, 1936, the labor court declared the company union of the Fundidora invalid. Three days later, the PNR formally nominated Anacleto Guerrero as its candidate for governor, rejecting once again Zuazua's attempt to gain the nomination. Then, on February 4, 1936, the arbitration board ruled against the company union in a representational election among furnace workers at the Vidriera Monterrey.[40] The arbitration board vote, following the Fundidora ruling and combined with the PNR decision, struck at a crucial element in the local power of the elite. The loss of authority over workers threatened the industrialists' sources of control. But the Garza-Sadas and their allies were not unprepared for the fight to retain their position. Headed by the Garza-Sadas, the furious elite put into action its well-laid plans of resistance to the Cardenista state.

V. On February 6, 1936, a virtual shutdown of the city's economy manifested the extent and capability of the elite's preparations to confront Cárdenas.[41] The few stores that remained open and the scarce traffic on major thoroughfares served to amplify the overwhelming quiet of the city, emphasizing the success of the elite's dramatic show of force. From throughout the country, business organizations lent their support to the *regiomontano paro* of the city. The day before (February 5), a crowd of nearly 40,000 demonstrated the ability of the *regiomontanos* to mobilize the city's population, including the vast majority of their workers, whether through genuine support, intimidation, or bribery. The impressive demonstration by the elite made clear the well-organized, resourceful opposition faced by the Cardenistas and their allies. Moreover, the gesture by the *regiomontano* businessmen undoubtedly enlivened the flickering hopes of the Callistas to recoup some of their influence. The enormous, effective show orchestrated by the elite, therefore, generated widespread reverberations throughout the volatile political context of Mexico in early 1936.

The strategy of the Monterrey industrialists made their February 6 *paro* the more effective. Rather than attacking Cárdenas directly, the elite's action centered on arousing public sentiment against labor by fomenting fears of communism. (This also made it easier for businessmen outside of Monterrey to support the elite.) Moreover, their anti-Communist sloganeering was wrapped in the mantle of Mexican nationalism.[42] By linking Lombardo with communism and Russian influence, *regiomontano* businessmen hoped to weaken labor's appeal and to associate their own action with patriotic duty. The elite's ploy immediately put Lombardo on the defensive, forcing him to disavow that he was an agent of the Soviet Union.[43] By stressing the issue of nationalism, the elite apparently intended to plumb the deep currents of nationalistic fervor promoted by Cárdenas himself. To save Mexico from the Communist menace, the *regiomontanos* cast themselves as the defenders of *patria*, family, and *mexicanismo*.

The effectiveness of the elite's action of February 6, seconded by businessmen throughout the country, was both a political and symbolic affront to Cárdenas. With the elections for governor only a month away and the CNDP meeting slated for late February, it appeared that the *regiomontanos* had taken the higher ground. What was intended to be a display of force for the president had mushroomed into a specific confrontation with the Monterrey elite. Cárdenas' key aims—to retain control over the governorship of Nuevo León and to solidify labor support—seemed seriously in jeopardy.[44] With the eyes of the nation's political interests focused on Monterrey, Cárdenas had few options but to take the Garza-Sadas head-on.

For a week, from February 7 to 14, 1936, Cárdenas' presence in Monterrey held center court in the attention of the country. His speech, enunciating his Fourteen-Point labor program, highlighted his stay in Nuevo León, earning him an enduring place in Mexican history. But that speech was preceded by a meeting on February 8 with representatives of the Centro Patronal and then again, two days later, on February 10. At the first meeting, Cárdenas primarily listened to the men from Monterrey.[45] They protested the vote of the arbitration board that had allowed the strike at the Vidriera to be declared legal. Furthermore, the businessmen emphasized the importance of *regiomontano* industries to the economic recovery of the nation, a recovery endangered by labor agitation. Finally, they stated their intention to maintain their "anti-Communist" campaign if necessary. In the subsequent meeting, members of the elite restated their objections to the arbitration court's decision to permit the strike at the glass plant and made a special plea for the removal of the head of the arbitration court (appointed by Morales Sánchez) for his prolabor bias. They concluded their presentation by stressing their exemplary labor record and accused labor leaders of promoting unions solely for reasons of self-aggrandizement.[46]

Finally, after hearing complaints for most of the two meetings, Cárdenas responded. The president stressed the necessity of a united labor front to the stability of the country. Confirming the perceptions of American observers, Cárdenas argued that the unification of the labor movement made its control easier and more efficient.[47] Thus, Cárdenas proposed, the disruptive consequences for business would end through the formation of a united labor front, which would facilitate the management of the economy. Cárdenas' views, however, failed to persuade *regiomontano* businessmen.[48] The following day, Cárdenas, in his threatening Fourteen-Point speech, made clear his intention to support labor, censured the actions of the elite, minimized its allegations, and discounted its anti-Communist rhetoric. With dramatic flourish, he ordered a recount of the workers' vote at the Vidriera that resulted in reaffirming the original findings of the arbitration court; Cárdenas then publicly endorsed the strike at the glass plant.[49]

The president's performance suited his political aims and showed his determination to risk support from capital in order to sustain his reforms. Still, his meetings with the Patronal Group indicated that Cárdenas looked for a resolution that would allow workers a victory without a complete loss of face for employers.[50] The *regiomontanos* refused to bow to an accord, compelling Cárdenas to his strong condemnation of capital that laced his Fourteen-Point speech of February 11, the day following his second meeting with the elite. Cárdenas left Monterrey on February 14, his prolabor image reinforced and his popularity among workers swelled by his public, dramatic demonstration endorsing their cause. Thus, the president departed from the city with an aura of political success. The president's departure, however, left in its wake a more determined opposition, strengthened by additional adherents and by the impetus provided by Cárdenas' decidedly prolabor performance. Cárdenas rekindled, as a result of his visit, the drive to curb state power by the *regiomontano* elite much in the same way that Calles provoked the formation of COPARMEX in 1929; but in this battle, the elite would be joined by much larger segments of the Mexican bourgeoisie.

VI. The response of the Monterrey elite to Cárdenas was spearheaded by the team that had led the battle over the labor law—Luis G. Sada and Joel Rocha. Rocha once again came out as spokesman, ideologue, and "front man" for the tactician, Sada. The parallel lines of reaction by the elite to the Cardenistas centered locally on retaking the hold over workers and on pressuring the new governor toward a more conciliatory position. At the national level, the elite attempted to galvanize anti-Cárdenas forces through support of various organizations and to mobilize capital against the Cárdenas regime. At both levels, the elite supported the rough tactics of the fascist *sinarquista* movement, funded a widespread campaign in print and radio to disseminate propaganda, and promoted the formation of various anti-Cárdenas, conservative organizations among students, women, and workers. The anti-Cárdenas campaign took place in a context in which the president strove to consolidate further his unsettled political base.[51] As a consequence, the national political situation remained an important factor in the effectiveness of the *regiomontano*-led opposition to Cárdenas. By taking such a visible position against Cárdenas, the *regiomontanos* became a pole of attraction to which anti-Cárdenas sentiment gravitated regardless of the motivation.

The primary, short-term objective of the elite was to break the growing though still limited strength of the CTM (Confederación de Trabajadores de México) in Monterrey. (The NL Federation of Workers was the local affiliate of the CTM; for purposes of the text, CTM in Monterrey and NLFW are used synonymously unless otherwise indicated.) The majority of the workers at key plants, such as the Cervecería and the Vidriera, remained under the thumb of their owners. The glassworks vote issue in fact involved essentially only one section of the Vidriera's large work force. Thus, the CTM "victory" at the glass plant was illusory and masked the uphill struggle facing Cetemista organizers.[52] In this regard, one problem stemmed from the residue of distrust and resentment among the leadership of the Nuevo León Federation of Workers toward Lombardo Toledano. Labor activists in the organization retained bitter memories of Lombardo's service to Morones and the CROM and their lack of support in past battles with the major employers of Monterrey, including their attempts to squash

Communist party efforts by Valentín Campa in Nuevo León.[53] The internecine fighting at the national level among rival labor groups further undermined the Cetemistas in Nuevo León. More importantly, such long-standing rifts provided an easy avenue for the elite to weaken Lombardo's influence in Monterrey.[54]

Businessmen employed a number of tactics to resist the Cetemistas' thrust into the city's largest companies. Using a network of workers as spies, the elite was able to anticipate moves by CTM organizers.[55] Utilizing these "moles" within the Cetemistas, employers also used them whenever convenient as provocateurs to foment division and debate that only exacerbated the wounds of the past between Cetemista sympathizers and unforgiving anti-Cromistas. Such divisions served to undermine morale among federation members and to discourage others from joining. Moreover, spies allowed the elite to identify workers being courted by the CTM as well as to finger Cetemista organizers within the plants. With this information, employers attempted to bribe recruits away from the CTM and/or to intimidate them to desert the organization.

If this were not enough, goons hired by businessmen offered yet another method of persuasion. To further their aim to crush the Cetemistas, the *regiomontano* businessmen supplied the *sinarquistas* with a crucial means of financial support to attack the "Communists." The *sinarquistas* were not initiated by the elite, but after February 1936 their organization was given a tremendous boost into national prominence by the aid provided by Monterrey's capitalists.[56] At the local level, the so-called Gold Shirts cast a physical, menacing pall over CTM efforts to organize *regiomontano* workers.

To complement the overt and covert campaign against the CTM, the elite initiated a steady barrage of propaganda against "outsiders," the "bolshevique" agitators, and "Moscow-controlled" Cetemistas. Employers, for instance, bought local newspapers in huge quantities and then distributed them for free or at a reduced price to workers; *El Porvenir*, and its sister paper, *El Sol*, were often reduced as a consequence to anti-Cetemista broadsides.[57] Given the burgeoning popularity of radio, *regiomontano* capitalists effectively used the air waves to dissuade workers from turning to the CTM, to convince wives of the dangers of the Communist menace to their husbands, and to paint a scenario where the city was being overrun by Communists.[58] Working within and outside local labor organizations, the elite mounted a wide-ranging, debilitating assault on the CTM in Monterrey that cajoled, intimidated, or deceived workers with telling results and that exhausted the resources of the Cetemistas to counter equally.

Nowhere was the anti-Cetemista drive more intense than at the Cervecería and Vidriera plants. The Garza-Sadas, as obvious targets of Lombardo's Monterrey effort, responded with full force. In addition to utilizing the tactics noted above, the owners of the glassworks and brewery escalated their wooing of workers with vacations, lotteries with cash prizes, and other types of incentives for employees to remain loyal to the company, to distract them from the appeals of the Cetemistas. In an insidious ploy, the Garza-Sadas also courted the wives of workers as a means of creating procompany sentiment within the workers' households. The women of the Garza-Sada clan pitched in, along with other elite females, by visiting homes, passing out anti-Communist literature, invoking the church's opposition to communism, and preaching the dangers to family life brought on by communism. In this context, the relations created by the well-honed paternalism of the Garza-Sadas toward workers were not easily broken by CTM organizers.[59]

Despite the myriad of schemes used to block the CTM, the elite realized that the effectiveness of these tactics was susceptible to the powers of Cardenista officials, especially the arbitration board. In this respect, the authority of the governor was pivotal. Thus, the elite invested much money and energy in the upcoming gubernatorial elections in April 1936. The Zuazua campaign, fueled by the industrialists' monies, reached into every corner of the state and permeated the daily life of the city, with banners, leaflets, newspaper advertisements, radio announcements, mobile public address units, and rallies continuously promoting Zuazua.[60] If necessary, Gold Shirts supplied an effective shield of protection to counter disruptions by Cetemistas. The attempt of interim governor Morales Sánchez to disband the *sinarquistas* was foiled when a court injunction neutralized the governor's ban.[61] Furthermore, Morales' effort to squash the *dorados* only compounded a situation thick with apprehension and rife with signs that the elite had retaken the upper hand. The tide in Monterrey was turning against the Cardenista forces.[62]

In early March 1936, the elite scored a coup by pushing through a tough statement from a meeting of private sector organizations that was sent to Cárdenas. The document amounted to a stinging indictment of Cárdenas' policies. The statement received national attention, with *Excelsior* leading the pack of newspapers that gave huge front-page play to the delivery of the document to Cárdenas on March 11, 1936.[63] Three days later, Cárdenas made a defiant response that included a thinly veiled threat of expropriation to recalcitrant businessmen.[64] But the private sector's statement had an effect, and the source of the Patronal Group's action was not lost on Cárdenas.

On March 16, the American consul reported to the secretary of state that the strike at the Vidriera had been settled "due to instructions received by both the governor of Nuevo León from authorities in Mexico City and labor leaders in the capital to local leaders in their demands."[65] Cárdenas had apparently considered the dangers that were implicit in the private sector's audacious statement. A signal was needed to deflate the tensions between his administration and businessmen, and to stave off the possibility of a capitalist alliance led by the men of Monterrey. Furthermore, Lombardo Toledano had succeeded in occupying the central role in the formation of the new labor confederation, the CTM, by being elected secretary general at its meeting (February 20–23, 1936). Worried about losing the beachhead established in Monterrey entirely, Lombardo perhaps decided that the time was propitious to back off from the deteriorating situation in Monterrey. Such a tack complemented Cárdenas' apparent desire to defuse the volatile situation there. Moreover, both Lombardo and Cárdenas were undoubtedly aware of Zuazua's overwhelming advantage in the upcoming elections and wanted to soften, perhaps, the opposition to the PNR candidate, Anacleto Guerrero. Finally, the specter of Calles remained in the background. Cárdenas was intent on avoiding any pretext for a Calles comeback through the possible alliance between the ex-president and the private sector. Cárdenas remembered the Sáenz affair in Querétaro in 1929. Nonetheless, he could not discount entirely that Calles and the *regiomontanos* would forget the past to salvage their aims for the future; stranger bedfellows had occurred in Mexican political history.[66]

The Garza-Sadas gloated over their triumph in the resolution of the Vidriera strike. Encouraged by this success, the elite pressed its advantage further.[67] The smug jubilance of the elite soared when in late March 1936 Morales Sánchez removed the staunchly prolabor judge of the labor tribunal and replaced him with a moderate. The change in the situation moved the U.S. consul in Monterrey to suggest to the State Department that the PNR had conceded the election to Zuazua.[68] In short, the elite had seemingly won another round in its battle against Cárdenas; but the president answered with his own counter.

The elections of April 1, 1936, resulted in Anacleto Guerrero winning the governorship of Nuevo León. The PNR's pervasive use of fraud made Zuazua's loss the more bitter for the *regiomontanos*. The following day, a large demonstration, composed primarily of women, protested Guerrero's victory, forcing Morales Sánchez to leave the governor's palace by the back door to escape the women's wrath. The complaints of the *regiomontanos*, including an avalanche of letters and telegrams to the Secretaría de Gobernación, failed to have any effect.[69] The elite, lulled into an expectant outlook for the election, was deprived once again of reasserting its influence over the governorship of Nuevo León. For Cárdenas, however, the fury of the industrialists of Monterrey over the election was secondary to a more immediate concern.

On April 11, 1936, Cárdenas expelled Calles from Mexico along with Morones and Melchor Ortega. With the ex-*jefe máximo* out of the way, and Lombardo Toledano in place at the head of the CTM, Cárdenas had strengthened his political hand. Still, he endeavored to solidify his position. Nuevo León, with the elite's implacable resistance, remained a weak link in the Cardenista defense against a Callista comeback. Cárdenas worked to preclude any ties that facilitated a Callista regrouping of forces.[70] (In fact, within days of the rupture of the Vidriera strike in February, Aarón Sáenz and José Benitez, two faithful Callistas, appeared in Monterrey, but their visit failed to elicit a favorable response from the *regiomontanos*.) The president's moves toward the elite, at once hostile and solicitous, reflected the aim to bring Nuevo León firmly into the Cardenista fold.

VII.   A month after the elections, tensions remained high as Anacleto Guerrero was installed on May 1, 1936, as the new governor of Nuevo León. To lessen the intense opposition of local industrialists, Guerrero made a series of obvious overtures to the elite. By June 30, 1936, the U.S. consul in Monterrey reported that "the local labor arbitration board has rendered several important decisions in favor of employers which has satisfied local business and industrial interests."[71] At the federal level, the Cárdenas administration announced a proindustry program of incentives for businessmen. The city's capitalists, however, gave no quarter. They chided the government plan for failing to deal with the key obstacle to industrial recovery—Communist agitation. The *regiomontanos'* main arm of anti-Cardenista activity, Acción Cívica, escalated its campaign to rid Monterrey of Lombardista "Communists." Headed by the old war horse Joel Rocha, and the legal counsel of the Cervecería, Virgilio Garza, Jr., Acción Cívica pressed its fight against the CTM's forces, undeterred by Cardenista blandishments or threats.[72] If any thoughts of rapprochement had been considered, they evaporated on the night of July 29, 1936.

Two meetings took place that night only a short distance from the other: one of the Acción Cívica, the other of the CTM affiliate in Monterrey. As the Cetemistas left their meeting, a large group passed by the hall where the Acción Cívica gathering continued. Rocks suddenly pelted the doors and windows of the building; guards stationed at the entry of the hall took cover as the men inside the hall drew their guns and rushed to the doorway. The ensuing volley of gunfire killed two Cetemistas while several others fell wounded. Where local authorities had been strangely absent, police suddenly appeared to arrest Acción Cívica members and round up others, 600 or so in all, and drove them off to the nearby army post barracks. What was apparently an attempt to harass the Acción Cívica had become instead a near massacre. The key target of the episode was Joel Rocha, who was arrested, along with the organization's leadership, including Virgilio Garza, Jr.[73] The next day, virtually all of those arrested posted bail and were released. Under pressure from workers, thousands of whom attended the funeral of the slain Cetemistas, Guerrero ordered the dissolution of the Acción Cívica. But the elite's immediate legal counter voided Guerrero's order.[74]

Relations between government and Monterrey's capitalists had reached a new low. (The proposed expropriation law, introduced to congress in September 1936 by Cardenistas, did little to assuage the distrust of the elite for the president.) The attempt by Cetemistas to muzzle the *regiomontano* businessmen backfired, for the elite seemed the more determined in its resistance to the Cardenistas. In the aftermath of the July 29 incident, local officials backed off from their harassment of the Acción Cívica. Once again conciliatory steps were taken to lessen the tensions between the Guerrero administration and the city's industrialists. The mayor of Monterrey resigned under pressure from the governor, who hoped to pacify an enraged elite.[75] Yet, for *regiomontano* capitalists, the threat of state retaliation lingered, a worry reinforced by the transparent punishment meted out in late 1936 to Callista landowners in the Laguna area under the aegis of the new expropriation law.[76] An abiding hatred for Cárdenas had supplanted the elite's distrust for the president.

VIII.   For political reasons, Cárdenas, like his mentor Calles in the Sáenz affair, risked relations with capital—or a fraction of it—to consolidate his own power and that of the state. But such actions were not intended to cripple Mexican capitalists, nor were these acts a reflection of government hostility toward Mexican business, or toward the Monterrey elite necessarily. Such considerations failed to sway the men of Nuevo León. The residue of the recent past had taken its toll. The economic recuperation of Mexico during the Cárdenas presidency held scant significance for the *regiomontanos'* view of his administration. The state's measures to promote native capital were seen as a natural function of government rather than extraordinary economic policy. Indeed, businessmen believed that Cárdenas fell far short of supplying sufficient support for Mexican capitalists. The president's agrarian reforms and his prolabor policies in particular eclipsed, in the eyes of Monterrey's industrialists, the president's aid to the private sector. In fact, the elite perceived its economic success as an indication of entrepreneurial prowess in the face of the constraints imposed by a "pro-Communist" president. Thus, while the Mexican economy improved—to the benefit of the elite—the men from Monterrey remained steadfast in their opposition to Cárdenas.[77] Profits were not enough.

The slights, resentments, disappointments, and frustrations accumulated over two decades came together in the elite's resistance to Cárdenas and steeled its resolve to confront his administration. This rupture between Cardenistas and the elite of Monterrey (i.e., the faction headed by the Garza-Sadas) had become irreversible. Cárdenas had gambled, with apparent political success, in his foray into Monterrey in February 1936. The president then attempted a short time later to repair his damaged relations with the business community, offering incentives to bring them into the fold. Recalcitrant capitalists, on the other hand, faced the consequences of Cárdenas' veiled threats. Still, the resistance of the *regiomontanos* remained. They were determined, it seems, to make the *michoacano* pay for his political ploy. Yet more than a personal vendetta spurred the elite's opposition to Cárdenas.

The *regiomontano* industrialists appeared convinced that Cárdenas was the harbinger of a socialistic regime where capital would be slowly squeezed into submission to the state. In a confidential memorandum filed on April 17, 1936, Thomas Bowman, the American consul general in Mexico City, noted the point of view of Mexican capitalists and their sense of exclusion from the Cardenista regime. Bowman went on to observe that "until recently each individual industry has carried on its own fight against the demands of labor with but indifferent success on the whole. There was no sign of cooperation among the capitalists to present an organized front until the strike in the Monterrey Glass works was invoked in February when the employer group of that city organized a huge demonstration against the striking laborers. . . . arising out of this bold move there has arisen an organization, . . . the Confederación Patronal de la República Mexicana, or Employers Confederation of Mexico."[78]

Bowman continued by describing the organization and its purpose. Among its tactics, the American consul general stated that "one of the reported plans is to organize a band of spies to be sent into the labor organizations to create discord and troubles of an internal character in them. . . . The labor organizations are looked upon by the organization as Communistic hotbeds. Financial and moral support will also be given the 'Gold Shirts.' . . . It is too soon, of course, to form any opinion as to its ultimate success but it is significant as a sign of awakening among employers of the necessity for concerted action."[79] Bowman went on to say (referring to the letter of March 1936 to Cárdenas) that capital had made gestures of conciliation. "The beneficial results of this new policy, if pursued, would appear to depend upon whether the laborers are motivated by the simple desire to improve their own standard of life or by the spirit of class warfare," Bowman argued, "which many of their leaders and supporters openly agitate for." However, Bowman concluded, "it is believed that most businessmen at present skeptically consider the latter motive predominant."[80]

The *regiomontanos* persisted in their resolve to roll back the Cardenistas from Nuevo León. Nearly a year after the president's celebrated journey to Monterrey, the U.S. consul in the city noted that the COPARMEX chapter "maintains a paid staff of labor observers whose business is to closely watch labor activities and prepare weekly bulletins for confidential distribution among members."[81] By February 1937, the American consul in Monterrey reported a discernible shift in the Cardenistas' stance in Monterrey as "strike agitation had noticeably diminished in the Monterrey industries."[82] Meanwhile, the consul continued, "the patronal association . . . [has] devoted practically all of [its] time to reports on communistic activities among labor organizations and political possibilities resulting therefrom."[83]

Thus, a year after Cárdenas' Fourteen-Point speech in Monterrey, his labor supporters appeared on the run; Cetemista strength had dwindled dramatically. Governor Anacleto Guerrero, apparently frustrated by the interminable feuding within the CTM and its disruptive consequences for PNR activities in Nuevo León, turned against the radical Cetemistas. Instead, Guerrero began to court the *blanco* unions for his PNR organization. The elite's disruptive tactics, coupled with the old animosities toward Lombardo Toledano, had rendered the Cetemista organization in Monterrey nearly impotent in its battle against the Garza-Sadas. In May 1937, Lombardo Toledano made a last-ditch effort to rally his forces in the city, to no avail. Despite Cetemista protests to PNR headquarters in Mexico City, Guerrero turned a deaf ear to their complaints, and a telling silence came from the presidential palace.[84]

In late May 1937, the U.S. consul reported an attempt by the militant or "red" wing of the CTM to remount a strike at the Vidriera. The arbitration board, with the obvious consent of Guerrero, ruled the action illegal. The Garza-Sadas took advantage of the ruling by "discharging a number of radical leaders and permitted the strikers to return to work on condition that the CTM labor contract be voided and workers agree to the provisions of the independent [*blanco*] syndicate's contract."[85] The American consul concluded that the "glass company appears to have completely broken the radical syndicate . . . and this with the approval of the government."[86] The American's observation, as it turned out, was also the epitaph of the CTM in the industries of the Garza-Sadas.

The elite was convinced that the weakening of the CTM in Monterrey stemmed from its efforts. In fact, the ebbing strength of the Cetemistas reflected to some extent a change in the posture of the Cárdenas regime. In July 1937, a month after the May visit of Lombardo to Monterrey, one observer remarked that the feuding among labor had subsided because of the "strong influence being brought to bear upon the President to look with disfavor on radical strike activities."[87] Nevertheless, bolstered by local success against the Cetemistas, the elite laid plans for larger prey. The presidential elections of 1940 afforded the Garza-Sadas and their cabal an opportunity to check the reformist impulse of the Mexican state spearheaded by Lázaro Cárdenas. Despite their experience with rigged elections, the men from Nuevo León had reason for optimism for their drive to deal Cardenismo a fatal blow.

IX.   The situation in Monterrey pointed to an initial retreat by Cardenista forces. As early as February 1937, the American consul reported remarks by business that indicated a "slowing down" of Cardenista reforms.[88] And in June 1937, the American consul noted that the PNR directorate was supporting conservative candidates in Nuevo León. Based on his observations in Nuevo León, the American went on to say that the "Cárdenas administration is now favoring a slowing down of radical labor movements and looks with disfavor on excessive strike activities of labor leaders."[89] In Nuevo León, according to the U.S. envoy, the Cetemistas were "not as popular with state and federal governments as heretofore and [that] the radical leaders of labor agitation are being placed in embarrassing positions with their membership."[90] A month later, the cordial relations between businessmen and Guerrero figured prominently in the U.S. consul's report (July 1937).[91] Thus, the unraveling of Cardenista strength was apparent in Nuevo León several months prior to obvious public indications of a conservative shift within the Cárdenas administration.[92]

Furthermore, the economic success of the Garza-Sadas afforded them yet another source of strength: a strength augmented by the federal government's fragile financial situation.[93] The deterioration of the state's finances was compounded by the expropriation of foreign oil companies in March 1938. The loss of export revenues made the federal treasury more vulnerable to the transfer of capital by Mexican businessmen to other countries. The precarious conditions of the Mexican economy therefore magnified the political pressures exercised by the elite. In this regard, the *regiomontanos* were not necessarily the only group that exerted financial pressure on the state for political gain. Rather, the political calculations of the elite turned on other factors, including international diplomatic opinion. For instance, the storm of protest over the expropriation by American interests raised the possibility that the United States would welcome a move away from Cardenista policies.[94]

Finally, by 1938, the president faced a vast reservoir of opposition. Although diverse in nature, this opposition held a key thread of unity— Lázaro Cárdenas. The Cedillo rebellion, though defeated quickly in 1938, revealed the undercurrents of anti-Cárdenas sentiments.[95] Given the assumption that Cárdenas would select his old friend and ideological ally, Francisco Múgica, as the next president, the anti-Cardenista fires burned still greater.[96] And, perhaps most important to the hopes of Monterrey's industrialists, there existed a man who possessed the attributes of an attractive candidate—Juan Andreu Almazán. From the standpoint of the elite, the possibilities of overwhelming the Cardenista regime appeared increasingly plausible by 1938 as the signs multiplied of Cárdenas' weakening political hold.[97] For among the problems facing Cárdenas were ominous stirrings of opposition from within his own ranks.

In the period 1934 to 1938, the relations between the businessmen of Monterrey and government revealed blatantly divergent forces within the state. On the one hand, Cárdenas pushed for the development of native capital, yet on the other he prompted the political organization of workers and peasants. For the president, these two elements of his administration went hand in hand and strengthened his position and that of his party. For the elite, Cárdenas' presidency represented a clear threat. The *regiomontanos* were not alone. From within the revolutionary family, criticism surfaced over Cárdenas' reforms: their ramifications provoked the concerns of bureaucrats, generals, and ex-officials who eyed enviously the rise of competing political actors. Furthermore, Cardenista reforms annoyed if not angered revolutionaries turned businessmen, whose interests dictated filling their pockets rather than fulfilling the stated aims of the revolution. The successor to Cárdenas, therefore, held important stakes for the elite; and for the Mexican state, as it turned out, the stakes were also high.

9. Epilogue as Preface to a New Era: The Monterrey Elite and the Elections of 1940

I. The 1940 elections capped over a decade of conflict between the Monterrey elite and the Mexican state. The political history of the presidential contest revealed the strengths and weaknesses of the two adversaries. Each side fielded its candidate, and they occupied the headlines and rhetoric of the time. Nonetheless, at a critical point in the campaign, the candidates themselves became secondary to the drama that unfolded over the relationship of the *regiomontano* elite to the post-Cárdenas state. At that pivotal juncture, the men of Nuevo León took center stage. Juan Andreu Almazán, the erstwhile champion of the group, was eclipsed by a larger struggle in which the Monterrey elite played a crucial role with enduring consequences for Mexico's political economy.

Lorenzo Meyer has argued persuasively that the foundations of the Mexican state were laid in the years from 1929 to 1940.[1] Significantly, this period also marked the consolidation of the Monterrey elite as a discernible fraction of the Mexican bourgeoisie and its identification as a potential political rival to government. Throughout this period, the *regiomontanos* sustained an adversarial position regardless of the faction that held sway in the presidential palace. Thus, the presidential race of 1940 represented a culminating point for both the elite and government. For the state, the elections signified a decisive step toward its political maturation. For the businessmen of Monterrey, the presidential contest offered an opportunity to influence the direction of state-capital relations after 1940. In the context of this key historical moment, the *regiomontanos'* resilient opposition contributed importantly to the formation and character of the post-Cárdenas state.

II. Almazán was a transparent opportunist whose popularity, charismatic image, and alleged effectiveness as military strategist, entrepreneur, and politician seem puzzling in hindsight. Still, the fact remains that he was convinced, or convinced himself, that the possibility existed of his election to the presidency. Almazán weighed his decision carefully; he had much to gain, but he also had a great deal to lose. The general by this time was enormously wealthy, politically influential, and well liked by many high-ranking officers of the Mexican military. In a meeting with Cárdenas in Monterrey in April 1939, Almazán received assurances that the elections, including the PRM nomination (the name of the party had changed to Partido de la Revolución Mexicana), would be conducted fairly. And Cárdenas' public pronouncements on the issue, though obligatory, reinforced the perception that he would allow an honest election. The emergence of Manuel Ávila Camacho, a moderate candidate for the party nomination, also augured well for Almazán: Ávila Camacho represented a conservative faction within the PRM. On July 29, 1939, Almazán announced his candidacy for the presidency.[2]

On September 1, 1939, *El Porvenir*, in an editorial, disputed the claim by the Mexican ambassador to the United States that the Roosevelt administration was indifferent to the results of the Mexican presidential elections.[3] The editorial reflected in fact the importance attached by Monterrey interests on American backing for the Almazanista effort. Unappreciated at the time, an ominous note appeared for the Almazán campaign on September 3, 1939, when *El Porvenir* headlined Britain's declaration of war against Germany. That same day, Ávila Camacho arrived in Monterrey.

In his visit, Ávila Camacho made a conscious, conspicuous attempt to court the businessmen of Monterrey to his side. Indeed, he began his speech with a glowing nod toward the *regiomontano* entrepreneurs, intending perhaps to deflect their drive to support an alternative, Almazanista party. The speech made an impression; a dent had been made in the wall of opposition in Monterrey toward the PRM.[4] Within four days, the federal government announced a new program of incentives and subsidies for Mexican industrialists.[5] Then, three weeks later, with grudging acknowledgment, *El Porvenir* lauded the administration's promotion of Mexican industry on the eve of Cárdenas' meeting with leading members of Mexico's private sector on September 27, 1939.[6]

Between Ávila Camacho's first trip to Monterrey in early September and Cárdenas' meeting with businessmen later that month, the *regiomontanos* had figured prominently at the meeting of the opposing Partido Acción Nacional on September 14–17, 1939, in Mexico City. Organized largely by Manuel Gómez Morín, a wealthy lawyer with close business ties with the elite, the PAN represented a conduit for anti-Cárdenas forces in the initial assembly of the party. Though resisted by Gómez Morín, Almazán received the backing of the new party, whose operations were funded in part by the capitalists of Monterrey. Since the PRM nominating convention would not take place until November 1939, the elite's support of the PAN and Almazán pointed to their suspicion that Múgica might still receive the nod of the PRM; the memories of Querétaro persisted.[7] (Múgica had announced his pulling out of contention for the PRM nomination in July 1939.) But the subsequent nomination of Ávila Camacho, in the minds of the elite, proved that the efforts had made an impact. Ávila Camacho undoubtedly reinforced the perception by his visits to Monterrey *after* the PAN's meeting in mid-September.

On October 5, 1939, the Cervecería Cuauhtémoc received several representatives of the PRM. On October 8, 1939, the brewery of the Garza-Sadas hosted a lunch for Ávila Camacho after he had toured the Cervecería and the Vidriera. Three days later, Ávila Camacho once again passed through the city, visiting the Fundidora and meeting with "some of the magnates of banking and industry of Monterrey."[8] And on October 14, 1939, Ávila Camacho appeared in Monterrey for the fourth time in a month, touring yet another company on that occasion.

The *regiomontanos* were not blind to the political currents that swirled within the PRM, the factionalism that tore at its unity. Yet, such divisions within the PRM, the residue of the conflicts between the Múgica and Ávila Camacho wings of the party, held no guarantees of an Almazán victory. Equally important, the *regiomontanos* realized their failure to galvanize sufficient support within the Mexican private sector to challenge the hold of the PRM.[9]

Throughout the previous three years, the Garza-Sadas and their allies had attempted to win over other powerful businessmen to their side in an open confrontation with the Mexican state. These efforts, however, drew a cautious if not sullen response from key fractions of the Mexican bourgeoisie. As the Cetemistas' thrust into Monterrey retreated in defeat in early 1937, the elite had redoubled its drive to organize capital into a united front against Cárdenas. Yet the clarion call in March 1937 for businessmen elsewhere to duplicate the elite's success in Nuevo León failed to elicit a resounding response by their private sector counterparts.[10] The following month (April 1937), with biting sarcasm, the *regiomontanos* chastized Mexican capitalists for their lack of courage openly to dispute government authority.[11] Such a quick, sharp criticism of their expected allies reflected the frustration of Monterrey's industrialists to arouse businessmen, the men of Mexico City in particular, to do battle with Cárdenas and the state. Nearly a year before (June 1936) in *Actividad*, the elite had made clear its dissatisfaction with its erstwhile counterparts in Mexico City for their unwillingness to join the COPARMEX campaign against Cárdenas.[12] Another criticism of capitalists of the Distrito Federal appeared in the July 1936 issue of the Nuevo León–based publication, along with an article entitled, tellingly, "Capital's Unification Is Urgent."[13]

The *regiomontanos'* efforts to unify capital compelled a response by Cárdenas when in August 1936 he introduced legislation that forced the Chambers of Commerce and Chambers of Industry to unite into one umbrella confederation. The Chambers Law of 1936 gave vast powers to the state that posed a clear threat to the business organization—an obvious attempt to keep Mexican capitalists in line and to isolate COPARMEX. The purpose of Cárdenas' tactic was not missed by the industrialists of Monterrey. In this respect, the Chambers Law of 1936 served as a warning to dissident businessmen, as Arnaldo Córdova has argued, but it failed to subdue the *regiomontanos.*[14]

As early as May 1936, the elite had alerted businessmen of Cardenista efforts to thwart capital's unity. In this light, Monterrey's industrialists understandably and caustically denounced Cárdenas' proindustry measures as a ploy to undermine the organization of businessmen, as a "divide and conquer" tactic.[15] In an article entitled "El mito de la cooperación patronal," published in May 1938 in *Actividad,* the elite repeated its condemnation of disunity among businessmen, with a tone of exasperation, urging capitalists once again to join COPARMEX in its battle against the Cardenista state.[16] Perhaps in retaliation, the CTM made a last-gasp, but disruptive effort to recoup lost ground in Monterrey two months later. The action enraged Nuevo León's businessmen to new heights of anti-Cardenista polemics, although the Cetemistas' effort fizzled into an ignominious failure.[17] Nevertheless, the repeated calls of the elite for capital's unity fell short of expectations due in part to the successful efforts of the Cárdenas administration to woo other capitalists from joining the ranks of COPARMEX.[18] Thus, the pleas of the *regiomontanos'* spokesman, Porfirio Ramos, in February 1939 for businessmen "to organize" was as much a lament as a rallying cry.[19] The constant calls of this type from 1936 through 1939 underscored the importance of capital's unity to the elite's designs to eliminate the reformist initiatives of the Cardenista state.

As the pivotal political moment arrived in late 1939, therefore, the elite was both apprehensive and hopeful over the response of other businessmen to the Almazán candidacy and his endorsement by the PAN convention. The response disappointed and embittered. In a revealing, biting editorial entitled "Ignorancia . . . ?" in *Actividad* in October 1939, the *regiomontanos* expressed their sense of betrayal, particularly at the hands of their Mexico City counterparts.[20] The business ties forged between the capitalists of the two cities failed to produce a binding political alliance. The inability of the industrialists of Monterrey to organize capital, especially the powerful fraction of the Distrito Federal, contributed decisively to the accommodation of the elite to Ávila Camacho. Thus, in the aftermath of Ávila Camacho's visits of September and October of 1939, the prevailing outlook of Monterrey businessmen was that "no independent candidate [had] much chance of becoming president of Mexico."[21]

Still, the elite pressed for a means to lessen further the power of the Cardenistas within the PRM. And the internal divisions of the PRM in the wake of the November convention allowed for political maneuvering by Nuevo León's businessmen. By supporting a large and effective campaign for Almazán, the *regiomontanos* seemed to have realized the impact of their pressure on a badly splintered PRM. As one student of Mexican politics at that time has concluded, "the opposition movement of 1939 had without doubt an important influence in the life of the party. During those months and under the influence of the divisiveness that developed then, two reactions took place: on the one hand, internal democracy became virtually nonexistent and, on the other hand, the official positions of the PRM became increasingly moderate."[22] In this light, the elite's continued support for Almazán and the PAN was apparently intended to influence Ávila Camacho and the PRM platform to move further away from Cardenismo. The effects of this ploy appeared clearly in the platform approved by the PRM convention in November as the six-year plan "seemed to be directed toward industrial development rather than social reforms. . . ."[23] Almazán's obvious popularity—that is, the force of the anti-Cardenistas—made the opposition's ploy the more effective. Despite the moderation of Ávila Camacho supporters, the expanding opposition continued to press his association with Cárdenas and to emphasize his early endorsement by the CTM.[24] The elite was convinced that Almazán would win an honest election.

If a deal had been struck with Ávila Camacho in his visits to Monterrey in late September 1939, the elite nonetheless played both sides against each other for several months. In fact, the Garza-Sadas and their cohort held onto a thread of hope that Almazán somehow, by military coup, would become president. But such a hope rested, in their eyes, on American backing for Almazán. The persistent portrayal of Ávila Camacho as a lackey of the "Communist" forces of Lombardo Toledano revealed an attempt to curry American favor for Almazán. Thus, members of the Garza-Sada clique continued to weigh and probe the possibilities of American support for their dream of an Almazán presidency.[25] But the war in Europe precluded such hopes. The United States wanted to avoid a revolt in its backyard as Europe, especially

Britain, required the full attention of the Roosevelt administration. Moreover, unknown to the *regiomontano* elite, the United States looked askance at the pro-German sentiments of the Monterrey business-men.[26] Hence, American interest in a coup for Almazán was virtually out of the question.

Nonetheless, the Garza-Sadas and their allies sustained their pres-sure as the PAN gained adherents and as Almazán's crowds grew larger, forcing the PRM candidate to take yet more moderate posi-tions.[27] In retaliation, Cardenistas in the spring of 1940 made constant threats and harassed the Garza-Sadas and their friends. In April 1940, for instance, the Rocha and Sada families requested safe passage across the border from the U.S. State Department in case of the need to make an emergency exit.[28] And in the month before the elections, the harassment of Almazán's business supporters compelled the gen-eral to lash out at the PRM for its effort to intimidate his backers.[29]

The complaints, however, were inconsequential to the results. The outcome of the elections in July 1940, as predicted by the elite, was a reflection of massive fraud; the lopsided victory of Manuel Ávila Camacho pointed to the practiced hand of PRM functionaries in rig-ging elections.[30] Despite the defeat of Almazán, however, the indus-trialists of Monterrey had won a crucial victory.

III.   In 1976, José López Portillo traveled to Nuevo León soon after his inauguration as president of Mexico to meet with the businessmen of Monterrey. The visit occurred in the wake of nearly three years of conflicts between former president José Luis Echeverría and the Grupo Monterrey. These clashes had precipitated the formation of a business organization (the Consejo Coordinador Empresarial) that brought together key segments of the Mexican private sector to op-pose the populist measures of the Echeverría regime. The journey of López Portillo recalled the trek of Ávila Camacho in 1939 to Mon-terrey; the CCE reminded of the origins of COPARMEX in 1929. Moreover, the visit of the newly installed president to Monterrey reconfirmed the historical, adversarial role of the Monterrey elite to the state. The near-mythic place of the *regiomontanos* among Mexican businessmen was once again affirmed, and specifically that of a par-ticular element of the Grupo Monterrey, the Garza-Sada family inter-ests. As one observer of Mexico has put it, "mention Monterrey and the Monterrey Group comes to mind; mention the Monterrey Group and a tightly-knit family of wealthy and conservative businessmen comes to mind."[31]

For most students of the Mexican past, the political identification of the Monterrey Group finds its origins in the celebrated confrontation with Lázaro Cárdenas in 1936. Few histories of modern Mexico fail to mention the event. Nonetheless, the importance of that moment generally rests on Cárdenas' position on labor—his famous Fourteen-Point speech—rather than on the roots and outcomes of the confrontation itself.[32] Similarly, the role of the *regiomontanos* in the labor law debate of 1929–1931 recedes in significance to the larger concern over the extension of government authority over workers as a result of the federal labor code of 1931.[33] In a related manner, the support of *regiomontanos* for the opposition in the 1940 elections becomes secondary to the consequences of the elections: the retreat of the dominant party from the reformist posture of the Cárdenas administration.[34] In the analysis of these events, the Monterrey elite becomes a prop or backdrop to the discussion usually centered on the evolution of the Mexican state. In short, the historical significance of the Grupo Monterrey is found in its relationship to pivotal turns in the development and direction of the Mexican state.[35] As a consequence, the definition of the Monterrey Group comes down to a series of snapshots of Mexican history—1929, 1936, 1940, and so on to the contemporary era. Crucial questions remain, however: why the Grupo Monterrey? Why the significance of the Garza-Sadas within the Monterrey Group? Why the leading role of the Monterrey Group, the Garza-Sadas specifically, in the contest between capital and the state in the postrevolutionary era?

As others have noted, powerful family groups exist in Mexico that parallel the Monterrey Group. And within such nuclei of economic interests, certain families hold decisive power.[36] Yet, in comparison to the businessmen of Monterrey, such family-based economic groups have been less forceful, less visible, less resilient in the conflicts between capital and the state. And rarely, it seems, based on the current evidence, has a group of industrialists so dominated a city in Mexico as effectively or as long as those of Monterrey. Indeed, they possess (or have possessed) a degree of power that approaches hegemonic proportions and clearly denotes them as an elite. Why, then, the recurring position of the Monterrey businessmen at the forefront of the opposition of the private sector to the Mexican state?

As this study has attempted to demonstrate, the historical importance of the *regiomontanos*, and the Garza-Sadas particularly, hinges on the development of this group within the larger framework of the evolution of capital-state relations. In this process, three interrelated factors emerge that are crucial to the singular place of the Monterrey elite in modern Mexican history: (1) the ability of the Monterrey elite, despite modifications in its composition, to sustain an extraordinary degree of cohesiveness—economic, social, and political—in which the concentration and coordination of its vast resources allowed it to bring inordinate pressure on capital-state relations; (2) the contradictions of the postrevolutionary state between the political imperatives of reform on the one hand and the consequences of the state's capitalist orientation toward economic development on the other; and (3) the differentiation within the private sector in its relations with the Mexican state.

The interconnections within the elite were critical to its economic success, its social distinctiveness, and its industrial origins. The pooling of economic resources, extending back to the times of Vidaurri in several cases, was reinforced by the multiplication of social ties that over time created a tight, thick complex of relations; an industrial elite formed on the basis of this interpenetration of relations. The implicit if not explicit competition represented by the proximity of the United States gave a regional bent to the formation of the Monterrey elite that was seconded by its initial orientation toward regional markets. If only inadvertently, the extractive nature of foreign investment in Monterrey served to further the insularity of the elite, its sense of mission, and its propensity to cooperate in the face of outside capitalists. Furthermore, the distance between Monterrey and Mexico City served to encourage the narrow vision of the men from Monterrey.

The social network underlying the economic ties among *regiomontano* businessmen underscored their social distinctiveness. The dependence of Monterrey's middle sectors contributed to the elite status of the businessmen of the city. More importantly, the emergence of an effective policy of labor paternalism in the major industries of Monterrey heightened the social as well as the economic power of *regiomontano* entrepreneurs. The prevailing, positivist intellectual currents of the time supplied the elite with an ideological underpinning to wealth and social position. In a nation long bereft of factories and native enterprise, the exceptional industrialization of Monterrey enhanced the image and substance of the elite to national proportions, fueling the elite's own growing sense of superiority.

Crucial to the elite's consolidation in the Porfiriato was the special role of government, namely, in the form of Bernardo Reyes during a critical period in the formation of the Monterrey elite. Reyes acted as political broker between the *regiomontanos* and the Porfirian government. Equally important, Reyes was primarily a promoter of the economic development of the city rather than a participant, leaving to the elite the economic reins of the city's industrialization. In the free enterprise notions of the *regiomontanos*, Reyes played perfectly the assigned role of government. Furthermore, the procapitalist posture of the Porfiriato reinforced the significance of the Reyes years in Monterrey. As a consequence, the incipient differences in the industries of Nuevo León in terms of their dependence on government were minimized by the convergence of interests between businessmen and the Porfiriato. The unobtrusive Reyes administration of Nuevo León therefore complemented the consolidation of the elite and completed its sense of control, its hegemony over the city.

In this context, the Garza-Sadas, more so than other fractions of the maturing elite, concentrated their economic, familial, and social resources on the Cervecería, the anchor of the group's fortunes. The vertical, logical growth of the brewery pushed its owners toward glass-making, and eventually the establishment of the Vidriera. Attendant activities, such as financing, packaging, and production of bottle caps, were natural extensions of their intent to develop the Cervecería. Hence, the preoccupation of the Garza-Sadas with the brewery gave their economic interests a greater focus, a center for their energies and investments in contrast to the more diffuse activities of their *regiomontano* counterparts in the Porfirian period. Unappreciated at the time, the unimportance of the state to the markets of the budding Garza-Sada empire gave the Cervecería a decided edge over those industries whose welfare stemmed in large measure from state protection, contracts, and support. The latent distinction between the Cervecería and the Fundidora, for example, and other firms of similar conditions, existed prior to 1910. Nonetheless, before 1910, the overriding factor in the rise of the Monterrey industrialists during the Porfirian era was the cohesion that derived from the elite's economic interconnections, social linkages, and common ideological outlook. The political dimension of its authority was provided by Reyes, who supplied the *regiomontanos* with governmental security and privilege. Thus, the apparent seamless web of power of the Monterrey elite seemed complete.

The revolution forced a wedge into the cohesive Porfirian front of the capitalists of Monterrey. The political assurances provided by Reyes eroded, then evaporated for a time after 1914. The reformist impulse of the new order destroyed the political harmony of business-government relations of the Porfiriato. The subsequent support of Victoriano Huerta, later of Aarón Sáenz, and still later of Almazán, reflected the attempts of the Monterrey elite to broker its relations between its economic interests and the postrevolutionary state. Similarly, the efforts of *regiomontano* businessmen to reassert their local dominance underscored their conflicts with governors and municipal officials, their extension of paternalistic labor controls, and their search for a new Reyes. Most importantly, after 1917 the new political and economic order touched a discordant element within the Monterrey elite, and among Mexican capitalists in general.

The progressive thrust of the new state—induced often by political necessity rather than by conviction—was juxtaposed with its drive for capitalist economic development, creating a tension in the state's relations with the private sector. The vulnerability of certain companies to the state assumed a critical importance in the ability and/or willingness of owners to counter the reformist initiative of the state. In this sense, the new state, despite its promotion of native capital, disrupted the congruence of the elite. The intrinsic rift between the Fundidora and the Cervecería became apparent in the wake of the state's determination to reconcile its economic reconstruction of the country with social reforms. The range of relations between capital and the state widened as a consequence of the shifting degrees of autonomy and/or dependence between businessmen and government. In the case of Monterrey's industries, the brewery and the city's steel plant provided a telling illustration of this change in the political economy of Mexico after 1910.

The Fundidora interests became an adjunct or ally to that segment of Monterrey's industrialists less dependent on the state rather than an integral part of the *regiomontano* bourgeoisie. The dependence of the Fundidora on the state facilitated the assumption of the Cervecería to a preeminent position within the industrial complex of Monterrey. In size, symbolic importance, and prowess, the Garza-Sadas had no other peers among firms owned largely or entirely by native capital in the city. The relatively small role of foreign investment in Monterrey—a pattern established prior to 1910—continued and furthered the prominence of the Cervecería clique. Moreover, through fortuitous economic success, coupled with competent leadership, the industries of the Garza-Sadas enjoyed an exceptional place in the city that redoubled their owners' clout within the Monterrey elite.

As a result, the reconstitution of the elite witnessed the emergence of a discernible core within the larger network of interests of the *regiomontano* business establishment. The Garza-Sadas composed the basis of that portion of the elite that disputed with increasing force the new state and its authority. This redefinition of the Monterrey elite reflected to a large extent the relative economic independence of the Garza-Sadas from the state as a source of protection or of profits. For the Garza-Sadas and their cohorts, this lack of reliance on the state for markets or defense from foreign competition also sustained the ideological outlook among *regiomontano* businessmen engendered by the Porfirian era. Moreover, the capable captains of the Cervecería, with their peculiar American cast, added to the preponderance of the Garza-Sadas within the elite of Monterrey in the postrevolutionary era. In this sense, the internal cohesion of the elite was redefined, or, perhaps more accurately, was refined in light of the new role of the state in the political economy of Monterrey and Mexico as a whole. In this realignment of the Monterrey elite, the state was an essential catalyst, an indispensable reference point. But the state was inconsistent in the conciliation of its economic aims with reform, endowing that fraction of Nuevo León's capitalists headed by the Garza-Sadas with greater meaning and power.

IV. The political economic context of the *regiomontano* elite changed substantially after 1917 with the end of the Porfiriato and the passing of the Maderista interlude. A key change stemmed from the contradictions of the new order, at once procapitalist and reformist. The return of the Cervecería to the Garza-Sadas in 1916 contrasted with the implications of the labor strikes of 1918 in Nuevo León and Article 123 of the new constitution. The concern for political consolidation of the postrevolutionary leadership compelled a reformist rhetoric, however unevenly implemented, that clashed implicitly if not explicitly with the goal of national economic development. The responses of the elite were several, but the underlying aim was to limit the state's power in the economy generally, and in the affairs of Monterrey businessmen in particular.

In this light, the elite sought to reproduce, however crudely, the past: to find a political *caudillo* in the mold of Reyes to mediate the interests of the elite with those of government. The *regiomontanos* desired a certain kind of arrangement or understanding with the state, not necessarily a political or economic divorce. Specifically, the men of Monterrey strove to negotiate a bargain of sorts with the new order that maintained the elite's local power and assured its national economic concerns. The new state proved incapable or unwilling to establish such an accord. The presence of brazenly corrupt officials, such as the governors in Nuevo León for most of the 1920s, revealed the concessions of the nascent state in order to acquire or sustain political support from ex-military chieftains. The concessions to Morones and the CROM showed the new order's need for sources of popular support; its occasional attempts at agrarian reform pointed to the effort to maintain a base among Mexican peasants. For the Monterrey industrialists, such acts of political consolidation by the new order undermined, indeed threatened, the aim of national economic reconstruction in which the interests of businessmen would be paramount.

Nonetheless, the key to the elite's concerns revolved around the issue of control over its local affairs. The arrival of Aarón Sáenz to the governorship of Nuevo León in 1927 offered *regiomontanos* a *caudillo* to intervene for the elite in political matters and to manage relations with the state. Sáenz' presidential contention after Obregón's death raised the hopes of the elite to greater heights. The history of intermittent friction between *regiomontano* capitalists and the state appeared to be near its end. The industrialists of Monterrey expected Sáenz to right the wrongs of the past and to guarantee the future.

But state interests intervened. The political situation following Obregón's death dictated a different tack by Calles. The *jefe máximo* jettisoned Sáenz' presidential bid. Instead, labor legislation for the codification of Article 123 was proposed that gave the state a decisive role in capital-labor relations. The presidency, seemingly so close to the grasp of the *regiomontanos*, was lost to the political maneuvering of Calles; their grip of Monterrey was once again in question. Hence, despite the increasingly probusiness stance of Calles-dominated administrations, the elite appeared determined to recoup its sense of control, to break the hold of Callistas specifically, and of the state generally in Monterrey. This motivation was bolstered by the passage in 1931 of a federal labor code decidedly proworker from the standpoint of *regiomontano* employers. The Monterrey-led efforts to block, then alter, the labor code underlined the emergence of the *regiomontano* elite as chief critics of the state from the private sector.

The events of 1929–1931, however, also indicated the reluctance of the state to confront the private sector. The state possessed the means, the instruments, to punish recalcitrant, overly critical businessmen. The government's lumber tax proposal of 1931—a transparent jab at Joel Rocha—showed that the Callistas' tolerance for criticism from the private sector had its limits. The point made, the Callistas consequently rescinded the lumber tax. Thus, condemnation of the state was not without costs for capitalists, and such considerations colored the frequency if not the severity of the criticism leveled against the state by businessmen. Still, the concern of the postrevolutionary leadership for economic recovery, and self-interest, blunted its willingness to retaliate fully against its capitalist critics.

But the Monterrey elite's confrontation with the state over the labor code—an extension of resentment over the Sáenz affair—also signaled a redefinition of the Mexican private sector that put the *regiomontanos* at the forefront of capital's opposition to the state. In this sense, the formation of COPARMEX reflected a clarification of the alignment of forces within the private sector as a consequence of state action. The state's political concerns framed a labor law that contradicted its capitalist economic goals—a contradiction that gave birth to COPARMEX. The inconsistency of the state opened the door for the elite's organization of COPARMEX and for its leadership of the Grupo Patronal.

This contradiction between capitalist economic development, on the one hand, and reform, on the other, was compounded by the growing role of postrevolutionary bureaucrats in the private sector. As time passed after 1917, the new state spawned its own "revolutionary capitalists" whose economic interests expanded and deepened *over time* and put them increasingly at odds with the reformist thrusts of the central government. As the Cárdenas administration entered office, therefore, the splintering of state interests between "revolutionary capitalists" and reformers blurred the cleavage between government and business, further complicating the jockeying for political power among the leadership of the state. By 1934, the state's "interests" were tied in part to those of the private sector. And, as in the contradiction within the state, the differences within the Mexican private sector offered the men of Monterrey advantages that redoubled their political strength. The fragmentation among businessmen magnified the cohesion of the *regiomontanos.*

V.   The relations between the Mexican private sector and the state varied in the two decades or so that followed the Mexican revolution. Indeed, the easy dichotomy between "capital" and "state" disintegrated in the face of Porfirian bankers who organized the postrevolutionary government's financial system and in light of large landowners who maintained their haciendas despite the din over agrarian reform. In fact, complexity marked the relationship between the new state and businessmen after 1917 as several factors impinged upon the interface between government and capitalists. First, for some segments of capital, the state held decisive power and influence. Second, for other elements of the private sector, industries in particular, the state's sway was enlarged by its importance as a source of profits and/or a defense against foreign competition. Third, the state's ability to manipulate workers and peasants gave it a means to influence a number of employers and landowners. Fourth, the postrevolutionary era witnessed the entry of government officials into the private sector. Thus, by the 1930s, the spectrum of relations involving government and businessmen vitiated any simple separation of interests into discrete categories of state and capital. And, in this context, the Monterrey elite, specifically the Garza-Sadas, held a distinct place.

The Cervecería and Vidriera in the 1920s benefited from the state's drive for industrialization and the promotion of native capital to counter the traditional and continuing dominance of the Mexican economy by foreign capital. But the necessity of protectionism from foreign competition was much less important to the brewery and its allied interests. Prohibition in the United States and exclusive rights to certain glass-making patents in Mexico gave the Cervecería a measure of immunity not available to many other firms. (In fact, the main problem for the brewery was its domestic competitors.) Furthermore, government did not constitute a key market for the brewery and its subsidiaries. In addition, notwithstanding their battles with the arbitration court, the labor paternalism of the Garza-Sadas blunted the impact of the state among the workers of the Cervecería and Vidriera. Finally, the Garza-Sadas held a tight rein over their interests that precluded the entry of government officials into the main holdings of the Garza-Sadas. Indeed, the evidence suggests that the Cervecería's owners, through their financial clout, were able to exercise their own kind of pressure on the state.

Hence, the Garza-Sada clan was able to keep the state at arm's length from its economic base, and, as a result, was less vulnerable to the government's use of instruments such as tariffs, contracts, or the mobilization of state-controlled unions. Consequently, the Garza-Sadas minimized the problems that plagued those that were forced to bow to political considerations. (Manuel Gómez Morín, for instance, quit his post as president of the Banco de México in 1929 due to the large loans extracted from the bank by favored officials, including the *jefe máximo* himself.)[37] In short, the relative autonomy of the Garza-Sadas from the state underlined their leadership of Monterrey's businessmen in the postrevolutionary years.

In this light, the events of 1929–1931 were pivotal for the position of the Garza-Sadas and their local allies in the spectrum of relations within and among government and capital. First, this period represented a break with the key faction of the state at that time, the Callistas. Second, the Monterrey elite broke ranks with the private sector and made its distinctiveness concrete through the formation of COPARMEX and its role in the ensuing labor code struggle.

The labor law issue confirmed the *regiomontanos'* irrevocable repugnance for the progressive, reformist elements of the state. More importantly, it also constituted a break with the more conservative Callistas, who, for reasons of political control over labor, fostered the codification of Article 123. The transformation of Sáenz from the darling of the elite in 1929 to architect of the passage of the federal labor code in 1931 revealed the estrangement between the elite and the least progressive elements of the state bureaucracy; Sáenz was one of the most visibly wealthy "revolutionary capitalists."[38] Sáenz and his counterparts demonstrated to members of the elite, if any proof was necessary, that their political interests were primary: their economic welfare was rooted in the state's domination if not control of Mexico's masses.[39]

The break with the conservative wing of the state in 1929–1931 paralleled the elite's redefinition within the broad framework of the Mexican private sector. The formation of COPARMEX reflected the delineation of fractions among Mexican businessmen that had remained largely ill defined through the 1920s. The labor law battle and the subsequent organization of COPARMEX gave definition to those segments of Mexican capital willing to follow the *regiomontano* lead. In this sense, the industrialists of Monterrey created a clearly visible and aggressive alternative to the previous configuration of capital-state relations. By default, the *regiomontanos* became the standard-bearers of a capitalist opposition to the state and provided Mexican businessmen (as well as foreigners) with a front or conduit to express their displeasure with state policies boldly. By conceding this assertive stand to the men of Nuevo León, the bulk of the Mexican private sector allowed the *regiomontanos* to give their extremely conservative stamp to capital's antigovernment positions. Thus, while some elements of Mexican capital were unwilling to come out explicitly on the side of the *regiomontano* elite in 1929, they nonetheless supported their position, if only implicitly.[40] Businessmen, in this respect, perhaps perceived the advantages of using the *regiomontano* elite as a lightning rod of capital-state relations, in which the risks involved were largely borne by the industrialists of Nuevo León.

VI.   The reformist thrust of Cárdenas created an open split within the state between the progressive and conservative camps of the PNR. This rift in the government's political center made a jumble of the intricate layers of relations among businessmen, government officials, and so-called revolutionary millionaires. For despite his reforms, Cárdenas continued to promote native capital, industry, and economic development and to allow "revolutionary capitalists" to prosper under his regime.[41] For those capitalists tied directly or closely to the state, the initial jockeying among Cardenistas and anti-Cardenistas led to a hesitant, tentative private sector. In this regard, contrary to the claim of Jorge Basurto, the industrialists of Monterrey opposed both Calles and Cárdenas as the dispute between the two men widened in the summer and fall of 1935.[42] In this delicate network of political and economic interests, the men of Monterrey made clear their position from the inception of the Cárdenas presidency.

In opposition to Cárdenas, the elite of Monterrey took the initiative early on in 1935 and provided anti-Cárdenas forces with a vehicle to vent their resistance, a conduit to funnel their resentment.[43] Indeed, the splits generated by the Cárdenas administration afforded the *regiomontanos* greater avenues of maneuver and influence. The pressures fostered by Monterrey's industrialists had a larger impact given the brittle, fissured condition of the PRM. And a splintered private sector furthered the elite's ability to occupy the high ground against the president *from the beginning,* as the anti-Cárdenas currents grew and swelled through 1938 and beyond. The political alternative engendered by the *regiomontanos*—touched off in February 1936, preceded by the gubernatorial conflict of 1935, and followed by recurring efforts to organize a capitalist front against Cárdenas—pushed the debate over the presidential succession away from reform in the crucial period from July 1939 to November 1939, from Almazán's debut as candidate to the PRM nominating convention.

In order to hold onto his political gains, Cárdenas was compelled to permit a man from the conservative wing of the party to become the next president of Mexico. Given the foreign and domestic conditions following the expropriation of the petroleum industry, Cárdenas' retreat from his reformist stance was understandable, but the opposition led by Monterrey's businessmen made his "move to the right" inevitable.[44] The determined opposition of the *regiomontano* elite facilitated a shift in the balance of power within the PRM in favor of the conservative wing of the party. Once in control, the anti-Cardenistas made few concessions to the progressives of the PRM. Indeed, the Monterrey-led reaction, as Robert Kaufman has suggested, "actually helped to preserve the capitalist system" in contrast to the pessimistic resignation that characterized the elite's accommodation with Ávila Camacho.[45] The danger posed by Almazán to the PRM forced the party's reformist camp to submit to the aegis of the conservatives. And, as the post-Cárdenas history of Mexico demonstrates, the conservatives took full advantage of their ascendancy.

In her insightful study of the Mexican state, Nora Hamilton has argued: "In general, the independence of the state is limited by the socio-economic structure in which it functions to promote private capital accumulation, by the economic power of private capital (both national and foreign), and by divisions within the state and the identification of certain state factions with dominant class interests."[46] In 1939–40, the Garza-Sadas and their allies made such a pattern manifest and contributed crucially to the conservative direction of the state after 1940. Clearly, the influence of the Monterrey elite at that time derived from the "divisions within the state" that stemmed from "the identification of certain state factions with dominant class interests." Yet the differences within the private sector, because of its identification with state interests, also contributed to the inordinate political weight of the *regiomontano* elite in that period.[47]

The latter factor, this differentiation within the private sector, conditions the notion of the uniformity of interests of Mexican capital before and after 1940.[48] It also suggests that the seeming unity of capital in more recent times must be scrutinized carefully, and certainly not projected simply onto the past without taking into account the variations, if not the latent rifts, that lie within the Mexican private sector.[49] The incoherence within the private sector, as Peter Smith has pointed out, marks the subtle—and not so subtle—fissures beneath the smooth veneer of Mexican capital.[50] The differences among business organizations underlie the initial formation of COPARMEX in 1929. Moreover, in the early maneuvering over the 1940 presidential elections, one must note the despair of the Monterrey elite over the *unwillingness* of other capitalists to join the *regiomontanos'* aggressive drive to block the possibility of a Cardenista from taking the office.

As Hamilton has noted, businessmen split their allegiances in the 1940 elections.[51] In this respect, the Fundidora's ownership, consistent with its position in 1929, failed to join the Cervecería clan in open opposition to the PRM's candidate. The political stance of the Fundidora revealed the elite's inability to mount a united capitalist front against the PRM in the presidential contest. If the *regiomontanos'* capitalist allies approved of the elite's political aims, such inclinations were not translated into direct, active support of Almazán. Nonetheless, if only inadvertently, the 1940 electoral process strengthened the bargaining position of Monterrey's industrialists with the state—a position established in 1929 and maintained through 1940 in contrast to that of other segments of the Mexican private sector.

The state attempted to contain the political leverage of the *regiomontano* elite. The 1936 Chambers Law reflected in part an effort to lessen the influence of the Monterrey group within Mexican capital. Similarly, the proindustry measures of Cárdenas, especially in the critical moments of the fall of 1939, were intended to induce businessmen away from the Almazán candidacy. These political lessons by Cárdenas were not lost on Ávila Camacho. In response to the *regiomontanos,* and consistent with Cárdenas' move of 1936, the state constituted a new business organization in 1941 (Cámara Nacional de la Industria de Transformación, or CANACINTRA) as a counterweight to COPARMEX. Tellingly, CANACINTRA embraced largely those enterprises highly dependent on the state.[52] Nevertheless, such actions on the part of the state, inducements as well as constraints, betrayed the singular influence of the Garza-Sadas and their cohort in the backdrop of a fractionalized private sector and a government eager to cement its political power.[53] Thus, the *regiomontanos'* resistance in the 1940 elections accrued to their benefit as the state endeavored to bring to heel the elite of Monterrey.

In the absence of detailed studies of other fractions of Mexican capital, the *regiomontanos'* significance has perhaps been exaggerated here and by others as well. Still, the historic, durable cohesiveness of this group of businessmen, anchored by that of the Garza-Sadas, underscores their extraordinary and powerful place in the political economy of Mexico in the postrevolutionary era, and it may also explain to a large extent their continuing importance in the period following the Cárdenas administration. What seems clear is that in losing the election of 1940, the nascent Grupo Monterrey and its leaders, the Garza-Sadas, gained a momentous, climactic victory.

The restoration of the Reyista "golden age" in Nuevo León must have appeared possible in 1940 to the men of Monterrey. And, as a result, their determination to keep it that way remained, in light of the past, the more trenchant and resolute.

Notes

The notes contain several abbreviations and acronyms for purposes of brevity. The citations for the Archivo General de la Nación (AGN) are from the Ramo presidentes unless otherwise indicated. I have kept the Spanish term *expediente* (Exp.) in most instances since it indicates more than the term "file" in American usage. Citations from the National Archives of the United States are usually from Record Group 59, State Department papers on the internal affairs of Mexico, primarily in file 812.00 concerning political issues. Useful information was also found in Record Group 84 regarding dispatches from the U.S. Embassy in Mexico City. (Unless otherwise indicated, citations from the National Archives are from Record Group 59 or Record Group 84.) It should be noted that the Federal Records Center at Suitland, Maryland (NAW/FRC) contained records that were still classified "confidential" at the time of the research for this manuscript. Also at that time, the Archivo General del Estado de Nuevo León contained records from the Archivo Municipal de Monterrey. Since then, both archives have been reorganized and relocated.

Abbreviations

AGENL   Archivo General del Estado de Nuevo León, Monterrey, Nuevo León
AGN   Archivo General de la Nación, Mexico City
BL   Bancroft Library, University of California, Berkeley, Berkeley, California
Condumex   Centro de Estudios de Historia de México, Condumex, Mexico City
     AVC   Archivo Venustiano Carranza
     ABR   Archivo Bernardo Reyes
LAC   Latin American Collection, University of Texas, Austin, Texas
NAW   National Archives of the United States, Washington, D.C.
NAW/FRC   National Archives of the United States, Federal Records Center, Suitland, Maryland

Preface

1. Irma Salinas Rocha, *Ni más ni menos* (Mexico City: Editorial Isaro, 1981), p. 53.

2. *Regiomontano* refers to someone from Nuevo León, particularly Monterrey.

3. The economic troubles of the Grupo Monterrey, since 1981 particularly, have led some observers to claim its imminent demise as a powerful element of the Mexican private sector. (See, for example, Carlos Martínez Assad, "Auge y decadencia del Grupo Monterrey," *Revista Mexicana de Sociología* 46:2 [abril–junio 1984]: 17–30.) In contrast, others are much less sanguine, such as Dale Story, who concludes: "Though the nationalization of the banks had left them more dependent on the state for credit and foreign currency, most Monterrey industrialists remained as combative as ever. . . . In 1983, the Monterrey Group was a shaken, but still powerful and autonomous, industrial force in Mexico whose support was still needed by the new administration" (*Industry, the State, and Public Policy in Mexico*, p. 92).

Introduction

1. Centro Patronal (Employers' Center) in Monterrey was part of the larger confederation of centers known as Confederación Patronal de la República Mexicana (COPARMEX) that was formed in 1929.

2. This account of the Vidriera strike synthesizes its extensive coverage in newspapers in Monterrey and Mexico City. A full treatment of the strike is found in chapter 8 with full citations. To date, an in-depth analysis of this important strike has yet to appear.

3. The Monterrey glassworks produced approximately 80% of Mexico's glass in 1936, virtually all of it for the national market.

4. The Centro Patronal was the local chapter of the larger, but Monterrey-dominated, business organization, Confederación Patronal de la República Mexicana (COPARMEX).

5. The CROM was the old labor organization headed by Luis Morones, whose dwindling power Cárdenas wanted to break entirely. Among several works on this topic, see Arnaldo Córdova, *La política de masas del cardenismo*, pp. 67–76.

6. After the assassination of president-elect Álvaro Obregón in 1928, outgoing president Plutarco Elías Calles called for a convention to select an interim president. But Aarón Sáenz, the original front-runner and Obregón supporter, was not elected—one reason was his close ties with Monterrey's industrialists. A full description of this event is found in chapter 7.

7. The founding board of directors of COPARMEX was dominated by Monterrey businessmen. This episode is analyzed in detail in chapter 7.

8. Almazán headed the Zona Militar in Nuevo León since 1926 and had married into a prominent *regiomontano* family. Later, under the banner of the Monterrey elite–supported Acción Nacional party, Almazán would run for president against the candidate of the ruling political party, selected by Cárdenas to be his successor. The 1940 presidential campaign is described in chapter 8.

9. Cárdenas was in the midst of a battle against ex-president Calles and his efforts to maintain his influence over Mexican politics. Though this

episode is explored more fully in a subsequent chapter, for a brief chronicle on this point, see Jan Bazant, *A Concise History of Mexico, from Hidalgo to Cárdenas, 1805–1940*, pp. 174–183.

10. Albert L. Michaels and Marvin Bernstein, "The Modernization of the Old Order: Organization and Periodization of Twentieth Century Mexican History," in *Contemporary Mexico*, ed. James W. Wilkie, Michael C. Meyer, and Edna Monzon de Wilkie (Berkeley: University of California Press, 1976), pp. 687–710.

11. As early as 1950, Sanford A. Mosk, in his *Industrial Revolution in Mexico*, noted the rise of a "new group" in Mexican business, yet few historical studies examined closely the inner workings of the Mexican private sector and its differences. In the analysis of the post-1940 economic boom, however, political economists have noted the variation in the business organizations within the Mexican private sector, pointing out the implications for business-government relations. For an overview, see Marco Antonio Alcázar, *Las agrupaciones patronales en México* (Mexico City: El Colegio de México, 1970).

12. This process is described in chapter 2.

13. Foreign investors were initially prominent in the Fundidora, but it eventually became primarily "Mexican" in its stockholders' composition.

14. See George Reid Andrews, "Toward a Re-evaluation of the Latin American Family Firm," *Inter-American Economic Affairs* 30 (Winter 1976): 23–40. Chapters 2 and 5 detail the development of the major business families of Monterrey.

15. The social ties among the elite are explored in chapter 3 for the period before 1910, and chapter 6 examines the same topic for the postrevolutionary years.

16. See Clark W. Reynolds, *The Mexican Economy: Twentieth Century Structure and Growth*.

17. Roger D. Hansen, *The Politics of Mexican Development*, pp. 165–168.

18. Ibid., p. 37.

19. Robert Jones Shafer, *Mexican Business Organizations: History and Analysis*, pp. 21–49.

20. For a general discussion of elites, see T. B. Bottomore, *Elites and Society* (London: C. A. Watts, 1964), especially pp. 28–47.

21. For a discussion of similar attitudes in the United States, see Robert Green McCloskey, *American Conservatism in the Age of Enterprise* (New York: Harper and Row, 1951).

22. This idea, and others, are analyzed in chapter 6.

23. A committee headed by Luis G. Sada was operating in the 1930s that set the groundwork for the establishment of the Instituto Tecnológico in Monterrey in 1942.

24. Among the works that sustain a generally monolithic view of the Grupo Monterrey for the years 1880 to 1940, see Juan Manuel Fragoso, Elvira Concheiro, and Antonio Gutierrez, *El poder de la gran burguesía* (Mexico City: Ediciones de Cultura Popular, 1979).

25. Dale Story, *Entrepreneurs and the State in Mexico: Examining the Authoritarian Thesis*, Technical Papers Series, no. 30 (Austin: Institute of Latin American Studies, University of Texas, 1980).

26. Ruth Berins Collier and David Collier, "Inducements versus Constraints: Disaggregating 'Corporatism,'" *American Political Science Review* 73 (December 1971): 967–986. It should be emphasized that the Colliers' use of these terms was related to state-labor relations; I have borrowed their terms and applied the concept to state-capital relations.

27. Two students of the relationship between the public and private sectors in Mexico have noted that the analysis of that relationship must "accommodate two dimensions: variation over time and variation according to the issue or policy area under consideration" (John F. H. Purcell and Susan Kaufman Purcell, "Mexican Business and Public Policy," in *Authoritarianism and Corporatism in Latin America*, ed. James M. Malloy, p. 191). The authors, however, tend to neglect the differentiation within the private sector in their search for general patterns of political behavior.

28. The conflict between the church and the federal government, the so-called Cristero Rebellion, 1926–1929, compounded the political troubles that resulted from the rebellion of Adolfo de la Huerta in 1923, the revolt headed by Gonzalo Escobar in 1929, and finally, in 1938, the rebellion led by Saturnino Cedillo.

29. The Banco de México was organized in 1925 and the Agricultural Credit Bank was formally opened in March 1926; the development bank was named Nacional Financiera and established in 1931.

30. Lorenzo Meyer, "El estado mexicano contemporáneo," in *Lecturas de política mexicana* (Mexico City: El Colegio de México, 1977), p. 10.

31. Hansen, *Politics of Mexican Development*, p. 169.

32. Córdova, *La política de masas*, pp. 146–176.

33. Ibid., pp. 197–201.

34. Fernando Henrique Cardoso, "On the Characterization of Authoritarian Regimes in Latin America," in *The New Authoritarianism in Latin America*, ed. David Collier, p. 47.

1. Commerce and Capital

1. This periodization follows, in general, that of several historians of Nuevo León. See Isidro Vizcaya Canales, *Los orígenes de la industrialización de Monterrey 1867–1920*, pp. v–xv.

2. For a description of this early period in Monterrey's history, see José P. Saldaña, *Estampas antiguas de Monterrey* (Monterrey: Impresora Monterrey, 1942).

3. Vizcaya Canales, *Orígenes*, p. vi.

4. Andrés Montemayor Hernández, *Historia de Monterrey*, p. 105.

5. Ibid., p. 97.

6. Vizcaya Canales, *Orígenes*, p. viii.

7. Ibid., p. ix.

8. Despite the damage to mines due to neglect and the chaos following independence, some mine owners and *hacendados* continued to have the means to buy imported goods, especially at the lower prices offered by smugglers.

9. Mary Catharine Megee, *Monterrey, Mexico: Internal Patterns and External Relations*, p. 19.

10. Montemayor Hernández, *Historia de Monterrey*, p. 145.

11. Daniel Cosío Villegas, ed., *Historia moderna de México, El Porfiriato, la vida económica*, vol. 1, books 1 and 2, pp. 399–400 (future references to this work are cited as *HM* and title of volume).

12. For a full treatment on this period, see Ronnie C. Tyler, "The Age of Cotton: Santiago Vidaurri and the Confederacy, 1861–1864" (Ph.D. dissertation, Texas Christian University, 1968).

13. Megee, *Monterrey*, p. 22.

14. Vizcaya Canales, *Orígenes*, p. xii.

15. Ibid., pp. xiii–xv.

16. See *HM, La república restaurada*, vol. 2, pp. 282–294; Vizcaya Canales, *Orígenes*, p. xiii.

17. Vizcaya Canales, *Orígenes*, p. 281.

18. Ibid., p. 282.

19. J. Fred Rippy, *The United States and Mexico*, p. 113.

20. Frank Lawrence Owsley, *King Cotton Diplomacy: Foreign Relations of the Confederate States of America*, p. 113.

21. Rippy, *United States and Mexico*, p. 235.

22. Ibid.

23. Ibid.

24. Owsley, *Diplomacy*, p. 115; Domenico Sindico, *Ensayo sobre problemas agrícolas en Nuevo León* (Mexico City: INAH, 1975), pp. 15–17.

25. Owsley, *Diplomacy*, p. 119.

26. Ibid.

27. Robert W. Delaney, "Matamoros, Port for Texas during the Civil War," *Southwestern Historical Quarterly* 58:4 (April 1955): 473–487.

28. Ibid.

29. Ibid., p. 478.

30. Ibid. Also Vizcaya Canales, *Orígenes*, p. xiv.

31. Delaney, "Matamoros," p. 478.

32. Owsley, *Diplomacy*, p. 133.

33. Roel, *Nuevo León*, p. 162.

34. Montemayor Hernández, *Historia de Monterrey*, pp. 195–196.

35. Santiago Roel, *Nuevo León: Apuntes históricos*, p. 174; Federic Mauro, "L'Economie de nord-est et la résistance à l'empire," in *La intervención francesa y el imperio de maximiliano*, pp. 61–69.

36. Ronnie C. Tyler, "Cotton on the Border, 1861–1865," *Southwestern Historical Quarterly* 73:4 (April 1970): 471. Also Tyler, "Las reclamaciones de Patricio Milmo," *Humanitas* 10 (1969): 561–563.

37. All of the major merchants discussed below arrived prior to 1860. A typical case was Eduardo Bremer, a German immigrant who arrived as the cotton boom began. A native of Hamburg, Bremer began a trade business in Matamoros and subsequently opened a store in Monterrey. By 1876, he also maintained a store in Brownsville, Texas. Later, Juan Reichmann, his son-in-law, ran the business for the aging Bremer, who died in 1904. Reichmann would

become a member of the Casino Monterrey and a leading member of the prosperous German colony in Monterrey (see *Voz de Nuevo León,* June 25, 1904, p. 1; on Reichmann, see *Voz de Nuevo León,* December 23, 1899, p. 3). See also José P. Saldaña, *Grandeza de Monterrey* (Monterrey: n.p., 1968), pp. 44–45. Another famous name also was enriched by the cotton trade—Evaristo Madero, who was a partner of Milmo's in 1862. On this point, see Saldaña, *Grandeza,* p. 45. On the Belden family, see Sara Aguilar Belden de Garza, *Una ciudad y dos familias,* p. 11.

38. See Agustín Basave, *Constructores de Monterrey,* pp. 57–60, 69–73, 79–81, 91–97. It was Calderón who would be the primary promoter of the brewery initiated by Isaac Garza and the German-American Joseph Schnaider.

39. Israel Cavazos Garza, "Las incursiones de los bárbaros en el noreste de Mexico, durante el siglo XIX," *Humanitas* 5 (1964): 350.

40. On the *regiomontano* economic problems of this period, see Vizcaya Canales, *Orígenes,* pp. 16–22; Montemayor Hernández, *Historia de Monterrey,* pp. 220–222; Roel, *Nuevo León,* pp. 207–210. See also on the whole issue of the Zona Libre, *HM, La república restaurada, la vida económica,* pp. 282–294.

41. *HM, La república restaurada, la vida económica,* pp. 292–293.

42. Ibid., p. 41. Also Vizcaya Canales, *Orígenes,* pp. 2–3.

43. *HM, La república restaurada, la vida económica,* pp. 80–81.

44. Ibid., pp. 115–136.

45. Lic. Genaro Garza, *Memoria que . . . , gobernador constitucional del estado de Nuevo León, presenta al soberano congreso del mismo, sobre el estado de los ramos de la administración pública* (Monterrey: Imprenta del gobierno, 1879), Document no. 34 (not paginated), AGENL. These *Memorias* were reports by the governors of their administration. Future references to this type of document are cited as *Memoria* and the year of publication.

46. Montemayor Hernández, *Historia de Monterrey,* p. 221.

47. *HM, La república restaurada, la vida económica,* p. 609.

48. *Periódico oficial,* December 9, 1874, p. 1, AGENL. See also *Memoria,* 1879, p. 38, AGENL.

49. *Memoria,* 1879, Document no. 34 (not paginated), AGENL, for the decline in number of businesses during this period.

50. Raymond Vernon, *The Dilemma of Mexico's Development,* p. 38.

51. *Memoria,* 1881, p. 22, AGENL; *Memoria,* 1886, special report, attached to the *Memoria,* issued on October 31, 1884, by the Cámara de Comercio (not paginated), AGENL.

52. Ibid.

53. *Memoria,* 1886, special report on the Zona Libre by a commission of the Cámara de Comercio, attached to *Memoria,* issued on March 4, 1885 (not paginated), and authored by Rodolfo Dresel, Otto Degetan, and Francisco Oliver, AGENL.

54. Ibid.

55. All of the literature on Monterrey's economic development emphasizes the importance of the city's rail connections. See Megee, *Monterrey,* p. 22.

56. *Voz de Nuevo León,* January 12, 1889, p. 2; February 16, 1889, p. 2.

57. Club de Sembradores, *Homenaje: 75* aniversario de la Cervecería Cuauhtémoc, S.A. 1890-1965* (Monterrey: n.p., 1965), pp. 7–9, 14–32.

58. *Memoria,* 1879, p. 38, AGENL.

59. *Memoria,* 1881, p. 18, AGENL.

60. Vizcaya Canales, *Orígenes,* pp. 29–30; HM, *La república restaurada, vida económica,* p. 101.

61. *Memoria,* 1883, Document nos. 7–49, passim, AGENL. In 1882, of ten tax exemptions made, six were made to *regiomontanos* who acted as partners and legal representatives for the new firms.

62. *Memoria,* 1886, p. 16, in an attachment written by the Cámara de Comercio, AGENL.

63. Vizcaya Canales, *Orígenes,* pp. 37–40. Also José Saldaña, *Apuntes sobre la industrialización de Monterrey,* p. 13.

64. *Voz de Nuevo León,* May 31, 1890, p. 2.

65. *Memoria,* 1889–1891, p. 536, AGENL.

66. HM, *El Porfiriato, la vida económica,* book 2, p. 723. See also pp. 722–724 for more on the reaction in Mexico.

67. *Voz de Nuevo León,* May 31, 1890, p. 1.

68. Harvey O'Connor, *The Guggenheims: The Making of an American Dynasty,* p. 89. O'Connor quotes Meyer Guggenheim as saying: "If we can't bring Mexican ore to Pueblo [Colorado], let us take a smelter to Mexico. I hear there are no smelters there? Very well, Mexico is ours for the taking."

2. The Making of an Industrial Elite

1. On the modernization of Mexico under Díaz, see *HM, El Porfiriato, la vida económica,* vol. 1, books 1 and 2. The abuses of the Porfiriato are well documented. See among dozens of works, John Kenneth Turner, *Barbarous Mexico* (Austin: University of Texas Press, 1969).

2. Perhaps the best treatment of the political economy of the Porfiriato in recent years is contained in Hansen's masterful book *Politics of Mexican Development,* particularly pp. 145–146.

3. Among many sources for the conditions of labor during the Porfiriato, see, for an overview, Luis González, "El liberalismo triunfante," in *Historia general de México* (Mexico City: El Colegio de México, 1981), vol. 2, pp. 970–977.

4. For a brief analysis of this process, see Mario Cerutti, "Monterrey y el desarrollo del capitalismo en el noreste de México," *Cathedra* 4 (enero–marzo 1978): 3–30.

5. Porfirian politics, including the triangle of Díaz, Reyes, and Limantour, are exhaustively covered in Cosío Villegas, *Historia moderna de México, El Porfiriato, la vida política interior,* vols. 8 and 9.

6. For an interesting discussion on regional elites and the Díaz administration, see James D. Cockcroft, "Social and Economic Structure of the Porfiriato: Mexico, 1877–1911," in *Dependence and Underdevelopment: Latin America's Political Economy,* ed. Cockcroft, Andre Gunder Frank, and Dale L. Johnson, pp. 44–70.

The statistics in the *Estadísticas económicas del Porfiriato: Fuerza de trabajo y actividad económica por sectores* (hereafter cited as *Fuerza de trabajo*) indicate in a number of categories significant variances between several states and regions. The differences between Nuevo León and other states are cited in subsequent notations.

7. See Celso Furtado, *Economic Development of Latin America* (London: Cambridge University Press, 1970), pp. 19–34; Vernon, *Dilemma*, pp. 55–58.

8. Fernando Rosenzweig, "El desarrollo económico de México de 1877 a 1911," *El Trimestre Económico* 32 (julio–septiembre 1965): 413–418; HM, *El Porfiriato, la vida económica*, book 2, pp. 1134, 1154.

9. Ibid., book 2, pp. 540, 628; David M. Pletcher, *Rails, Mines, and Progress: Seven American Promoters in Mexico, 1867–1911* (Ithaca, N.Y.: Cornell University Press, 1958), pp. 21–25; John Coatsworth, *Growth against Development: The Economic Impact of Railroads in Porfirian Mexico* (DeKalb: Northern Illinois Press, 1981).

10. *Fuerza de trabajo*, p. 46; *Estadísticas sociales del Porfiriato, 1877–1910* (Mexico City: El Colegio de México, 1956), p. 74 (hereafter cited as *Estadísticas sociales*).

11. *Estadísticas sociales*, pp. 7, 9, 69; Keith A. Davies, "Tendencias demográficas urbanas durante el siglo XIX en México," in *Ensayos sobre el desarrollo urbano de México*, ed. Alejandra Moreno Toscano (Mexico City: Sep/Setentas, 1974), pp. 158–160; Vernon, *Dilemma*, pp. 41–42; *El Economista Mexicano*, March 9, 1907, p. 492.

12. *Fuerza de trabajo*, pp. 128, 45, 131, 86; *El Economista Mexicano*, January 16, 1904, p. 389. Statistics for 1903 showed Nuevo León a poor eighth in livestock production; *Estadísticas sociales*, pp. 64–65, 40–41, 217–219.

13. Clark W. Reynolds, *The Mexican Economy: Twentieth Century Structure and Growth*, pp. 15–26; also William P. Glade, Jr., and Charles W. Anderson, *The Political Economy of Mexico*, pp. 13–15. The north in general enjoyed a period of intense economic development, but only Monterrey became highly industrialized, according to figures on industrial production for the Porfiriato; see Rosenzweig, "Desarrollo económico," p. 421. On the degree of native capital in Monterrey, see Isidro Vizcaya Canales, *Orígenes*, p. 74.

14. *Voz de Nuevo León*, July 23, 1892, p. 3. *El Economista Mexicano*, November 23, 1901, p. 117, mentions the activity of the smelters and the need for more laborers; whereas textile workers were laid off, other industries continued to employ new workers, or at least maintain their work force; see *El Economista Mexicano*, March 15, 1902, pp. 378–379. By November of 1902, drought effects had been overcome in Nuevo León; see *El Economista Mexicano*, November 8, 1902, p. 120.

15. See *Memoria*, 1908–1909, pp. 17, 20, 24–25, 32–33, AGENL. See also *El Economista Mexicano*, September 9, 1905, p. 522; February 24, 1906, p. 410; August 25, 1906, p. 449; November 10, 1906, pp. 119–120; December 1, 1906, pp. 187–188; March 28, 1908, p. 514; September 19, 1908, p. 527; March 19, 1909, p. 522; March 27, 1909, pp. 567–568; October 9, 1909, p. 13. The effects on workers, though, was another matter. See chapter 3.

16. *Memoria*, 1889–1891, pp. 457–481, AGENL.

17. O'Conner, *The Guggenheims*, p. 90.

18. Ibid., pp. 92, 94–95; HM, *El Porfiriato, la vida económica*, book 1, p. 561.

19. Marvin D. Bernstein, *The Mexican Mining Industry, 1890–1950*, p. 38; *Memoria*, 1889–1891, p. 38, AGENL.

20. Bernstein, *Mexican Mining*, p. 38; Vizcaya Canales, *Orígenes*, p. 76; *Memoria*, 1889–1891, Document no. 32 (not paginated), AGENL.

21. *Monterrey News*, April 21, 1907, p. 1.

22. *HM, El Porfiriato, la vida social*, p. 25; *La Defensa*, January 14, 1894, p. 1. See also *Memoria*, 1895–1899, pp. 241–248. Census figures of 1895 contained in *Memoria*, 1895–1899, Document 72, addenda 1131–1133, p. xliv, AGENL. On Mexico as a whole, see *HM, El Porfiriato, la vida económica*, book 1, pp. 411–414.

23. Pablo Livas, *El estado de Nuevo León* (Monterrey: Imprenta de J. Cantú Leal, 1910), p. 71. See *Memoria*, 1899–1903, pp. xlff., AGENL; Roel, *Nuevo León*, p. 231; *Estadísticas sociales del Porfiriato*, pp. 15, 39, 43, 57.

24. Vizcaya Canales, *Orígenes*, p. 100; *Memoria*, 1912, p. 20; Livas, *Estado*, pp. 15–48 passim; Montemayor Hernández, *Historia de Monterrey*, pp. 225–267 passim; Saldaña, *Apuntes*, pp. 24–25.

25. *Memoria*, 1879, Document no. 34 (unpaginated), put the figure of 348 commercial establishments for the year ending 1879, AGENL; the 1910 figure is from Livas, *Estado*, p. 28. Many of the new businesses clustered near the railway junction to the north and close to the industry springing up on the northern perimeter of the city.

26. Livas, *Estado*, p. 28. Several sources relate the change in the city's commerce and its location. See Megee, *Monterrey, Mexico*, pp. 43–48; Samuel N. Dicken, "Monterrey and Northeastern Mexico," *Annals of the Association of American Geographers* 29 (June 1939): 139, 144.

27. *La Defensa*, August 25, 1893, pp. 1–2.

28. *La Defensa*, August 26, 1893, p. 3.

29. *HM, El Porfiriato, la vida económica*, book 2, p. 746.

30. Livas, *Estado*, p. 28.

31. *Monterrey News*, April 23, 1907, p. 1; November 10, 1907, p. 16. Such visits were numerous; see also *Voz de Nuevo León*, March 3, 1900, p. 3. The Hernández family, among others, had stores along the Texas border.

32. Livas, *Estado*, p. 76. These land values were probably underassessed to lower property taxes; very likely, the value of such properties was even higher.

33. Percy Martin, *Mexico of the Twentieth Century* (London: Edward Arnold, 1907), vol. 3, p. 83.

34. *Voz de Nuevo León*, March 23, 1895, p. 2.

35. *Voz de Nuevo León*, October 5, 1901, p. 3.

36. *HM, El Porfiriato, la vida económica*, book 1, pp. 329–377. See also Martin, *Mexico*, p. 83; Vizcaya Canales, *Orígenes*, pp. 83–84.

37. To take but one example, a review of real estate transactions finds few foreigners in the booming property market. Here again, local businessmen were avidly involved as foreigners concentrated on a few pursuits rather than diversifying their interests.

38. Robertson was born in 1849 to a noted family in Tennessee whose father founded Nashville. He served in the Confederate army (thus the "Colonel"), later was a lawyer in St. Louis, Missouri, and then went to Mexico to direct

construction of the Gulf Railroad. See Basave, *Constructores de Monterrey*, pp. 26ff.; *La Defensa*, January 26, 1893, p. 2; *Voz de Nuevo León*, November 17, 1894, p. 1; August 11, 1900, p. 1.

39. *Voz de Nuevo León*, December 20, 1890, p. 1. Two years later, Robertson started his own newspaper in both English and Spanish editions.

40. *La Defensa*, April 18, 1894, p. 3.

41. Martin, *Mexico*, p. 82.

42. Cited in Vizcaya Canales, *Orígenes*, pp. 24–25.

43. Ibid., p. 74; see also Saldaña, *Apuntes*, p. 30.

44. As mining towns boomed, Rivero, like other Monterrey merchants, was soon profiting from the increase in the area's commerce; *Voz de Nuevo León*, December 26, 1888, p. 2; January 2, 1889, p. 2; January 12, 1889, pp. 2–3; February 16, 1889, p. 2; April 27, 1889, p. 1. Rivero personified the apparent strategy of accumulation of capital and then reinvesting in new ventures, using profits from previously established enterprises. This process was noted in the *Monterrey News*, April 22, 1907, p. 4. The Hernández brothers were perhaps the most commercially oriented family and continued to adhere to their commercial roots. See Livas, *Estado*, p. 28; and Vizcaya Canales, *Orígenes*, pp. 82, 90–97; *HM, El Porfiriato, la vida económica*, book 1, p. 23.

45. Cerutti, "Monterrey y el desarrollo del capitalismo," pp. 11–14. There was wide variation in the interest in real estate among the elite.

46. Again, variation occurred in individual interest. Isaac Garza and Francisco G. Sada were rarely involved in buying urban properties, as opposed to Muguerza.

47. Mario Cerutti, "Los Maderos en la economía de Monterrey (1890–1910)," *Cathedra* 4 (abril–junio 1978): 29–93.

48. Cantú Treviño's success stemmed largely from his store founded in 1891; later he acquired the La Leona textile mill. Salinas y Rocha began their furniture operations in 1906. Unfortunately, to date, a detailed treatment of their business histories has yet to appear; Vizcaya Canales, *Orígenes*, pp. 85, 86, 90.

49. For an overview, see Mario Cerutti, "Concesiones estatales, industrias y modalidades del capitalismo en Monterrey (1890–1910)," *Cathedra* 5 (abril–junio/julio–septiembre 1979): 45–76.

50. This native-supported facility was preceded two years earlier by the opening of a branch of the Banco Nacional de México and was managed by Valentín Rivero and Francisco Armendaiz.

51. The Banco de Nuevo León opened branches throughout the region, including the towns of Saltillo, Parras, Piedras Negras, Monclova, Torreón, Tampico, Ciudad Victoria, and Nuevo Laredo. As early as 1903, the banks of Nuevo León were the fourth largest in the country in terms of total assets.

52. *Monterrey News*, April 27, 1907, p. 4; *Estadísticas económicas del Porfiriato: Comercio exterior de México, 1877–1911*, p. 182; Livas, *Estado*, pp. 32–33. The strength of Monterrey's banks was a common theme in local newspapers (e.g., *Monterrey News*, April 22, 1907, p. 4; July 22, 1907, p. 4). Monterrey's major merchants maintained their short-term credit operations, and their banking interests as well. Rivero, who managed the branch of the Banco Nacional, also conducted semibanking facilities in his store in addition

to being a major investor in the Banco Mercantil. The Monterrey banks were strong; the Banco de Nuevo León was one of the most respected in the country; see *HM, El Porfiriato, la vida económica,* book 2, pp. 813–814; Vizcaya Canales, *Orígenes,* pp. 87–90.

The Banco Mercantil demonstrated the growing interest of Mexico City businessmen in the thriving northern metropolis. Casasús was well tied to Mexican banking interests since he was appointed to the national banking commission in 1896 by Limantour.

53. Livas, *Estado,* pp. 32–33; *El Economista Mexicano,* March 28, 1908, p. 514; September 19, 1908, p. 527.

54. Cerutti, "Los Maderos en la economía de Monterrey," pp. 67–70.

55. A close examination of table 6 shows that Monterrey businessmen, especially Ferrara, were involved in export-related activities as well as those indicated by their mining interests.

56. Rivero's son represented his father in the administration of the Banco Mercantil; similarly, Gustavo and Ernesto Madero helped their father, Evaristo, direct the Banco de Nuevo León. These are but two examples.

57. This trend would expand in the 1920s, the example of Luis G. Sada, noted later in this chapter, setting the pattern for the others. Moreover, Joel Rocha, of the Salinas y Rocha firm, worked in a furniture factory in Chicago and learned bedstead-making processes; *El Porvenir,* March 1, 1926, p. 5.

58. *Correspondencia con el Ministro de Fomento,* 1902 (Box 1), pp. 02–1 to 02–5, AGENL.

59. Ernest Henry Gruening, *Mexico and Its Heritage,* p. 59.

60. Hansen, *Politics of Mexican Development,* pp. 150–153.

61. See Abelardo Villegas, *Positivismo y porfirismo* (Mexico City: Sep/ Setentas, 1972).

62. On Reyes, see E. V. Niemeyer, Jr., *El general Bernardo Reyes.*

63. Carleton Beals, *Porfirio Díaz: Dictator of Mexico,* p. 328. For more on the *científicos,* see Hansen, *Politics of Mexican Development,* pp. 154–155.

64. Niemeyer, *Reyes,* pp. 51–57.

65. Bernardo Reyes apparently enjoyed a reputation for honesty that contrasted with the venality of most other generals and *caciques* accorded political and economic power by Díaz. On this point, see Anthony Bryan, "El papel del Gen. Bernardo Reyes en la política nacional y regional de México," *Humanitas* 13 (1972): 331–340. For a different view, see Gruening, *Mexico and Its Heritage,* p. 59: here the author notes that Reyes received two salaries as governor and regional military commander, a bonus of 2,000 pesos a year, plus an expense account for his troops "without accounting" so that "these sums represented but a fraction of his income." Nonetheless, to take real estate sales as an example, Reyes was very rarely involved; locally, as opposed to his federal income, Reyes was unobtrusive.

66. Bernardo Reyes, *Informe del gobernador de Nuevo León . . . al XXXIII congreso del estado, en la apertura del primer período de sesiones ordinarias el 16 de septiembre de 1905* (Monterrey: Tipografía del Gobierno del Estado, 1905), p. 29; see *Memoria,* 1889–1891, pp. 329–332, for the initial proposal for school reform; also *Memoria,* 1899–1903, p. xxiv, AGENL.

67. U.S. Consular Reports, Dispatch no. 84, October 28, 1901, Monterrey, Nuevo León. This view is echoed in the following remarks: "In Nuevo León . . . civil and criminal justice passed through the hands of his son-in-law if he wanted to win" (from Gruening, *Mexico and Its Heritage*, p. 59); "Rodolfo's connections netted him $900,000 pesos for his first year's law practice. To win cases in states under Reyes' jurisdiction, it was almost obligatory to hire the services of Rodolfo or Reyes' son-in-law" (Beals, *Díaz*, p. 356). Cipriano Madrigal was Bernardo Reyes' son-in-law (Beals, *Díaz*, p. 356).

68. *El Hijo del Ahuizote*, May 20, 1894, p. 7; October 16, 1898, p. 671.

69. Rodolfo Reyes, for example, was used to make the deal for the Monterrey steel mill.

70. The visit of Porfirio Díaz in 1898 was the ultimate example of this practice, repeated often during and after the Porfirian era.

71. The visit of Díaz in 1898 reflected the elite's efforts to appease the dictator (this is treated in the subsequent chapter); José P. Saldaña, "El Gral. Don Porfirio Díaz in Monterrey," *Humanitas* 11 (1970): 413–452.

72. Niemeyer, *Reyes*, pp. 66–70. The major works on Bernardo Reyes assume the elite supported Reyes unquestionably. This was not always necessarily true. For a differing view, see Adolfo Duclos Salinas, *Méjico pacificado, El progreso de Méjico y los hombres que lo gobiernan, Porfirio Díaz, Bernardo Reyes*. For example, while the governor attended a conference, Manuel Rivero was selected as interim governor for a very short time in 1902. Rivero, a member of the elite Rivero clan, refused to permit the graft and embezzlement that he discovered while in office. Rivero was disgusted by the corruption among Reyista officeholders—to the political embarrassment of Reyes and his appointees; see Duclos Salinas, *Méjico pacificado*, pp. 220–221.

73. Vizcaya Canales, *Orígenes*, pp. 85–87; Livas, *Estado*, pp. 28–58 passim.

74. HM, *El Porfiriato, la vida económica*, book 1, p. 378.

75. Reyes to Limantour, December 2, 1899, Condumex, Archivo de Bernardo Reyes, #15682 (hereafter cited as ABR and number).

76. Bryan, "El papel del Gen. Bernardo Reyes en la política nacional y regional de México," *Humanitas* 13 (1972): 331–340.

77. Reyes to Limantour, December 6, 1899, ABR, #15683.

78. HM, *El Porfiriato, la vida económica*, book 1, pp. 454–455, 460–465; see also Dawn Keremitsis, *La industria textil mexicana en el siglo XIX*, pp. 110–115.

79. Reyes to Limantour, December 6, 1899, ABR, #15683; *Voz de Nuevo León*, June 24, 1899, p. 1.

80. Reyes to Limantour, December 21, 1899, ABR, #15691.

81. Reyes to Díaz, May 4, 1899, ABR, #16113.

82. *Voz de Nuevo León*, October 26, 1899, pp. 1–2; November 25, 1899, pp. 1–2.

83. Reyes to Díaz, December 21, 1899, ABR, #16153.

84. Ibid.

85. Reyes to Díaz, January 3, 1900, ABR, #16160.

86. HM, *El Porfiriato, la vida económica*, book 1, p. 379; on Milmo and Kelly ties, *Voz de Nuevo León*, May 23, 1896, p. 3.

87. *Voz de Nuevo León*, May 19, 1900, p. 1.

88. *Correspondencia con el Ministro de Fomento, 1900,* Box 4, Vicente Ferrara to Ministry of Development, May 30, 1900, AGENL (hereafter cited as *Correspondencia* with appropriate year and location).

89. *Correspondencia, 1902,* Box 4, Ferrara to Ministry of Development, May 13, 1902, AGENL.

90. *Correspondencia, 1902,* Box 4, telegram dated July 17, 1902, AGENL.

91. Ibid., response from Ferrara dated July 18, 1902.

92. *Correspondencia, 1903,* Box 1, Ferrara to Ministry of Development, March 21, 1903, AGENL.

93. Ibid., Reyes to Ministry of Development, May 16, 1903.

94. *El Economista Mexicano,* February 6, 1904, pp. 477–478; February 27, p. 557.

95. Ibid., February 18, 1905, p. 430.

96. Phillip Hanna, U.S. consul in Monterrey, noted as early as May 1904 the importance of the governmental protection extended to the Fundidora "against competition of older and richer countries"; Hanna went on optimistically, if somewhat regretfully, to speculate as to the potential of Mexican industries to supply Latin America "with all sorts of manufactured articles of competition with other countries of the world" (from U.S. Consular Reports, Dispatch no. 223, May 31, 1904, Monterrey, Nuevo León). Later, in 1909, the Fundidora would receive a boost from the contract to supply the national railway with steel, a beneficial contract magnified by a recession of that time.

97. *El Economista Mexicano,* December 1, 1906, pp. 187–188.

98. *Monterrey News,* April 13, 1907, p. 1.

99. Ibid., April 28, 1907, p. 1.

100. Hugo Scherer, Pablo Macedo, and Fernando Pimentel y Fagoaga were all financially involved in the Fundidora and also intimately tied with the *científicos;* on this group and their governmental power, see Beals, *Díaz,* pp. 329–331.

101. *Memoria,* 1889–1891, pp. 506–507, AGENL.

102. *HM, El Porfiriato, la vida económica,* book 1, pp. 361, 374, 413, 445, 458, for information on the brewery.

103. Salvador Novo, *Crónica regiomontana: Breve historia de un gran esfuerzo* (Monterrey: n.p., 1965), unpaginated.

104. *New York Times,* June 14, 1891, sec. 9, p. 5; February 4, 1899, sec. 6, p. 5. Beer production in the United States went from 30.5 million barrels in 1891 to 39.5 in 1900 and 59.5 million barrels in 1910; *Historical Statistics of the U.S., Colonial Times to 1970,* pt. 2 (Washington, D.C.: Government Printing Office, 1975), p. 690.

105. *El Economista Mexicano,* October 22, 1904, p. 56; March 25, 1905, p. 539; November 10, 1906. *Voz de Nuevo León,* October 22, 1904, p. 2; *El País,* November 4, 1906, p. 2.

106. *El Economista Mexicano,* August 5, 1899, p. 4; May 31, 1902, p. 149.

107. By 1910, over 1,500 workers were at the brewery, indicating a *tripling* of the work force between 1900 and 1910.

108. Novo, *Crónica; El Economista Mexicano,* March 15, 1902, pp. 378–379; *Voz de Nuevo León,* August 15, 1903, p. 3.

109. *El Economista Mexicano,* November 10, 1906, pp. 119–120.

110. This reflects Reyes' view of the greater importance of the steel mill.

111. Bernardo Reyes' correspondence shows a remarkable lack of interest in the Cervecería.

112. Pletcher, *Rails, Mines, and Progress,* p. 27; William F. Cole, *Steel and Economic Growth in Mexico* (Austin: Institute of Latin American Studies, University of Texas Press, 1967), pp. 7–10.

113. It should be stressed that Garza and Sada invested together in virtually every joint venture in which either participated.

114. Real estate transactions show Muguerza very active, as opposed to either Garza or Sada; Muguerza went on his own without either Garza or Sada in several investments; see *Homenaje,* pp. 6–32, especially pp. 23–25.

115. *El Imparcial,* May 17, 1900, p. 2.

116. *El Economista Mexicano,* February 7, 1903, pp. 3–4.

117. *Voz de Nuevo León,* April 22, 1905, p. 1.

118. *Voz de Nuevo León,* January 14, 1905, p. 1. Vizcaya Canales puts the figure of 80% as the share of native capital in Monterrey's industrial development.

119. See Mark Wasserman, "Foreign Investment in Mexico, 1876–1910: A Case Study of the Role of Regional Elites," *Americas* 36 (July 1979): 3–21.

120. Virgilio Garza, Jr., "Brief Sketch of the Industrial Development of Monterrey," in *Basic Industries in Texas and Northern Mexico,* pp. 100–101. Garza was a wealthy lawyer for several of the major businessmen of Monterrey from the 1920s to the 1940s.

3. El patriotismo verdadero

1. Francisco G. de Cosmes, "¿De qué lado está el verdadero patriotismo?" in *Positivismo y porfirismo,* ed. Abelardo Villegas, p. 130.

2. Ibid. For a more racial view of Mexican society, see Francisco Bulnes, "Las tres razas humanas," in ibid., pp. 137–158.

3. For the classic work on this subject, see Leopoldo Zea, *El positivismo en México: Nacimiento, apogeo y decadencia* (Mexico City: Fondo de Cultura Económica, 1968).

4. Guillermo Beato, "Jalisco: Economía y estructura social en el siglo XIX," in *El siglo XIX en México* (Mexico City: Claves Latinoamericanas, 1985), pp. 149–199.

5. The rise of the elite of San Luis Potosí showed a different trajectory, though with similar results. See James D. Cockcroft, "Social and Economic Structure of the Porfiriato, 1877–1911," in *Dependence and Underdevelopment,* ed. Cockcroft, Frank, and Johnson, pp. 47–70.

6. Michael C. Meyer and William L. Sherman, *The Course of Mexican History,* 2nd ed. (New York: Oxford University Press, 1983), pp. 473–475. The text and photos of Anita Brenner's *The Wind That Swept Mexico* (Austin: University of Texas Press, 1971) capture Porfirian elite social life well, especially pp. 14–18.

7. Jesús Luna, *La carrera pública de Don Ramón Corral* (Mexico City: Sep/Setentas, 1975), pp. 34–36.

8. Much of the information on the Casino Monterrey comes from Carlos Pérez-Maldonado, *El Casino Monterrey* (Monterrey: Impresora del Norte, 1958).

9. The three men were prominent guests of the elite throughout Reyes' rule in Nuevo León. In 1892, both Sepúlveda and García Chavarrí were elected to the casino executive board; *Voz de Nuevo León*, December 26, 1892, p. 2.

10. *Diario del Hogar*, April 22, 1903, p. 1; April 29, 1903, p. 2.

11. Two members of the Madero family were on the casino board of directors by 1910; *Monterrey News*, special Sunday edition, September 16, 1910 (unpaginated).

12. *Voz de Nuevo León*, January 2, 1897, p. 1.

13. Carlos (Karl) Holck was a key member of the business establishment and an original member of the casino in 1866. He and Eduardo Bremer paved the way for later Germans to enter high social circles. Bremer's son-in-law, Juan Reichmann, carried on this "tradition" after the death of Bremer in 1904; *Voz de Nuevo León*, June 25, 1904, p. 1. On Reichmann, see *Voz de Nuevo León*, December 23, 1899, p. 3.

14. Brewmasters were all Germans, supervised by John Schmidt of Munich; *Voz de Nuevo León*, November 19, 1903, p. 1.

15. *Voz de Nuevo León*, December 24, 1892, p. 3.

16. *Voz de Nuevo León*, August 27, 1892, p. 3.

17. *Monterrey News*, April 21, 1909, p. 5; *Homenaje*, p. 33.

18. Basave, *Constructores de Monterrey*, pp. 99–102; Juan R. Vega G., ed., *Personalidades de Monterrey*, p. 117.

19. The Hernández clan was another hub of such ties that embraced the Mendirichagas and Maderos. See Mario Cerutti, "Los Maderos en la economía de Monterrey (1890–1910)," *Cathedra* 8 (abril–junio 1978): especially 47–52.

20. Vizcaya Canales, *Orígenes*, pp. 108, 112–119.

21. *La Defensa del Pueblo*, January 25, 1893, p. 2; December 28, 1893, p. 3; *Monterrey News*, April 28, 1907, p. 8; May 1, 1907, p. 8; November 7, 1907, p. 7.

22. *Monterrey News*, September 16, 1910, special Sunday edition (unpaginated); also Vizcaya Canales, *Orígenes*, pp. 108–110.

23. Pérez-Maldonado, *Casino Monterrey*, pp. 213–215; *Monterrey News*, July 10, 1907, p. 1; July 13, 1907, p. 8; October 4, 1907, p. 8.

24. Pérez-Maldonado, *Casino Monterrey*, p. 202.

25. Vizcaya Canales, *Orígenes*, pp. 119–120. See note 20 for examples.

26. Examples of citations are too lengthy to enumerate here, but the *Monterrey News* tended to do more "social notes" type of reporting, whereas the *Voz de Nuevo León* was a drier sort of paper.

27. Among numerous examples: *Voz de Nuevo León*, June 21, 1890, p. 2, dedicated nearly an entire page to a dance at the casino, including a description of the dresses worn by the women. *Monterrey News*, July 13, 1907, p. 8, devoted an entire article to a *gran tertulia* attended by the "best families" of the city with a list of the people involved.

28. *Monterrey News,* September 21, 1910, p. 1.

29. Aguilar Belden de Garza, *Una ciudad y dos familias,* pp. 29–38.

30. Some of the homes went as high as $40,000, as in the case of the Madero home bought in 1906, making for exclusivity.

31. Topo Chico was a resort development promoted by Joseph Robertson that had its own tramway from downtown Monterrey; *Monterrey News,* July 12, 1907, p. 1.

32. The description of Díaz' visit is a synthesis of various sources, chief among them, José P. Saldaña, "El Gral. Don Porfirio Díaz en Monterrey," *Humanitas* 11 (1970): 413–452.

33. The Padilla family of the manager of the Banco de Nuevo León appeared in the group (Rómulo and Enrique) as well as Arturo and Greta Houser, offspring of a wealthy German family; *El Imparcial,* December 18, 1898, p. 1; December 19, 1898, p. 1; December 20, 1898, p. 1; December 21, 1898, p. 1; December 22, 1898, p. 1; December 23, 1898, p. 1.

34. The Villarreal family was politically important, with Viviano Villarreal serving a stint as governor prior to Reyes' arrival. On the family ties between them and the Maderos, see Cerutti, "Los Maderos."

35. *Monterrey News,* September 16, 1910, special edition (unpaginated). Despite the appearance of other clubs, all of the elite continued to participate in the casino.

36. Villarreal and de Tárnava may have been included because of their particular expertise in certain matters that made them better representatives for the interests that were behind them.

37. Vizcaya Canales, *Orígenes,* puts the number at about 500 or so; however, the membership of the elite club often crossed over, and many casino members were also members of the Centro Español, Club Alemán, and so forth.

38. *Voz de Nuevo León,* March 2, 1895, pp. 2–3.

39. Ramón E. Ruiz, *The Great Rebellion: Mexico, 1905–1924,* p. 45.

40. *Memoria,* 1879, Document nos. 22–27, 34 (unpaginated); *Memoria,* 1895–1899, pp. xxiv–xlvi, pp. 781–782, AGENL.

41. *Memoria,* 1895–1899, pp. 241–254.

42. Ibid., p. 255.

43. *Voz de Nuevo León,* December 14, 1889, p. 3. On the "envidia" of the middle class, see *Voz de Nuevo León,* December 13, 1902, p. 3; March 4, 1903, p. 1; April 4, 1903, p. 2.

44. *El Hijo de Ahuizote,* May 20, 1894, p. 7.

45. Beals, *Díaz,* p. 350.

46. *Voz de Nuevo León,* December 28, 1902, p. 1.

47. The newspaper *Redención* headed the opposition.

48. *Redención,* February 27, 1903, pp. 1–2.

49. Ibid., March 1, 1903, p. 3.

50. Ibid., March 22, 1903, p. 4.

51. "Manifesto to the Nation," p. 2, contained in the U.S. Consular Reports, Dispatch no. 153, April 29, 1903.

52. E. V. Niemeyer, in his biography of Reyes, suggests that the opposition had much to gain from any adverse publicity involving Reyes and thus might

have deliberately provoked the incident: "Since the weight of the evidence falls on the opposition, it is probable that the incident might have been provoked accidentally by irresponsible or drunk persons present at the plaza" (*Reyes*, p. 122). I disagree, but Reyes apparently realized his mistake very soon after his fit of rage.

53. *El País*, May 29, 1903, pp. 1–2; Beals, *Díaz*, p. 358; reaction to the decision was cited in *Diario del Hogar*, May 29, 1903, p. 2.

54. *Diario del Hogar*, April 30, 1903, p. 2; June 10, 1903, p. 2. Mendirichaga tried to evade more contributions by going to Europe in order not to give to the Reyes postelectoral campaign (e.g., the paying-off of promised bribes); see *Diario del Hogar*, June 30, 1903, p. 2.

55. By August 1903, the elite was once again making "contributions" to Reyes; *Voz de Nuevo León*, August 26, 1903, p. 1; September 2, 1903, p. 1. According to various sources, it was the April 2 incident that sparked Francisco I. Madero's initial interest in politics. See Stanley R. Ross, *Francisco I. Madero: Apostle of Democracy*, p. 34; Gruening, *Mexico and Its Heritage*, p. 93.

56. *Voz de Nuevo León*, December 26, 1891, p. 2; January 2, 1892, pp. 2–3; July 8, 1893, p. 2.

57. *Memoria*, 1887, AGENL; *Voz de Nuevo León*, March 30, 1889, p. 1; July 20, 1889, p. 1; March 29, 1890, p. 1; May 1, 1894, p. 2; March 21, 1896, p. 3; October 31, 1896, p. 2. Given that the minimum wage was around 30 cents a day, a few cents were significant to a worker.

58. *Voz de Nuevo León*, November 27, 1897, p. 2.

59. *El País*, November 9, 1906, p. 3.

60. *Monterrey News*, July 12, 1907, p. 8.

61. *Voz de Nuevo León*, August 12, 1903, p. 3; May 16, 1907, p. 4; *Monterrey News*, January 16, 1907, p. 4; September 15, 1907, p. 8; *El Economista Mexicano*, November 23, 1901, p. 117.

62. *Voz de Nuevo León*, July 4, 1891, pp. 1–2; March 3, 1894, p. 3; August 12, 1903, p. 1; August 15, 1903, p. 3; November 19, 1903, p. 1; *El Economista Mexicano*, March 15, 1902, pp. 378–379 (noted that over fifty German families were brought over in initial glass-making effort).

63. The number of German employees in Monterrey reached the point that vacations to Germany were organized in large groups; *Monterrey News*, April 12, 1907, p. 3. Austrian workers were also brought in to work in the Fundidora; *Voz de Nuevo León*, October 4, 1902, pp. 1–2. On the hotel for its European workers, see *Voz de Nuevo León*, May 16, 1903, p. 4.

64. It appears that the Holck interests were critical in the formation and prominence of the German colony. See note 13.

65. J. F. Bergier, "The Industrial Bourgeoisie and the Rise of the Working Class, 1700–1914," in *The Fontana Economic History of Europe: The Industrial Revolution*, ed. Carlo Cipolla (London: Collins/Fontana Books, 1973), p. 436.

66. *Voz de Nuevo León*, November 13, 1897, p. 1; May 12, 1900, p. 1; August 20, 1902, p. 1; October 4, 1902, pp. 1–2.

67. Labor activity in this period was apparently confined largely to companies not of the elite. Reyes' major biographer, E. V. Niemeyer, sees Reyes as prolabor. Yet Reyes' record on labor shows obvious contradictions that can be

explained largely by Reyes' political motivations. As Niemeyer himself cites (*Reyes,* pp. 136–141), Reyes was intimately involved in the formation of a railway brotherhood in Monterrey; as Barry Carr notes, it was "with the intention of exercising control over the organization from behind the scenes" (*El movimiento obrero y la política en México, 1910–1929,* vol. 1, p. 43). If Reyes was sympathetic to the plight of workers, he was also aware of their potential political power. Again, as Carr notes, Reyes "demonstrated an enormous ability of clairvoyance in his handling of the growing labor movement" (*El movimiento obrero,* p. 43). For Díaz' handling of the situation, see Rodney D. Anderson, *Outcasts in Their Own Land: Mexican Industrial Workers, 1906–1911,* pp. 210–212, 300–302. Anderson also notes Reyes' attempt to control the railway workers organization, yet he states: "General Reyes was the most sensitive to the problems of the workers of his state" (p. 211), a highly debatable conclusion.

68. *El Economista Mexicano,* March 25, 1911, p. 557; Máximo de León Garza, *Monterrey, Un vistazo a sus entrañas* (Monterrey: n.p., 1966), pp. 24–29; on foreign labor versus Mexican labor and wages, see *El Economista Mexicano,* July 1, 1899, p. 255; *El País,* May 28, 1903, p. 1; Ramón E. Ruiz, *Labor and the Ambivalent Revolutionaries: Mexico, 1911–1923,* pp. 11–16. Reyes' approach to labor was seen in several instances, two in particular involving railway workers in 1898 and 1902; *Voz de Nuevo León,* March 26, 1898, p. 1; April 2, 1898, p. 1. The 1898 strike revolved around the issue of discrimination against Mexican workers by the American-owned Gulf Railroad. Strikers were jailed, while others fled to other cities. Two weeks later, the *Voz de Nuevo León* (in its April 23, 1898, edition, p. 1) criticized another newspaper for its defense of the rights of Mexican workers. The Reyista-controlled *Voz de Nuevo León* stressed the tenets of economic liberalism that allowed the employer to hire and fire whomever he wished.

The 1902 strike of firemen of the National Railway concerned a demand by workers for a raise to counter the devaluation of that year. Strikers were suspended from their jobs. State troops made sure "no trouble" occurred. The strike was broken when the railway callously hired new men at higher pay while refusing to rehire workers; see *El Imparcial,* October 8, 1902, p. 1, and subsequent issues: October 9, 1902, p. 2; October 10, 1902, p. 1; October 12, 1902, p. 1; October 15, 1902, p. 1; October 18, 1902, p. 1; also *Voz de Nuevo León,* October 11, 1902, p. 1.

The repression of labor by the Reyes government included the suppression of news items on labor. In reviewing Monterrey newspapers, the extent of this policy by the Reyes-controlled press was apparent. Indeed, for example, on the 1902 *fogonero* strike cited above, the Mexico City paper *El Imparcial* gave extensive coverage in contrast to the one item in the *Voz de Nuevo León.* To some extent, this policy reflected the politics of the Reyes versus Limantour rivalry, where such a strike would prove embarrassing to Reyes and his ability to maintain "peace and order" in Nuevo León.

69. *El Imparcial,* May 16, 1907, p. 6; *El País,* June 12, 1907, p. 1; *Monterrey News,* June 21, 1907, p. 8; June 12, 1907, p. 4.

70. See de León Garza, *Monterrey,* pp. 17–29.

71. Of Monterrey's total labor force of about 5,000, 13 companies represented about 3,900 of the total number of workers.

72. *Monterrey News,* October 7, 1907, p. 1.

73. Among many citations: *Monterrey News,* November 7, 1907, p. 4; December 22, 1907, p. 14; January 13, 1909, p. 4; January 19, 1909, p. 4.

74. *Monterrey News,* October 7, 1907, p. 1.

75. *Voz de Nuevo León,* November 3, 1900, p. 2.

76. *Voz de Nuevo León,* May 26, 1900, p. 1.

77. *Monterrey News,* May 6, 1907, p. 6.

78. Ibid.

79. *Monterrey News,* November 7, 1907, p. 1.

4. The Survival of a Porfirian Elite

1. The degree to which the Mexican revolution was indeed a revolution has sparked a long and vigorous debate among scholars. For a summary of the contending schools of thought, see Hector Aguilar Camin, ed., *Interpretaciones de la revolución mexicana* (Mexico City: Editorial Nuevo Imagen, 1981).

2. The Madero visits to Monterrey are based on the following: José P. Saldaña, *Casos y cosas de Monterrey,* pp. 144–156; Aguilar Belden de Garza, *Una ciudad y dos familias,* pp. 122–125; Charles C. Cumberland, *Mexican Revolution: Genesis under Madero,* pp. 108–111; Ross, *Madero,* pp. 104–107; José C. Valadés, *Imaginación y realidad de Francisco I. Madero* (Mexico City: Antigua Librería Robredo, 1960), pp. 246–261; *El Imparcial,* June 8, 1910, p. 1; June 9, 1910, pp. 1, 3, 7; June 10, 1910, p. 3; June 12, 1910, pp. 1, 7; June 16, 1911, p. 1; June 17, 1911, p. 4; October 19, 1911, p. 1; October 20, 1911, p. 4; October 21, 1911, pp. 1, 10; October 22, 1911, p. 2.

3. The quote is from Saldaña, *Casos y cosas,* p. 155. The telegram referred to appeared in the *Monterrey News,* May 10, 1911, p. 1, and May 11, 1911, p. 7.

4. Ruiz, *The Great Rebellion,* p. 120.

5. Ibid.

6. Bazant, *Concise History,* pp. 118–124.

7. Hansen, *Politics of Mexican Development,* p. 151.

8. Ibid.

9. Ibid., p. 154.

10. Ibid., p. 156.

11. Ibid., p. 155.

12. Ibid.

13. Bazant, *Concise History,* p. 121.

14. Bazant, *Concise History,* p. 120; Juan Felipe Leal, *México: Estado, burocracia y sindicato* (Mexico City: Ed. El Caballito, 1975), p. 27.

15. Beals, *Díaz,* pp. 389–390.

16. Cumberland, *Mexican Revolution,* p. 48; Ross, *Madero,* pp. 46–49.

17. Cumberland, *Mexican Revolution,* pp. 55–69.

18. Beals, *Díaz,* p. 411; Cumberland, *Mexican Revolution,* pp. 84–85.

19. Ibid.

20. Ross, *Madero*, p. 73; Niemeyer, *Reyes*, pp. 178–179; Luis González, "El liberalismo triunfante," in *Historia general de México*, vol. 3 (Mexico City: El Colegio de México, 1976), pp. 256–258, where he stresses the importance of the period's economic problems.

21. Ross, *Madero*, p. 51.

22. Ibid.; see also Cumberland, *Mexican Revolution*, pp. 88, 108–109.

23. Ross, *Madero*, p. 51; in July 1909, Evaristo Madero still refused to give his grandson money for the campaign. In the *Monterrey News*, December 5, 1910, p. 1, Ernesto Madero disclaimed Madero family involvement in any political movements in Mexico. See Beals, *Díaz*, pp. 419–420, where he notes that Díaz "suspected the entire family" and "unsuccessfully tried to promote a civil suit against the family properties." Moreover, Díaz "moved to break the Maderos financially" by sending a federal official to look into the Maderos' huge debt owed to the Banco de Nuevo León.

24. *Monterrey News*, June 9, 1909, p. 1; Niemeyer, *Reyes*, p. 177.

25. Luis G. Sada to Secretaría de Gobernación, August 25, 1916; Secretaría de Gobernación to L. G. Sada, October 11, 1916, AGN, Ramo Gobernación, Box 78/Exp. 13.

26. William Weber Johnson, *Heroic Mexico: The Narrative History of a Twentieth Century Revolution*, pp. 137–142.

27. On the business activities of the Monterrey elite during the revolution, see U.S. Congress, Senate, Committee on Foreign Relations, *Investigations of Mexican Affairs, Hearings and Preliminary Report*, 2 vols. (Washington, D.C.: Government Printing Office, 1920), pp. 1920–1935, 2885. According to reports, the Fundidora was sending shipments as far away as San Francisco, California; see *Excelsior*, January 5, 1918, p. 1. In addition, see José Fuentes Mares, *Monterrey, Una ciudad creadora y sus capitanes*, pp. 126–128.

28. Ruiz, *Great Rebellion*, pp. 153–166.

29. Montemayor Hernández, *Historia de Monterrey*, pp. 321–322; Gilberto Álvarez Salinas, *Pancho Villa en Monterrey*, pp. 33–45; Álvarez notes that the Cervecería and the Fundidora paid 20,000 pesos each to Villa, p. 44.

30. *San Antonio Express*, April 7, 1914, p. 1; April 21, 1914, p. 2; *Correspondencia con el Ministro de Gobernación*, 1914–1918, Number 8167, March 24, 1914, AGENL.

31. *San Antonio Express*, April 25, 1914, p. 1; Montemayor Hernández, *Historia de Monterrey*, pp. 314–318.

32. *San Antonio Express*, May 25, 1914, p. 2.

33. Prior to his trip to Washington, Schnaider had telegrammed, then written to the American consul in Monterrey, Phillip C. Hanna, to explain his allegations; Joseph M. Schnaider to Phillip C. Hanna, April 8, 1914; also April 9, 1914, NAW, RG 59.350.

34. William J. Bryan to Phillip C. Hanna, June 2, 1914; Hanna to W. J. Bryan, June 4, 1914; W. J. Bryan to Hanna, June 5, 1914, NAW, RG 59.350.

35. Hanna to Pablo González, June 9, 1914, NAW, RG 59.350.

36. Pablo González to Phillip C. Hanna, June 10, 1914, NAW, RG 59.350.

37. Phillip C. Hanna to Venustiano Carranza, June 11, 1914; Phillip C.

230 Notes to Pages 109–113

Hanna to Pablo González, June 11, 1914; Isidro Fabela to Phillip C. Hanna, June 14, 1914, NAW, RG 59.350.
    38. T. Ayres Robertson to Phillip C. Hanna, June 18, 1914; Joseph M. Schnaider to Phillip C. Hanna, June 15, 1914; June 17, 1914, NAW, RG 59.350.
    39. Telegram, Phillip C. Hanna to Secretary of State, June 20, 1914, NAW, RG 59.312.11/4795; Wilbur J. Oarr to Phillip C. Hanna, June 26, 1914, NAW, RG 59.312.11/4783.
    40. For all of his nationalism, Carranza was sensitive to the importance of foreign investment to the Mexican economy; Phillip C. Hanna to Secretary of State, March 2, 1916, NAW, RG 59.350.
    41. The international context included World War I and the success of the Bolshevik revolution. Both events had obvious implications for the Carranza administration, particularly for its relation to the United States.
    42. *Correspondencia con el Ministerio de Relaciones Exteriores,* 1914, Venustiano Carranza to Antonio I. Villarreal, August 24, 1914, AGENL; Valentín Rivero to Venustiano Carranza, November 26, 1915, Condumex, AVC, Bundle 61/Document 6810.
    43. Luis G. Sada to Venustiano Carranza, August 25, 1916; Secretaría de Gobernación to L. G. Sada, October 11, 1916; Ana Gorostieta de G. Sada to Venustiano Carranza, September 24, 1918; Secretaría de Gobernación to Ana Gorostieta de G. Sada, October 17, 1918; Luis G. Sada to Secretaría de Hacienda, September 6, 1916, AGN, Ramo Gobernación, Box 78/Exp. 13.
    44. Ruiz, *Great Rebellion,* p. 372.
    45. Randolph Robertson to Secretary of State, August 16, 1917, where the vice-consul notes that the Fundidora was shipping 75% of its production to the United States, NAW, RG 84.812.113/9124. See also note 27.
    46. Florentino Cantú Treviño to Departamento de Trabajo, February 27, 1917. The portfolio contained a series of letters and telegrams on the protests of textile workers and responses by owners such as Florentino Cantú Treviño; *Correspondencia con el Ministro de Fomento,* 1919–1920, AGENL.
    47. Gremios Unidos de la Fundidora to Pablo de la Garza, March 4, 1917; Pablo de la Garza to Gerente, Fundidora, March 8, 1917; Director General, Fundidora to Sec. General de Gobierno, March 10, 1917, *Varios particulares de la provincia,* 1912–1926, AGENL.
    48. Thomas Bowman to Secretary of State, February 9, 1920, noted that Nicéforo Zambrano was a Carrancista who worked to oust politicians who were antibusiness, NAW, RG.59.
    49. *Memoria . . . Nicéforo Zambrano, gobernador . . . de Nuevo León . . . 30 de Junio de 1917 al 3 de Octubre, 1919* (Monterrey: Imprenta del Gobierno, 1921), pp. xviii, 194–197, AGENL.
    50. Ibid., p. xix.
    51. Ibid., p. 639.
    52. Ibid.
    53. Ibid., p. xix.
    54. Javier Rojas, "Luchas obreras y sindicalismo blanco en Monterrey," *Cuadernos de Cultura Obrera* 1 (May 1980): 1–42.

55. Pablo de la Garza to Secretaría de Fomento, February 28, 1917, *Correspondencia con el Ministro de Fomento*, 1919–1920, AGENL.

56. AGN, Sección de Trabajo. The archives of the Department of Labor contain much material on complaints of workers from Monterrey in which the Cantú Treviños appear frequently during the 1920s. For example: Box 444/ Exp. 11, Antonio Sánchez to Álvaro Obregón, December 17, 1922.

57. Ruiz, *Great Rebellion*, pp. 160–166.

5. The Redefinition of Power

1. For an overall view of this period, see among many other works Lorenzo Meyer, *Historia general de México* (Mexico City: El Colegio de México, 1976), vol. 4, pp. 111–154.

2. See Enrique Krauze, Jean Meyer, and Cayetano Reyes, *Historia de la revolución mexicana, 1924–1928*, vol. 10, *La reconstrucción económica*.

3. Ibid., pp. 107–132, 183–199.

4. For a brief analysis, see Bazant, *Concise History*, pp. 158–165.

5. See Hansen, *Politics of Mexican Development*, pp. 156–171.

6. Edwin Lieuwin, *Mexican Militarism: The Political Rise and Fall of the Revolutionary Army, 1910–1940* (Albuquerque: University of New Mexico Press, 1968), pp. 57–65.

7. Gruening, *Mexico and Its Heritage*, p. 486.

8. In 1920, Obregón led the coup that ousted Venustiano Carranza from office. Three years later, with many of his former supporters betraying him, Obregón had to fight off the coup of Adolfo de la Huerta; Ruiz, *Great Rebellion*, p. 177.

9. Henry Bamford Parker, *A History of Mexico* (Boston: Houghton Mifflin Company, 1938), pp. 377–379.

10. Krauze, Meyer, and Reyes, *La reconstrucción económica*, pp. 289–292.

11. *El Porvenir*, February 16, 1925, p. 3. As table 14 makes clear, the smelters of Monterrey remained the overwhelming source of American capital in the city in the early 1920s.

12. The Vidriera in a series of letters in 1924 attempted to block any attempt by foreign imports to break its monopoly of glass-making; AGN, 104-V-15; R. G. Sada to Calles, October 8, 1924; R. G. Sada to Calles, August 21, 1924; similar letters sent to Secretaría de Hacienda on August 21 and October 6, 1924.

13. Given the power of the *caudillo*-type presidency in the early 1920s, such an approach was not surprising, especially in light of the elite's Porfirian experience with the political system under Díaz; see Lorenzo Meyer, "Historical Roots of the Authoritarian State in Mexico," in *Authoritarianism in Mexico*, ed. José Luis Reyna and Richard S. Weinert, pp. 4–11.

14. Krauze, Meyer, and Reyes, *La reconstrucción económica*, pp. 83–97.

15. Thomas D. Bowman to Secretary of State, Monterrey, May 18, 1920, NAW.812.00/24079.

16. Thomas D. Bowman to Secretary of State, Monterrey, July 27, 1920,

NAW.812.00/24426. From June to July 1920, Monterrey's industrialists confronted a series of work actions, particularly at the metal refining plants, including the Fundidora. Despite the intensity of the workers' efforts, the intransigence of the industrialists to a labor federation forced the workers to concede to the formation of company (*blanco*) unions. In exchange, the companies involved gave raises to the workers, including a 20% to 50% salary hike for workers at the Fundidora. It should be emphasized that the drive to form a labor federation at this time in Monterrey received no aid from the state or federal government. See Paco Ignacio Taibo II, *La gran huelga del verano de 1920 en Monterrey,* Cuadernos de Cultura Obrera, num. 4 (Monterrey: OIDMO, 1981).

17. Thomas D. Bowman to Secretary of State, Monterrey, April 30, 1921, NAW.812.00/24974.

18. Thomas D. Bowman to Secretary of State, Monterrey, May 7, 1921, NAW.812.50/83.

19. Cámara de Comercio, Industria y Minera de Nuevo León to Álvaro Obregón, Monterrey, July 7, 1921; Álvaro Obregón to Cámara de Nuevo León, Mexico City, July 8, 1921, AGN.814-M-23. Five months later, the situation remained much the same: Thomas D. Bowman to Secretary of State, Monterrey, November 15, 1921, NAW.812.50/94.

20. *El Porvenir,* July 23, 1927, pp. 1, 4; July 24, 1927, p. 4.

21. Cámara Nacional de Comercio, Industria y Minera del Estado de Nuevo León to Álvaro Obregón, Monterrey, September 15, 1921; Obregón to Cámara, Mexico City, September 22, 1921, AGN.808-N-4; Cámara to Álvaro Obregón, Monterrey, June 17, 1921; Obregón to Cámara, Mexico City, June 20, 1921, AGN.424-M-2; Cámara to Álvaro Obregón, Monterrey, November 30, 1922, AGN.824-M-6. On the beer tax issue: Enrique Sada Muguerza to Álvaro Obregón, Monterrey, May 13, 1922, AGN.808-C-29; Governor Ramiro Tamez wrote to Obregón to argue the case for the brewery as well; Tamez to Obregón, Monterrey, December 5, 1922, AGN.424-C-7.

22. Krauze, Meyer, and Reyes, *La reconstrucción económica,* p. 43. José R. Calderón served on the first board of directors of the Banco de México. Two of Monterrey's banks ranked third and fourth in the country in 1924, the Banco de Nuevo León and the Banco Mercantil (*Excelsior,* January 31, 1924, pp. 1, 8). The Monterrey elite was also active in the meetings leading up to the formation of the Banco de México (*Excelsior,* February 1, 1924, pp. 1, 8; February 2, 1924, pp. 1, 7).

23. Gruening, *Mexico and Its Heritage,* p. 319.

24. Ibid., p. 320.

25. Ibid., p. 468.

26. Thomas D. Bowman to Secretary of State, Monterrey, May 18, 1920, NAW.812.00/24079.

27. This was a disruptive time in Nuevo León politics that included for a while two "legislatures" meeting simultaneously and a shoot-out between supporters of Siller and González on the streets of the city; Porfirio G. González to Plutarco Elías Calles, Monterrey, March 21, 1925, AGN.243-N2-G-2; Paul Foster, U.S. Consul to Secretary of State, Monterrey, April 29, 1925,

NAW.812.00/27530; *Excelsior,* July 3, 1925, pp. 1, 8; July 4, 1925, pp. 1, 4; July 5, 1925, pp. 1, 11; July 8, 1925, pp. 1, 4; July 9, 1925, p. 1; July 11, 1925, p. 1; July 14, 1925, pp. 1, 8; July 15, 1925, p. 1; July 16, 1925, p. 1; July 17, 1925, pp. 1, 3. On the Sáenz meeting with businessmen, see *El Porvenir,* June 2, 1925, p. 4.

28. Montemayor Hernández, *Historia de Monterrey,* p. 343.

29. *El Porvenir,* June 2, 1925, p. 4; August 23, 1926, p. 1; January 26, 1927, p. 4; February 1, 1927, p. 4; February 28, 1927, p. 4; March 12, 1927, p. 1. On the Sáenz meeting with businessmen, see May 13, 1927, p. 1; May 14, 1927, p. 4; on Sáenz comments, see May 16, 1927, p. 4.

30. On Sáenz probusiness measures, see *El Porvenir,* August 12, 1927, p. 4; October 16, 1927, p. 4; October 19, 1927, p. 4. On beer tax issue, see Correspondencia del General Aarón Sáenz, Monterrey, December 31, 1927, Box 3, Exp. 101–130 and Exp. 114 (1928), AGENL; Francisco G. Sada to Aarón Sáenz, Monterrey, February 15, 1928; Enrique Sada M. to Aarón Sáenz, Monterrey, February 23, 1928; Francisco G. Sada to Sáenz, Monterrey, February 25, 1928, AGENL. On the tax question, see *El Porvenir,* March 5, 1928, p. 4. On tourism, Sáenz was responding to an idea long touted by businessmen as a result of the road construction program in the region that had stimulated auto traffic between Monterrey and Texas via Laredo; *El Porvenir,* May 13, 1928, p. 4. On the elite's participation in Sáenz' economic plans, see *El Porvenir,* June 16, 1928, p. 4; June 17, 1928, pp. 3, 4; June 19, 1928, p. 4; June 22, 1928, p. 4.

31. *El Porvenir,* April 3, 1928, p. 4; June 23, 1928, p. 4; June 24, 1928, p. 4; June 26, 1928, p. 4.

32. Thomas D. Bowman to Secretary of State, Monterrey, January 7, 1921, NAW.812.00/25303.

33. Ibid.

34. Ibid. As the U.S. consul put it, "it becomes known that the matter was settled to the satisfaction of the brewery. . . . It has since become known that the brewery's exclusive agency in Tampico, the most profitable representation at their command, had been given to private representatives of Governor García."

35. Thomas D. Bowman to Secretary of State, Monterrey, November 15, 1921, NAW.812.50/94. A detailed history of the beverage and beer industries in Mexico is beyond the scope of this study. Briefly, several indications existed at the time that the glass plant and the brewery held distinct advantages. Prohibition in the United States offered a clandestine market, for example, for beer along the Texas border. The year before Prohibition (1917), beer production in Texas was nearly 800,000 barrels, almost double the amount made in 1905. It is conceivable that some of that demand was filled after 1918 by the Cervecería Cuauhtémoc (and other breweries located near the border). As an indication of the demand for beer, and necessity, several breweries in the United States relocated to border towns. Demand in Mexico for beer prompted breweries to increase their capacity and/or improve their equipment. Finally, the soft drink industry continued to be popular in Mexico. For instance, bottlers in Aguascalientes in 1923 were turning out 250,000 bottles of soda a month—all the

bottles were made in Monterrey by the Vidriera. See *Beverage Journal* 57:1 (July 1921): 45; 57:3 (September 1921): 117; 57:5 (November 1921): 219; 58:4 (April 1922): 63; 59:3 (March 1923): 51; 59:7 (July 1923): 84; 62:5 (April 1926): 78; and *Western Brewer* 69:9 (September 1933): 89.

Interestingly, some breweries moved back to Texas with the repeal of Prohibition (1933), but the illicit trade in beer probably continued for a time—99 counties in Texas remained "dry" as late as 1937. See *Western Brewer* 70:3 (March 1934): 60; *Beverage Journal* 67:9 (September 1931): 32; 76:2 (February 1937): 47.

36. Paul H. Foster to Secretary of State, Monterrey, November 22, 1922, NAW.812.50/125.

37. *Excelsior*, February 4, 1924, p. 8; February 21, 1924, sec. 2, p. 8; February 25, 1924, pp. 1, 6.

38. The Fundidora's increased production did not necessarily mean prosperity for the steel plant. The Fundidora's productive capacity rarely reached over 50% in the 1920s. Without government support, the plant would have been extremely hard-pressed to continue operations. This is underscored by the effects of the rebellion headed by Adolfo de la Huerta. A full discussion of the rebellion is beyond the scope of this book, but its impact highlights the Fundidora's precarious footing. On the business aspects of the Fundidora, see *Report, Compañía Fundidora de Fierro y Acero de Monterrey, S.A.* (Mexico City: Compañía Fundidora, 1930), LAC. This was a stockholders' report with information covering the years 1903 to 1929. For a detailed account of the Huertista rebellion, see Dulles, *Yesterday in Mexico*, pp. 204–263.

39. Among several cases of protest was the one registered in January 1925 by businessmen as reported in *El Porvenir*, January 3, 1925, p. 4; January 5, 1925, p. 4; January 6, 1925, pp. 1, 4; January 8, 1925, p. 1. See table 15 on elite interests in 1922.

40. The Junta de Arbitraje y Conciliación is referred to in the rest of the text as the labor board or labor tribunal or in related terms rather than using the full formal title in every instance.

41. *El Porvenir*, May 29, 1925, p. 3; June 27, 1925, p. 3; July 18, 1925, p. 5.

42. Ibid., July 24, 1925, p. 1; July 25, 1925, p. 4; July 26, 1925, pp. 1, 4; August 1, 1925, p. 4; August 6, 1925, p. 4.

43. Ibid., August 13, 1925, p. 4; August 14, 1925, p. 1; September 3, 1925, p. 4. Joel Rocha, in Mexico City at the time, also blasted the governor's new appointment in *Excelsior*, July 18, 1925, p. 1.

44. Juan Guzmán, Secretary General of Workers Federation of Nuevo León, to Álvaro Obregón, Monterrey, June 28, 1924, AGN; Sección de Trabajo, Box 726/Exp. 7; Sociedad Cooperativa de la Cervecería Cuauhtémoc to Álvaro Obregón, Monterrey, June 24, 1924, AGN.811-C-165.

45. José Cavazos to Álvaro Obregón, June 25, 1924, AGN.811-C-165; Porfirio González to Álvaro Obregón, Monterrey, June 25, 1924, AGN.811-C-165; Department of Labor to Juan Guzmán, August 21, 1924, AGN, Sección de Trabajo, Box 726/Exp. 7.

46. One reason for such speedy decisions was the low number of cases. For example, in 1928, salary disputes before the arbitration court totaled 5

cases in Monterrey as opposed to 1,129 cases in the Distrito Federal. Firings composed 34 cases of the Monterrey court as opposed to over 3,000 cases in the Distrito Federal, 139 cases in Puebla, and 212 cases in Veracruz; AGN, Sección de Trabajo, Box 1647/Exp. 2.

47. In a letter to Obregón, workers' representatives said of the arbitration court's proceedings: "for such meetings, we three humble workers stand in representation of workers to protect our situation, and in representation of . . . a lawyer, Virgilio Garza. . . ." In a case involving the Vidriera, the glass plant let go over sixty workers, with over fifty of them receiving indemnities; eventually without support from the governor, and with a lack of confidence in arbitration court, the workers who were fired for their prounion sentiments were forced to accept an indemnity equaling two months' pay; AGN, Sección de Trabajo, Box 650/Exp. 10 (1923).

48. *El Porvenir,* March 2, 1925, sec. 2, p. 2.

49. Ernest Gruening, usually a perceptive observer of Mexico, notes that the workers at the Fundidora "are fully satisfied with conditions" and goes on to describe the local arbitration court as "fair and without definite bias in favor of one or the other" (*Mexico and Its Heritage,* p. 354). The Cervecería also offered relatively high wages: AGN, Departamento de Trabajo, Box 280/Exp. 3; Box 436/Exp. 3; Box 636/Exp. 3.

50. *El Porvenir,* December 5, 1924, p. 1; December 6, 1924, p. 3.

51. Ibid., March 6, 1925, p. 3. Strike reported on March 26, 1925, p. 1. The Modelo printery was owned by the editor of *El Porvenir.*

52. *El Porvenir,* April 2, 1925, p. 1.

53. *El Porvenir,* April 3, 1925, p. 1; April 9, 1925, pp. 1, 4.

54. *El Porvenir,* April 10, 1925, p. 1.

55. *El Porvenir,* April 13, 1925, p. 4.

56. *Excelsior,* April 16, 1925, pp. 1, 7, 11.

57. *Excelsior,* April 20, 1925, sec. 2, p. 7; April 21, 1925, sec. 2, p. 3.

58. *El Porvenir,* November 12, 1925, p. 3. This comment reflected the intense concern of Nuevo León's businessmen over the introduction of new proposals by the CROM for labor legislation (e.g., the notion of a six-hour day); *El Porvenir,* November 4, 1925, p. 1; November 7, 1925, p. 1; November 8, 1925, p. 3; November 11, 1925, p. 3, where the editorial, after lamenting recent labor troubles, observed: "Regardless, we assume that the highest authorities will now be ready to suppress with a heavy hand any anarchic intentions." This is of course a reference to Calles and the CROM.

59. As early as August 1925, the elite of Monterrey was sounding the alarm over the codification of labor laws and their adverse effect on industry if they remain "socialistic" in nature; *El Porvenir,* August 21, 1925, p. 1.

60. This was not unique to the men from Monterrey. As one observer has put it: "As the weaknesses of the state laws and their administration became glaringly manifest, labor and capital were compelled to turn more and more to the federal government for decisions in their disputes"; as a result, both sides wanted a federal labor code (Marjorie Ruth Clark, *Organized Labor in Mexico,* pp. 214–215).

61. Confederation of Industrial Chambers to Secretary of Industry,

Commerce, and Labor, Mexico City, November 13, 1925, AGN, Sección de Trabajo, Box 856/Exp. 2. Note that the timing of this letter coincided with *El Porvenir*'s criticism of Calles and Morones in note 58. Like most businessmen, the *regiomontanos* were well aware that the CROM had made important inroads in several parts of the country because of its political connections, resulting in favorable decisions by local labor tribunals. See Carr, *El movimiento obrero*, pp. 174–175.

6. Elite and Society in the Postrevolutionary Era

1. *El Porvenir,* September 15, 1926, p. 4.
2. See Arnaldo Córdova, *La ideología de la revolución mexicana: La formación del nuevo régimen,* pp. 31, 37.
3. Carlos Pérez Maldonado, *Nuestra Señora de Monterrey* (Monterrey: n.p., 1946), p. 193.
4. Carlos Pérez Maldonado, *El Casino de Monterrey* (Monterrey: n.p., 1951), pp. 96–97.
5. Note should be taken of the ties between the Garza-Sadas within their own circle as well as with other "well-placed" families. For example, note the marriage of Roberto G. *Sada* Treviño with Irma *Salinas Rocha;* Roberto *Garza Sada* with Margarita *Sada;* see also figure 4.
6. See Thomas C. Cochran and William Miller, *The Age of Enterprise: A Social History of Industrial America,* rev. ed. (New York: Harper and Row, 1961), pp. 323–331.
7. These men often traded places as officers of the club. When the international president of the Rotary Club arrived in Monterrey, he was met by Roberto G. Sada, Joel Rocha, and Jorge Rivero; *El Porvenir,* March 15, 1927, p. 5.
8. *El Porvenir* regularly had an article on its fourth page when the Rotary Club met; for example, *El Porvenir,* October 1, 1927, p. 4.
9. *El Porvenir,* April 3, 1926, p. 5.
10. *El Porvenir,* February 28, 1926, p. 4.
11. Begun in 1918 by Barragán, the magazine had a circulation hovering near two thousand until the Cárdenas years, when circulation reached about six thousand. The magazine featured many articles on American entrepreneurs; Henry Ford was a favorite topic (e.g., *Actividad* 6 [September 1923]: 1123–1125).
12. *El Porvenir,* August 20, 1925, p. 4; August 20, 1926, p. 4; May 12, 1927, p. 5; August 21, 1927, sec. 2, p. 1.
13. *El Porvenir,* June 8, 1926, p. 4; June 9, 1926, p. 1; June 16, 1926, p. 4; August 18, 1926, p. 5.
14. *El Porvenir,* January 3, 1926, sec. 1, p. 4; June 24, 1926, p. 1.
15. *El Porvenir,* February 4, 1925, p. 3.
16. *El Porvenir,* April 3, 1925, p. 3; July 3, 1925, p. 3.
17. The notion of welfare capitalism, despite its touting by the elite, had in fact a short and ineffective popularity in the United States, in spite of the near worship of Taylorism among American businessmen.
18. Robert H. Wiebe, *The Search for Order, 1877–1920* (New York: Hill and Wang, 1967), p. 294.

19. Fundidora Legal Department to Aarón Sáenz, July 31, 1928, Box 10/ Exp. 452, AGENL; Adolfo Prieto to Plutarco Elías Calles, July 2, 1928, AGN, 728-C-56.

20. Richard Hofstadter, *The Age of Reform: From Bryan to F.D.R.* (New York: Vintage Books, 1955), p. 243.

21. Ibid.

22. *El Porvenir*, November 29, 1926, p. 3. The migration of Mexican workers was a frequent issue in Monterrey newspapers; for example, *El Porvenir*, May 11, 1926, p. 3. In this light, the rewards given to workers were perhaps more effective, such as the fiestas for employees of the Cervecería (*El Porvenir*, August 9, 1926, p. 8) or a trip for seventy workers to Tampico (*El Porvenir*, June 6, 1926, p. 6) paid for by the brewery.

23. *El Porvenir*, January 1, 1926, sec. 2, p. 1.

24. One of the more popular bands in the mid-1920s in Monterrey was "La Victor Jazz" (*El Porvenir*, January 4, 1926, sec. 1, p. 4).

25. Among many examples, see *Excelsior*, July 9, 1925, p. 9.

26. An early sign of economic nationalism was an editorial in *El Porvenir*, April 14, 1926, p. 3, calling on the Mexican government to "buy Mexican," especially from the Fundidora. Perhaps coincidentally, the Vidriera a few months later featured the *hecho en México* logo (*El Porvenir*, September 16, 1926, p. 6).

27. The tone of *Actividad* articles betrays the sense of the elite on this issue, with repeated illustrations of the "American way" as superior—this at a time when businessmen in the United States enjoyed unprecedented prestige and considerable power.

28. For example, in 1926, the Nuevo León Cámara volunteered to aid President Calles in economic planning with an implicit suggestion that he needed their aid; *El Porvenir*, April 4, 1926, p. 3; Luis Estrada to Plutarco Elías Calles, May 28, 1926, AGN.731-M-10.

29. *Actividad* published in June 1922 a long article on the industrial giants in the United States and the benefits that they generated as a result for American society, not unlike the attitude of the Garza-Sadas.

30. Among many examples of this type of activity, elite women spearheaded a toy drive for the poor at Christmas in 1926 (*El Porvenir*, December 25, 1926, p. 4) in cooperation with the Rotary Club.

31. The editor of *Excelsior* for several years in the 1920s was Manuel Barragán, an intimate crony of the elite, Rotary Club member, and ally of the Garza-Sadas.

32. Irma Salinas Rocha, *Nostro grupo* (Monterrey: Editorial Isaro, 1978), pp. 17–27. It should be noted that the Cervecería's owners cultivated an elitist image for themselves and their products. Their advertising included female imagery that emphasized a highbrow look and message (while using an American ad agency). And aside from the usual radio and newspaper spots, they also used a direct mail campaign "to the 50,000 most prominent people in Mexico . . ." (*Brewers Journal* 75:1 [July 1936]: 33). They were quick to invite Americans to tour their facilities through their contacts with the U.S. brewing industry. José F. Muguerza, for instance, even addressed the U.S. Brewers

Association in its meeting in 1940 at San Antonio (see *Brewers Journal* 72:4 [April 1935]: 30–33; 73:4 [October 1935]: 38; 83:4 [October 1940]: 48; 83:5 [November 1940]: 60–62).

33. Montemayor Hernández, *Historia de Monterrey,* pp. 327–330, 351–354.

34. Jean Meyer, *Historia de la revolución mexicana, 1924–1928,* vol. 11, *Estado y sociedad con Calles,* p. 311.

35. The Nuevo León Chamber of Commerce encompassed three sections on industry, commerce, and mining. The largest one was the commercial section that embraced most businesses, large and small.

36. On this marriage, see *El Porvenir,* June 6, 1925, p. 6. For other aspects of his career, see *El Porvenir,* December 12, 1924, pp. 1, 8; his job as legal counsel of the Cervecería began with his defense of the firm before the labor court in 1925 (*El Porvenir,* September 3, 1925, p. 4).

37. Wiebe, *Search for Order,* p. 135.

38. This attitude was clearly visible in the special section in *El Porvenir* on the international Rotary Club meeting held in Monterrey in 1925 (*El Porvenir,* March 1, 1925, sec. 2, pp. 6–7; March 2, 1925, sec. 2, pp. 2–3; March 4, 1925, sec. 2, p. 2).

39. For an example, see *Actividad* 5 (August 1922): 812. In 1927, *El Porvenir* published a series of interviews with businessmen on how they would deal with the problems of the Mexican economy (e.g., *El Porvenir,* April 20, 1927, p. 3). The series ran through May on nearly a daily basis.

40. Among many examples of this attitude was the editorial in *El Porvenir,* April 17, 1927, p. 3, on government corruption and its adverse economic impact.

41. For a typical example, see *El Porvenir,* April 13, 1927, p. 3.

42. Barragán became editor of *Excelsior* (Mexico City) in 1928.

7. A Fateful Time

1. *Excelsior,* November 18, 1928, p. 1.

2. *Excelsior,* November 14, 1928, p. 1. In this article, Sáenz played his role as a cautious candidate, indicating that he would wait for the PNR convention to discuss his presidential plans.

3. *Excelsior,* November 3, 1928, p. 1; December 8, 1928, p. 1.

4. *Excelsior,* December 15, 1928, pp. 1, 3.

5. Lorenzo Meyer, *Historia de la revolución mexicana,* vol. 12, *Los inicios de la institucionalización,* pp. 55–58.

6. *Excelsior,* March 2, 1929, p. 1; March 3, 1929, pp. 1, 3.

7. *Excelsior,* March 4, 1929, p. 1.

8. Dwight Morrow to Secretary of State, Mexico City, November 21, 1928, NAW.800/1149. In this communication, Morrow questioned Calles' support for Sáenz while virtually all political observers assumed Sáenz would be the next president of Mexico. Indications that the Sáenz nomination was in trouble were further described in a letter less than a month before the Querétaro convention; Dwight Morrow to Secretary of State, Mexico City, February 12, 1929, NAW.800/1431. For a general review of this episode, see Dulles, *Yesterday in Mexico,* pp. 414–435.

9. William Chapman, American Consul, to Secretary of State, Monterrey, October 8, 1927, NAW/FRC.800/3; Dwight Morrow to Secretary of State, Mexico City, February 12, 1929, NAW.800/1431; Luis Javier Garrido, *El partido de la revolución institucionalizada: La formación del nuevo estado en México (1928–1945)*, pp. 83–109; Carlos Roel to Álvaro Obregón, Monterrey, September 18, 1923, AGN.408-N-9, Bundle 4.

10. *Excelsior*, November 5, 1928, p. 6.

11. *Excelsior*, March 2, 1929, p. 3.

12. Emilio Portes Gil, *Autobiografía de la revolución mexicana* (Mexico City: Instituto Mexicano de Cultura, 1964), p. 452.

13. Dwight Morrow to Secretary of State, Mexico City, November 29, 1929, NAW.800/2027.

14. Ibid., also Stokeley W. Morgan, Chargé d'Affaires, to Secretary of State, Mexico City, May 24, 1929, NAW.800.1/1651.

15. *Excelsior*, July 10, 1929, p. 1.

16. This view is found in the transcript of the sessions on the federal labor code held from November 15 to December 8, 1928, AGN, Sección de Trabajo, Box 1676/Exp. 2.

17. *El Porvenir*, September 13, 1926, p. 1; September 14, 1926, p. 3.

18. Carr, *El movimiento obrero*, pp. 158–175.

19. *El Porvenir*, August 14, 1925, p. 3; November 6, 1926, p. 3.

20. Dulles, *Yesterday in Mexico*, pp. 356–357.

21. H. F. Arthur Schoenfeld to Secretary of State, Mexico City, December 8, 1928, NAW.800, Telegram #318.

22. *Excelsior*, November 5, 1928, p. 1.

23. *Excelsior*, December 6, 1928, p. 1.

24. *Excelsior*, December 8, 1928, p. 1; H. F. Arthur Schoenfeld to Secretary of State, Mexico City, December 13, 1928, NAW.800, Telegram #326.

25. *Excelsior*, December 8, 1928, p. 1.

26. H. F. Arthur Schoenfeld to Secretary of State, Mexico City, December 12, 1928, NAW.850.4/1229.

27. *Excelsior*, February 9, 1929, p. 1.

28. *New York Times*, July 10, 1929, p. 14.

29. *Excelsior*, January 28, 1929, p. 5; July 15, 1929, p. 5.

30. Tzvi Medin, *El minimato presidencial: Historia política del maximato (1928–1935)*, pp. 60–66.

31. *Excelsior*, July 26, 1929, p. 5.

32. *Excelsior*, July 29, 1929, p. 5. It should be kept in mind that the editor of *Excelsior* at this time was Manuel Barragán, ex–secretary general of the Nuevo León Chamber of Commerce and well-known friend of the Monterrey elite.

33. *Excelsior*, August 5, 1929, p. 5.

34. *Excelsior*, July 26, 1929, p. 11.

35. *New York Times*, August 2, 1929, p. 22.

36. *Excelsior*, September 14, 1929, p. 5.

37. Again, the connection to Manuel Barragán was important.

38. Robert Jones Shafer, *Mexican Business Organizations: History and Analysis*, pp. 30–35.

39. Ibid., p. 37.
40. *Excelsior,* September 10, 1929, p. 1.
41. *Excelsior,* September 13, 1929, pp. 1, 2.
42. Ibid., p. 1.
43. Ibid., p. 2.
44. *Excelsior,* September 14, 1929, pp. 1, 4; September 16, 1929, p. 1; September 17, 1929, pp. 1, 10; September 19, 1929, pp. 1, 10.
45. *Excelsior,* September 19, 1929, p. 1.
46. *Excelsior,* September 20, 1929, p. 1.
47. *Excelsior,* September 21, 1929, pp. 1, 7.
48. *Excelsior,* September 22, 1929, pp. 1, 3.
49. *Excelsior,* September 21, 1929, p. 1.
50. *Excelsior,* September 27, 1929, p. 1.
51. Shafer, *Mexican Business Organizations,* p. 39.
52. Ibid.
53. *Excelsior,* October 11, 1929, pp. 1, 4.
54. The Grupo Patronal and COPARMEX maintained representatives after the conclusion of the assembly of representatives and delegates from member organizations.
55. Hershel V. Johnson, Chargé d'Affaires, to Secretary of State, Mexico City, September 10, 1929, NAW.850.4/1865.
56. *Excelsior,* September 26, 1929, p. 1.
57. *New York Times,* August 17, 1929, p. 21; September 27, 1929, p. 42; Meyer, *Inicios de la institucionalización,* pp. 237–238.
58. Lorenzo Meyer, *Historia de la revolución mexicana, 1928–1934,* vol. 13, *El conflicto social y los gobiernos del maximato,* pp. 148–151.
59. Carr, *El movimiento obrero,* pp. 258–262.
60. Edward Nathan to Secretary of State, Monterrey, June 1, 1931, NAW/FRC.800/31.C16.1.
61. Henry H. Balch to Secretary of State, Monterrey, December 30, 1930, NAW.800/314.
62. Edward Nathan to Secretary of State, Monterrey, September 8, 1931, NAW/FRC.851.51.C16.1.
63. Shafer, *Mexican Business Organizations,* p. 40.
64. J. Reuben Clark, Jr., to Secretary of State, Mexico City, March 13, 1931, NAW.850.4/249.
65. *Excelsior,* April 26, 1931, p. 1.
66. J. Reuben Clark, Jr., to Secretary of State, Mexico City, April 24, 1931, NAW.850.4/373; May 12, 1931, NAW.850.4/408; May 16, 1931, NAW.850.4-F; June 12, 1931, NAW.850.4F/503.
67. *Excelsior,* June 10, 1931, p. 1.
68. *Excelsior,* June 11, 1931, p. 3; June 12, 1931, p. 1.
69. *Excelsior,* June 27, 1931, p. 1.
70. As early as mid-May, Calles had agreed to help in the passage of the codification legislation: J. Reuben Clark, Jr., to Secretary of State, Mexico City, May 16, 1931, NAW.850.4-F; May 22, 1931, NAW.850.4F/443; *Excelsior,* July 11, 1931, p. 1.

71. *Excelsior,* July 22, 1931, p. 1; August 6, 1931, p. 3.

72. *Excelsior,* August 11, 1931, p. 1; August 14, 1931, p. 4.

73. *Excelsior,* August 17, 1931, p. 1.

74. *Excelsior,* August 22, 1931, p. 1; August 29, 1931, p. 1.

75. By this time, several patriarchs of the elite had died or retired. Isaac Garza would die in 1933, José H. Muguerza in 1939. Francisco G. Sada was seventy-five years old by 1931 and was not active in the direction of the Cervecería by that time.

76. *Excelsior,* October 27, 1929, p. 1.

77. *Excelsior,* October 7, 1929, sec. 2, p. 1.

78. Henry H. Balch to Secretary of State, Monterrey, November 5, 1929, NAW.800.C8.37.

79. *Excelsior,* October 3, 1929, p. 9; October 7, 1929, pp. 1, 10, sec. 2, p. 1; October 19, 1929, pp. 1, 3, 4.

80. *Excelsior,* October 7, 1929, pp. 1, 10.

81. Ibid.

82. *New York Times,* October 7, 1929, p. 9.

83. *Excelsior,* September 10, 1929, p. 1.

84. Arnaldo Córdova, *La clase obrera en la historia de México,* vol. 9, *En una época de crisis (1928–1934),* p. 96.

8. Confrontation

1. See Arnaldo Córdova, *La política de masas del cardenismo,* for an overview of this period and its importance; Samuel León, "Alianza de clase y cardenismo (junio de 1935–febrero de 1936)," *Revista Mexicana de Ciencias Políticas y Sociales* (julio–septiembre 1977): 25–76.

2. Garrido, *El partido de la revolución institucionalizada,* pp. 177–211.

3. Edward Nathan, U.S. Consul, to Secretary of State, Monterrey, August 31, 1934, NAW/FRC.800/458; November 30, 1934, NAW/FRC.800/503; H. W. Carlson, U.S. Vice-Consul, to Secretary of State, Monterrey, January 31, 1935, NAW/FRC.800/515.

4. Edward Nathan, U.S. Consul, to Secretary of State, Monterrey, June 18, 1934, NAW/FRC.800/422.

5. Arturo Anguiano, *El estado y la política obrera del cardenismo,* pp. 22–36.

6. Lázaro Cárdenas, *Palabras y documentos públicos, 1928–1940,* pp. 86–87.

7. Medin, *El minimato presidencial,* pp. 137–144.

8. R. Henry Norweb, Chargé d'Affaires, to Secretary of State, Mexico City, January 17, 1936, NAW.812.00/303229.

9. Alicia Hernández Chavez, *Historia de la revolución mexicana, 1934–1940,* vol. 16, *La mecánica cardenista,* pp. 87–89.

10. Edward Nathan, U.S. Consul, to Secretary of State, Monterrey, June 15, 1935, NAW/FRC.800/573.

11. Hernández Chavez, *La mecánica cardenista,* pp. 91–105.

12. Jorge Basurto, *Cárdenas y el poder sindical,* pp. 51–56.

13. Hernández Chavez, *La mecánica cardenista,* pp. 140–141.

14. Basurto, *Cárdenas y el poder sindical,* pp. 52–53.

15. Dulles, *Yesterday in Mexico*, pp. 640–646.

16. Anguiano, *El estado y la política obrera*, pp. 119–125.

17. Hernández Chavez, *La mecánica cardenista*, p. 131.

18. Anguiano, *El estado y la política obrera*, pp. 70–72.

19. Edward Nathan to Secretary of State, Monterrey, September 18, 1931, NAW/FRC.800/76.

20. Edward Nathan to Secretary of State, Monterrey, October 5, 1931, NAW/FRC.800/75.

21. J. Reuben Clark to Secretary of State, Mexico City, March 5, 1931, NAW/FRC.800/236; Edward Nathan to Secretary of State, Monterrey, October 20, 1933, NAW/FRC.800/344; December 26, 1933, NAW/FRC.800/361.

22. Edward Nathan to Secretary of State, Monterrey, June 18, 1934, NAW/FRC.800/422; August 31, 1934, NAW/FRC.800/468.

23. Edward Nathan to Secretary of State, Monterrey, October 2, 1934, NAW/FRC.800/1818; October 3, 1934, NAW/FRC.800/472; October 4, 1934, NAW/FRC.800/473; October 10, 1934, NAW/FRC.800/475; Secretary of State to Edward Nathan, Washington, D.C., November 13, 1934, NAW/FRC.800/103.

24. Edward Nathan to Secretary of State, Monterrey, April 13, 1935, NAW/FRC.800/542; May 6, 1935, NAW/FRC.800/558; May 9, 1935, NAW/FRC.800/560.

25. Edward Nathan to Secretary of State, Monterrey, May 31, 1935, NAW/FRC.800/567; June 15, 1935, NAW/FRC.800/573.

26. Edward Nathan to Secretary of State, Monterrey, June 17, 1935, NAW/FRC.800/574.

27. Dulles, *Yesterday in Mexico*, pp. 635, 646.

28. Edward Nathan to Secretary of State, Monterrey, July 31, 1935, NAW/FRC.800/592; August 10, 1935, NAW/FRC.800/598.

29. Edward Nathan to Secretary of State, Monterrey, November 18, 1935, NAW/FRC.800/623.

30. Edward Nathan to Secretary of State, Monterrey, December 31, 1935, NAW/FRC.800/639; Cesar Gutiérrez González, "Hegemonía, lucha sindical y movimiento obrero en Nuevo León, febrero, 1936" (unpublished manuscript), pp. 1–4.

31. C. C. Acosta to Jefe de la Oficina de Información Política y Social, Secretaría de Gobernación, Mexico City, November 22, 1935, AGN, Gobernación, Box 277; December 2, 1935, AGN, Gobernación, Box 277.

32. William Cameron Townsend, *Lázaro Cárdenas: Mexican Democrat* (Ann Arbor: George Wahr Publishing Co., 1952), pp. 129–130.

33. Edward Nathan to Secretary of State, Monterrey, September 18, 1931, NAW/FRC.800/76; September 8, 1931, NAW/FRC.851.51.

34. Edward Nathan to Secretary of State, Monterrey, April 30, 1932, NAW/FRC.800/161; February 28, 1933, NAW/FRC.800/255; May 29, 1934, NAW/FRC.800/411.

35. H. W. Carlson, Vice-Consul, to Secretary of State, January 31, 1935, NAW/FRC.800/515.

36. Edward Nathan to Secretary of State, Monterrey, April 24, 1935, NAW/FRC.850.4/550; April 12, 1935, NAW/FRC.850.4/541.

37. Edward Nathan to Secretary of State, Monterrey, January 31, 1936, NAW/FRC.800/649.

38. Basurto, *Cárdenas y el poder syndical*, pp. 55–56; C. C. Acosta to Jefe de la Oficina de Información Política y Social, Secretaría de Gobernación, Monterrey, December 23, 1935, AGN, Gobernación, Box 278.

39. Edward Nathan to Secretary of State, Monterrey, January 31, 1936, NAW/FRC.800/649.

40. Edward Nathan to Secretary of State, Monterrey, February 4, 1936, NAW/FRC.800/650; Jane Walter, "Lázaro Cárdenas y la fuerza de trabajo: Tres huelgas en 1936," *Historias* 5 (enero–marzo 1984): 77–88.

41. Edward Nathan to Secretary of State, Monterrey, February 7, 1936, NAW.800/652.

42. Edward Nathan to Secretary of State, Monterrey, February 6, 1936, NAW.800/651; Gregorio Morales Sánchez, Provisional Governor of Nuevo León, to Lázaro Cárdenas, Monterrey, February 6, 1936, AGN.432.2/184.

43. *Excelsior*, February 7, 1936, pp. 1, 4.

44. Emilio Portes Gil to Luis I. Rodríguez, Secretario Particular del Presidente, February 4, 1936, AGN.432.2/184.

45. Edward Nathan to Secretary of State, Monterrey, February 10, 1936, NAW.800/655.

46. Edward Nathan to Secretary of State, Monterrey, February 12, 1936, NAW.800/654.

47. Ibid. Also in January 1936, one U.S. official had noted that Cárdenas' intent was "to organize one large labor union under government control, so to end inter-union disputes and to create a unified element for its own protection—and for his political support"; R. Henry Norweb, Chargé d'Affaires to Secretary of State, Mexico City, January 17, 1936, NAW.812.30329.

48. *El Porvenir*, February 12, 1936, pp. 1, 7; February 14, 1936, p. 1.

49. *El Porvenir*, February 13, 1936, p. 1; February 15, 1936, p. 4.

50. Edward Nathan to Secretary of State, Monterrey, February 12, 1936, NAW.800/654.

51. Edward Nathan to Secretary of State, Monterrey, February 13, 1936, NAW.800/657; February 26, 1936, NAW.800/667.

52. *El Porvenir*, February 1, 1936, p. 8. It should be noted that the representation vote at the Vidriera was very close. Because office workers were not allowed to vote, the CTM group was able to win by the slim margin of twenty votes or so.

53. *El Porvenir*, February 12, 1936, p. 4; Agustín Ávila Ortíz to Jefe, Depto. del Trabajo, Monterrey, October 27, 1936, AGN.Sección de Trabajo, Box 63/Exp. 8.

54. Basurto, *Cárdenas y el poder sindical*, pp. 82–83.

55. Thomas D. Bowman, U.S. Consul General, to Department of Labor, Mexico City, April 17, 1936, NAW/FRC.850.4 (Box 1).

56. Edward Nathan to Secretary of State, Monterrey, February 18, 1936, NAW.800/661; February 29, 1936, NAW.800/668.

57. Edward Nathan to Secretary of State, Monterrey, February 13, 1936, NAW.800/657.

244   *Notes to Pages 183–187*

58. *El Porvenir,* February 10, 1936, p. 4; Gregorio Morales Sánchez to Lázaro Cárdenas, February 6, 1936; Ramón Villarreal to Lázaro Cárdenas, March 9, 1936; Sindicato de Choferes, Mecanicos y Similares to Lázaro Cárdenas, March 20, 1936, AGN.432.2/184.

59. Vicente Lombardo Toledano to Lázaro Cárdenas, Mexico City, March 10, 1936, AGN.432.2/184.

60. AGN, Gobernación, Dirección General de Gobierno, 2.312(16)11. This file contained various materials from the Zuazua campaign.

61. Edward Nathan to Secretary of State, Monterrey, March 2, 1936, NAW.800/670.

62. Edward Nathan to Secretary of State, Monterrey, March 31, 1936, NAW.800/678.

63. Edward Nathan to Secretary of State, Monterrey, March 14, 1936, NAW.800/673.

64. Cárdenas, *Palabras y documentos públicos,* pp. 200–206.

65. Edward Nathan to Secretary of State, Monterrey, March 16, 1936, NAW.800/674.

66. Edward Nathan to Secretary of State, Monterrey, March 31, 1936, NAW.800/678.

67. Ibid.

68. Ibid.

69. Edward Nathan to Secretary of State, Monterrey, April 16, 1936, NAW.800/685; April 20, 1936, NAW.800/686.

70. Edward Nathan to Secretary of State, Monterrey, February 14, 1936, NAW.800 (telegram); *Actividad* 160 (May 1936): 7, 14–15; 161 (June 1936): 7–8. It should also be noted that Cárdenas was also concerned with Calles' criticism while the ex-president was in the United States, especially American perceptions of Cardenista reformism. On this point, see Walter, "Lázaro Cárdenas," pp. 87–88.

71. Edward Nathan to Secretary of State, Monterrey, April 30, 1936, NAW.800/691; H. W. Carlson, U.S. Vice-Consul, to Secretary of State, Monterrey, June 1, 1936, NAW.800/696. Quote is from Nathan to Secretary of State, Monterrey, June 30, 1936, NAW.800/703. In late July, Anacleto Guerrero made a speech that criticized radical labor activists: businessmen were quick to praise the governor; *El Porvenir,* July 25, 1936, pp. 4, 8; July 28, 1936, p. 3; July 29, 1936, p. 5.

72. Edward Nathan to Secretary of State, Monterrey, June 30, 1936, NAW.800/703; *El Porvenir,* July 14, 1936, p. 3; July 15, 1936, p. 3.

73. On the July 29 incident, elements of this description are taken from Cesar Gutiérrez González, "29 de julio de 1936 en Monterrey: Un caso de lucha de clases" (unpublished manuscript), Oficina de Investigación y Difusión del Movimiento Obrero, Monterrey, Nuevo León; also Edward Nathan to Secretary of State, Monterrey, July 30, 1936, NAW.800/711.

74. Edward Nathan to Secretary of State, Monterrey, July 31, 1936, NAW.800/712; August 3, 1936, NAW.800/714.

75. Edward Nathan to Secretary of State, Monterrey, August 31, 1936, NAW.800/727; *El Porvenir,* August 13, 1936, p. 4. Guerrero's ousting of the

mayor added to his problems with the more militant factions of the local CTM organization that supported the mayor.

76. Edward Nathan to Secretary of State, Monterrey, September 30, 1936, NAW.800/737; *Actividad* 165 (October 1936): 7–8.

77. *Actividad* 160 (May 1936): 7; editorial in this issue was entitled "Socialismo o fomento industrial"; also *Actividad* 162 (July 1936): 37–38; 164 (September 1936): 7–8.

78. Thomas D. Bowman, U.S. Consul General, to Department of Labor, Mexico City, April 17, 1936, NAW/FRC.850.4.

79. Ibid.

80. Ibid.

81. William P. Blocker, U.S. Consul, to Secretary of State, Monterrey, March 13, 1937, NAW.800/68.

82. William P. Blocker to Secretary of State, Monterrey, February 27, 1937, NAW.800/52.

83. Ibid.

84. William P. Blocker to Secretary of State, Monterrey, March 31, 1937, NAW.800/77; April 28, 1937, NAW.800/95; May 29, 1937, NAW.800/112.

85. William P. Blocker to Secretary of State, Monterrey, May 29, 1937, NAW.800/112.

86. Ibid.

87. William P. Blocker to Secretary of State, Monterrey, July 29, 1937, NAW.800/145.

88. William P. Blocker to Secretary of State, Monterrey, February 27, 1937, NAW.800/52.

89. William P. Blocker to Secretary of State, Monterrey, June 29, 1937, NAW.800/128.

90. Ibid.

91. William P. Blocker to Secretary of State, Monterrey, July 29, 1937, NAW.800/145.

92. Many observers emphasize that Cárdenas' retreat from his reformist push occurs primarily as an outcome of the expropriation of petroleum companies in March 1938. For an analysis, see Nora Hamilton, *The Limits of State Autonomy: Post-Revolutionary Mexico*, pp. 237–239.

93. Hernández Chavez, *La mecánica cardenista*, pp. 190–192.

94. Lorenzo Meyer, *México y los Estados Unidos en el conflicto petrolero, 1917–1942* (Mexico City: El Colegio de México, 1972), pp. 330–345. The elite badly misread the U.S. stance toward Mexico and Cárdenas during this period, overestimating the significance of anti-Cárdenas tracts published in the United States and underestimating the implications of the Good Neighbor policy of the Roosevelt administration.

95. Hamilton, *Limits of State Autonomy*, pp. 225–227.

96. Hernández Chavez, *La mecánica cardenista*, pp. 187–189; Tzvi Medin, *Ideología y praxis política de Lázaro Cárdenas* (Mexico City: Siglo Veintiuno Editores, 1972), pp. 211–214; William P. Blocker to Secretary of State, Monterrey, June 1, 1938, NAW.800/277.

97. H. W. Carlson, U.S. Vice-Consul, to Secretary of State, January 28, 1939, NAW.800/351.

9. Epilogue as Preface to a New Era

1. Lorenzo Meyer, "Historical Roots of the Authoritarian State," in *Authoritarianism in Mexico*, ed. Reyna and Weinert, pp. 4–16.

2. Doyle C. McDonough, U.S. Consul General, to Secretary of State, Monterrey, March 30, 1939, NAW.800/16; April 20, 1939, NAW.800/29; April 27, 1939, NAW.800; July 31, 1939, NAW.800/74.

3. *El Porvenir*, September 1, 1939, p. 3.

4. *El Porvenir*, September 4, 1939, p. 4.

5. *El Porvenir*, September 7, 1939, p. 1.

6. *El Porvenir*, September 27, 1939, p. 3.

7. *Actividad* maintained a suspicious view in several articles during this period (e.g., editorial in *Actividad* 291 [October 1, 1939]: 5–7).

8. *El Porvenir*, October 6, 1939, p. 4; October 8, 1939, p. 7; October 11, 1939, p. 2; October 15, 1939, p. 7; Doyle McDonough to Secretary of State, Monterrey, September 6, 1939, NAW.800/96.

9. Doyle McDonough to Secretary of State, Monterrey, October 31, 1939, NAW.800/136.

10. *Actividad* 231 (March 15, 1937): 5.

11. *Actividad* 232 (April 1, 1937): 5.

12. *Actividad* 161 (June 1936): 7–8.

13. *Actividad* 162 (July 1936): 7–8, 37–38.

14. Córdova, *La política de masas*, pp. 197–201.

15. *Actividad* 160 (May 1936): 7.

16. *Actividad* 257 (May 1, 1938): 9–10.

17. H. W. Carlson to Secretary of State, Monterrey, August 1, 1938, NAW/FRC.800/308; August 5, 1938, NAW/FRC.800/309; August 9, 1938, NAW/FRC.800/312; August 10, 1938, NAW/FRC.800/314; September 1, 1938, NAW/FRC.800/321. The last communication noted that a serious flood of the city fatally crippled the momentum of the CTM effort.

18. Anguiano, *El estado y la política obrera*, pp. 99–100.

19. Cited in José Ariel Contreras, *México 1940: Industrialización y crisis política*, p. 160.

20. *Actividad* 291 (October 1, 1939): 5–7.

21. Ibid.

22. Garrido, *El partido de la revolución*, p. 277.

23. Ibid., p. 285. See also Franz A. von Sauer, *The Alienated "Loyal" Opposition: Mexico's Partido Acción Nacional* (Albuquerque: University of New Mexico Press, 1974), pp. 109–110; Donald J. Mabry, *Mexico's Acción Nacional: A Catholic Alternative to Revolution* (Syracuse: Syracuse University Press, 1973), pp. 34–39.

24. *Actividad* 293 (November 1, 1939): 9, 39; 294 (November 15, 1939): 2–3.

25. Doyle C. McDonough to Secretary of State, Monterrey, December 1, 1939, NAW.800/159; January 31, 1940, NAW/FRC.800/204; March 25, 1940,

NAW/FRC.800/237; April 20, 1940, NAW/FRC.800/266; Romeyn Wormuth, U.S. Consul, Nuevo Laredo, to Secretary of State, April 27, 1940, NAW/FRC.800/1231. The American business magazine *Fortune* noted the fears surrounding Lombardo's role in Mexico's political future ("Mexico in Revolution," *Fortune* 18 [October 1938]: 136).

26. Doyle C. McDonough to Secretary of State, Monterrey, July 31, 1940, NAW/FRC.800/344; June 30, 1940, NAW/FRC.800/318. The Nazi concern had dated since 1938; Paul Demille, U.S. Vice-Consul, to Secretary of State, March 25, 1938, NAW/FRC.820.02.

27. Doyle C. McDonough to Secretary of State, Monterrey, May 13, 1940, NAW.800/282; May 31, 1940, NAW/FRC.800/303.

28. Romeyn Wormuth, U.S. Consul, Nuevo Laredo, to Secretary of State, April 27, 1940, NAW/FRC.800/1231; Doyle C. McDonough to American Embassy (Mexico City), April 11, 1940, NAW/FRC, Telegram #800.

29. *New York Times,* July 15, 1940, p. 5.

30. Doyle C. McDonough to Secretary of State, Monterrey, July 9, 1940, NAW/FRC.800/325; Michael Scully, "Behind the Mexican Crisis," *Current History* 52:53 (November 7, 1940): 18.

31. Alan Riding, in *New York Times,* October 21, 1974.

32. A typical example of this neglect of what happened in the aftermath of the Fourteen-Point speech is found in Basurto, *Cárdenas y el poder sindical,* pp. 59-64.

33. Córdova provides an example of this concern in his *En una época de crisis (1928-1934),* pp. 90-121.

34. An example is found in the book by Contreras, *México 1940.*

35. See Hamilton, *Limits of State Autonomy,* especially chapter 9.

36. For example, see Juan Manuel Fragoso, Elvira Concheiro, and Antonio Gutiérrez, *El poder de la gran burguesía* (Mexico City: Ediciones de Cultura Popular, 1979).

37. Krauze, Meyer, and Reyes, *La reconstrucción económica,* p. 50.

38. For example, in one dispatch on Sáenz from a U.S. embassy official, he noted that Sáenz accepted the endorsement of the agrarian party for his presidential bid with appropriate radical rhetoric, although "he is likely," the same official suggested, "to make some effort to check those destructive features of the agrarian program" (H. F. Arthur Schoenfeld to Secretary of State, Mexico City, January 28, 1929, NAW.800/1377).

39. Arnaldo Córdova, *La formación del poder político en México* (Mexico City: Ediciones Era, 1974), pp. 42-44.

40. It should be noted that the economic interests in Mexico City failed to institute a COPARMEX chapter in 1929. Their meeting of October 1929, reported in *Excelsior,* reflected a much more prudent stance than that of the *regiomontano* elite (*Excelsior,* October 11, 1929, pp. 1, 4).

41. Anguiano, *El estado y la política obrera,* pp. 99-100.

42. Basurto, *Cárdenas y el poder sindical,* p. 59, where he states that the bourgeoisie sided with Calles.

43. Note should be taken that Cárdenas was particularly angered by the elite's mobilization of other businessmen to criticize his policies; Edward

Nathan to Secretary of State, Monterrey, February 12, 1936, NAW.800/654; also *El Porvenir,* February 12, 1936, p. 1.

44. For a sympathetic treatment of Cárdenas' dilemma, see Albert L. Michaels, "The Crisis of Cardenismo," *Journal of Latin American Studies* 2 (May 1970): 51–79.

45. Robert Kaufman, "Mexico and Latin American Authoritarianism," in *Authoritarianism in Mexico,* ed. Reyna and Weinert, p. 229; Garrido, *El partido de la revolución,* pp. 281–286.

46. Hamilton, *Limits of State Autonomy,* p. 31.

47. Contreras, *México 1940,* pp. 170–171. See also the trenchant remarks in Valentín Campa A., *Mi testimonio: Experiencias de un comunista mexicano* (Mexico City: Ediciones de Cultura Popular, 1978), pp. 271–272.

48. An example of this tendency to lump the private sector together is found in Salvador Cordero H., *Concentración industrial y poder económico en México* (Mexico City: Centro de Estudios Sociológicos, #18, Colegio de México, 1977).

49. Fragoso, Concheiro, and Gutiérrez in their *El poder de la gran burguesía* offer important insights to the fractions among capital that point to the need for more historiographical work on the formation of economic groups in Mexico and their specific relations to the state over time. Current works continue to underestimate the significance of the differentiation of the private sector over time. In this respect, Dale Story's recently published analysis of state-industry relations in Mexico provides only an incomplete view. Story rightly emphasizes the importance of "privileged or elitist sectors" and their relative autonomy from the Mexican state. On the other hand, to prove his thesis, Story concentrates on industrial groups and organizations rather than on particular elites. In fact, the one major fraction of the private sector that Story examines carefully is the Grupo Monterrey. Thus, Story's disaggregating of the private sector remains insufficient. This shortcoming of an otherwise fine study underscores the need for more historical research on the distinct segments of the Mexican private sector and their relations with the state. See Story, *Industry, the State, and Public Policy in Mexico,* especially pp. 79–105.

50. Peter Smith, "Does Mexico Have a Power Elite?" in *Authoritarianism in Mexico,* ed. Reyna and Weinert, p. 148. See also on this point Miguel Basáñez, *La lucha por la hegemonía en México, 1968–1980* (Mexico City: Siglo Veintiuno Editores, 1981), pp. 81–86.

51. Hamilton, *Limits of State Autonomy,* p. 264.

52. Marcos Antonio Alcázar, *Las agrupaciones patronales en México* (Mexico City: El Colegio de México, 1970), pp. 35–36.

53. On this point, see David Collier and Ruth Berins Collier, "Inducements versus Constraints: Disaggregating 'Corporatism,'" *American Political Science Review* 73:4 (December 1979): 967–986.

Selected Bibliography

Archival Material

Archivo General de la Nación, Mexico City, Mexico.
Archivo General del Estado de Nuevo León, Monterrey, Nuevo León.
Archivo Municipal de Monterrey, Monterrey, Nuevo León.
Bancroft Library, University of California, Berkeley.
Centro de Estudios de Historia de México, Condumex, Mexico City, Mexico.
Latin American Collection, University of Texas, Austin.
National Archives of the United States, Washington, D.C.

Periodicals

Actividad (Monterrey), 1922–1940.
Beverage Journal (Chicago), 1922–1940.
La Defensa (Monterrey), 1883–1893.
El Diario del Hogar (Mexico City), 1908–1913.
El Economista Mexicano (Mexico City), 1887-1911.
Excelsior (Mexico City), 1917–1940.
El Hijo del Ahuizote (Mexico City), 1890–1903.
El Imparcial (Mexico City), 1898–1911.
Monterrey News (Monterrey), 1893–1911.
El País (Mexico City), 1906.
El Periódico Oficial (Monterrey), 1874–1910.
El Porvenir (Monterrey), 1918–1940.
El Pueblo (Mexico City), 1918.
Redención (Monterrey), 1903.
La Voz de Nuevo León (Monterrey), 1888–1909.

Books and Articles

Aguilar Belden de Garza, Sara. *Una ciudad y dos familias.* Mexico City: Ed. Jus, 1970.
Aguilar Camin, Hector. *La frontera nomada: Sonora y la revolución mexicana.* Mexico City: Siglo Veintiuno Editores, 1977.

Aguilar M., Alonso, and Fernando Carmona. *México: Riqueza y miseria.* Mexico City: Editorial Nuestro Tiempo, 1967.

Alperovich, M. S., and B. T. Rudenko. *Ensayos de historia de México.* Mexico City: Ediciones de Cultura Popular, 1974.

Álvarez Salinas, Gilberto. *Pancho Villa en Monterrey.* Monterrey: Ediciones Continentes, 1969.

Anderson, Rodney D. *Outcasts in Their Own Land: Mexican Industrial Workers, 1906–1911.* DeKalb: Northern Illinois Press, 1976.

Andrews, George Reid. "Toward a Re-Evaluation of the Latin American Family Firm: The Industry Executives of Monterrey." *Inter-American Economic Affairs* 30 (Winter 1976): 23–40.

Anguiano, Arturo. *El estado y la política obrera del cardenismo.* Mexico City: Ediciones Era, 1975.

Balán, Jorge, Harley L. Browning, and Elizabeth Jelin. *Men in a Developing Society: Geographic and Social Mobility in Monterrey, Mexico.* Austin: University of Texas Press, 1973.

Basave, Agustín. *Constructores de Monterrey.* Monterrey, 1945.

Basurto, Jorge. *Cárdenas y el poder sindical.* Mexico City: Ediciones Era, 1983.

Bazant, Jan. *A Concise History of Mexico, from Hidalgo to Cárdenas, 1805–1940.* New York: Cambridge University Press, 1977.

Beals, Carleton. *Porfirio Díaz: Dictator of Mexico.* Philadelphia: J. B. Lippincott Co., 1932.

Bernstein, Marvin D. *The Mexican Mining Industry, 1890–1950.* Albany: State University of New York, 1964.

Berrueto Ramón, Federico. "Santiago Vidaurri y el estado de Nuevo León y Coahuila." *Humanitas* 6 (1965): 407–420.

Bryan, Anthony. "El papel del Gen. Bernardo Reyes en la política nacional y regional de México." *Humanitas* 13 (1972): 331–340.

Cárdenas, Lázaro. *Palabras y documentos públicos, 1928–1940.* Vol. 1. Mexico City: Siglo Veintiuno Editores, 1978.

Carr, Barry. *El movimiento obrero y la política en México, 1910–1929.* Mexico City: Ediciones Era, 1981.

Carrion, Jorge, and Alonso Aguilar M. *La burguesía, la oligarquía y el estado.* Mexico City: Editorial Nuestro Tiempo, 1972.

Cavazos Garza, Israel. "Las incursiones de los bárbaros en el noreste de México, durante el siglo XIX." *Humanitas* 5 (1964): 343–356.

Cerutti, Mario. *Burguesía y capitalismo en Monterrey (1850–1910).* Mexico City: Claves Latinoamericanas, 1983.

Chavez, Elías. "Hay prominentes panistas que sirven al Grupo Monterrey." *Proceso,* April 17, 1978, pp. 6–10.

Clark, Marjorie Ruth. *Organized Labor in Mexico.* Chapel Hill: University of North Carolina Press, 1934.

Cockcroft, James D., Andre Gunder Frank, and Dale L. Johnson. *Dependence and Underdevelopment: Latin America's Political Economy.* Garden City, N.Y.: Doubleday and Company, 1972.

Collier, David, ed. *The New Authoritarianism in Latin America.* Princeton: Princeton University Press, 1979.

Contreras, José Ariel. *México 1940: Industrialización y crisis política*. Mexico City: Siglo Veintiuno Editores, 1980.

Córdova, Arnaldo. *La clase obrera en la historia de México*. Vol. 9, *En una época de crisis (1928–1934)*. Mexico City: Siglo Veintiuno Editores, 1980.

———. *La ideología de la revolución mexicana: La formación del nuevo régimen*. Mexico City: Ediciones Era, 1973.

———. *La política de masas del cardenismo*. Mexico City: Ediciones Era, 1974.

Cortés Conde, Roberto. *The First Stages of Modernization in Spanish America*. New York: Harper and Row, 1974.

Cosío Villegas, Daniel, ed. *Historia moderna de México*. 9 vols. Mexico City: Editorial Hermes, 1955–1972.

Cossio, David Alberto. *Historia de Nuevo León: Evolución política y social*. 6 vols. Monterrey: J. Cantú Leal, 1925–1933.

Cumberland, Charles C. *Mexican Revolution: Genesis under Madero*. Austin: University of Texas Press, 1952.

Delaney, Robert W. "Matamoros, Port for Texas during the Civil War." *Southwestern Historical Quarterly* 58:4 (April 1955): 473–487.

de la Peña, Sergio. *La formación del capitalismo en México*. Mexico City: Siglo Veintiuno Editores, 1975.

Dicken, Samuel N. "Monterrey and Northeastern Mexico." *Annals of the Association of American Geographers* 29 (June 1939): 127–158.

Duclos Salinas, Adolfo. *Méjico pacificado: El progreso de Méjico y los hombres que lo gobiernan, Porfirio Díaz, Bernardo Reyes*. Saint Louis: Imprenta de Hughes y Cía, 1904.

Dulles, John W. F. *Yesterday in Mexico: A Chronicle of the Revolution, 1919–1936*. Austin: University of Texas Press, 1961.

Estadísticas económicas del Porfiriato: Comercio exterior de México, 1877–1911. Mexico City: El Colegio de México, 1960.

Estadísticas económicas del Porfiriato: Fuerza de trabajo y actividad económica por sectores. Mexico City: El Colegio de México, 1964.

Fuentes Mares, José. *Monterrey, Una ciudad creadora y sus capitanes*. Mexico City: Editorial Jus, 1976.

Garrido, Luis Javier. *El partido de la revolución institucionalizada: La formación del nuevo estado en México (1928–1945)*. Mexico City: Siglo Veintiuno Editores, 1982.

Garza, Virgilio, Jr. "Brief Sketch of the Industrial Development of Monterrey." In *Basic Industries in Texas and Northern Mexico*. Austin: University of Texas, 1950.

Glade, William P., Jr., and Charles W. Anderson. *The Political Economy of Mexico*. Madison: University of Wisconsin Press, 1963.

González Navarro, Moisés. *Estadísticas sociales del Porfiriato 1877–1910*. Mexico City: Secretaría de Economía, 1956.

Gruening, Ernest Henry. *Mexico and Its Heritage*. New York: Century Co., 1928.

Guadarrama, Rocio. *Los sindicatos y la política en México: La CROM (1918–1928)*. Mexico City: Ediciones Era, 1981.

Hamilton, Nora. *The Limits of State Autonomy: Post-Revolutionary Mexico*. Princeton: Princeton University Press, 1982.

Hansen, Roger D. *The Politics of Mexican Development.* Baltimore: Johns Hopkins University Press, 1971.

Hernández Chavez, Alicia. *Historia de la revolución mexicana, 1934–1940.* Vol. 16, *La mecánica cardenista.* Mexico City: El Colegio de México, 1979.

Johnson, William Weber. *Heroic Mexico: The Narrative History of a Twentieth Century Revolution.* Garden City, N.Y.: Doubleday and Company, 1968.

Katz, Friedrich. "Labor Conditions on Haciendas in Porfirian Mexico: Some Trends and Tendencies." *Hispanic American Historical Review* 54 (February 1974): 1–47.

Keremitsis, Dawn. *La industria textil mexicana en el siglo XIX.* Mexico City: Sep/Setentas, 1973.

Krauze, Enrique, Jean Meyer, and Cayetano Reyes. *Historia de la revolución mexicana, 1924–1928.* Vol. 10, *La reconstrucción económica.* Mexico City: El Colegio de México, 1977.

León, Samuel, and Ignacio Marvan. *La clase obrera en la historia de México: En el cardenismo (1934–1940).* Mexico City: Siglo Veintiuno Editores, 1985.

Livas, Pablo. *El estado de Nuevo León.* Monterrey: J. Cantú Leal, Imp., 1910.

Malloy, James M., ed. *Authoritarianism and Corporatism in Latin America.* Pittsburgh: University of Pittsburgh Press, 1977.

Mauro, Frederic. "Le Développement économique de Monterrey (1890–1960)." *Caravelle* 2 (1964): 35–126.

———. "L'Economie du nord-est et la résistance à l'empire." In *La intervención francesa y el imperio de maximiliano.* Mexico City: IFAL, 1965.

Medin, Tzvi. *El minimato presidencial: Historia política del maximato (1928–1935).* Mexico City: Ediciones Era, 1982.

Medina, Luis. *Historia de la revolución mexicana, 1940–1952.* Vol. 18, *Del cardenismo al avilacamachismo.* Mexico City: El Colegio de México, 1978.

Megee, Mary Catharine. *Monterrey, Mexico: Internal Patterns and External Relations.* Chicago: University of Chicago Press, 1958.

Meyer, Jean. *Historia de la revolución mexicana, 1924–1928.* Vol. 11, *Estado y sociedad con Calles.* Mexico City: El Colegio de México, 1977.

Meyer, Lorenzo. *Historia de la revolución mexicana, 1928–1934.* Vol. 12, *Los inicios de la institucionalización.* Mexico City: El Colegio de México, 1978.

———. *Historia de la revolución mexicana, 1928–1934.* Vol. 13, *El conflicto social y los gobiernos del maximato.* Mexico City: El Colegio de México, 1978.

Michaels, Albert L. "The Crisis of Cardenismo." *Journal of Latin American Studies* 2 (May 1970): 51–79.

Montemayor Hernández, Andrés. *Historia de Monterrey.* Monterrey: Asociación de Editores y Libreros de Monterrey, 1971.

Morales Gómez, Antonio. *Cronología de Nuevo León, 1527–1955.* Mexico City: Editorial Benito Juárez, 1955.

Moseley, Edward H. "Santiago Vidaurri: Héroe de la Reforma." *Humanitas* 11 (1970): 685–695.

Mosk, Sanford A. *Industrial Revolution in Mexico.* Berkeley: University of California Press, 1950.

Niemeyer, E. V., Jr. "Bernardo Reyes en la historia de México." *Humanitas* 5 (1964): 469–475.

————. *El general Bernardo Reyes.* Monterrey: Centro de Estudios Humanísticos de la Universidad de Nuevo León, 1966.

Nuncio, Abraham. *El Grupo Monterrey.* Mexico City: Editorial Nueva Imagen, 1982.

Ober, Frederick. *Twenty Years among the Mexicans.* Cincinnati: Chase and Hall, 1875.

O'Connor, Harvey. *The Guggenheims: The Making of an American Dynasty.* New York: Covici-Friede Publishers, 1937.

Ortiz Pinchetti, Francisco. "Del echeverrismo surgió todopoderoso el Grupo Monterrey." *Proceso*, May 1, 1978, pp. 16–19.

Owsley, Frank Lawrence. *King Cotton Diplomacy: Foreign Relations of the Confederate States of America.* Rev. ed. Chicago: University of Chicago Press, 1959.

Packard, Gordon. "Roots of Monterrey's Industrial Growth." MA thesis, University of California, Berkeley, 1961.

Pereyra, Carlos. "Misión empresarial: Subyugar al poder político." *Proceso*, April 3, 1978, pp. 34–35.

Puente Leyva, Jesús. *Distribución del ingreso en una ciudad urbana: El caso de Monterrey.* Mexico City: Siglo Veintiuno Editores, 1969.

Reyes, Rodolfo. *De mi vida: Memorias políticas.* Madrid: Biblioteca Nueva, 1929–30.

Reyna, José Luis, and Richard S. Weinert, eds. *Authoritarianism in Mexico.* Philadelphia: Institute for the Study of Human Issues, 1977.

Reynolds, Clark W. *The Mexican Economy: Twentieth Century Structure and Growth.* New Haven: Yale University Press, 1970.

Riding, Alan. *Distant Neighbors: A Portrait of the Mexicans.* New York: Alfred A. Knopf, 1985.

Rippy, J. Fred. *The United States and Mexico.* Rev. ed. New York: F. S. Crofts, 1931.

Robles, Vito Alessio. *Monterrey en la historia y en la leyenda.* Mexico City: José Porrua e Hijos, 1936.

Roel, Santiago. *Nuevo León: Apuntes históricos.* 3d ed. Monterrey: Imprenta del Bachiller, 1948.

Rosenzweig, Fernando. "El desarrollo económico de México de 1877 a 1911." *El Trimestre Económico* 32 (1965): 405–454.

Ross, Stanley R. *Francisco I. Madero, Apostle of Mexican Democracy.* New York: Columbia University Press, 1955.

Ruiz, Ramón E. *The Great Rebellion: Mexico, 1905–1924.* New York: W. W. Norton, 1980.

————. *Labor and the Ambivalent Revolutionaries: Mexico, 1911–1923.* Baltimore: Johns Hopkins Press, 1976.

Saldaña, José P. "Apuntes politicos y socio-económicos de Monterrey." *Humanitas* 15 (1974): 447–490.

————. *Apuntes sobre la industrialización de Monterrey.* Monterrey: Centro Patronal de Nuevo León, 1961.

———. *Casos y cosas de Monterrey.* Monterrey: Impresora Monterrey, 1942.

———. *Episodios contemporáneos.* Monterrey, 1955.

———. *Episodios de ayer.* Monterrey: Sistemas y Servicios Técnicos, 1959.

———. "El Gral. Don Porfirio Díaz en Monterrey." *Humanitas* 11 (1970): 413–452.

Shafer, Robert Jones. *Mexican Business Organizations: History and Analysis.* Syracuse: Syracuse University Press, 1973.

Solís M., Leopoldo. "Hacia un análisis general a largo plazo del desarrollo económico de México." *Demografía y Economia,* 1967, pp. 40–53.

Story, Dale. *Industry, the State, and Public Policy in Mexico.* Austin: University of Texas Press, 1986.

Tyler, Ronnie C. "Cotton on the Border, 1861–1865." *Southwestern Historical Quarterly* 73 (April 1970): 456–477.

———. "Las reclamaciones de Patricio Milmo." *Humanitas* 10 (1969): 561–583.

———. *Santiago Vidaurri and the Southern Confederacy.* Austin: Texas State Historical Association, 1973.

Vega G., Juan R., ed. *Personalidades de Monterrey.* Monterrey: Vega y Asociados, 1967.

Vellinga, Menno. *Industrialización, burguesía, y clase obrera en México: El caso de Monterrey.* Mexico City: Siglo Veintiuno Editores, 1979.

Vernon, Raymond. *The Dilemma of Mexico's Development.* Cambridge: Harvard University Press, 1963.

Villegas, Abelardo. *Positivismo y porfirismo.* Mexico City: Sep/Setentas, 1972.

Vizcaya Canales, Isidro. *Los orígenes de la industrialización de Monterrey, 1867–1920.* Monterrey: Librería Tecnológico, 1971.

Wasserman, Mark. *Capitalists, Caciques, and Revolution: The Native Elite and Foreign Enterprise in Chihuahua, Mexico, 1854–1911.* Chapel Hill: University of North Carolina Press, 1984.

Womack, John. *Zapata and the Mexican Revolution.* New York: Alfred A. Knopf, 1969.

INDEX